The Power to Manage?

The crucial role of employers and managers in the development of industrial relations has been the focus of much recent research. However, there remains little consensus on key issues such as the determinants of managerial strategies, or employers' contribution to differing national patterns of industrial relations.

The Power to Manage? argues that many of these difficulties stem from the limitations of the theoretical frameworks within which the research has been carried out. Both Marxist and mainstream perspectives subordinate managerial choices to the pressures of the market or the broader patterns of business development. In consequence, these approaches cannot explain the persistent diversity of employers' labour policies or the prevalence of contradictory and incoherent strategies.

Using the 'peculiarities' of British industrial relations as a point of departure, the contributors to this volume present detailed empirical studies of employer labour policies in a variety of countries. These, together with the substantial introduction and conclusion by the editors, establish a comparative framework within which the distinctiveness of British developments can be evaluated and point the way towards a new interpretation of the employer's role in industrial relations.

Steven Tolliday is Assistant Professor at the Graduate School of Business Administration, Harvard University. Jonathan Zeitlin is Lecturer in Modern Social History at Birkbeck College, University of London. From September 1991, he will be Associate Professor of History and Industrial Relations at the University of Wisconsin–Madison.

The Power to Manage?

Employers and industrial relations in comparative-historical perspective

Edited by
Steven Tolliday and Jonathan Zeitlin

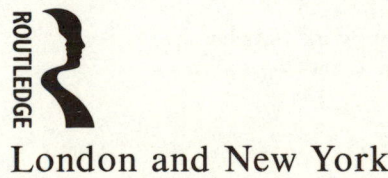

London and New York

First published 1991
by Routledge
11 New Fetter Lane, London EC4P 4EE

Simultaneously published in the USA and Canada
by Routledge
a division of Routledge, Chapman and Hall, Inc.
29 West 35th Street, New York, NY 10001

Typeset in 10/12pt Times by Witwell Ltd, Southport
Printed in Great Britain by Biddles Ltd, Guildford

British Library Cataloguing in Publication Data
The power to manage?: employers and industrial relations in
  comparative historical perspective
  1. Europe. Industrial relations
  I. Tolliday, Steven II. Zeitlin, Jonathan
  331.094

Library of Congress Cataloging in Publication Data
The power to manage?: employers and industrial relations in
  comparative-historical perspective/edited by Steven Tolliday and
  Jonathan Zeitlin.
        p.   cm.
  Includes bibliographical references and index.
  1. Industrial relations. 2. Employers' associations.
  3. Industrial relations – Great Britain. 4. Employers' associations –
  Great Britain. I. Tolliday, Steven. II. Zeitlin, Jonathan.
  HD6971.P83 1991
  331–dc20   90-24513

ISBN 0–415–02625–3

Contents

List of contributors   vii
Preface   ix

Introduction
Employers and industrial relations between theory and history
Steven Tolliday and Jonathan Zeitlin   1

Part I The peculiarities of the British?

1 Employers' strategies and craft production: the British
shipbuilding industry 1870–1950
Alastair Reid   35

2 The internal politics of employer organization: the
Engineering Employers' Federation 1896–1939
Jonathan Zeitlin   52

3 Ford and 'Fordism' in postwar Britain: enterprise management
and the control of labour 1937–1987
Steven Tolliday   81

Part II National models, historical contrasts

4 Employers' collective action in the open-shop era: the Metal
Manufacturers' Association of Philadelphia *c.* 1903–1933
Howell Harris   117

5 The 'human factor' and the limits of rationalization: personnel
management strategies and the rationalization movement in
German industry between the wars
Heidrun Homburg   147

6 Employers' associations and industrial relations in postwar
Germany: the case of Ruhr heavy industry
Werner Plumpe   176

7 Enterprise management and employer organization in Italy: Fiat,
  public enterprise and *Confindustria* 1922–1990
  Giovanni Contini   204

Part III Against convergence

8 Technological convergence and the limits to managerial control:
  flexible manufacturing systems in Britain, the USA and Japan
  Bryn Jones   231

9 Employers and the structure of collective bargaining: distinguishing
  cause and effect
  Keith Sisson   256

  Conclusion
  National models and international variations in labour management
  and employer organization
  Steven Tolliday and Jonathan Zeitlin   273

  Index   344

List of contributors

GIOVANNI CONTINI is an Industrial Archivist and Head of the Audio-Visual Section, Superintendancy of Archives for Tuscany, Florence.

HOWELL HARRIS is Senior Lecturer in History at the University of Durham.

HEIDRUN HOMBURG is currently a Visiting Research Fellow at the Maison des Sciences de l'Homme, Paris. She taught previously in the Department of History at the University of Bielefeld.

BRYN JONES is Senior Lecturer in the School of Social Science, University of Bath.

WERNER PLUMPE teaches in the Department of History at the Ruhr University of Bochum.

ALASTAIR REID is Fellow and Lecturer in History at Girton College, University of Cambridge.

KEITH SISSON is the Director of the Industrial Relations Research Unit at the University of Warwick.

STEVEN TOLLIDAY is Assistant Professor at the Graduate School of Business Administration, Harvard University.

JONATHAN ZEITLIN is Lecturer in Modern Social History at Birkbeck College, University of London. From September 1991, he will be Associate Professor of History and Industrial Relations at the University of Wisconsin–Madison.

Preface

This volume draws on the selected and revised proceedings of a conference held at Girton College, Cambridge, in September 1987 under the auspices of the Centre for Economic Policy Research. We are pleased to acknowledge the generous funding provided by the European Commission (DG IV), the Nuffield Foundation and CEPR itself. We would also like to thank the following people for their assistance and support: Alastair Reid, our co-organizer; John Morley of DG IV; Richard Portes, Wendy Thompson and Stephen Yeo of CEPR; Leslie Cadwell, who helped prepare the index; Nancy Marten and Claire L'Enfant of Routledge; and the other conference participants, particularly those whose fine papers could not be included in this volume.

Steven Tolliday and Jonathan Zeitlin

1 Introduction

Employers and industrial relations between
theory and history

Steven Tolliday and Jonathan Zeitlin

The central role of employers in the development of industrial relations commands increasing recognition from historians and social scientists alike. A growing body of empirical research has focused on the evolution of managerial strategies at the level of the enterprise and the activities of employers' associations in the labour market and the political arena. But little consensus has so far emerged on such key issues as the determinants of management strategies, the propensity of employers for collective action, or their contribution to differing national patterns of industrial relations.[1]

Much of the difficulty stems from the limitations of the theoretical approaches within which research has been conducted. Despite their apparent variety, we argue below, most analyses of business behaviour share certain fundamental features. First, they regard the conduct of the firm as a more or less functional response to changing environmental pressures. Second, this functional vision of the firm typically goes hand in hand with a unilinear evolutionary model of the stages of business development. Thus, despite their ostensible emphasis on the importance of employer strategies for industrial relations, such approaches in practice give little causal weight to managerial choices as opposed to the pressures of the market and the broader trajectory of business development. As a result, none is well equipped to explain the persistent differences in employer labour policies between apparently similar developed nations. Nor can they account convincingly for situations in which management has failed to implement, or at times even to formulate, a coherent labour strategy.

These weaknesses in the dominant approaches to the analysis of employer labour policies are highlighted by the history of British industrial relations since the late nineteenth century. Recent studies suggest that British employers have been internationally distinctive in three important respects. They have been unable or unwilling to establish direct control over the production process on the shop floor; they have failed to develop complex managerial and supervisory hierarchies in the enterprise; and they have not constructed effective associations for collective action in relation to trade unions and the state.[2] Despite major changes in business organization over the course of the twentieth century, this pattern appears to have characterized much of British industry into the 1970s, and it remains to be seen how far the developments of the 1980s mark a decisive shift in management policies and practice.[3]

This book serves a double purpose. First, it brings together detailed empirical studies of employer labour policies in Western Europe, the United States and Japan in order to establish a comparative-historical framework within which the distinctiveness of British developments can be evaluated and explained. How great are international variations in managerial strategies within the enterprise and what are their consequences for industrial relations? How far have employers in other developed countries been able to combine effectively and what factors have made this cohesion possible? The chapters in this volume shed new light on these questions whose answers are of crucial importance for current debates about both the past and the future of industrial relations in Britain and other advanced economies. Second, at a deeper level this book points the way towards a reinterpretation of the employers' role in the development of industrial relations in the light of empirical research. In contrast to prevailing approaches, we argue that firms and employers' associations, like trade unions and the state, must be treated as complex institutions whose decisions are the product of the internal political processes as well as external pressures. More fundamentally still, we suggest, employers and managers must be treated as potentially autonomous historical actors whose substantive choices can modify as well as reflect their environment.

The book is divided into five main parts. This introductory chapter examines the major theoretical approaches to the study of the enterprise and considers the limitations of their analysis of employers' labour strategies and collective organization; only by discarding their underlying assumptions, it contends, can the persistent diversity revealed by empirical research such as that presented in this volume be convincingly accommodated. Chapters 1–3 explore the distinctiveness of British employers through detailed case studies of key sectors such as shipbuilding, engineering and motor vehicles. Chapters 4–7 develop the notion of contrasting national models through fine-grained historical accounts of labour management and employer organization in the United States, Germany and Italy. Chapters 8–9 adopt an explicitly comparative framework, scrutinizing work organization and collective bargaining across a variety of countries, and rejecting the notion of a tendency towards the convergence of managerial strategies across nations. The concluding chapter returns to the problem of the 'peculiarities of the British', building on the findings of the preceding chapters to assess the nature, causes and consequences of international variations in employer labour policies.

LABOUR MANAGEMENT AND THE THEORY OF THE FIRM

Dominant interpretations of employer labour policies, as we have already suggested, depend on deeper theoretical assumptions about the nature of the business enterprise. Despite their many differences, most theories of the firm – economic and sociological, Marxist and liberal – largely concur in viewing its behaviour as a series of more or less functional adaptations to the external environment. Markets and technology, it is widely agreed, determine a narrow range of appropriate organizational forms and business strategies at any moment in time. These imperatives in turn are held to shape employers' individual labour strategies and their wider associational activities. As with all simple but powerful theories, their most sophisticated exponents hedge these assumptions round with innumerable qualifications and relax them substantially in the course of empirical research; but as we shall see, in framing more general claims they typically return to their original positions.[4]

An adaptational theory of the firm does not in itself imply any necessary historical trajectory. Organizational structures and business strategies might be held to remain in constant flux in response to random changes in the external environment. For most versions of the theory, however, long-term historical trends – notably the extension of the market and the diffusion of large-scale technologies – impose a distinctive evolutionary dynamic on the development of the business enterprise. At the company level, this dynamic centres on the rise of large corporations based on the professionalization of management, the internalization of market transactions, and the separation of conception from execution at all levels of the organization. On the shop floor, it implies a progressive tendency towards an ever more refined division of labour, the fragmentation of manual tasks, the dilution of craft skills and the elaboration of managerial control over the organization of production. As economic development proceeds, the leading sectors of successful industrial economies are expected to converge on a common model of efficient business organization. Divergences from this pattern in industrial structure, business strategy and work organization are usually attributed to three main sources. They may result from the residual survival of declining firms which will soon be eliminated by competitive pressures, differences in the suitability of particular industries for large-scale production and distribution, or variations in the level of development reached by individual national economies.

The simplest and still perhaps most widespread approach to the theory of the firm is that of neo-classical economics. For this school, exemplified in the methodological writings of Milton Friedman, the firm is explicitly conceived as a 'black box', a passive respondent to market signals whose internal processes are wholly devoid of theoretical significance. Exogenously determined price changes, on this view, cause firms to adjust their output, substitute factors of production and shift between available technologies according to well-defined rules of optimization. Whatever the observable evidence, Friedman argues, 'under a wide range of circumstances individual firms behave *as if* they were seeking rationally to maximize their expected returns' because the 'natural selection' of the market forces them to do so. 'Let the apparent immediate determinant of business behaviour be anything at all – habitual reaction, random chance, or whatnot', he observes in a celebrated passage,

> Whenever this determinant happens to lead to behaviour consistent with rational and informed maximization of returns, the business will prosper and acquire resources with which to expand; whenever it does not, the business will tend to lose resources and can be kept in existence only by the addition of resources from outside.[5]

The patent inadequacy of this position for the analysis of large-scale enterprises has given rise to a variety of 'managerial' theories of the firm which take as their point of departure the separation of ownership and control within the modern corporation.[6] Drawing on organizational sociology[7] and business history as well as industrial economics, the central feature of most managerial theories is the extension of the neo-classical model of economic behaviour inside the black box of the firm. Alternative goals such as growth or sales may be substituted for that of profits; orthodox assumptions of perfect information may be relaxed and oligopolistic competition accommodated; and sociological contingencies or transaction costs may replace the direct price discipline of the market as the driving force behind enterprise decision-making. Yet despite appearing to take account of a wider range of motives and behavioural patterns, the managerial firm in these theories normally remains a more or less straightforward maximizer of an objective function whose conduct is determined by the constraints of the external environment.[8]

Thus Alfred Chandler in history and Oliver Williamson in theory both treat the evolution of successive forms of business organization as a necessary consequence of changing markets and technology. In Chandler's view, for example, the emergence and diffusion of the modern corporation was a functional response to the organizational demands of wider markets and larger-scale technologies, manifest first in the United States and then on a global scale.[9] The construction of the American railways, he argues, unified this vast continental market, creating the conditions for mass production and distribution at the same time as it gave rise to the managerial hierarchies required to coordinate the throughput of goods within the new large-scale enterprises. As businesses diversified, moving into new spheres of activity, the multi-divisional or 'M-Form' corporation then appeared as a solution to the problem of reconciling centralized capital allocation and performance monitoring with decentralized administration of day-to-day operations. The development of these 'organizational capabilities' gave first-movers significant advantages of scale and scope and enabled them to establish oligopolies which created formidable barriers to entry. Oligopoly did not, however, lead to predatory and exploitative behaviour: rather, it enabled firms to overcome problems of risk and uncertainty and to use their large market share and vertical integration to achieve lower costs and higher productivity through administrative co-ordination. In particular industries, to be sure, technological characteristics proved unfavourable to corporate consolidation, and alternative forms of business enterprise have accordingly persisted. But international competition has driven the core sectors of other advanced economies to converge towards the American model, with limited variations associated with their individual routes to managerial capitalism.[10]

Chandler himself has little to say about corporate labour policies but others like William Lazonick have sought to draw out the implications of his 'managerial revolution' in this area. Just as the new managerial structures sought to take control of supply, production and distribution, so they sought to take control of work organization away from the shop floor through deskilling technology, attacks on craft unions and the construction of elaborate hierarchies for the coordination, supervision and direction of the labour force. At the same time, however, the new high-throughput technology created new concerns about the quality of worker effort, and oligopolistic firms were therefore willing to share some of their gains with labour through the internalization of training, promotion and reward within the boundaries of the corporation. In this way, it is argued, the leading corporations came to exercise effective control over their workforce even if they could not win its wholehearted loyalty.[11]

For Oliver Williamson, on the other hand, transaction costs and asset specificity rather than production costs and economies of scale are the crucial determinants of changes in the structure of the enterprise.[12] Mass markets and large-scale technologies alone cannot account for vertical integration since the interdependent phases of production and distribution could still be performed by separate firms on a contractual basis. But under conditions of uncertainty, Williamson argues, firms must regularly undertake investments in task-specific non-redeployable assets, while imperfect information and potential opportunism make it impossible to 'cross all possible bridges in advance' through a comprehensive set of contingent claims contracts. Hence recurrent contracting between interdependent firms is subject to a variety of transaction costs from haggling over unforeseen contingencies to monitoring performance, and market exchange is progressively supplanted by internal governance structures as asset specificity deepens and capital investments become more difficult to turn to alternative uses.[13] The central assumption is that the selection of governance structures is determined by efficiency in reducing overall transaction costs, and firms shift across a spectrum of alternatives from spot-market contracting to administrative hierarchy according to the type of transaction involved. Thus managers constantly balance the costs of using the market against those of internal organization, while competition ensures that the most transactionally efficient governance structure will eventually be adopted.[14]

The organization of work, in Williamson's model, is no different from any other transaction, and the rise of the factory system can be explained by the efficiency of authority relations in restraining opportunism and economizing on costly bargaining when adaptation to a changing environment is required. As human capital assets such as skills and knowledge have become increasingly firm-specific or 'idiosyncratic' in Williamson's terms, management and workers' shared need to safeguard costly investments in on-the-job training has led in turn to the widespread development of internal labour markets characterized by administrative rules governing layoffs, promotion and discipline.[15]

Like Chandler, Williamson emphasizes the dependence of economic efficiency on the internal organization of the firm. But while Chandler has less faith in the 'marvels of the market' and examines the dynamic interaction of organization, technology and strategy in economic success, Williamson's transaction-cost approach is more static and concerned with 'adaptive, sequential decision-making'.[16] Beneath these differences, however, the outcome of the process for the two authors is otherwise the same: the internalization of a growing range of economic activities inside large, hierarchical organizations. In both cases, moreover, there is a uniquely efficient form of business enterprise at each stage of economic development. Those firms that fail to conform to the requirements of their environment either by adapting their structures to the needs of strategy or by minimizing transaction costs will decline and disappear, while choices between markets and hierarchies are themselves ultimately determined by the natural selection of the market.[17]

For Marxists, unlike mainstream theorists of the firm, class interest rather than the neutral pursuit of efficiency is the motor of changes in business organization and management strategy, but the substantive picture that emerges is surprisingly similar. At the heart of the capitalist enterprise, Marxists argue, stands a structural antagonism between workers and employers, rooted in the struggle to extract surplus value from the production process. The law of value leaves little room for managerial discretion, and the organization of work is shaped by the resulting imperative for control over labour. Labour power, on this view, is not just another commodity or factor of production but the pivotal component of the production process because of its unique capacity both to create additional value and to resist managerial direction by varying the intensity of work effort. Like mainstream theorists, however, Marxists generally maintain that competitive market pressures force each firm to adopt improved methods of production in order to match the socially necessary labour time required for the manufacture of its products and that this process of increasing efficiency will continue until the potential development of the forces of production under capitalism has reached its social limits.[18]

Despite their many variations, modern Marxists typically subscribe to an evolutionary model of capitalist development whose basic lines were laid down by Marx himself. The dynamics of competition and accumulation, Marx argued, give rise to a progressive tendency towards the centralization of capital in fewer hands and its concentration in larger installations. At the level of the production process, these developments are accompanied by a parallel trend towards the separation of conception from execution and the increasing subjection of labour to capital. The transformation of the labour process can thus be understood as a series of stages in capitalists' appropriation of knowledge, skill and discretion from the direct producers, and the ever-closer approximation of the latter to the ideal of abstract labour power. Marx himself distinguished three main steps in this process: 'simple cooperation', 'manufacture' and machine production or 'modern industry', as workers lose control first over the product itself, then over the labour process as a whole, and finally over the specific tasks on which they are engaged.[19]

Subsequent Marxists, most notably Braverman, have updated and extended this unilinear model to cover the era of 'monopoly capitalism' by focusing on the impact of 'scientific management' and the application of science and technology to industrial production.[20] Following principles first enunciated by Frederick W. Taylor at the turn of the century, Braverman argues, management has consciously set out to reduce the knowledge and initiative of the individual worker, centralize the planning and direction of production in its own hands, and impose a fragmented and tightly supervised distribution of tasks on the shop floor. At the same time, the introduction of ever more advanced forms of mechanization and automation has removed the last vestiges of skill and discretion from the labour process, reducing the worker to a passive attendant of the machine. For Braverman as for Marx, however, the incidence of these tendencies is extremely uneven across industries, as labour tends to pile up in relatively unmechanized sectors which are then transformed in turn. A variety of forms of work organization – from the most 'archaic' to the most 'advanced' – will therefore coexist at any given moment in time. But this apparent diversity is merely transitory and the central tendencies will sooner or later be extended to all other sectors of the economy as well.[21]

Other recent neo-Marxist writers, by contrast, have sought to modify Marx's schematic model of capitalist development to accommodate a wider range of observed managerial behaviour while preserving its fundamental principles. Thus Andrew Friedman links variations in managerial control strategies to the evolution of the product cycle as well as the wider economy. 'Direct control' of labour through job fragmentation, mechanization and tight supervision becomes only one type of managerial strategy rather than the sole form of capitalist control over productive activity, as Braverman maintained. Under conditions of relative monopoly power, as during the ascending phases of the product cycle when demand is expanding and production remains relatively unstandardized, worker resistance and insulation from competitive pressures induce managers to apply an alternative strategy of 'responsible autonomy' to the core sections of their labour force. In this strategy, managers seek to harness rather than eliminate the

variability of labour power by acknowledging workers' discretionary intervention in production while seeking to win their active support for the firm's
commercial objectives. As the product cycle turns downwards, however,
demand is saturated and production becomes more standardized, competitive pressures reassert themselves, the scope for discretionary behaviour
is reduced, and managers are obliged to revert to direct control strategies for
dealing with labour. Managerial choice remains primarily a search for
comprehensive methods of work control moving through alternate phases in
response to the dictates of the market. Since neither strategy usually appears
in a pure form, these shifts can be presented as movements along a spectrum
according to changes in competitive and technological conditions, mediated
by the expectations of managers.[22]

A second major current, associated with the work of radical economists
such as Marglin, Edwards, Gordon and Reich, is distinguished by its
emphasis on the priority of power over efficiency in the organization of the
capitalist enterprise. The radicals argue that the hierarchical organization of
production – from the rise of the factory system to the job structures of the
modern corporation – is rooted less in any contribution to technological
advance than in capitalists' attempts to control the work-force and appropriate a larger share of the surplus product.[23] But if, on this view, power
rather than efficiency shapes the division of labour under capitalism, power
is conceived not as an end in itself but as a means of maximizing profits; and
few radicals would deny that capitalists are driven by the competitive
process to introduce the most profitable form of productive organization
currently available.[24] Hence for all their emphasis on the labour process as
an historically contingent power struggle between employers and workers,
the radicals ultimately concur with their more orthodox critics – whether
Marxist or liberal – that the logic of capitalism itself obliges firms to adopt
the form of organization that most efficiently serves their economic
interests.[25]

Like Marx, Braverman and Friedman, the radicals also discern an
historical logic in the evolution of the labour process as a result of the
dynamics of capital accumulation and workers' continuing resistance to
managerial control. Thus Edwards, Gordon and Reich distinguish three
main systems of labour management: 'simple' or 'hierarchical' control
through direct supervision by the boss or foreman; 'technical' control
through the introduction of managerial planning and deskilling machinery;
and 'bureaucratic' control through impersonal rules governing the operation
of internal labour markets within large enterprises. All of these control
systems may coexist within the economy as a whole, giving rise to distinctive
patterns of segmentation within the labour force; but with the transition
from competitive to monopoly capitalism, bureaucratic systems of control
have become progressively dominant in large 'core' corporations enjoying a
significant degree of market power. Each control system, however, has its
own internal contradictions, and the high fixed costs of bureaucratic control

render it particularly vulnerable to cyclical downturns which erode corporate profitability, forcing firms to renege on implicit guarantees of job security and reintroduce more coercive systems of labour control.[26]

A final influential Marxist schema is Michael Burawoy's typology of 'factory regimes' which vary with the political and ideological apparatuses regulating production as well as with the organization of work itself.[27] In capitalist societies, where the apparatuses of factory and state remain institutionally separate, Burawoy distinguishes three main types of factory regime, 'market despotic', 'hegemonic' and 'hegemonic despotic', depending on the forms of competition and state intervention at work.[28] Under market despotism, the prototypical regime of competitive capitalism, the subordination of labour to capital is secured through the 'economic whip of the market' and the state regulates only the external conditions of exchange without intervening directly in the factory apparatus itself. Under hegemonic regimes, characteristic of monopoly capitalism, the subordination of labour requires a measure of consent and the state shapes the factory apparatus through the development of new systems of labour law and social insurance.[29] With the resurgence of competitive pressures in advanced capitalism, finally, despotic features reappear within the hegemonic regime, as the interests of capital and labour are still coordinated through the state, but workers are now forced to make rather than receive concessions on the basis of their employers' relative profitability.[30] Thus for Burawoy, as for Friedman and Edwards, the evolution of the capitalist enterprise towards increasingly bureaucratic and consensual modes of labour control is undercut by the reassertion of crisis tendencies in the wider economy, while the revival of market competition pushes firms back towards the coercive modes of labour control held by Marx to be an inherent feature of capitalism itself.

By the mid-1970s, then, both Marxist and mainstream analyses had largely converged on a common vision of the developmental trajectory of the capitalist enterprise and its labour strategies – the progressive extension of task fragmentation, managerial control and bureaucratic employment practices within large, vertically integrated corporations enjoying a substantial degree of market power. But just as this teleological model of capitalist development was being embodied in ever more elegant and comprehensive theoretical syntheses, the world it was intended to describe was changing in ways that made the model seem increasingly unsatisfactory even to its staunchest proponents. Pervasive instability in markets, technologies and industrial relations have stimulated experiments with new hybrid forms of enterprise management and work organization that blur established boundaries between markets and hierarchies and undermine traditional divisions of labour. New strategies and practices, from joint ventures and 'just-in-time' component supply to teamworking and multiskilling, have spread rapidly among the world's largest corporations and cannot easily be dismissed as archaic survivals of a previous stage of development or marginal phenomena confined to peripheral firms and sectors. At the same time, moreover, this movement of managerial labour strategies away from deskilling and direct control has been associated with an intensification of competitive pressures on firms rather than their relative insulation from them.[31]

Hence, as in the past, both mainstream and Marxist writers have responded by reworking their models of capitalist development to accommodate discordant empirical phenomena while remaining faithful to the theoretical assumptions which underlie them. Thus among the managerialists, for example, Williamson now argues that under certain conditions – such as rapid innovation in products and processes or recurrent purchasing of customized material – 'relational contracting' between loose networks of firms or managers held together by a 'clan' culture may prove competitively superior to coordination through either markets or hierarchies.[32] And even where competitive conditions are otherwise similar, as in the case of the international automobile industry, he now acknowledges that the existence of cultural and institutional checks on opportunism may permit a greater degree of vertical disintegration in Japan than in the United States by reducing the trading hazards associated with subcontracting.[33] But while this last example suggests that a plurality of organizational solutions may prove compatible with the demands of a given external environment, Williamson none the less continues to maintain that the competitive process will select out those forms that most efficiently minimize transaction costs – at least in the longer term.

Among Marxists, too, there is widespread retreat from claims that contemporary forms of work organization show an unambiguous trend towards deskilling and direct control. Recurrent experiments in job redesign, the recomposition of tasks and the devolution of greater autonomy to individuals or work groups have shifted the terrain of debate from the 'degradation of work' to its transformation.[34] Many Marxists, to be sure, continue to regard these phenomena as temporary exceptions to the deeper tendencies of capitalist development which can be expected to reassert themselves in the long run,[35] but other writers in this tradition are prepared to consider more significant theoretical innovations. Thus, for example, Paul Edwards (who calls himself a 'materialist' rather than a Marxist) distinguishes between 'detailed' and 'general' control of the labour process, arguing that firms are concerned less with control over the 'details of work tasks' than with 'the accommodation of workers to the overall aims of the enterprise', however the latter may be obtained.[36] And John Storey likewise maintains that there may be a diversity of overlapping and countervailing means of management control within the 'totality' of political, economic and ideological structures of capitalist production which place objective limits on workers' ability to challenge managerial plans.[37]

More radically still, John Kelly locates the roots of job redesign experiments in the 'disarticulation' between the different 'moments' of the 'circuit of capital' (the purchase of labour power in the labour market, the extraction of surplus value in the labour process and the realization of surplus value in the product market) with no moment necessarily dominant over the others and no reason to expect a unitary response from firms to this dilemma.[38] In a similar vein, finally, Richard Hyman sees the plurality of observable managerial strategies as a product of the structural contradictions of capitalism itself. Hence 'for individual capitals – as for capital in general – there is no "one best way" of managing these contradictions, only different routes to partial failure', and 'managerial strategy can best be conceptualized as the programmatic choice among alternatives none of which can prove satisfactory'. Managerial concerns with improved design or product quality may conflict with desires for greater control, and there are irresolvable tensions between other objectives such as direction and delegation within the labour process, discipline and consent of the work-force, securing and obscuring the commodity status of labour, and individual and collective representation of workers.[39]

On these assumptions, as Hyman and others have recognized, any notion of a managerial 'control imperative' becomes problematic.[40] Even under the most favourable conditions, with stable markets, standardized products and special-purpose machinery, direct control strategies remain necessarily incomplete, as Tolliday shows in his chapter on Ford in Britain. However elaborate a firm's planning, it appears inherently impossible to predict all the contingencies in a complex manufacturing process, and a variety of unforeseen factors – fluctuations in the mix of products, the state of equipment and the particular set of employees who show up for work each day – all combine to demand greater discretion from even 'unskilled' workers than their formal job descriptions specify.[41] Nor is this difficulty obviated by advances in automation: for as Bryn Jones's chapter demonstrates, the importance of such 'tacit skills' is if anything enhanced with flexible manufacturing systems because of their increased complexity and vulnerability to breakdown. Hence managers typically require an ineradicable measure of consent and cooperation from even the most deskilled work-force. Yet if management explicitly incorporates its dependence on worker initiatives into the organization of production, as in a strategy of responsible autonomy, there can be no guarantee that the resulting autonomy will remain 'responsible'.[42]

Such writers have moved a long way towards accepting that there can be no 'one best way' to competitive success. Yet they remain unwilling to jettison their deterministic assumptions, however nuanced by the introduction of 'multiple', 'overlapping' or 'contradictory' determinations. At the deepest level, therefore, these writers continue to insist that management's oscillation between alternative labour strategies is itself determined by the contradictory structure of capitalist production, and that managerial options are narrowly constrained by the requirements of surplus extraction. Thus even the most sophisticated Marxists, like their mainstream counterparts, remain unwilling to concede a genuine scope for managerial choice in the face of the objective constraints imposed by the external environment.[43]

ECONOMIC 'NATURAL SELECTION' AND THE LIMITS OF DETERMINISM

Dominant theories of the enterprise are thus largely agreed in deriving employers' labour strategies from the imperatives of markets and technology. But how robust is this widely shared assumption? Empirical studies of firms' internal operations typically reveal complex political processes involving both conflict and cooperation between individuals, departments and interest groups rather than a clearly defined hierarchical structure of command corresponding to the formal organizational chart. The business enterprise, in Cyert and March's influential formulation, should therefore be understood not as unitary actor but rather as a 'political coalition' whose objectives are determined by a bargaining process resulting in a 'quasi-resolution of conflict' which may be renegotiated at any time.[44] Business decisions, on this view, are deeply influenced by non-economic factors such as company history, power struggles, personalities and ideology, and they are often based on routinized decision mechanisms such as standard operating procedures, 'rules of thumb' and accounting conventions rather than an assessment of each problem on its individual merits. In neither case, therefore, can such decisions be convincingly represented as the product of a strictly rational and objectively valid calculation of prospective costs and benefits in the light of predetermined organizational goals. Labour management, in this respect, is no different from any other sphere of enterprise activity, such as finance, marketing, product design or choice of technology.

Many contemporary students of management such as contingency theorists acknowledge the force of these observations but regard them as imperfections to be overcome so that organizations can be steered towards more 'rational' forms of decision-making. Such writers recognize the complexity of firms' internal operations while seeking to retain a core 'logic of effectiveness'. Contingency theorists are therefore concerned with mismatches between external change and organizational structure or between company strategy and company culture, and their diagnoses focus on the problem of effective business leadership in winning support for 'contextually appropriate action' or making organizations 'congruent with their environment'. The requirements of market competition thus remain the driving force behind organizational change, but its imperatives are mediated by cognitive and political processes which may impede or facilitate the necessary adjustments.[45]

But empirical studies of business behaviour are less sanguine than prescriptive theorists about the prospects of overcoming organizational disfunctions within the enterprise. For the internal politics of the firm, these studies suggest, are not confined to 'routine' decisions about pricing, output or work assignments, but also extend to more fundamental 'strategic' decisions. As Williams *et al.* have demonstrated, for example, the management of nationalized enterprises such as British Leyland, British Steel and the National Coal Board justified disastrous large-scale additions to capacity during the 1970s by building optimistic assumptions about future demand into their investment-appraisal models. At the same time, these companies also pursued reductions in direct labour costs well beyond their importance in total costs or their strategic relevance for competitive performance.[46] In the private sector, similarly, a recent study by a team at the London Business School of strategic investment decisions in large diversified companies found that formal capital-budgeting procedures and financial-appraisal techniques were rarely followed rigorously, while outcomes depended heavily on organizational structure, divisional interests, *ad hoc* intervention by senior management and the overall 'corporate climate'. Strategic planning in these companies, the authors concluded was more 'emergent' than 'deliberate', and it was difficult to view investment decisions, however major, as 'the implementation of an explicit prior strategy'.[47]

The standard reply to these observations, whether from neo-classical economists, managerialists or Marxists, is that whatever their truth as empirical descriptions, the internal decision-making processes of the firm are irrelevant to the long-term operation of the economy because the market selects through competition only those firms which, by whatever methods, hit upon the optimally efficient solution for profit maximization. More concretely, firms pursuing suboptimal strategies will be either eliminated by bankruptcy or take-over or forced to imitate their more successful competitors in order to forestall this fate.[48]

To what extent, however, does the market act as an effective mechanism for 'natural selection' among competing firms? Empirical research on business failure casts substantial doubt upon the claim that surviving firms are necessarily the most efficient or even the most profitable in some objective sense. Thus studies of stock-market takeovers in postwar Britain, for example, have consistently found that size, gearing and share prices rather than profitability or technical efficiency are the distinguishing characteristics of surviving firms, while merged companies have generally proved less profitable than their separate constituents.[49] Similarly, studies of the diffusion of the M-Form corporation from the United States to Great Britain, West Germany and Japan have failed to find any systematic association between multi-divisionalization and economic performance.[50] Even in the United States, where Chandler argued that the corporate consolidations of the turn of the century only proved successful in sectors where they permitted the realization of economies of scale, more recent research by Lamoreaux has demonstrated that market power, oligopolistic pricing and the erection of artificial barriers to entry played a crucial role in the creation and survival of the largest merged companies such as US Steel.[51]

Mergers, takeovers and bankruptcy proceedings are strongly influenced by the institutional organization of the capital market, competition policy, company law and the accounting conventions that define the valuation of capital assets and the assessment of profit and loss. All of these vary considerably from country to country, notably between stock-market systems such as the US and the UK on the one hand and bank-based systems such as the Federal Republic of Germany and Japan on the other, and these variations in turn shape the criteria for business success and failure in different national contexts.[52] But mergers, takeovers and bankruptcy proceedings also depend on quintessentially subjective judgements about management quality, the value of a business as a 'going concern' versus the break-up value of its assets, and the potential returns to alternative configurations of company structure and strategy. The larger and more diversified the enterprise, too, the more controversial becomes the allocation of costs and revenues among its constituent parts, and the greater the weight of such subjective factors in assessing proposals for closures or restructuring, as recent debates about hostile take-overs and leveraged buy-outs in the US or the retrenchment programmes of nationalized companies in the UK graphically illustrate.[53] In none of these cases, therefore, can business failure be properly regarded as an impersonal mechanism whereby unsuccessful firms are eliminated on the basis of objective judgements about past performance rather than subjective assessments of future prospects.[54]

At a deeper theoretical level, it is doubtful whether the market could ever act as an effective mechanism of 'natural selection' imposing profit-maximizing decisions on firms under any set of empirically plausible circumstances. For, as Sidney Winter has shown, information costs ensure that firms can never know *ex ante* whether or not they are pursuing optimal strategies in any given situation: under conditions of uncertainty, an alternative strategy might always prove more profitable, but the costs involved in its discovery might well outweigh the prospective returns. It is for this reason, Winter argues, that firms adopt routinized decision rules such as mark-up pricing and aim at satisfactory rates of return rather than seeking to discover the highest payoff in each new situation.[55]

Other theorists have suggested that such 'satisficing' behaviour should be interpreted as a more sophisticated form of maximization or 'bounded rationality' once the costs of information are taken into account. But this approach offers no solution to the problem since, as Winter points out, the optimal level of search activity cannot itself be determined without incurring additional information costs. 'Bounded rationality', like the Marxist concept of the 'relative autonomy of the state', is thus a contradiction in terms: either behaviour is rational in the strict sense of being the best possible choice under the circumstances or it is not; and a decision procedure which provides no means for assessing the limits of the information on which it is based can hardly be considered a higher form of optimization.[56]

If firms themselves are not capable of determining optimal strategies *ex ante*, neither is it likely that the 'natural selection' of the market will impose profit maximization on them *ex post*. For, as Winter has formally demonstrated, such characteristic features of modern economies as production economies of scale, product differentiation, variations in access to external finance and divergent expansion policies might all prevent maximizing firms from driving non-maximizers out of business. Conversely, he suggests, business policies that might approximate to profit maximization under one set of market conditions will not necessarily do so under another. Under conditions of rapid innovation or extreme cyclical fluctuations, for example, the situation 'may present decision problems totally unlike those on which the selection process has been doing its work'. Hence, if environmental changes exceed the range of past experience,

> the selection process may discriminate *against* those firms that would approach profit maximizing behaviour over a wide range of situations, and in favour of those which happen, by virtue of their rules of thumb, to achieve profit maximization in a restricted range of situations.[57]

Since firms' decision procedures are embedded in organizational routines, a period of time will normally elapse before their behaviour adjusts to the demands of the new conditions; by that point, however, the environment might once again have changed in unanticipated ways. At any given moment, therefore, the population of firms in the economy will typically consist of a heterogeneous amalgam of maximizers and non-maximizers with respect to current market conditions, and this pattern can be expected to persist indefinitely in the absence of some long-term trend to static equilibrium.[58]

But what of technology? Is there an immanent logic of technological efficiency that imparts to the economy a developmental trajectory – for example towards larger-scale production methods – that market processes alone do not possess? Here, too, recent research supports a sceptical response. Detailed studies show that in the formative stages of the automobile, office equipment and computer industries, to take some notable examples, there was an abundance of competing solutions to the key technical problems. Each was potentially better on some dimensions than the others; and its advantages reflected the particular circumstances and favoured the interests of its sponsors over the other competitors. Typically an exercise of economic power decided the outcome. Some firm or group of firms with enough control over the emerging market to ensure an indispensable minimum of demand for its solution and enough capital to cover the costs of its mistakes pressed ahead and imposed its plan. Once its products were established, competitors had reason to emulate them more or less completely, since development of radically different but promising lesigns was costly; and the prospects that costly innovation would be rewarded were steadily diminished as customers became habituated to existing solutions. Although the winning design had to meet some minimum performance standard, the sweep of its success was thus no proof of its unrivalled technical superiority; other variants could have served as well.[59] But however overwhelming the triumph of a particular design solution, its hegemony was never permanent: a sudden shift in the conditions of competition such as the discovery of a new technology, a change in the price of raw materials or a realignment of demand might always reopen debate on the definition of the product. Nor did victory in one stage of technological competition provide any guarantee of equal success in the next, as can be seen, for example, from the relative performance of American and Japanese manufacturers during the current phase of 'dematurity' in the international automobile industry.[60]

At a more general level, similarly, as we have argued elsewhere, the ascendancy of mass production over craft production in industrial economies through most of this century was not the result of its inherent technological superiority. Under favourable circumstances, a growing body of historical evidence suggests, craft production – understood as the combination of skilled workers and general-purpose equipment to manufacture customized products – could prove as technologically innovative and economically dynamic as mass production – understood as the manufacture of standardized products by unskilled workers using special-purpose equipment.[61] Where markets were diversified, skills abundant and local institutions geared to balancing competition and cooperation among economic actors – as in many of the most famous industrial regions of the nineteenth century – craft producers, whether organized in large, internally flexible firms or interdependent networks of small ones, demonstrated a sustained capacity for innovation in products and processes over long periods of time.[62] But from the late nineteenth century onwards, the concurrent and competing development of mass production exerted an increasingly unfavourable influence on the wider environment confronting craft producers in a variety of spheres from retail distribution and the shaping of consumer tastes through systems of training and industrial relations to government policies. The result, as in the parallel case of industrial innovation, was the gradual abandonment of potentially viable technological alternatives that under different background conditions might have played a more important role in subsequent developments. Craft production, to be sure, persisted wherever markets were too small or too unstable to justify investment in special-purpose equipment and bureaucratic management methods, but even its own practioners now acknowledged their effective subordination to the technological dynamic of mass production.[63]

As in individual industries, however, apparently closed debates about the general trajectory of technological development may be reopened by unexpected changes in the conditions of competition, such as the upheavals in the international economy during the 1970s and 1980s. Mass production requires a large, homogeneous market for standardized goods and a stable, predictable environment in order to realize economies of scale and cover the high fixed costs of product-specific investments. But since the mid-1970s, these requirements have become increasingly problematic in a world economy characterized by slowly growing national markets, intensified international competition and fragmentation of demand for manufactured products, as well as by sharp fluctuations in exchange rates and raw material prices. This persistent volatility of international markets, together with concurrent advances in micro-electronics and computerization, has arguably shifted the trajectory of technological development towards 'flexible specialization', a revitalized form of craft production based on the use of flexible, modern equipment and skilled, adaptable workers to turn out a wide and changing array of semi-customized goods. Thus the mass-production paradigm of technological development that had been taken for granted for so long has itself been fundamentally challenged.[64]

At a deeper theoretical level, finally, as Brian Arthur among others has shown, the technology that wins out in any given contest is not necessarily the one with the greatest potential for long-term development. Most technologies, he argues, are characterized by increasing returns, once adopted, for a variety of well-known reasons ranging from learning by using and network externalities through production economies of scale and informational advantages to technological interrelatedness. Under these conditions small 'historical' events may give one technology an initial edge which becomes cumulatively larger as additional adopters are attracted who might otherwise have gone along with one of its rivals, until the market 'tips' in its favour. Where such increasing returns are unbounded, the dominant technology will drive out all others and create a monopoly, while under less extreme assumptions certain sequences of adoption could bid up the returns to both technologies more or less in concert, leading to a shared market. In either case, however, it is the contingent outcome of historical events – themselves a product of the choices and expectations of the actors involved – rather than current or potential efficiency which shapes the trajectory of technological development and the resulting market structure.[65]

Theoretically as well as empirically, then, there seems little reason to assume that technology or markets impose a narrow range of appropriate strategies on the enterprise, whether in relation to labour management or to any other sphere of business activity. Competition, to be sure, rewards some firms and penalizes others, while the least successful enterprises may be eliminated from contention altogether. But the degree to which any particular feature of firm performance is 'selected out' by the market is difficult to determine, and the criteria for competitive survival are often quite loose.[66] Within these broad efficiency constraints, a variety of managerial strategies may be pursued, and as we shall see in subsequent chapters, a considerable diversity of labour policies may therefore be observed at any historical moment.

EMPLOYER ORGANIZATION AND THEORIES OF COLLECTIVE ACTION

Despite their many differences, as we have seen, mainstream and Marxist theories of the firm substantially agree that the interests of individual employers are determined by their objective position in wider economic (and, for Marxists, social) structures. Hence both schools likewise concur in treating collective organization, whether in relation to workers or the state, as a simple aggregation of employers' underlying interests rather than as a contingent political process in which these interests are redefined as well as expressed. These common premises have none the less given rise to a variety of contrasting views about the associative behaviour of employers and their propensity for collective action.

The most widespread approach to the analysis of interest group activity remains that of classical pluralism. In this view, the development of organization among businessmen, like other 'potential' groups, is a direct product of the latent interests shared by their individual members. These interests exist prior to and independent of organization.[67] The pluralist approach may then be refined by tracing observable conflicts within the business community to prior differences in economic position, as in the recent literature on the politics of industrial sectors. Drawing on theories of the product cycle and the Marxist notion of class fractions as well as on pluralism itself, writers such as Kurth, Ferguson, Abraham and Gourevitch have accordingly sought to derive the divergent political orientations of business groups – such as free trade or protectionism and acceptance or rejection of collective bargaining – from the underlying characteristics of particular sectors in terms of markets, technology, labour force and capital requirements.[68]

If collective organization, for pluralists and sector analysts alike, arises directly from the existence of common interests, this link has been challenged by rational-choice theorists such as Mancur Olson.[69] For even if all members of a group may have a common interest in a good obtainable through collective action, Olson argues, they have no common interest in paying for the cost of this collective good, and will not contribute to it if they can obtain the benefits without so doing. The existence of this 'free rider' problem means that such collective goods will not normally be provided except under special circumstances: where all members of a group are obliged to contribute to the common good through some form of coercion; where individual members are large enough to provide some measure of the good for themselves; where a group is small enough to provide social as well as economic incentives for membership compliance; or where collective solidarity is underpinned by the provision of 'selective incentives' – such as low-cost insurance or expert advice – to members of the group on an individual basis. Collective organization, on Olson's analysis, is thus inherently problematic for employers and workers alike, but business organizations are advantaged in many industries by oligopolistic concentration which reduces the size of the potential group and increases its cohesion, as well as by their superior ability to provide selective incentives. At the national level, conversely, he suggests, the business community as a whole forms a large group which is neither particularly well organized nor disproportionately powerful. In each case, however, the success or failure of collective action remains a simple consequence of group members' rational pursuit of their predetermined economic interests.[70]

From a Marxist perspective, Offe and Wiesenthal have taken up Olson's analysis of the logic of collective action, while insisting on a fundamental difference in its application to the interests of capitalists and workers.[71] Capital, in their view, is already 'organized' within the firm, while labour instead is atomized by competition. The asymmetrical dependence of labour on capital arising from workers' inability to reproduce themselves outside the labour market means that a broader range of 'life-interests' is involved in organization for workers than for capitalists, while the interests of the former are also more heterogeneous than those of the latter. 'Compared to that of any individual member of the working class', they assert, 'the interest of a capitalist is far less likely to be ambiguous, controversial, or wrongly perceived.' Hence there are two distinct 'logics of collective action'. Workers, unlike capitalists, can only overcome the higher costs of collective action by creating a collective identity which changes the standards according to which these costs are assessed by each individual member of the group. Thus workers' interests 'can only be met to the extent that they are partially redefined', and their organizations must 'simultaneously express and define the interests of their members'. 'Capital associations', by contrast, need only aggregate and specify the 'given and fixed' interests of their members, whose formation takes place outside of and prior to the organization. Divergences may well arise within business associations – for example, between large and small firms, exporters and home-market producers, or competitors in labour, capital and product markets. But such internal conflicts are easily resolved through the provision of selective incentives because of the limited engagement of members' 'central life-interests' within the organization. Thus business organizations, unlike trade unions or political parties, have no need for explicit ideology, and

> even if the need to rely on some explicit common understanding of interests should come up, the task is an easier one to solve because one can assume a presupposed consensus of social, cultural and political values, to which one can always refer.

The only uncertainty lies in finding the most effective means of securing these ends in any given situation.[72]

Whatever their disagreements, each of the approaches examined so far assumes that collective organization plays a strategically significant function for employers, whether in relation to trade unions or the state. But a number of writers have recently questioned this assumption from a variety of perspectives. Thus Howard Gospel, for example, argues that collective bargaining by employers' associations represents a 'delegated' form of labour management which is tendentially displaced as industrial relations are internalized within large, hierarchical corporations engaged in mass production and distribution.[73] Paul Windolf conversely sees an evolutionary tendency towards the growth of enterprise-level bargaining arising from the new, flexible forms of work organization and decentralized 'productivity coalitions' demanded by the changing markets and technologies of the 1980s.[74] And theorists of 'disorganized capitalism' likewise discern a secular decline of employer organization as a result of global trends towards the internationalization of capital and the disintegration of mass unionism based on working-class collective identities.[75] But in each case, as in the previous approaches considered, it is employers' prior economic interests – assumed once again to be fixed and unambiguous – that determine their now-declining propensity for collective action.

The most significant departure from this widespread interpretation of business organization as a collective expression of pre-determined interests can be found within recent theorizations of neo-corporatism. Early versions of this approach, whether advanced by liberals or Marxists, regarded collective organization among employers and workers alike as a functional response to growing systemic demands for the incorporation of organized interest groups in the economic and political management of advanced industrial societies.[76] But as the geographical and temporal variability of neo-corporatist arrangements has become more apparent, sophisticated proponents of this approach such as Schmitter and Streeck have come to see effective employer organization as a necessary condition for their success whose existence cannot be taken for granted.[77] In contrast to Offe and Wiesenthal, these writers argue that employer interests are everywhere extremely heterogeneous and their solidarity inherently provisional and precarious. Hence, as Streeck observes,

> To speak on behalf of their members, employers associations seem to need the support of strong interlocutors, in particular trade unions and governments. They also seem to depend on the presence of favourable institutional and economic conditions that induce similar individual responses of their members and thereby help associations contain the strong centrifugal tendencies among their membership.[78]

This shift in perspective in turn depends on a fundamental modification of the received understanding of interest-group organization as a simple aggregation of membership preferences. Thus, as Streeck and Schmitter argue, both employers' associations and trade unions are '*producers* of group interests'.

> Contrary to their dominant image as 'voluntary organizations', they are much more than passive recipients of preferences put forward by their constituents and clients. Empirical observations of neo-corporatist practice, as well as theoretical reasoning, show that organized group interests are not given but emerge as a result of a multi-faceted interaction between social and organizational structure – whereby the substance of the collective interest depends at least as much on the way it is organized, as does the structure of the organization on the interest it is to represent.[79]

At this point, however, collective action among employers can no longer be derived from their prior economic interests, and the constitutive role of organization in redefining those interests must therefore be acknowledged for capitalists as for workers.

Dominant approaches to collective action among employers characteristically assume that their organizations represent a simple aggregation of predetermined social and economic interests. But, as we have seen, markets and technology do not determine a uniquely effective labour strategy for enterprise management, nor do they impose on employers an unambiguous set of objective interests in relation to their work-force. Broad goals such as profitability or business success may be pursued by a variety of means, while differences in institutional structures, expectations and forms of calculation will shape perceptions of the optimal course of action in any given circumstances. It follows, therefore, that quite similar business groups can arrive at radically divergent definitions of their underlying interests in any particular situation.[80]

At a deeper theoretical level, it is highly questionable whether objective interests can ever be imputed to social actors without reference either to their conscious interpretations or to some specific context. There is no self-evident reason to assume that social actors' own assessment of their interests should necessarily correspond – even in the long run – to an abstract definition put forward by an external observer. Even if interests could be taken as given, moreover, their 'rational' pursuit by individual actors may give rise to collectively sub-optimal outcomes, as in the well-known case of the 'prisoner's dilemma'. Only by recognizing the limits of their own rationality, sophisticated rational-choice theorists argue, can human actors overcome these difficulties through the development of suitably 'cooperative games'.[81] More radically still, much recent work on the methodology of the social sciences suggests that interests should be regarded as inherently ambiguous, context-dependent and potentially incoherent. From this perspective, interests emerge from an interaction between social actors' prior interpretative framework and the specific situation in which they find themselves, a context which includes the discourses and practices of institutions such as employers' associations and trade unions as well as social and economic relationships. From these reflections it follows that whatever the objective bases for individualism or collective action among employers – as among workers themselves – there can be no way to determine in advance which tendency will prove more fundamental.[82]

But even if we could ascribe objective interests to employers in relation to their labour force, collective organization among them could never be a simple aggregation of such interests. On the one hand, some impulses towards collective action remain ineradicable for employers because of the persistence of problems that cannot be resolved by the internalization of functions within the individual enterprise. Questions such as the regulation of local labour markets, the reform of labour law and the political representation of business interests all potentially require some degree of coordination among separate firms. As we shall see in the conclusion such coordination, tacit or formal, can in fact be observed even in those cases where the internalization of economic activity has proceeded furthest, as in Japan and the United States.

On the other hand, however, collective organization among employers is also inherently difficult because of the underlying heterogeneity of business interests arising from inter-firm differences in size, market position and geographical location. Employer organization is thus intrinsically problematic, and yet it occurs – often on a large scale over long periods of time. Nor should it be imagined – *pace* Offe and Wiesenthal – that collective action is necessarily of secondary importance for individual employers. For employers, as for workers, collective organization can, on occasion, exert a decisive influence over the 'central life-interests' of the individual members. Thus participation in protracted industrial disputes may bring particular enterprises to the brink of bankruptcy, as in the case of the British engineering industry between 1897 and 1922, or on a larger scale, the wage policies of national employers' associations may systematically contribute to the demise of weak firms or sectors who could not afford to pay the centrally agreed rates, as in Sweden through most of the postwar period.[83]

Employers' associations, like trade unions, are therefore obliged to construct solidarity among their members, building coalitions among potentially conflicting interests which are redefined by the process of collective organization itself. Such associations are thus inherently political bodies whose policies are shaped by internal conflicts in which contingent factors such as organizational structure, ideology and leadership may play crucial roles, as well as by their relationship with external actors such as trade unions and the state.[84] Hence, as the rest of this book demonstrates, these relationships form the basis of any understanding of how and why collective organization among employers, like their individual labour strategies, has varied and continues to vary so widely across sectors and countries at different points in time.

NOTES

1 For previous surveys of the literature on employers and industrial relations, see H. F. Gospel and C. R. Littler (eds), *Managerial Strategies and Industrial Relations* (London, 1983); K. Thurley and S. Wood (eds), *Industrial Relations and Management Strategies* (Cambridge, 1983); and J. P. Windmuller and A. Gladstone (eds), *Employers' Associations and Industrial Relations* (Oxford, 1984). Two comparative studies which emphasize the role of employers in the development of industrial relations are H. A. Clegg, *Trade Unionism under Collective Bargaining* (Oxford, 1976); and K. Sisson, *The Management of Collective Bargaining* (Oxford, 1987).

2 See, for example, H. Phelps Brown, *The Origins of Trade Union Power* (Oxford, 1983), esp. pp. 98–131; and J. Zeitlin, 'From Labour History to the History of Industrial Relations', *Economic History Review*, 2nd series, 51 (1987).

3 For careful reviews of recent developments, see J. MacInnes, *Thatcherism at Work* (Milton Keynes, 1987); and E. Batstone, *The Reform of Workplace Industrial Relations* (Oxford, 1988).

4 For related critiques of the theory of the firm, see J. D. Tomlinson, 'Economic and Sociological Theories of the Enterprise and Industrial Democracy', *British Journal of Sociology* 35 (1984); *idem* 'Democracy Inside the Black Box? Neo-classical Theories of the Firm and Industrial Democracy', *Economy and Society* 15 (1986); G. Thompson, 'The Firm as a "Dispersed Social Agency" ' *Economy and Society* 11 (1982); and R. Whitley, 'Taking Firms Seriously as Economic Actors: Towards a Sociology of Firm Behaviour', *Organization Studies* 8 (1987).

5 M. Friedman, 'The Methodology of Positive Economics', in *Essays in Positive Economics* (Chicago, 1953) p. 22; cf. also F. Machlup, 'Marginal Analysis and Empirical Research', *American Economic Review* 36 (1956). A close parallel to the neo-classical approach in organizational sociology is population-ecology theory which holds that the distribution of organizational forms across the economy is determined by competitive selection processes. See M. T. Hannan and J. Freeman, *Organizational Ecology* (Cambridge, Mass., 1989).

6 Useful surveys can be found in J. Wildsmith, *Managerial Theories of the Firm* (London, 1973); and M. C. Sawyer, *Theories of the Firm* (London, 1979), esp. ch. 7.

7 The convergent approach within organizational sociology is that of contingency theory. Reacting against previous approaches that sought to discover a universal model of organizational efficiency, contingency theorists argue that the appropriateness of different organizational forms is determined by structural features of the external environment, notably technology and markets. For helpful critical surveys of the literature, see J. Child, 'Organizational Structure, Environment and Performance: The Role of Strategic Choice', *Sociology* 6 (1972); S. Wood, 'A Reappraisal of the Contingency Approach to Organization', *Journal of Management Studies* 16 (1979); and G. Schreyögg, 'Contingency and Choice in Organization Theory', *Organization Studies* 1 (1980).

8 A partial exception to these strictures is the behavioural approach elaborated by Richard Cyert, James March and Herbert Simon in Cyert and March, *A Behavioural Theory of the Firm* (Englewood Cliffs, NJ, 1963); and March and Simon *Organizations* (New York, 1958). In principle, the behaviourists depart significantly from orthodox theories of the firm by adopting an empirical approach to its goals, acknowledging a diversity of influences on business decision-making and rejecting the possibility of maximization. In practice, however, they circumscribe the radical implications of these postulates in

developing formal models of business behaviour by 'greatly reducing the potential number of goals and the number of decisions taken by the firm', and explaining decision-makers' actions as a simple product of 'the internal states they bring to their situations and the environmental stimuli generated by these situations'. See the critical discussion in Tomlinson, 'Economic and Sociological Theories of the Enterprise', p. 593; and R. Whittington, 'Environmental Structure and Theories of Strategic Choice', *Journal of Management Studies* 25 (1988), pp. 530–1, from which these quotations are taken respectively.

9 A. D. Chandler, Jr, *Strategy and Structure: Chapters in the History of American Enterprise* (Cambridge, Mass., 1962); *The Visible Hand: The Managerial Revolution in American Business* (Cambridge, Mass., 1977).

10 A. D. Chandler, Jr, *Scale and Scope: The Dynamics of Industrial Capitalism* (Cambridge, Mass., 1990).

11 W. Lazonick, *Competitive Advantage on the Shop Floor* (Cambridge, Mass., 1991). For applications to Britain which stress the role of factor and product markets in determining employer labour policies, see H. F. Gospel, *Markets, Firms and the Management of Labour: The British Experience in Historical Perspective* (forthcoming); *idem*, 'The Management of Labour: Great Britain, the US, and Japan', *Business History* 30 (1988); and R. Fitzgerald, *British Labour Management and Industrial Welfare, 1846–1939* (London, 1988).

12 O. E. Williamson, *Markets and Hierarchies* (New York, 1975); *The Economic Institutions of Capitalism* (New York, 1985).

13 For a clear statement, see *Economic Institutions of Capitalism*, ch. 3, esp. p. 70. Internal organization nevertheless remains for Williamson something of an unhappy necessity where market-mediated contracts break down. The costs of internal governance structures may rise and they are vulnerable to bureaucratic deformations since firms can only 'mimic the high-powered incentives of the market' (ibid., ch. 6, esp. p. 140).

14 'more efficient modes will eventually supplant less efficient modes – though entrenched power interests can sometimes delay the displacement' (ibid., p. 236; cf. also pp. 22–3).

15 ibid., chs 9–10; *Markets and Hierarchies*, ch. 4.

16 See Lazonick's comparison of the two approaches in *Competitive Advantage on the Shop Floor*, and the authors' assessments of each other's work in O. E. Williamson, 'Emergence of the Visible Hand: Implications for Industrial Organization', in A. D. Chandler, Jr, and H. Daems (eds), *Managerial Hierarchies: Comparative Perspectives on the Rise of the Modern Industrial Enterprise* (Cambridge, Mass., 1980); and A. D. Chandler, 'The Evolution of the Large Industrial Corporation: An Evaluation of the Transaction-Cost Approach', *Business and Economic History*, 2nd ser., 11 (1982).

17 For an incisive overview of the structure of the argument, see C. F. Sabel, 'The Re-emergence of Regional Economies', in P. C. Schmitter (ed.), *Experimenting with Scale* (Cambridge, forthcoming).

18 The classic statement is of course K. Marx, *Capital*, esp. vol. I (trans. B. Fowkes, Harmondsworth, 1976). An increasing number of writers have sought to abandon the labour theory of value while preserving Marx's account of the contradiction between labour and capital within the production process. For a powerful demonstration of the centrality of value categories within Marx's analysis of capitalism and their theoretical indefensibility, see A. Cutler, B. Hindess, P. Hirst and A. Hussain, *Marx's 'Capital' and Capitalism Today*, 2 vols (London, 1977–8), esp. vol. I, pts I–II.

19 ibid., chs 13–15.

20 H. W. Braverman, *Labor and Monopoly Capitalism: The Degradation of Work in the Twentieth Century* (New York, 1974).

21 See, for example, the discussion of the incipient Taylorization of clerical and service work, ibid., pp. 259–377.
22 A. L. Friedman, *Industry and Labour: Class Struggle at Work and Monopoly Capitalism* (London, 1977); 'Management Strategies, Market Conditions and the Labour Process', in F. H. Stephen (ed.), *Firms, Organization and Labour* (London, 1984); 'Developing the Managerial Strategies Approach to the Labour Process', *Capital and Class* 30 (1986).
23 S. A. Marglin, 'What Do Bosses Do? The Origins and Functions of Hierarchy in Capitalist Production', *Review of Radical Political Economics* 6 (1974); K. Stone, 'The Origins of Job Structures in the Steel Industry', ibid.; S. A. Marglin, 'Knowledge and Power', in Stephen, *Firms, Organization and Labour*; R. Edwards, *Contested Terrain: The Transformation of the Workplace in the Twentieth Century* (New York, 1979); D. M. Gordon, R. Edwards and M. Reich, *Segmented Work, Divided Workers: The Historical Transformation of Labor in the United States* (Cambridge, 1982).
24 See, for example, D. M. Gordon, 'Capitalist Efficiency and Socialist Efficiency', *Monthly Review* (1976). For a broader attempt to analyse the division of labour as a product of power relations, see D. Rueschmeyer, *Power and the Division of Labour* (Cambridge, 1986); and for the inherent limitations of 'power' as an analytic category, see B. Hindess, 'Power, Interests and the Outcome of Struggles', in *Political Choice and Social Structure* (Aldershot, 1990).
25 Indeed, as one organization theorist has remarked, 'it is not easy to distinguish' the radical analysis of Edwards from the transaction-cost approach: see J. Pfeffer, *Organizations and Organization Theory* (Marshfield, Mass., 1982), p. 166. For restatements of the priority of efficiency over power or control in the organization of work under capitalism, from a Marxist and a liberal perspective respectively, see S. Cohen, 'A Labour Process to Nowhere?', *New Left Review* 165 (1987); and D. S. Landes, 'What Do Bosses Really Do?', *Journal of Economic History* 46 (1986).
26 Edwards, *Contested Terrain*; Gordon, Edwards and Reich, *Segmented Work*. While acknowledging the limitations of particular managerial strategies, these authors none the less tend to assume that an effective substitute will always be forthcoming: see the discussion of the 'panacea fallacy' in C. Littler and G. Salaman, 'Bravermania and Beyond: Recent Theories of the Labour Process', *Sociology* 16 (1982).
27 M. Burawoy, *The Politics of Production: Factory Regimes under Capitalism and Socialism* (London, 1985).
28 In state socialist societies, the fusion of factory and state apparatuses generates a fourth type of regime, 'bureaucratic despotism': ibid., ch. 4. Burawoy also acknowledges significant variations within as well as across regime types: see esp. chs 2–3.
29 ibid. Under an hegemonic regime, worker resistance can itself become functional for capital, stimulating the emergence of bargaining arrangements and legal rules required for the mobilization of consent. Cf. Burawoy's earlier work, *Manufacturing Consent* (Chicago, 1979), which placed greater emphasis on the factory rather than the wider society as the crucial site for the production of hegemony under monopoly capitalism.
30 Burawoy, *Politics of Production*, pp. 148–52.
31 For general overviews of these developments, see M. J. Piore and C. F. Sabel, *The Second Industrial Divide* (New York, 1984); C. F. Sabel, 'Flexible Specialization and the Re-emergence of Regional Economies', in P. Hirst and J. Zeitlin (eds), *Reversing Industrial Decline? Industrial Structure and Policy in Britain and her Competitors* (Oxford, 1989); and *idem*, 'Skills without a Place: The Reorganization of the Corporation and the Experience of Work', paper

presented to the British Sociological Association Conference, Guildford, 2–4 Apr. 1990. For a case study of a key sector, see S. Tolliday and J. Zeitlin (eds), *The Automobile Industry and Its Workers: Between Fordism and Flexibility* (Cambridge, 1986).

32 Williamson, *Economics Institutions of Capitalism*, pp. 71–3, 83–4, 141–4, 158–9; O. E. Williamson and W. G. Ouchi, 'The Markets and Hierarchies Program of Research: Origins, Implications, Prospects', in A. H. Van de Ven and W. F. Joyce (eds), *Perspectives on Organization Design and Behavior* (New York, 1981); W. G. Ouchi, 'Markets, Bureaucracies, and Clans', *Administrative Science Quarterly* 25 (1980); and the discussion in Sabel, 'Flexible Specialization', pp. 29–31.

33 Williamson, *Economic Institutions of Capitalism*, pp. 120–3; Ouchi, 'Markets, Bureaucracies, and Clans'.

34 Compare S. Wood (ed.), *The Degradation of Work? Skill, Deskilling and the Labour Process* (London, 1982), and *idem* (ed.), *The Transformation of Work? Skill, Flexibility and the Labour Process* (London, 1989). The labour process debate is commonly acknowledged to have 'run into the sand' as a result of the diversity revealed by empirical studies and the undermining of the logical architecture of Braverman's argument: see J. Storey, 'The Means of Management Control', *Sociology* 19 (1985), esp. p. 194; P. Thompson, 'Crawling from the Wreckage: The Labour Process and the Politics of Production', in D. Knights and H. Wilmott (eds), *Labour Process Theory* (London, 1989); and Cohen, 'Labour Process to Nowhere?'.

35 See, for example, P. Armstrong, 'Labour and Monopoly Capital: The Degradation of Debate', in R. Hyman and W. Streeck (eds), *New Technology and Industrial Relations* (Oxford, 1988).

36 P. K. Edwards, *Control at Work: A Materialist Analysis* (Oxford, 1986), esp. p. 6.

37 Storey, 'Means of Management Control'.

38 J. Kelly, 'Management's Redesign of Work: Labour Process, Labour Markets and Product Markets', in D. Knights, H. Wilmott and D. Collinson (eds), *Job Redesign: Critical Perspectives on the Labour Process* (Aldershot, 1985).

39 R. Hyman, 'Strategy or Structure? Capital, Labour and Control', *Work, Employment and Society* 1 (1987), esp. p. 30.

40 Cf. also P. Cressy and J. MacInnes, 'Voting for Ford: Industrial Democracy and the Control of Labour', *Capital and Class* 11 (1980). But for a last-ditch defence of labour control as an unavoidable imperative of capitalist production, see P. Thompson, Jr, *The Nature of Work: An Introduction to the Labour Process Debate* (2nd edn, London, 1989), pp. 234–46.

41 For the general argument, see T. Manwaring and S. Wood, 'The Ghost in the Machine: Tacit Skills in the Labour Process', in Knights *et al., Job Redesign*.

42 For a fuller elaboration of this argument, see J. Zeitlin, 'Shop Floor Bargaining and the State: A Contradictory Relationship', in S. Tolliday and J. Zeitlin (eds), *Shop Floor Bargaining and the State* (Cambridge, 1985), pp. 14–15.

43 For an agnostic position in the face of the diversity of experience and plurality of theoretical positions, see Wood, *Transformation of Work?*, ch. 1.

44 Cyert and March, *Behavioral Theory of the Firm*; J. G. March, 'The Business Firm as a Political Coalition', *Journal of Politics* 24 (1962).

45 See, for example, P. R. Lawrence and J. Lorsch, *Organization and Environment* (Boston, 1967); *idem, Developing Organizations* (Reading, Mass., 1969); A. Pettigrew, *The Awakening Giant: Continuity and Change at ICI* (Oxford, 1985), esp. p. 439; and C. Prahalad and Y. Doz, 'Managing Managers: The Work of Top Management', in J. G. Hunt, D. M. Hosking, C. A. Schriesheim and R. Stewart (eds), *Leaders and Managers: International Perspectives on Managerial Behaviour and Leadership* (New York, 1984), pp. 373–4. For the relationship

between the positive and normative dimensions of contingency theory, see Schreyögg, 'Contingency and Choice in Organization Theory', and his exchange with L. Donaldson in *Organization Studies* 3 (1982).

46 K. Williams, C. Haslam, A. Wardlow and J. Williams, 'Accounting for Failure in the Nationalized Enterprises – Coal, Steel and Cars since 1970', *Economy and Society* 15 (1986); K. Williams, C. Haslam and J. Williams, *The Breakdown of Austin-Rover* (Leamington Spa, 1987).

47 P. Marsh, P. Barwise, K. Thomas and R. Wensley, *Managing Strategic Investment in Large Diversified Companies* (Centre for Business Strategy Report Series, London Business School, 1988), p. 55; extended version published in A. M. Pettigrew (ed.), *Competitiveness and the Management Process* (Oxford, 1988).

48 For the strongest statements of this view, see Friedman, 'Methodology of Positive Analysis', and Machlup, 'Marginal Analysis and Empirical Research'.

49 For a comprehensive review of the evidence, see A. Hughes, 'The Impact of Merger: A Survey of Empirical Evidence for the UK', in J. Fairburn and J. Kay (eds), *Mergers and Merger Policy* (Oxford, 1989).

50 While the M-Form corporation does appear to be positively associated with superior performance in the United States, the evidence is contradictory in the case of Britain and negative in those of the Federal Republic of Germany and Japan. For the US, see D. J. Teece, 'Internal Organization and Economic Performance: An Empirical Analysis of the Profitability of Principal Firms', *Journal of Industrial Economics* 30 (1981). For the UK, see P. Steer and J. Cable, 'Internal Organization and Profit: An Empirical Analysis of Large UK Companies', *Journal of Industrial Economics* 27 (1978); R. S. Thompson, 'Internal Organization and Profit: A Note', *Journal of Industrial Economics* 30 (1981); P. H. Grinyer, M. Yassai-Ardekani and S. Al-Bazza, 'Strategy, Structure, the Environment and Financial Performance in 48 United Kingdom Companies', *Academy of Management Journal* 23 (1980); and C. W. L. Hill and J. F. Pickering, 'Divisionalization, Decentralization and Performance of Large United Kingdom Companies', *Journal of Management Studies* 23 (1986). On the Federal Republic of Germany and Japan, see J. Cable and M. J. Dirrheimer, 'Hierarchies and Markets: An Empirical Test of the Multidivisional Hypothesis in West Germany', *International Journal of Industrial Organization* 1 (1983); J. Cable and H. Yasuki, 'Internal Organisation, Business Groups and Corporate Performance: An Empirical Test of the Multidivisional Hypothesis in Japan', *International Journal of Industrial Organization* 3 (1985).

51 Chandler, *Visible Hand*, pp. 320–39; N. Lamoreaux, *The Great Merger Movement in American Business, 1895–1904*, (Cambridge, 1985); cf. also R. B. Du Boff and E. S. Herman, 'Alfred Chandler's New Business History: A Review', *Politics and Society* 10 (1980).

52 For a useful discussion of international differences in capital market organization and the implications for economic policy and performance, see J. Zysman, *Governments, Markets and Growth* (Ithaca, NY, 1983).

53 On the American debate over hostile take-overs and leveraged buy-outs, see J. C. Coffee, Jr, L. Lowenstein and S. Rose-Ackerman (eds), *Knights, Raiders and Targets: The Impact of the Hostile Takeover* (New York, 1988); and on the accounting problems of retrenchment in British Coal, see D. Cooper and T. Hooper (eds), *Debating Coal Closures: Economic Calculation in the Coal Dispute, 1984–1985* (Cambridge, 1988), esp. chs 5, 7, and 8.

54 For fuller discussions of the theoretical issues, see A. Singh, 'Take-overs, Economic Natural Selection, and the Theory of the Firm: Evidence from the Postwar United Kingdom Experience', *Economic Journal* 85 (1975); A. Hughes and A. Singh, 'Takeovers and the Stock Market', *Contributions to Political*

Economy 6 (1987); R. E. Caves, 'Mergers, Takeovers and Economic Efficiency: Foresight vs. Hindsight', *International Journal of Industrial Organization* 7 (1989); and D. Helm, 'Mergers, Take-overs and the Enforcement of Profit Maximization', in Fairburn and Kay, *Mergers and Merger Policy*.

55. S. G. Winter, Jr, 'Economic "Natural Selection" and the Theory of the Firm', *Yale Economic Essays* 4 (1964), pp. 261–5, drawing on H. Simon, 'A Behavioural Model of Rational Choice', *Quarterly Journal of Economics* 69 (1955).

56 W. Riker and P. C. Ordeshook, *An Introduction to Positive Political Theory* (Englewood Cliffs, NJ, 1973); Winter, 'Economic "Natural Selection" ', pp. 264–5; and J. Elster, *Ulysses and the Sirens* (2nd edn, Cambridge, 1984), esp. pp. 58–9, 133–7. For the parallel with the Marxist concept of the 'relative autonomy of the state', see Cutler *et al.*, *Marx's 'Capital'*, pt III; and Zeitlin, 'Shop Floor Bargaining and the State', p. 25.

57 Winter, 'Economic "Natural Selection" ', pp. 242–5, 258, 265–6, esp. p. 266.

58 ibid., pp. 245–61, 268–9. In subsequent work undertaken independently and with Richard Nelson, Winter has attempted to generate an evolutionary theory which closely approximates to the notion of natural selection in which firms are profit-seekers and the more successful drive the less successful out of business, without assuming either profit maximization or equilibrium. The central difficulty, as Winter noted in his original article (ibid., pp. 266–7), is the relative stability of market conditions: the more stable the environment, the more closely surviving firms approximate to profit maximization, the more volatile the less so. See S. G. Winter, Jr, 'Satisficing, Selection and the Innovating Remnant', *Quarterly Journal of Economics* 85 (1971); 'Optimization and Evolution in the Theory of the Firm', in R. H. Day and T. Groves (eds.), *Adaptive Economic Models* (New York, 1975); and R. Nelson and S. G. Winter, Jr, *An Evolutionary Theory of Economic Change* (Cambridge, Mass., 1982), esp. pts I–II.

59 Well-documented examples include the automobile engine, the typewriter key-board and the personal computer: see C. C. McLaughlin, 'The Stanley Steamer: A Study in Unsuccessful Innovation', in H. G. J. Aitken (ed.), *Explorations in Enterprise* (Cambridge, Mass. 1967); P. David, 'Understanding the Economics of QWERTY: The Necessity of History', in W. N. Parker (ed.), *Economic History and the Modern Economist* (Oxford, 1986); and R. T. DeLamarter, *Big Blue: IBM's Use and Abuse of Power* (London, 1988). For a fuller discussion, see C. Sabel and J. Zeitlin, 'Historical Alternatives to Mass Production: Politics, Markets and Technology in Nineteenth-Century Industrialization', *Past and Present* 108 (1985); and W. B. Arthur, 'Competing Technologies: An Overview', in G. Dosi, C. Freeman, R. Nelson and G. Silverberg (eds), *Technical Change and Economic Theory* (1988).

60 Tolliday and Zeitlin, *Automobile Industry*, esp. pt III.

61 Sabel and Zeitlin, 'Historical Alternatives'; Piore and Sabel, *Second Industrial Divide*. For a vigorous critique from the standpoint of orthodox economic history, see D. S. Landes, 'Small is Beautiful. Small is Beautiful?', in Fondazione ASSI di Storia e Studi sull'Impresa-Instituto per la Storia dell'Umbria Con-temporanea, *Piccola e grande impresa: un problema storico* (Milan, 1987).

62 Important examples include silks in Lyon; ribbons, hardware and speciality steels in St Etienne; edge-tools, cutlery and speciality steel in Solingen, Rems-cheid and Sheffield; watches in the Swiss Jura; cottons in Mulhouse and Pawtucket, Rhode Island; woollens in Roubaix; and textiles of all kinds in Philadelphia. Detailed studies of many such cases will appear in C. Sabel and J. Zeitlin (eds), *Worlds of Possibility: Flexibility and Mass Production in Western Industrialization* (forthcoming), a collective volume based on papers presented to the International Working Group on Historical Alternatives to Mass Produc-tion, Maison des Sciences de l'Homme, Paris.

63 Sabel and Zeitlin, 'Historical Alternatives to Mass Production', esp. pp. 156–61. Two of the best documented cases are Solingen cutlery and Philadelphia textiles: see R. Boch, 'The Rise and Decline of "Flexible Production": The Cutlery Industry of Solingen since the Eighteenth Century', and P. Scranton, ' "Have a Heart for the Manufacturer!" Production, Distribution, and the Decline of American Textile Manufacturing', in Sabel and Zeitlin, *Worlds of Possibility*.

64 On the development of flexible specialization, see Piore and Sabel, *Second Industrial Divide*; Hirst and Zeitlin, *Reversing Industrial Decline?*, esp. Sabel, 'Flexible Specialization'; Sabel, 'Skills without a Place'; and P. Hirst and J. Zeitlin, 'Flexible Specialization versus Post-Fordism: Theory, Evidence and Policy Implications', *Economy and Society* 20 (1991). For representative critiques, see K. Williams, T. Cutler, J. Williams and C. Haslam 'The End of Mass Production?', *Economy and Society* 16 (1987); A. Pollert, 'Dismantling Flexibility', *Capital and Class* 34 (1988); R. Hyman, 'Flexible Specialization: Miracle or Myth?', in Hyman and Streeck, *New Technology and Industrial Relations*; and Wood, *Transformation of Work?*.

65 See the discussions of the literature in Arthur, 'Competing Technologies'; M. Storper, 'Big Structures, Small Events, and Large Processes in Economic Geography', *Environment and Planning A* 20 (1988); and T. P. Hughes, 'The Evolution of Large Technological Systems', in W. E. Bijker, T. P. Hughes and T. J. Pinch (eds), *The Social Construction of Technological Systems: New Directions in the Sociology and History of Technology* (Cambridge, Mass., 1987).

66 Cf. recent attempts to explain 'permanently poor performance' by firms in M. W. Meyer and L. G. Zucker, *Permanently Failing Organizations* (London, 1989).

67 As David Truman puts it in his influential formulation, 'The existence of neither the group nor the interest is dependent upon formal organization . . . organization in the formal sense represents merely a stage or degree of interaction', *The Governmental Process* (New York, 1951), p. 51, quoted in A. L. Saxenian, 'In Search of Power: The Organization of Business Interests in Silicon Valley and Route 128', *Economy and Society* 18 (1989), an insightful and convergent discussion of businessmen's collective political activities, on which we have drawn.

68 J. Kurth, 'The Political Consequences of the Product Cycle: Industrial History and Political Outcomes', *International Organization* 33 (1979); T. Ferguson, 'From Normalcy to New Deal: Industrial Structure, Party Competition, and American Public Policy in the Great Depression', *International Organization* 38 (1984); D. Abraham, *The Collapse of the Weimar Republic* (2nd edn, New York, 1986); and P. Gourevitch, *Politics in Hard Times* (Ithaca, NY, 1986). These theorists also characteristically emphasize the importance of coalitions between different sectoral interest groups in determining political outcomes.

69 M. Olson, *The Logic of Collective Action: Public Goods and the Theory of Groups* (Cambridge, Mass., 1965).

70 ibid., pp. 141–8. For an unconvincing attempt to integrate values other than economic self-interest into Olson's utilitarian calculus of collective action, see T. M. Moe, *The Organization of Interests* (Chicago, 1980), and Saxenian's comments in 'In Search of Power', n. 5.

71 C. Offe and H. Wiesenthal, 'Two Logics of Collective Action', in M. Zeitlin (ed.), *Political Power and Social Theory* I (1980); reprinted in C. Offe, *Disorganized Capitalism* (Cambridge, 1985), from which citations are taken.

72 ibid., pp. 179, 183–4, 189–91. As we have seen, however, Hyman, 'Strategy or Structure?', concludes from similar Marxist premises that capitalists' interests in relation to labour are objectively contradictory.

73 Gospel, *Management of Labour*; 'The Management of Labour'; and 'The

Development of Management Organization: A Historical Perspective', in Thurley and Wood, *Industrial Relations and Management Strategy*.

74 P. Windolf, 'Productivity Coalitions and the Future of European Corporatism', *Industrial Relations* 28 (1989); for a milder, less evolutionary formulation, see W. Streeck, 'Neo-Corporatist Industrial Relations and the Economic Crisis in West Germany', in J. Goldthorpe (ed.), *Order and Conflict in Contemporary Capitalism* (Oxford, 1984).

75 S. Lash and J. Urry, *The End of Organized Capitalism* (Cambridge, 1987); S. Lash and P. Bagguley, 'Labour Relations in Disorganized Capitalism: A Five-Nation Comparison', *Environment and Planning D: Society and Space* 6 (1988).

76 For a selection of classic formulations, see P. C. Schmitter and G. Lembruch (eds), *Trends towards Corporatist Intermediation* (London, 1979).

77 P. C. Schmitter and W. Streeck, 'The Organization of Business Interests: A Research Design to Study the Associative Action of Business in the Advanced Industrial Societies of Western Europe' *IIM/LMP Discussion Paper* 81–3 (Wissenschaftszentrum Berlin, 1981); W. Streeck and P. C. Schmitter (eds), *Private Interest Government: Beyond Market and State* (London, 1985); W. Streeck, 'Between Pluralism and Corporatism: German Business Associations and the State', *Journal of Public Policy* 3 (1983); 'The Uncertainties of Management in the Management of Uncertainty: Employers, Labour Relations and Industrial Adjustment in the 1980s', *Work, Employment and Society* 1 (1987); and 'Interest Heterogeneity and Organizing Capacity: Two Logics of Collective Action?', *IIM Discussion Paper* FS I 89–4 (Wissenschaftszentrum Berlin, 1989).

78 Streeck, 'Uncertainties of Management', p. 283.

79 Streeck and Schmitter, 'Community, Market, State – and Associations? The Prospective Contribution of Interest Governance to Social Order', in *Private Interest Government*, p. 19.

80 For a striking case in point, see Saxenian's discussion of the contrasting political outlooks of business associations in Silicon Valley and Route 128 in 'In Search of Power'.

81 See J. Elster, *Logic and Society* (New York, 1978), ch. 5; *idem, Ulysses and the Sirens*, esp. pt II; B. Barry and R. Hardin (eds), *Rational Man and Irrational Society* (London, 1982); R. Axelrod, *The Evolution of Cooperation* (New York, 1984). For applications to employers and industrial relations, see M. Aoki, *The Cooperative Game Theory of the Firm* (Oxford, 1984); and J. R. Bowman, *Capitalist Collective Action: Competition, Cooperation and Conflict in the Coal Industry* (Cambridge, 1989). For a penetrating critique of this approach for its underlying structural determinism and its inattention to actors' internal processes of deliberation, see B. Hindess, *Choice, Rationality and Social Theory* (London, 1988); and *idem, Political Choice*.

82 For fuller statements of this position, see B. Hindess, ' "Interests" in Political Analysis', in *Political Choice; idem, Politics and Class Analysis*; C. F. Sabel, *Work and Politics* (Cambridge, 1982), esp. chs 1 and 4; and Zeitlin, 'Labour History', pp. 167–9.

83 On the British engineering industry, see Zeitlin's chapter (2) in this volume. On the impact on employers of Sweden's 'solidaristic wage policy', see A. Martin, 'Trade Unions in Sweden: Strategic Responses to Change and Crisis', in P. Gourevitch, A. Martin, G. Ross, S. Bornstein, A. Markovits and C. Allen (eds), *Unions and Economic Crisis: Britain, West Germany, and Sweden* (London, 1984); and L. Bengtsson, A. C. Eriksson and P. Sederblad, 'The Associative Action of Swedish Business Interests: The Swedish Employers' Confederation and Centralized Collective Bargaining in 1980, 1981 and 1983', *IIM/LMP Discussion Paper* 84–24 (Wissenschaftszentrum Berlin, 1984).

84 For a parallel analysis of trade unions, see C. F. Sabel, 'The Internal Politics of Trade Unions', in S. Berger (ed.), *Organizing Interests in Western Europe* (Cambridge, 1981).

Part I

The peculiarities of the British?

1 Employers' strategies and craft production

The British shipbuilding industry 1870–1950

Alastair Reid

INTRODUCTION

Until recently, most accounts of the division of labour in capitalist economies have assumed that its development led both to the reduction of levels of skill possessed by employees and to an increase in the effective control of production by their employers. More careful historical research over the last decade has thrown a great deal of doubt on the former assumption, as it has been repeatedly discovered not only that technical innovation does not always completely dispense with old skills and usually requires new ones, but also that large sectors of even the most advanced economies remain committed to a variety of customer-specific products and hence to an experienced and adaptable work-force.[1] This revision of assumptions about skill levels automatically implies a need to reassess the effectiveness of employers' control of production, for workers' retention of skill and discretion, even in the context of machine production, undermines all the processes by which it has normally been assumed that the development of capitalism increases the power of the capitalist. For example, theories based on the progressive sub-division of tasks, on the imposition of clearly defined rules and on the separation of conception from execution all appear more doubtful in the light of recent historical studies of actual divisions of labour.

If these studies of the workplace imply increasingly serious limitations to the power of the capitalist, it is necessary to look more directly at the common assumption that there was an inevitable tendency towards greater employers' control of production. In the following discussion of the British shipbuilding industry, this will be done by focusing on what can be seen as a series of obstacles, first at the industry level where it will be argued that employers' associations were surprisingly weak in their dealings with trade unions, and second at the level of the individual firm where it will be stressed that there were real difficulties involved in reducing work-group autonomy within the context of craft production. Finally, after considering their inability to overcome obstacles, it will be suggested that employers in the British shipbuilding industry, while continually attempting to eliminate troublesome behaviour on the part of their work-force, were fundamentally not prepared to undertake that direct involvement in the production process without which they could not hope for real control.

THE SHIPBUILDING EMPLOYERS

From the last decade of the nineteenth century the shipbuilding industry was well known for its strong and aggressive employers' organization. Eventually emerging in 1899 from among the earliest of the regional bodies of this type in Britain, the Shipbuilding Employers' Federation (SEF) was, as John Lovell has shown, to be regularly involved in fierce national confrontations with the industry's major unions, most notably in 1908, 1910 and 1923. However, despite its appearance as a united and determinedly aggressive force in industrial relations, the SEF was unable to establish a common policy of any substance over the long-term question of innovation in production. The conflicts of the 1900s were largely concerned with resisting inter-regional wage leap-frogging by the Boilermakers' Society, and with establishing a united bargaining procedure. Their outcome was indeed largely formal and procedural, dealing with the fixing of national standard time rates but leaving piece-rates and bonuses to be determined at the level of the individual firm. Similarly, although these years saw the increasingly coherent formulation of a set of employers' demands for the relaxation of demarcation lines and the more flexible use of skilled labour, this too was largely a formal approach – indeed, it was specifically designed to leave actual practice up to *ad hoc* arrangements in individual yards.[2] The development of the SEF, and its behaviour during national disputes, certainly deserves further attention, but the initial impression given both by the national agreement of 1909 and by the nature of the records preserved in the archives, is that the regional employers' associations, in close communication with the individual firms, remained the central pivot in collective bargaining in shipbuilding and that the national parent body was much more of a figure-head than in the engineering industry. In any case, the Boilermakers' Society only tolerated the national procedure for four years, unilaterally withdrawing in 1913, so that it had little time to take hold as a major determinant of industrial relations.

The main explanation for this strategic weakness in employers' organization, in shipbuilding as in so many other British industries, lay in the large number of relatively small and independent companies and the divergences of interest between them. There was, for example, a straightforward division of economic interest between merchant-shipbuilders and war-shipbuilders, making quite different products and competing in quite different markets, which was to lead to friction among the employers during and immediately after the First World War. Neither of the markets was perfectly competitive, for a large proportion even of merchant-ship contracts were arranged between shippers and builders who had institutional or long-standing personal links. However war-shipbuilding was an even more closed set-up, with a list of Admiralty-approved builders and informal agreements between firms on the level of cost estimates to be submitted to the government. The war-shipbuilders tended to be more heavily capitalized and more broadly equipped with machinery, as much to satisfy the Admiralty's exacting standards as to reach new levels of technical efficiency, and, as a result, they pushed ahead more eagerly with pneumatic machinery introduced from the United States in the 1900s which was used for closing the rivets which held the steel hull plates together.[3] By the outbreak of the First World War the war-shipbuilders therefore had, in almost every case, extensive pneumatic plant operated on wage and working agreements that had been negotiated independently within each company, usually in the form of percentage deductions from the previous standard hand rates for the job and with non-union labour employed on the preparatory 'screwing up' of the plates.[4]

When the pressures of war production led the government to push for a general introduction of this machinery throughout the shipbuilding industry in 1917, the SEF was faced with a series of difficult negotiations: first, because the main union of structural steelworkers, the United Society of Boilermakers and Iron and Steel Shipbuilders (USBISS) was so strong after three years of wartime full employment that it was able to swing the balance towards its own preferred definitions of manning and wage rates; and second, because, as a consequence, the employers' negotiating committee was forced to concede national conditions which required the war-ship-builders to make significant increases over their existing yard wage agreements and to replace their preparatory labourers with USBISS members. In effect, faced with a dual pressure from the government and the wartime labour market, the merchant-shipbuilding majority of the SEF had sacrificed the interests of the war-shipbuilding part of its membership that had practical experience of working pneumatic tools. Indeed, it had conceded to union demands to such a degree that the machinery in question was to become significantly less attractive as an investment. Thus in pressing the Clyde delegates of the Boilermakers' Society to work harder to get their members fully to accept the new agreement, the Chairman of the SEF confessed that there had been much disunity on their side too:[5]

Certain of the big firms who have done more than anybody else in pneumatic riveting for many years past have worked on better terms than that [new] agreement gave them, but, whilst you had difficulty in getting your Members to work it, we have had a good deal of difficulty in getting our people to think that the agreement which we came to was one which we should have done, and I personally have come in for a dressing-down for having been a Party to it.

Another important division between shipbuilding employers was that between regions, especially between the two main sites of the industry on the Clyde in the west of Scotland and the rivers of the Tyne, Wear and Tees on the north-east coast of England. This had an economic component, since the Clyde was more biased towards passenger-liner building and the north-east coast towards general cargo shipbuilding,[6] but overlaid on that was a deep divergence in attitudes towards industrial relations which was equally strong in the other industries in each region. Broadly speaking, the west of Scotland employers were more authoritarian and more anti-union, keen to seize any opportunity to weaken or even destroy labour organizations. By contrast, employers on the north-east coast tried to avoid conflicts with their men over basic principles and were almost always prepared to enter negotiations: it was therefore no accident that the head offices of the main shipbuilding unions gradually moved to Newcastle upon Tyne. The precise explanation for this regional divergence is not yet clear, but it is worth pointing out that Glasgow was also notorious for the authoritarianism of its local government, and it may well be that this had deep roots in the distinctive political and religious development of Scotland, with its significantly less paternalistic social legislation and its more intrusive post-Reformation church.[7]

At any rate, the difference in attitudes became particularly marked on the industrial front in the 1900s when, in the aftermath of the famous engineering lock-out of 1897–8, many Clyde employers wanted to impose the same strict rules on 'managerial prerogatives' as they felt the engineering employers had won.[8] Accordingly, they began to work out detailed proposals on yard management which, on the one hand, followed the bargaining procedures by then in force in engineering, but, at the same time, made amendments with regard to work organization to adapt it to shipbuilding conditions, emphasizing employers' control over the numbers of apprentices and the lines of demarcation between occupations much more than machine manning. At first the shipbuilding employers on the Tyne followed this initiative with interest, but when it became clear that some of the Clyde shipyards actually wanted to do something about it and were prepared to face up to a national strike, the employers on the north-east coast backed off rapidly. Something of this divergence was revealed in an interesting correspondence between G. V. Hunter of Tyneside and John Inglis of Clydeside.[9] According to Hunter:

We in the North of England . . . want to work by agreement with the Trade Unions, we think we can manage the men better by so doing . . . I think it will be necessary for some of the Scottish shipbuilders, who are more in earnest and more advanced in their ideas than we are to discuss the business with all our Members in this district and try to convert those among us who are opposed to action being taken at present . . .

to which Inglis replied in a more aggressive tone:

For my part I believe the Union leaders only require to be convinced that they have a united body of employers to face – they are all mighty fearful of their funds . . . Personally I have no objection to begin by trying to work with the Unions – if they will not hear reason I am equally ready to fight them.

While their internal resolve was weakened by this divergence of attitude, the proposed shipbuilding employers' offensive over managerial power was finally undermined by a further factor: their inability to get joint action from employers in the neighbouring engineering industry with its over-lapping labour market. The dominant factions within the Engineering Employers' Federation felt they had achieved their aims in 1897–8 and were therefore unwilling to prejudice either that achievement itself or their members' market positions by closing down boiler shops in which members of the major shipbuilding unions were working outside marine engineering. Because of the large numbers of men involved, the absence of such a guarantee meant that the shipbuilding employers could not be sure that the balance of power really was on their side, and the whole scheme quietly faded away early in 1905. Although a bargaining procedure similar to that imposed by the engineering employers was later enforced after a series of disputes in shipbuilding between 1906 and 1909, there was to be no major victory for the employers over the organization of work and the elaborate structure of bargaining was itself eventually abandoned in 1913, once the Boilermakers' Society had been able to rebuild its financial base in the prewar boom.[10]

Finally, we may note a further division between employers simply over the extent to which they showed a real interest in the radical reorganization of production. One striking instance of this has been demonstrated by Alan McKinlay in the case of Clydeside shipbuilding employers' attitudes in the 1920s towards new technology for punching rivet holes in plates.[11] Because the machines could greatly increase productivity in this one aspect of platers' work, some firms began to propose a more rigid sub-division of these men's tasks, involving the dissolution of the traditional squads and the incorporation of their leading men into the supervisory and technical staff of the firm. However, given the strength of the Boilermakers' Society, such a step could only be taken on an industry-wide basis and this was not forthcoming as most of the firms, even in this hard-line region, were concerned that such a division of labour would be too inflexible and therefore lead to higher overheads. The importance of this case is that the difference of attitude cannot be traced to the most obvious divergences of economic interest in the industry, as major war-shipbuilding firms like John Brown and Beardmore found themselves on opposite sides of the fence, and even though it was small firms which were the most vocal in demanding radical changes, large firms, like Brown, were also associated with them. It seems, then, to have been simply a difference of opinion, possibly the result of those who happened to be in charge of the yards at the time, possibly the product of distinct traditions of company management.

Thus despite the existence of a permanent national body representing the employers in industrial bargaining, their interests were in fact sufficiently divergent to make unity around a common policy that went beyond standard rates and hours very difficult to maintain. We have noted differences over the introduction of machinery, divergences of attitude between regions leading to divergences over the degree of managerial authority desired and a difference of opinion even between employers in the same region and product market over the extent to which rationalization ought to be pursued. That this disunity between the employers was a large part of the explanation of their lack of effective power in the shipbuilding industry was very clear to James Lithgow, the major cargo-shipbuilder on the Clyde. Writing to another company in 1914 during a conflict caused by severe competition between the two employers over skilled labour, he stated:[12]

Our opinion is that Shipbuilders have themselves very largely to thank for Ninety per cent of the trouble which takes place with workmen. When trouble arises the interests of the various Shipbuilders appear so antagonistic, that our experience has shown that in a great many cases, some individual firm is left to do the fighting and if they are not strong enough to do so, all kinds of unreasonable demands are conceded, and whatever is done in one yard is used as a precedent in other cases.

And with even more penetration, William Denny had remarked as early as 1877:[13]

The Clyde has fought with the Tyne, the Thames and the Mersey, and on the Clyde every master has contested with every other for the work to be done. . . . This free competition of master against master has been the secret of this country's advance as a manufacturing nation. . . . A single master dreads his workmen less than his fellow-master, and his profits are more reduced by their competition than by any amount of strikes and shortening of hours.

THE LOGIC OF CRAFT PRODUCTION

Despite these divergences over specific issues which made common action between firms over the organization of work unusual, British shipbuilding employers did share a common commitment to the general features of craft production, that is, the use of labour-intensive methods with a devolved structure of management.[14] Once again a large part of the explanation for these features of the industry can be formulated in terms of a series of obstacles to the employers' direct control of the production process.

First of all, there was the fundamental, but frequently overlooked, problem of the inadequacy of the available technology. For although the inventors and promoters of new machinery were always confident of its ability to displace manual skills, its actual application in particular industrial situations frequently led to much less satisfactory results. This was particularly the case in shipbuilding where the production process was dispersed over a wide area and the product was subjected to unusually severe stresses in use. Thus the central technical problem to be solved was that of the efficient and sound assembly of the various components, especially the steel items composing the basic structure of the vessel. Hydraulic methods of riveting, which had increased per capita output by up to nine times in boiler shops as early as the 1860s, turned out to be of little use in shipyards because any equipment with the necessary reach to rivet hull plates was impossibly heavy to move around, and, in any case, could not produce the flush effect required to reduce water resistance without distortions in the plates during assembly. It was therefore restricted to heavy internal items and by the 1900s was still only being used on under 5 per cent of shipyard riveting.[15] Similarly, pneumatic riveting, quite apart from the question of its economic efficiency under union-imposed wage rates and working conditions, and even though it was considerably easier to move around the yard, was suspected of not producing a tight enough bonding of hull plates to guarantee water tightness. As a result it was restricted to lighter internal and superstructural items amounting, as late as the 1920s, to only 25 per cent of shipyard riveting.[16] A further technical breakthrough in this area of shipyard activity was the process of welding plates together by using high temperatures to melt a bonding agent along the joints. But although this held out the prospect of an even smoother surface and an even lighter vessel, it was many years before the customers were convinced that ship design and work practices had advanced sufficiently to guarantee a safe and lasting product: in 1936, less than 1 per cent of shipyard labour used welding equipment. And, as Edward Lorenz has shown, even when this technology was more widely introduced during and after the Second World War in the context of standardization and rationalization of yard layout, it still could not replace skilled hand labour at dispersed work sites.[17] Similar problems at the assembly stage afflicted the major outfitting trades, so that in marine engineering, plumbing, electrical work, joinery, and even in painting, as in boilermaking, the workers involved in shipbuilding have been required to possess high levels of manual skill right up to the present day. Even the extreme pressures of the First World War, normally thought to have led to a marked reduction in skill levels through dilution with female labour, made little impression on shipbuilding.[18] The words of the naval architect David Pollock in the 1880s applied throughout our period:[19]

Since the early days of iron shipbuilding, when hand labour entered largely into almost all the operations of the shipyard, the field of its application has been gradually narrowed by the employment of machinery. The past few years have been uncommonly fruitful of changes in this direction, and many things point to the likelihood of manual work still more largely superseded by machine power in the immediate future. Such changes, however, have not, as might be assumed, had any very sensible effect in diminishing the number of operatives generally employed. The influence has rather been absorbed in the greatly increased rate of production, and the elaboration and enhanced refinement of detail demanded by the much more exacting standard of modern times. The need for skilled handicraftsmen may not now be so general, but the skill which is still indispensable is of a higher calibre, and has called into existence several almost entirely new classes of shipyard operatives.

The second feature of the industry which might also be considered as a major obstacle to managerial rationalization was the intensity of fluctuation in the demand for the product. There were a number of contributory factors to this, including the low level of replacement demand for capital goods and the long period of construction of even the average type of vessel, and their precise weighting in the final outcome has been much debated by economists. However, the result for shipbuilding employers was clear: in view of the long periods of idleness in the industry and its very sharp peaks of intense activity, it was preferable for an employer to rely as much as possible on manual labour which could be dispensed with when not required, rather than to invest in capital equipment which could become an intolerable financial burden.[20] Closely interconnected with these severe fluctuations was the employers' continued commitment to particular customers and to highly specialized products tailored to their needs. Here again it is probably futile to search for ultimate causes, but it is clear both that firms producing for narrow and specialized markets are more prone to fluctuations in output, and that attachment to particular customers provided some sort of safeguard against the full impact of depressions. The net result, once again, was to intensify the employers' dependence on skilled labour which could absorb experiments with new designs and the changing needs of valued customers, even in the course of construction of a single vessel.

Thus one of the most deeply entrenched features of the industry was the subcontracting of whole sections of the work on the vessel to squads of skilled workmen who were given only the vaguest of instructions and then left to organize the work among themselves. Right up to the 1960s it was far from uncommon for squads of platers to take the measurements of plates required from the gaps left in the half-completed hull, and it was unusual for squads in any trade to be given a precise time-limit for the completion of their tasks.[21] As John Hill, leader of the boilermakers' union between the wars put it:[22]

[squad leaders] are not only highly skilled craftsmen, but they have that other qualification of being capable organisers of squads. They take the whole care and responsibility from the management and staff very largely. It is simply a matter, when the job comes along, of the foreman saying to Mr. So-and-so, 'Here you are; these are plans of that job: get along with it' and there is no need to look after them and watch them and see if they are doing it right, or to hurry them on with the job. The whole work is taken and managed so successfully that it is not so much the price as the skill and organisation of the squad that tells in the long run.

These then, in outline, were the central problems at the level of the firm, and though a minority of owners and managers might periodically project some major rationalization of shipyard production, the majority were practical enough to realize that that would not be feasible short of further major progress in the technology of steel assembly and a decisive shift of production preferences towards standardization. Since neither of these was evident in the industry until the 1950s, the shipbuilding employers in the period under consideration continued to make do with an archetypal case of craft production and, though they might try to increase their control through stricter supervision, improved incentive payments and schemes for reducing labour turnover, these could at best provide only tactical improvements in a situation in which they had already conceded strategic autonomy to their skilled workers.

Moreover, because of their adoption of labour-intensive methods as a response to severe fluctuations in output they were deprived of one major weapon in the battle for control: paternalism. Shipyards were indeed large enough, both physically and economically, to dominate the surrounding neighbourhood, as is clear in the virtual identification of yards and communities on the down-river sites: Dennystown on the Clyde, Vickerstown in Barrow, and most famous of all, Palmerstown at Jarrow on the Tyne. In these and other localities the firm was not only the biggest local employer but usually also financed local amenities like public parks, libraries and hospitals. However, because of the policy of regularly laying off large sections of the labour force, it was impossible to build up an effective relation of paternalism with the work-force: company housing was usually provided only for foremen and a minority of key technical workers, company welfare was usually restricted to minimal contributory accident insurance, and there is little evidence of any deep-seated loyalty to firms among the mass of their employees.[23] Since even the steadiest of men spent only around a third of their working lives in the yard nearest their homes and relied for welfare provision on their union up to the First World War, and increasingly on the state thereafter, there was no effective basis for employers to establish a leverage of persuasion or coercion outside the immediate relationship of the short-term employment contract.

Within that context their main agents of labour discipline were the foremen but these supervisors were, as Joseph Melling has shown, far from being simple tools of management. Given the *ad hoc* nature of craft production, foremen had to be capable of efficient work in the trade that they supervised in order to demonstrate what was required. They were therefore almost universally recruited from among the skilled workers, and they frequently remained as members of their original trade unions in order to retain their entitlements to sickness pay and retirement pensions. During the 1900s the shipbuilding employers tried very hard to detach foremen from the influence of the skilled men and their unions by joining an employers' welfare fund known as the Foremen's Mutual Benefit Society, but this had only partial success: the foremen were still to be found siding with the workers under them, especially over issues of demarcation between occupations, and they temporarily formed an independent trade union of their own during the First World War.[24] Even during the inter-war years of high unemployment, the foremen proved to be an unreliable tool of supervisory control, for they preferred to carry on offering customary allowances for obstructed riveting work and employing the usual numbers of skilled journeymen, in the face of employers' pressure to cut back wages to the standard rates and employ more juvenile labour.[25]

In the absence of an unmediated system of supervision, shipyard employers attempted to increase their control over production by intro-ducing systems of incentive payment. However, remuneration by the amount produced rather than by the hours worked was ultimately no solution, for despite the enthusiasm with which many employers greeted them in the 1870s, piece-rate systems were soon undermined by contra-dictory pressures. If the rates offered were genuinely rewarding and the men responded by working really hard, they ended up by earning wages which were regarded as ridiculously high, not only because they added to yard costs but also because they undermined the status hierarchy between manual workers, white-collar workers and supervisory staff. When, on the other hand, the employers took steps to avoid such an outcome and to reduce the total wages by cutting the rate per item, the men simply responded by developing deeply entrenched restrictions on output in order to avoid having to work harder for the same take-home pay.[26] The Premium Bonus System, introduced in metalworking increasingly after 1897, seemed at first to offer a way out of this situation for, by systematically reducing the wage increment for each extra unit of time saved on a task, it promised to set an automatic upper limit on manual workers' earnings whilst still providing an incentive for effort. However, when introduced into a context riddled with restrictive practices, bonus systems fell foul of exactly the same contradictory pressures as piece-rates: the initial standard times set for tasks could be beaten by large margins when workers put in a real effort, the employers' response was to reduce the standard time allowed and the men therefore immediately re-imposed restrictive practices.[27] In any case neither piece-rates nor the Premium Bonus System were entirely suitable for the bulk of shipbuilding tasks as most of the industry's workers could not be observed at one work-site, and the time taken for essentially similar tasks could vary enormously depending on where they were performed, thus requiring a complex system of customary bonuses for obstructed work which undermined the basic principle of incentive payments.

The most obvious symptoms of this double failure to impose either an effective system of supervision or an effective method of incentive payment were chronic absenteeism and very high levels of labour turnover. Not only was it rare for the squads to return from their periods of holiday promptly, it was common for them to take substantial amounts of time off within the normal working week, most commonly on a Monday. In contemporary discussions, an excessive weight of blame was usually laid on heavy drinking at the weekends, but while it may be valid to emphasize a relatively high leisure preference behind this practice, it was also bound up with strategies for maintaining weekly earnings, either by pushing as much work as possible into periods of overtime pay, or by restricting output to maintain piece-rates, or both. Thus figures from the Clyde indicate a significant increase in rates of absenteeism in periods of greater output, when it reached an average of a day a week in the case of piece-working boilermakers and a quarter of a day a week even in the case of time-working shipwrights and joiners.[28]

As if this was not bad enough, shipbuilding employers were also confronted by their skilled workers' excessively independent movement around the labour market from firm to firm, frequently leaving their current contracts uncompleted after the most remunerative parts had been done. Once again, they frequently sought an explanation in the moral failings of the work-force, but again the truth was to be found in more mundane and rational economic calculation. Whereas in the case of absenteeism within the working week the root cause was the employers' unwillingness to give a genuine reward for effort, in the case of labour mobility the root cause was their willingness to offer bonuses and extras to attract skilled labour from their rivals in periods of high activity. Thus in both cases they really only had themselves to blame, and if in the one case the solution would have been to offer more generous wages, in the other it would have been to reach some agreement between themselves to divide up the labour supply more rationally. However, just as their collective organization at national level foundered over differences of economic interest, so attempts at coordination of local labour markets were usually hindered by the intense competition between firms. The preferred device was the 'character' or 'discharge' note that each workman was to be required to get whenever he left a yard and each employer was to insist on seeing before taking on a new workman, in order to check on whether he had completed his previous contract. Until 1906 these had been operating only at the discretion of particular firms, but thereafter the regional employers' associations attempted to operate a more coherent surveillance of the labour market. This continued up to the First World War but in periods of prosperity and full employment, when it was needed the most, the discharge-note scheme tended to break down, not only because of union resistance but also because of the urgency of each employer's demand for labour: there is evidence that they accepted men without notes, took on men they knew were using aliases and frequently sent their own agents to poach skilled workers from outside each other's yard gates.[29]

CONCLUSIONS

Given the limited nature of the technology available, their own preference for customer-specific production and their inability to organize a united front within the industry, British shipbuilding employers were inevitably committed to labour-intensive, low-supervision methods and to a work-force with high levels of technical skill and task discretion. Thus the industry's work-force was not confronted with any significant pressures towards a major transformation in technology or work organization, and the main characteristics of craft production were not determined by the existence of strong craft unions – rather the contrary. The industry's very strong trade unions developed partly as a result of the real skills and functional importance of the craftsmen and partly as a result of the high levels of labour mobility in such a fluctuating industry, which required generous union welfare and unemployment benefits. However, on the basis of their intrinsically strong bargaining-position and their large financial reserves the unions, especially the Boilermakers' Society, were able to take substantial control over the lines of demarcation between occupations, the regulation of apprenticeship training and the manning of machinery, thus making a significant negative impact on industrial efficiency at the margin.[30] Moreover, on the foundation of their strategic autonomy, shipbuilding workers have been able to mount some of the country's most effective protests against company closures in years of recession – for example, the Jarrow March of 1936 and the work-in at Upper Clyde Shipbuilders in 1971, both of which threatened to undermine employers' freedom of action even in the sphere of investment decisions.[31]

Why then did the shipbuilding employers tolerate such a situation? One part of the answer is that despite all of the problems and difficulties which they faced in the management of skilled labour, they too were able to push the margin of efficiency in their favour by means other than a complete transformation of production. For example, the increasing scale of vessels, especially in the 1890s and 1900s, automatically gave rise to increases in productivity, as volume increased more rapidly than surface area, so that carrying capacity increased more quickly than the amount of work required for construction. At the same time many employers deliberately pursued working-methods which made use of larger steel plates, thus reducing the amount of cutting and bending required and even more substantially reducing the amount of riveting required in joining them together. Further ways of reducing the amount of riveting, without mechanizing the trade, included overlapping the plates rather than joining them with 'butt-straps' (which required only one rather than two rows of rivets) and 'joggling' the plates by kinking the edges of the outer rows to bring them closer to the frames (which eliminated packing between frames and plates and reduced the size of the rivets required).[32]

There was considerably less improvement among the outfitting trades, although even here a gratuitous benefit was gained through the increasing division of labour and application of machinery in the production of components: pipes, paint and, above all, wooden items, where the wood-cutting machines introduced from the United States in the 1870s led to an overall increase in the efficiency of the joinery department by as much as 60 per cent.[33] Finally, we may note that whereas machinery rarely displaced skill, it did frequently either supplement or replace manual effort. Thus while the hydraulic plate-shaping and beam-bending equipment introduced from the 1870s did not reduce the status and indispensability of the platers, it did reduce the physical effort required from their large gangs of helpers. Similarly, the improvement of cranes and haulage equipment, especially in the 1920s, led to a substantial cost saving in the least skilled groups of fetching and carrying labour.[34]

However, important as these other avenues for increasing efficiency were, they do not account for the whole of the shipbuilding employers' attitudes. Perhaps, strange as it may at first seem, they were in fact deeply committed not only to a high level of manual skill but also to a high level of independence on the part of their work-force. We have already seen some of the economic bases for such a preference, above all the desire for flexibility in the work process and the choice of low overheads in depressions rather than a paternalistic employment strategy. To these may also be added an almost instinctive dislike for the extra burden of white-collar salaries implied by the more systematic costing and supervision of manual labour, an objection which was usually sufficient to sink any such proposals brought up before the industry's regional technical associations.[35]

But might it not be that there were even deeper instincts involved, which produced a distinctive set of managerial values stressing not only high quality in the product but also a high level of self-reliance and independence in the work-force? Documenting this more precisely is a difficult task, especially as so many of the lengthy employers' statements on record in the twentieth century are forceful attacks on craft privileges and restrictions. However, it may be suggested that even from these it emerges that the central objection to trade unionism was formulated in terms of its impo-sition of collective restrictions on individual initiative which, if left to itself, would reap the full rewards of piece-rates.[36] Similarly, during the introduc-tion of piece-work in the 1870s, its most vocal champions among the employers argued that it would produce a more independent, intelligent and innovative attitude among the work-force which would have its roots in a more open employment contract:[37]

> You never see a piece-worker running to his work at the approach of his employer or foreman. He knows he is giving an equivalent for his wages, and that he has the right to choose his own way of doing his work, and in his own time too. This makes a marked distinction between the piece-worker and the time-worker. The former feels that he and his master have contracted and fulfilled a bargain, and that all scores are clear between them.

Perhaps these attitudes were unique to shipbuilding or to the craft sections of the economy, but it may be that they were a wider manifestation within the organization of production itself of that liberal mainstream in British social and political life which Alan Fox has emphasized in his recent account of the development of collective-bargaining institutions.[38] International comparison certainly indicates a relatively slow development of bureaucratic management and mass production in Britain, without making it entirely clear where the emphasis should be placed in analysing the interaction between employers' attitudes and strong occupational trade unions.[39] One of the implications of this study is that more weight ought to be placed on the lack of a strong desire among the employers to move away from established craft methods, not only for sound economic reasons but possibly also for political and social ones.

This study of the British shipbuilding industry therefore throws further doubt on the most commonly prevailing assumptions about the development of capitalist economies. For not only did employees retain high levels of skill and workplace autonomy, it also appears that their employers made no sustained attempts to increase their effective control of production and may even have had an implicit commitment to the independence of skilled labour. It therefore becomes important to clarify the intellectual origins of our common assumptions, and here the root of the problem is that most of the major theories about historical trends in modern economies have been devised by intellectuals deeply disenchanted with them and determined to demonstrate that Western European countries were not, contrary to establishment claims, generating more genuine human freedoms. As a result their theories, especially those of Marx and Weber, have usually been designed to show how an early phase of individualism and apparent freedom would inevitably be replaced by a later phase of ever-tightening organization which would reveal the true nature of modern capitalism, whether as a result of monopolies emerging out of markets or of bureaucracies emerging from the search for efficiency. Unfortunately, even scholars with different political outlooks have tended to capitulate before the superficially systematic approach of these theorists, and their assumptions, which are certainly inappropriate for the British case, have consequently become almost universal. Surely the time has now come, with the accumulation of so many empirical counter-examples, to move on from qualification and revision to a fundamental recasting of our basic assumptions about the development of modern societies? And surely this must also involve not only the now customary criticism of economic determinism but also a radical reconsideration of the dynamics of economic change itself?

NOTES

1 S. Wood (ed.), *The Degradation of Work? Skill, Deskilling and the Labour Process* (London, 1982); R. Harrison and J. Zeitlin (eds), *Divisions of Labour: Skilled Workers and Technological Change in Nineteenth Century England* (Brighton, Sussex, 1985).

2 J. Lovell, 'Confronting the Union: The Emergence of National Employer Organization in the British Shipbuilding Industry, 1899–1910' (unpublished paper, University of Kent, 1986); and for another account of these years see R. Okayama, 'Employers' Labour Policy and Craft Unions: A Study of British Industrial Relations in Shipbuilding from the 1870s to the War', *Bulletin of the Institute of Social Sciences Meiji University* 3 (1979).

3 S. Pollard and P. Robertson, *The British Shipbuilding Industry, 1870–1914* (Cambridge, Mass., 1979), pp. 72–86, 92–106.

4 This account of pneumatic riveting is based mainly on the Clyde Shipbuilders' Association (CSA) papers, in Strathclyde Regional Archives TD 241/12/41.

5 TD 241/12/41: Proceedings in Central Conference Between SEF and USBISS, Edinburgh, 12 Sept. 1918, pp. 33–4.

6 Pollard and Robertson, *British Shipbuilding*, pp. 59–64.

7 T. C. Smout, *A History of the Scottish People 1560–1830* (London, 1969), esp. pp. 72–100.

8 This account of managerial pressures is based mainly on CSA papers in TD 241/12/1.

9 TD 241/12/1: Hunter to Inglis 24 Dec. 1902, Inglis to Hunter 27 Dec. 1902.

10 J. E. Mortimer, *History of the Boilermakers' Society, Volume II. 1906–1939* (London, 1982), pp. 8–13, 34–8, 54–5; Lovell, 'Confronting the Union', pp. 9–10, 15–17, 20.

11 A. McKinlay, 'Employers and Skilled Workers in the Inter-War Depression: Engineering and Shipbuilding on Clydeside 1919–39' (D. Phil. thesis, Oxford University, 1986), pp. 272–81.

12 CSA papers in TD 241/12/8: Russell & Co. to Swan Hunter 22 Dec. 1914.

13 W. Denny, *The Worth of Wages* (Dumbarton, 1877), pp. 10, 11–12.

14 For a seminal analysis see A. L. Stinchcombe, 'Bureaucratic and Craft Administration of Production: A Comparative Study', *Administrative Science Quarterly* 4 (1959), pp. 168–87; and for earlier studies of shipbuilding see R. K. Brown, R. Brannen, J. M. Cousins and M. L. Samphier, 'The Contours of Solidarity: Social Stratification and Industrial Relations in Shipbuilding', *British Journal of Industrial Relations* 10 (1972), pp. 12–41; and F. Wilkinson, 'Demarcation in Shipbuilding' (Cambridge University, Department of Applied Economics working paper, 1974), especially pp. 1–39.

15 A. J. Reid, 'The Division of Labour in the Shipbuilding Industry 1880–1920' (Ph.D. thesis, Cambridge University, 1980), pp. 131–3.

16 J. McGovern, 'Some Notes on Shipbuilding Methods', *Transactions of the North East Coast Institution of Engineers and Shipbuilders* 38 (1921–1922), pp. 349–402, especially p. 371; CSA papers in TD 241/12/41: Clyde Pneumatic Riveting Returns 11 June 1918, Report of the Third Meeting of the SEF Pneumatic Riveting Committee 3 July 1918.

17 J. McGoldrick, 'Crisis and the Division of Labour: Clydeside Shipbuilding in the

Inter-War Period', in T. Dickson (ed.), *Capital and Class in Scotland* (Edinburgh, 1982), pp. 143–85, esp. pp. 168–80; E. H. Lorenz, 'The Labour Process and Industrial Relations in the British and French Shipbuilding Industries, from 1880 to 1970' (Ph.D. thesis, Cambridge University, 1983), pp. 156–78.

18 A. J. Reid, 'Dilution, Trade Unionism and the State in Britain during the First World War', in S. Tolliday and J. Zeitlin (eds), *Shop Floor Bargaining and the State: Historical and Comparative Perspectives* (Cambridge, 1985), pp. 46–74.

19 D. Pollock, *Modern Shipbuilding and the Men Engaged in It* (London, 1884), p. 129.

20 Pollard and Robertson, *British Shipbuilding*, pp. 25–30.

21 J. R. Parkinson, *The Economics of Shipbuilding in the United Kingdom* (Cambridge, 1960), pp. 118–19; R. K. Brown, R. Brannen, J. M. Cousins and M. L. Samphier, 'Leisure in Work: The "Occupational Culture" of Shipbuilding Workers' in M. A. Smith, S. Parker and C. S. Smith (eds), *Leisure and Society in Britain* (London, 1973), pp. 97–110, especially p. 102; and, for the widespread use of internal contracting in British industry, H. Gospel 'The Development of Management Organisation in Industrial Relations: A Historical Perspective', in K. Thurley and S. Wood (eds), *Industrial Relations and Management Strategy* (Cambridge, 1983).

22 Quoted in McKinlay, 'Employers and Skilled Workers', p. 236.

23 J. Melling, 'Employers, Industrial Housing and the Evolution of Company Welfare Policies in Britain's Heavy Industry: West Scotland, 1870–1920' *International Review of Social History* 26 (1981), pp. 255–301.

24 J. Melling, ' "Non-Commissioned Officers": British Employers and their Supervisory Workers, 1880–1920', *Social History* 5 (1980), pp. 183–221.

25 McKinlay, 'Employers and Skilled Workers', pp. 289–331.

26 Webb Trade Union Collection, in British Library of Political and Economic Science, Webb Coll. E.A. vii (1) pp. 28–9, viii (4) p. 298; W. A. Riddell, *Adventures of An Obscure Victorian* (Greenock, 1964), pp. 16–18, 114–115, 134–5.

27 *Trades Union Congress Joint Committee on the Premium Bonus System. Report* (Manchester, 1910), pp. 7, 23–4, 30–1.

28 CSA papers in TD 241/8/10: 'Chart showing average percentage of time lost by workers for each month during fortnightly and weekly pays 1899–1911'.

29 CSA papers in TD 241/12/3: Memorandum on the Discharge Note System (undated); TD 241/12/8: CSA circular 18 Jan. 1913; S. Price, 'Labour Mobility in Clyde Shipbuilding, 1889–1913' (unpublished paper, Scottish Development Agency 1981).

30 K. McClelland and A. J. Reid, 'Wood, Iron and Steel: Technology, Labour and Trade Union Organisation in the Shipbuilding Industry, 1840–1914', in Harrison and Zeitlin (eds), *Divisions of Labour*, pp. 151–84.

31 E. Wilkinson, *The Town that was Murdered. The Life-Story of Jarrow* (London, 1939); J. Foster and C. Woolfson, *The Politics of the UCS Work-In* (London, 1986); B. Strath, *The Politics of De-Industrialisation: The Contraction of the West European Shipbuilding Industry* (London 1987), especially pp. 125–8.

32 D. Pollock, *The Shipbuilding Industry* (London, 1905), pp. 97–9; J. R. Hume, 'Shipbuilding Machine Tools', in J. Butt and J. T. Ward (eds), *Scottish Themes, Essays in Honour of Professor S. G. E. Lythe* (Edinburgh, 1976), pp. 158–80, esp. pp. 163–4.

33 G. T. Jones, *Increasing Return* (Cambridge, 1933), p. 94; R. Samuel, 'The Workshop of the World: Steam Power and Hand Technology in Mid-Victorian Britain', *History Workshop* 3 (1977), pp. 6–72, esp. pp. 31, 37.

34 Reid, 'Division of Labour', pp. 107, 112–113, 115–116.

35 See, for example, the discussion following McGovern, 'Notes on Shipbuilding Methods', pp. 367–402.
36 See, for example, Lithgow's comments as President of the SEF in 1921, quoted at length in J. M. Reid, *James Lithgow: Master of Work* (London, 1964), pp. 79–84.
37 Denny, *Worth of Wages*, p. 22.
38 A. Fox, *History and Heritage: The Social Origins of the British Industrial Relations System* (London, 1985).
39 R. Bean, *Comparative Industrial Relations* (Beckenham, 1985), especially pp. 63–8; D. Gallie, *In Search of the New Working Class* (Cambridge, 1978).

2 The internal politics of employer organization
The Engineering Employers' Federation 1896–1939

Jonathan Zeitlin

INTRODUCTION

British employers have become notorious for their lack of collective solidarity. By contrast to their German, Scandinavian and even American counterparts, it is widely agreed, employers' associations in Britain have typically lacked internal coherence and capacity for sustained offensive action, whether at the peak or the sectoral level. As a result, it is often argued, British employers have proved less successful in defending managerial authority within the enterprise and maintaining orderly bargaining arrangements within the wider labour market than their competitors in many (but by no means all) advanced industrial economies.[1]

These international contrasts have evident force when applied to the postwar world of fragmented workplace bargaining and strong shop-steward organizations in which they were originally formulated. But how far do they hold good for the period before the Second World War, when Britain's national bargaining system was widely admired by foreign observers and her employers' associations often served as a model for similar organizations abroad? No case is better placed to test the limits of employer collective action among employers in prewar Britain than that of the Engineering Employers' Federation (EEF). Alone among British employers' associations, the EEF mounted successful national lock-outs against trade unions to enforce recognition of managerial prerogatives in 1897–8 and again in 1922, while the disputes procedure it imposed at the turn of the century remained in place with minimal modification until 1971. By the 1920s, the Federation had also constructed a centralized system of national wage bargaining which it maintained intact through depression and recovery well into the postwar period.[2] However much the subsequent decline of national bargaining has tarnished the EEF's image, before 1939 it is surely there if anywhere in British industry that a unified, cohesive and effective example of employer solidarity might be found.

Despite the EEF's undoubted achievements, however, an examination of its internal politics reveals a rather more complex and problematic picture. Engineering employers, as this chapter seeks to demonstrate, were deeply divided amongst themselves by sectoral and regional cleavages as well as inter-firm rivalries. The creation of a national employers' organization in the late 1890s was thus a delicate and contingent exercise in coalition-building rather than a natural consequence of some underlying unity of interests. Only in exceptional circumstances, as its leaders realized, could the EEF mobilize its diverse membership behind a national lock-out, while the growing possibility of government intervention increased still further the risks of a confrontational strategy. The Federation leadership was thus drawn towards the pursuit of a durable accommodation with organized labour – particularly during the highly politicized years of reconstruction after the First World War. But the EEF's freedom of manoeuvre in implementing this strategy was circumscribed by internal dissent as well as by the unions' inability to deliver their members' compliance with national agreements. The reassertion of managerial authority through a renewed lock-out in 1922 was thus a second-best solution to the stalemate in national negotiations, and the Federation's resounding victory over the unions paradoxically laid the foundations for the subsequent decay of employer solidarity by undermining the leverage of the central authorities on both sides over their members.

A DIFFICULT BIRTH, 1850–98

Few industries are so heterogeneous as engineering. Indeed, it is less a single industry than a congeries of distinct but overlapping sectors linked by a common set of metalworking processes and the manual skills associated with them. In late nineteenth and early twentieth-century Britain, the most important such sectors were textile, railway and marine engineering, though significant clusters of firms could also be found specializing in the manufacture of armaments, machine tools and many other types of capital equipment. Motor vehicles, cycles and electrical engineering already accounted for a sizeable proportion of output before 1914, and their share of the total would increase dramatically between the wars. Product markets differed considerably from sector to sector, resulting in major variations in profitability, exposure to competition, experience of the trade cycle, and the mix of skills employed. Individual sectors were typically concentrated in particular districts, and regional patterns of growth and development were highly uneven. Within each sector and district, finally, there were pronounced disparities in size and resources between companies, with a handful of giant enterprises employing 5,000 workers or more at one extreme, and several thousand small and medium-sized general engineering firms, often operating as subcontractors, at the other. Yet the boundaries of particular sectors remained fluid, and firms and workers alike might move between them at different points of the trade cycle, giving rise to interconnected labour markets across the industry as a whole.[3]

Under these conditions, it is hardly surprising that it proved so difficult to construct a national organization of engineering employers during the second half of the nineteenth century. Periodic attempts at national collaboration among employers failed to overcome persistent sectoral and regional divisions, while bitter rivalries between individual firms often undermined collective responses to union demands at a local level. In 1852 a coalition of masters in Lancashire and London, the two major centres of the industry, crushed the newly formed Amalgamated Society of Engineers (ASE) in a major lock-out over craft regulation and managerial control, imposing the non-union 'document' on the defeated workers. But no permanent organization followed this victory, while the expansion and diversification of demand for British engineering products gradually re-established employers' dependence on skilled labour in the production process. These trends in turn allowed the ASE to rebuild its membership and revive its regulation of wages and working conditions by picking off individual employers during the 1850s and 1860s. While local employers' associations had been formed in a number of engineering centres during the 1860s, it was the unexpected success of the nine-hours strikes in 1871 which sparked off the first serious attempt to establish a national organization. Although the initiative for inter-regional collaboration came from New-castle manufacturer William Armstrong, the movement foundered on conflicts between inland and marine districts, and most of the latter held aloof from what became the Iron Trades Employers' Association (ITEA). By the mid-1880s, this organization had branches in seventeen districts, and played an active role in promoting resistance to union demands by providing financial support to individual firms, supplying blackleg labour, and using black lists and 'enquiry notes' to prevent strikers from obtaining employment elsewhere. But the ITEA did not engage in collective bargaining and remained a loose confederation of local employers' associations without the power to undertake national action.[4]

During the depressed years of the 1870s and 1880s, British engineering employers had sought with considerable success to cheapen and intensify skilled labour within the existing organization of production, through methods such as piece-work, systematic overtime, the multiplication of apprentices and the promotion of semi-skilled 'handymen' and boys onto simpler types of machinery. As the trade cycle turned up from the late 1880s, the ASE and other unions launched a major offensive to regain ground lost to the employers during the previous decades and re-establish their control over the labour market. This movement was centred above all in the marine districts, whose connection with the sharp cyclical fluctuations of the shipbuilding industry encouraged workers to take the fullest possible advantage of the leverage afforded by a boom by pressing for wage advances, hours reductions and tighter restrictions on overtime, piece-work, machine manning, demarcation and apprenticeship ratios. The sharp downturn of trade after 1893 shifted the focus of union militancy to reductions in working hours aimed at containing unemployment. Only deepening recession in 1895 halted the national campaign for an eight-hour day, but not before a significant body of employers had acceded to union demands.[5]

It was this resurgence of craft militancy which provided the impetus for renewed attempts to create a national organization of engineering employers. In 1889 the Clyde masters, who had remained outside the ITEA, invited firms throughout the country to participate in a new National Federation of Engineering and Shipbuilding Employers. But the response was disappointing outside the marine districts, and the emergent organization was dominated by firms whose primary interests lay in shipbuilding. Meanwhile, the local employers' associations on the three rivers of the north-east coast had been developing wider forms of coordination and mutual support to counteract the unions' leap-frogging tactics, including regional black lists, sympathetic lock-outs and a strike insurance scheme. By the mid-1890s the north-east employers too were seeking closer cooperation with other districts, but the decisive step towards national organization was taken in the Clyde–Belfast dispute of 1895, where support from the Clyde masters proved instrumental in forcing the ASE to moderate its demand for a wage advance on the other side of the North Channel.[6]

The success of concerted action in the Clyde–Belfast dispute prompted employers from the major marine districts to place their collaboration on a more permanent footing, and the Engineering Employers' Federation (EEF) was formed officially in April 1896. The new organization was governed by an elected Executive Board with regional representatives, while subscriptions and voting power were proportional to the total wage bill of each association. The EEF took as its objective the coordination of employer resistance to union demands across the whole spectrum of contested issues from wages and hours to machine manning, payment systems and 'interference with foremen'. Federation decisions were to be binding on local associations, which were prohibited from independent action on matters of general importance without consulting the executive, and central authority was given added teeth by powers to subsidize firms for strike losses incurred while following its instructions.[7]

At the outset, membership was confined to Barrow, Belfast, the Clyde and the north-east coast, but the Federation's leaders – notably its first President, Colonel Dyer of Armstrong's – soon set out to build it into a truly national organization. They were assisted in this project by the mounting tensions between employers and skilled workers associated with the diffusion from the mid-1890s of American-model machine tools such as capstan and turret lathes, grinders and milling machines. The ASE was determined to capture the new equipment for its members, and a series of strikes over machine manning ensued. One such dispute provoked the EEF to threaten a national lock-out in August 1896, and by November it had embarked on a coordinated campaign of resistance to union claims in the name of employers' property rights in the machines. While the practical impact of the new technology remained limited, the ASE's demands for exclusive rights to work it raised issues of principle which also applied to a much wider range of equipment. In the context of growing fears of foreign competition, these conflicts over mechanization proved a powerful force for convincing engineering employers in different sectors that common interests outweighed historic antagonisms, and Manchester became the first inland district to join the EEF in March 1897.[8] In the event, however, it was not the machine question but the revival of union demands for the eight-hour day that triggered the national lock-out of 1897–8. The weakly organized London employers had remained outside the EEF, and metropolitan resistance to the eight-hour day began to collapse in the face of pressure from a joint committee of engineering and shipbuilding unions during the spring of 1897. In a desperate effort to staunch the flow of defeats, the London employers applied for membership in the EEF, which seized the opportunity to widen its sphere of influence by threatening to lock out union members nationally until the shorter-hours demand was withdrawn. The ASE stood its ground and the lock-out began in July 1897.[9]

The EEF was well prepared for this confrontation. Plans had been laid for a strike levy on member firms, a benefit society to detach supervisors from the unions, an ample supply of blacklegs and the generalization of the 'enquiry note' system. Resistance to the eight-hour day provided propitious ground on which to mobilize employers from diverse sectors and districts, since a substantial reduction in working hours would reduce productivity, raise costs and undermine the competitive position of firms across the industry as a whole. Employers facing very different material circumstances could likewise rally behind the Federation's principled defence of managerial prerogatives, while the disputed machine question enabled the EEF to brand the ASE as enemies of progress and property in the eyes of public opinion. Most of the provincial branches of the ITEA affiliated to the EEF during the course of the lock-out, and membership of the Federation expanded from 180 firms at the outset to 702 at its close. Yet the solidarity and unanimity among engineering employers during the dispute should not be exaggerated. Leading employers such as Benjamin Browne and William Mather sought to broker a compromise settlement through the Board of Trade, and there were notable abstentions and defections from Federation membership among textile-machinery manufacturers, marine engineers and the great railway workshops. At the height of the lock-out only 25 per cent of ASE members were affected, with considerable variations in the proportion from district to district.[10]

But the chinks in the employers' armour were minor compared to the glaring weaknesses the lock-out exposed in the ASE. Despite growing membership, the ASE had organized fewer than half the skilled engineers in the industry and none of the burgeoning army of handymen capable of working the new machine tools. Equally, the ASE's fierce defence of the boundaries of the engineer's trade had isolated the union from the other great craft societies which held aloof from the dispute. The cost of financing the six-month conflict brought the ASE to the verge of bankruptcy and forced its leaders to sue for peace.[11] The 'Terms of Settlement' accepted by ASE members in January 1898 conceded a legitimate role for collective bargaining over wages in return for a sweeping recognition of managerial prerogatives in other spheres. Employers were henceforth free to hire non-unionists, to institute piece-work systems at prices agreed with the individual worker, to demand up to forty hours of overtime per man per month, to pay non-unionists at individual rates, to employ as many apprentices as they chose, and to place any suitable worker on any machine at a mutually agreed rate. In addition, the Terms of Settlement established a novel disputes procedure which enshrined the Federation's strategy of elevating all disputes from the firm to the regional and, ultimately, the national level: henceforth the ASE could not sanction any strike until it had gone through a national conference between the union executive and the EEF.[12] These procedural arrangements were designed to discourage local resistance on questions of principle by forcing the ASE executive to discipline its members through the constant threat of a renewed national lock-out.

THE LIMITS OF EMPLOYER DOMINANCE, 1898–1914

The overwhelming scale of the EEF's victory in 1897–8 inaugurated a long period of employer dominance of industrial relations in engineering. Yet the emergent national system of collective bargaining and dispute resolution set in motion by that victory proved a major source of internal tensions within the Federation just as it did within the unions themselves. One set of tensions was rooted in the relationship of EEF officials with external bodies – above all trade unions but increasingly also the state. As guardians of the collective interests of engineering employers as a whole, the Federation's leaders had to judge the precise balance of concession and coercion most likely to preserve the settlement of 1898 as trade-union organization revived and governments became less tolerant of employer unilateralism in the run-up to the First World War. And as in any trade union, the policies adopted by the central authorities of the EEF, whether militant or conciliatory, inevitably provoked dissent from firms and associations whose sectional interests they cut across. A second and related set of tensions arose from the growing integration of collective bargaining, particularly over wage questions, among separate districts and between different trades within each district. Although the impetus for wider coordination in wage disputes emanated from the associations themselves, these centripetal pressures placed great strain on employer solidarity and, as in the unions, touched off reactions from defenders of local autonomy. Since the EEF remained a voluntary organization with a representative constitution and limited sanctions over its members, the Federation's leaders, like their union counterparts, were obliged to pay close heed to the discontents of the rank and file in framing their national strategies.

As I have sought to show elsewhere, the reassertion of management prerogatives in 1897–8 did not lead to a wholesale transformation of work organization across the engineering industry. Where firms were large, demand buoyant and products relatively standardized, as in newer, lighter sectors such as cycles, motors and electrical engineering or parts of armaments, textile machinery and other older sectors, employers might undertake large-scale investments in deskilling equipment and introduce new systems of supervision and incentive payment designed to rationalize and speed up work. But in the bulk of British engineering, industrial structure and market conditions discouraged major retooling, so that innovation consisted rather in the introduction of new machine tools and management practices within a workshop organization that remained structurally unchanged. In such cases, employers' attempts to free themselves of craft restrictions were more an extension of their traditional strategies for work intensification and cost-cutting than any breakthrough into a new 'Taylorist' mode, and they remained substantially dependent on the intervention of skilled workers in the production process right up to the First World War. Hence the ASE was soon able to rebuild its organization, and issues such as machine manning, payment by results, overtime and apprenticeship continued to dominate industrial conflict in engineering after 1898 as they had before.[13]

In the years immediately following the lock-out, the EEF's central aim was to protect the Terms of Settlement against local encroachments by developing the procedure for avoiding disputes into a binding framework for labour relations in the industry. Since no strike could 'constitutionally' take place until a deadlock had been reached at central conference, the Federation could use its national strength to choke off local flare-ups of craft militancy even during periods of high demand for skilled labour such as the Boer War. Conscious of its dominant position, the EEF generally refrained from open threats of a national lock-out, preferring to isolate local resistance by bringing informal pressure to bear on the union leadership and by offering financial support to the firm concerned. While the Federation's strategy proved highly successful in containing local strikes for over a decade, its effectiveness depended in no small part on maintaining the credibility of the disputes procedure in the eyes of the union. Hence the EEF was careful to insist on the observance of central conference decisions even when these were unfavourable to particular employers. In order to secure a more voluntary adherence to the Terms of Settlement by the ASE, the Federation leaders were likewise prepared to offer concessions on substantive issues such as piece-rate fixing, overtime limits and the displacement of skilled workers by machinery. At the same time, however, they rejected amendments that would have compromised the underlying principles of managerial prerogative, insisting for example that the disputes

procedure remain retrospective, triggered only after a managerial innovation.[14]

Behind this tactical flexibility lay EEF officials' awareness of the problems involved in mobilizing their membership for a renewed confrontation
over any but the most vital issues as the organizational strength of the ASE
revived and unrest mounted in the districts in the years following the lock-
out. Thus, as A. P. Henderson, the Federation's Executive Chairman,
observed in 1906.[15]

> It would be a very difficult thing to get the Federation lined up against
> the ASE. . . . I think we should do everything we possibly can to avoid
> lining up the Federation, because we might be disappointed to find what
> the lining up was when the flag was raised. We need a very strong case to
> put before the Federation before we will get them to be as prepared to go
> into the sacrifice as they did on the previous occasion.

If the concessions offered by the EEF Executive were far from sufficient
to satisfy the restive districts of the ASE, they were often too much for the
Federation's own members. In 1907, for example, manufacturers of agricultural machinery in Lincoln and East Anglia resigned *en masse* from the
EEF in protest at the provision for overtime and night-shift payments to
piece-workers in the revised Terms of Settlement agreed with the ASE.[16]
The Federation also faced the converse problem of firms or associations
prepared to concede more generous conditions than those permitted
nationally. Thus the EEF was forced to reconsider its position on working
hours after 1902 by the growing diffusion of the 'one-break system' in which
the traditional breakfast stoppage was eliminated in exchange for a later
starting-time. Despite the opposition of a majority of local associations,
important members in centres like Manchester were anxious to introduce
the system, and the General Electric Company, its most committed
proponent, resigned from the Federation when ASE members refused to
accept a proposed agreement on the issue in 1907.[17]

But it was the growing entanglement of wage questions with the disputes
procedure that proved the greatest threat to the Terms of Settlement in the
decade following the lock-out. The founders of the EEF had initially
proposed to confine its scope to matters of principle, leaving adjustments of
wages to the districts, but it was eventually agreed to permit local
associations to appeal for assistance from the Federation in disputes over
wages as well. After 1898 the associations realized that they could use the
procedure to stall district movements for wage advances when demand was
brisk, while demanding immediate reductions when the trade cycle turned
downwards. Under these conditions, local deadlocks could quickly raise the
spectre of a national confrontation. Thus in 1903 on the Clyde and 1908 on
the north-east coast, ASE district committees struck against proposed wage
cuts in defiance of the orders of George Barnes, the union's General
Secretary, who was committed to working within the Terms of Settlement.

A series of decisions by internal bodies of the highly democratic ASE had progressively circumscribed the executive's powers to control local disputes, and Barnes himself resigned in 1908 when he was unable to compel the north-east strikers to return to work. The Federation remained reluctant to elevate a local wage dispute into a national issue, but after six months' impasse, pressure from the north-east association forced it to threaten a full-scale lock-out, and a compromise settlement was only reached through the intervention of Lloyd George and the Board of Trade.[18]

The progressive integration of collective bargaining on a wider scale raised serious internal problems for the EEF just as for the ASE. In Lancashire, for example, employers' associations were narrowly constituted around the old textile centres, and attempts to establish a broader combination for bargaining purposes ran aground on the continuing attachment to local autonomy in many districts.[19] In the marine districts, too, proposals for formal collaboration in wage negotiations between shipbuilders and engineers were rejected as a potential threat to the cohesion of the EEF, while the north-west and north-east associations themselves proved no more successful in sustaining a coordinated bargaining strategy.[20] For many Federation leaders, the protracted strike on the north-east coast in 1908 had brought to light the underlying weakness of the industry's wage determination procedures. It seemed increasingly unlikely, observed Allan Smith, then assistant secretary of the Federation, that the EEF's diverse membership would support a national lock-out over small adjustments of wages in a single district, while the movement of public opinion and government policy towards compulsory arbitration and a minimum wage raised the possibility of outside intervention in any strike of large proportions. Smith therefore proposed the constitution of a national wages board in which an impartial arbitrator would be given binding authority to adjudicate local wage movements based on objective indicators of trading conditions. But any such scheme implied greater central coordination of wage bargaining, and a Federation subcommittee identified the major obstacle as the 'want of common interest on the part of firms', observing that 'textile machinery might be very busy when marine depressed. Similarly with other branches of trade a serious difficulty would accordingly arise in the way of getting the Federation to act as a body on a wage question.' When the local associations were consulted in 1909, they rejected any departure from the existing procedure by a wide margin.[21]

The north-east coast dispute of 1908 signalled a period of mounting challenge to the policies developed by the EEF over the preceding decade. With the erosion of executive authority in the ASE, and the rapid tightening of labour markets after 1911, craft militancy in engineering enjoyed a dramatic resurgence. Its effects could be seen first of all in an intensified militancy in disputes over machine manning and payment systems, which both mushroomed in number and proved vastly more successful for skilled workers than at any time since 1898. ASE negotiators began to win growing numbers of compromise settlements and even victories on these issues through the disputes procedure, as they were rarely prepared to drop a case before the final failure to agree; and positive results were also achieved by official strikes after the exhaustion of the procedure. In a number of instances, large firms that had played a leading role in the assault on craft practices were forced to accept limitations on their rights to promote handymen or introduce new payment systems. This process culminated in the ASE's unilateral termination of the 1898 settlement and the renewal of its demand for a 48-hour week at the end of 1913, an offensive tempered only by its grudging acceptance of an interim disputes procedure.[22]

The Federation's response to these unwelcome developments was predominately one of caution. Individual firms faced with a protracted strike might demand a national lock-out and aggressive associations like the north-west (Clyde) proclaim their willingness 'to give all active support necessary to maintain and, if needful, enforce . . . the employers' rights and discretion as to the manning of machines and the employment of handymen generally'.[23] But the Federation leaders were not yet prepared to abandon the tactics which had proved satisfactory during the preceding decade. Long experience under the disputes procedure had bred a habit of negotiation that was not easily broken, and the broad coalition necessary to sustain a national lock-out would be especially difficult to mobilize in the context of a boom which tipped the balance of power in favour of local militancy.

One reason for the EEF's caution was the growing tendency of public officials to intervene in industrial relations which had already become evident in the north-east coast dispute of 1908.[24] As the secretary of the Shipbuilding Employers' Federation (SEF) observed to the EEF in 1911,[25]

> Within recent years, this Federation, and over a longer period both your Federation and this Federation have had difficulty in preventing the Board of Trade coming into questions at issue with their workmen under conditions which, it was considered, would have imperiled, if not sacrificed, the interests of the employers.

EEF leaders themselves believed that the Liberal government was considering the introduction of compulsory arbitration 'on all questions, whether of fact or of principle', a move which would subject managerial prerogatives as well as wages to the interference of an outside party. To deflect this threat, the EEF executive put forward new proposals for a central wages board, with a neutral chairman empowered to give binding decisions on advances and reductions, which were to be kept to a minimum, based on the state of trade. This scheme was accepted by the associations in 1913, but could not be implemented before the war because of long-term wage-stabilization agreements in a number of the districts.[26]

At the same time, however, the EEF was also seeking to strengthen its hand in disputes with the ASE by increasing the financial resources available for supporting the firms affected. In 1908 the north-east coast association had proposed the creation of a more formal subsidy scheme to indemnify firms against strike losses 'so as to avoid as far as possible the necessity for such extreme measures as a general lockout by the Federation'. But no action was taken until 1912, when the mounting cost of machine-manning disputes obliged the Federation to impose an extraordinary levy on its members and devise plans for a permanent subsidy scheme with contributions based on each firm's annual wage bill. While the local associations overwhelmingly approved this scheme the following year, many firms opposed the additional expense and feared lest they be forced to finance strikes arising, as one letter put it, 'from employers' want of tact'; as a result, membership of the Federation fell from 810 firms in 1913 to 744 in 1914.[27]

There were thus sound reasons, both external and internal, for the leadership of the EEF to avoid a renewed confrontation with the ASE. Even when the new union executive unilaterally repudiated the Terms of Settlement, the Federation's response was to reopen negotiations rather than call for a general lock-out, and the interim procedural agreement made no reference to managerial prerogatives. At the same time, to be sure, the Federation also warned the ASE executive against the risks of unilateral action in the districts on sensitive issues such as the closed shop. But when the SEF proposed a joint lock-out in opposition to the 48-hour week, the EEF executive instead obtained its members' authority to negotiate a more modest reduction in exchange for concessions from the unions on other contested questions. Thus, on the eve of the First World War, all the major questions that appeared to have been settled in 1897–8 had once more been reopened. The pressures towards a renewed trial of strength between the EEF and the ASE were certainly mounting, but a negotiated solution was also possible and the outcome far from certain.[28]

THE CRUCIBLE OF WAR, 1914–18

The First World War was a period of unprecedented difficulty for British engineering employers and their organizations. Government policies and the priorities of war production placed a premium on the cooperation of organized labour, while employers' representatives were largely excluded from key decisions. Full employment and cost-plus contracts touched off a desperate scramble for scarce skilled workers, and established forms of employer solidarity in the labour market came close to collapse. Prewar tensions within the Federation erupted into open revolt, and the EEF leaders – above all, Allan Smith – were obliged to reconstruct their organization and rethink its policies in preparation for the challenges of the postwar world.

Far from being a pliant tool of industrial capital, the wartime state proved distinctly resistant to employer influence, even where manufacturers were seconded as advisers to the war departments. Throughout the war, the central concern of government planners was to obtain the munitions and manpower required for military victory, and commercial considerations were relegated to the margins of policy-making. By contrast, the representation of union officials at all levels of the state machinery was explicitly geared to winning labour support for government policies. The framework for wartime labour policy was established by the Treasury Agreement of March 1915, a bilateral compact between Lloyd George and the unions, and the employers were not consulted despite the obligations undertaken on their behalf, which included limitation of profits and legal guarantees of the restoration of prewar practices.[29]

Wartime conditions undermined the position of engineering employers in the local labour market as in the national political arena. As the War Office and the Admiralty placed ever larger munitions contracts, the major armaments firms and their subcontractors were drawn into a frenetic and increasingly unprincipled search for skilled labour which threatened to destroy the cohesion of their local employers' associations. Engineering employers had never proved very successful in restraining competition amongst themselves for labour in periods of high demand. Prewar attempts to extend the 'enquiry note' from a simple blacklist of strikers to a comprehensive system for preventing workers from changing jobs without their employer's consent had broken down repeatedly in the face of determined union opposition and divisions among firms themselves.[30] Hence even the best organized local associations were thus ill prepared to cope with the unprecedented strains caused by the munitions boom. On the Clyde, for example, the north-west association passed a series of resolutions in 1914–15 urging its members to use the enquiry note and to defend the district rate, but given the pressures in the labour market these remained very much a dead letter. On the north-east coast, too, enquiry notes fell into disuse and even so staunch an exponent of employer solidarity as Armstrong-Whitworth was prepared to hire men on strike from other local firms. Perhaps the most serious breach of Federation practice was committed by the recently formed Coventry association, which unilaterally agreed in June of 1916 to a general wage increase for men on time rates, provoking demands for its expulsion by the other West Midlands districts and formal censure from the EEF executive.[31]

It was thus the failure of solidarity among engineering employers themselves which lay behind their demands for official restrictions on labour mobility in 1915 and after. Local associations on the Clyde and in Birmingham appealed to the Admiralty and the War Office to stop their contractors paying 'illegitimate' bonuses to attract labour and prevent men on munitions work from changing jobs in search of higher wages. In response to this pressure, the Munitions Act of 1915 prohibited employers from taking on workers from government-controlled firms without a leaving certificate from their previous employer. But these provisions were quickly watered down as a result of opposition from the unions and the leaving certificates were dropped entirely after the strike wave of May 1917.[32] In negotiations with the Ministry of Munitions over the amendment of the Munitions Act the EEF sought desperately to obtain some continuing government backing for limitations on competition for labour between its members; as Allan Smith told the Ministry 'we want to subject ourselves to discipline as much as anybody else, because we have to protect ourselves from ourselves.' But the Ministry would not permit local employers' associations to implement collective restrictions on worker mobility, while its own hesitant efforts to impose an embargo on competitive bidding-up of wages touched off a major industrial crisis in the summer of 1918. By March 1918 the EEF had accepted that many munitions firms could not hold out against a threatened stoppage for even a few hours, and asked only that its members notify Federation officials of their concessions after the fact so that representations could be made to the government authorities.[33]

The inability of the Federation leaders to prevent these reverses sparked open conflict over the direction of policy for the first time in the EEF's history. From the early months of the war, Allan Smith, the Federation secretary, was closely involved in negotiations with the ASE and the War Office over measures to accelerate the output of munitions. His central objective was to obtain the relaxation of trade-union restrictions on urgent war work while safeguarding the autonomy of the Federation and its bargaining procedures as far as possible. Conscious of employers' limited influence with the government and convinced of trade-union leaders' underlying patriotism, Smith favoured a conciliatory approach to the ASE executive which took into account the internal constraints on its freedom of manoeuvre.[34] Nor were Smith's policies wholly unsuccessful. The ASE was persuaded first to allow female labour on 'purely automatic machinery', and then to concede a further extension of dilution in exchange for various safeguards. Although the Federation was not consulted in the drafting of the Munitions Act, the resulting measure incorporated modified versions of a number of Smith's proposals – including the abolition of strikes and lock-outs, the suspension of restrictive practices and the establishment of munitions tribunals – and he himself was coopted onto numerous official bodies by the newly formed Ministry of Munitions.[35]

But where the industrial situation was most acute, as on the Clyde, Smith's emollient gradualism failed to satisfy local engineering employers thirsting for sterner measures. The north-west association had been up in arms over the authorities' inability to restrict the movement of labour, and its members were deeply shocked by wage concessions granted to unofficial strikers in February 1915. William Weir, whose firm had been in the forefront of the prewar struggles over managerial prerogatives, drafted draconian proposals for the abolition of illegitimate bonuses and induce-ments, the stabilization of wages, the suspension of trade unions and employers' federations, and the generalization of industrial conscription. In June 1915 the north-west association decided to press these proposals on the government in hopes of influencing the deliberations on the Munitions Act, but the Emergency Committee of the EEF got wind of these plans and enjoined the association against any independent action. The Clyde employers reluctantly complied, but complained bitterly that 'no lead had been given by the Federation to Local Associations in regard to a uniform wages policy or anything else in the present critical times.'[36] After a long series of concessions to the unions on dilution and the Munitions Act, the government's creation of a central Labour Advisory Committee precipitated a renewed burst of outrage from the Clyde in August 1916. J. R. Richmond, Weir's half-brother and north-west representative on the Emergency Committee, wrote to the Federation pillorying 'the supine and inactive policies . . . during the last two years', demanding greater consultation with the local associations, and questioning the value of Smith's association with the Ministry of Munitions. Nor were these views confined to the Clyde: furious about government decisions on women's wages, the Birmingham association echoed this call for the reconsideration of Smith's position on the official bodies responsible. But the Emergency Committee expressed its confidence in Smith's connection with the Ministry, reaffirming its support for his policies, and Richmond himself resigned the following month.[37]

This incipient revolt of the membership provoked a swift response from Smith, and the EEF leadership aimed at safeguarding the cohesion of the organization. Already before 1914, the direction of Federation policy was largely set by an appointed Emergency Committee and the full-time secretariat rather than the elected Executive Board, but the centralization of wartime negotiations had tended to concentrate decision-making power still further in the hands of Allan Smith. Now the constitution of the Federation was revised to reconcile the imperatives of professional administration with demands for greater accountability to the constituent associations. The Emergency Committee was replaced by a Management Committee composed of twelve elected members of the Executive Board together with office bearers and trustees; and the Board itself was reconstructed to provide for representation of the associations in closer proportion to their wage bill. Smith himself became the full-time chairman of the EEF, presiding over all its committees, and he was directed to devote 'all his time, attention and abilities to the business of the Federation,' though he remained a member of many official bodies. Smith's authority was thus reaffirmed and in some ways enhanced, but so too was his dependence on the support of the associations, a point underlined by Richmond's election to the Management Committee.[38]

The reorganization of the Federation went hand in hand with the reorientation of its policies. As the chief spokesman for engineering interests on the Ministry of Munitions Employers' Advisory Committee, Allan Smith put himself squarely behind his members' grievances and emerged as a much more forceful critic of government labour policies than hitherto. Government orders on women's wages, the privileged position of the ASE, the abolition of leaving certificates, the encouragement of shop committees and the extension of bonuses to skilled timeworkers all came in for bitter complaint, together with the lack of coordination among government departments and the Ministry's persistent failure to consult the employers until crucial decisions had already been taken.[39] But Smith also sought to give a positive direction to EEF policy by concluding national agreements with the unions on wage determination and shop-steward recognition despite the bitter opposition of important sections of the membership.[40]

These agreements formed part of a broader project aimed at preparing the Federation for postwar reconstruction. Although membership had increased rapidly during the war as growing numbers of employers felt the need for formal representation in their dealings with the state, internal surveys revealed the extent of disarray within the Federation. Beneath the unanimous adherence to the abstract principle of managerial prerogative, deep divisions were apparent across a broad spectrum of vital issues, from the future basis of wage determination and the length of the working day to the acceptability of shop committees. A number of associations also expressed doubts about the possibility of restoring the prewar position on key questions such as payment systems, overtime, training, the closed shop and the restrospective character of the disputes procedure.[41] Under these circumstances, concluded Allan Smith, employers' collective interests could only be safeguarded through a bold national strategy aimed at reaching a durable accommodation with the unions even at the price of substantial reductions in hours and a greater degree of joint regulation over wages and working conditions. Thus an EEF report in January 1918 accepted the inevitability of the 48-hour week, acknowledged that 'regard must be had to the claims of the skilled turner' in machine manning, envisaged the introduction of a grading system for all operations and recommended consideration of trade-union representation of apprentices. The Federation also advocated the continuation of binding arbitration on wages after the war, and was prepared to accept the compression of regional wage differentials as well as the establishment of minimum rates for unskilled labour.[42]

At the same time, however, Smith also sought to rebuild the EEF's capacity for collective action by internal reforms to improve its cohesion and by forging closer links with other employers' organizations. Thus six regional Joint Standing Committees were created in 1917–18 to 'bring about a closer community of interest amongst the local associations and bring [them] into closer touch with the Federation'; and in areas such as Lancashire, full-time regional organizers were appointed to increase recruitment and coordinate bargaining strategy across districts.[43] In 1918, the EEF absorbed the National Employers' Federation, whose 700-odd members were concentrated in the Midlands where Federation organization had historically been weak; and talks were underway with the SEF for a joint approach to postwar negotiations on working hours.[44] But Smith was also seeking to create a broader framework for cooperation on labour issues with employers outside the metal trades, and his efforts bore fruit in early 1919 with the formation of the National Confederation of Employers' Organizations (NCEO).[45]

THE FAILURE OF COOPERATIVE BARGAINING, 1918–22

At the end of the First World War there was little sense that the EEF was preparing for a renewed confrontation with the unions. Although membership had doubled from 744 firms in 1914 to 1,469 in 1918, solidarity within the local associations had largely collapsed and central authority stood at a low ebb, despite the efforts of Allan Smith to reorganize the Federation on stronger lines. Thrown onto the defensive by government policies which they expected to continue after the war, EEF leaders were seeking a comprehensive settlement with the unions in return for significant concessions on wages, hours and working conditions. It was only with the onset of a major depression, a pronounced shift in the political climate, and the demonstration of the unions' inability to ensure the observance of national agreements that the EEF turned towards a unilateral reimposition of managerial prerogatives. Even then, a considerable measure of internal opposition had to be overcome before its membership could be mobilized in support of a national lock-out.

The pursuit of Smith's 'national programme' dominated the Federation's bargaining strategy in the immediate postwar years. Faced with mounting industrial unrest in the wake of the armistice, the EEF and SEF conceded a 47-hour week in November 1918 in exchange for general promises by the trade-union leaders to promote maximum output and negotiate seriously on the introduction of payment by results.[46] But these promises proved virtually unenforceable in 1919–20 as district committees and shop stewards broke free from central union control, and engineering employers experienced a growing tide of unilateral restrictions on machine manning, payment systems, apprenticeship ratios and overtime working. Throughout this period, however, Smith and the EEF leaders maintained a cautious posture, conscious of the Lloyd George government's reluctance to antagonize the unions and the continuing disarray within their own ranks. Thus a Federation circular of August 1919 urged employers to exercise 'the utmost discretion and tact' and afford 'workpeople the opportunity of raising any question in a constitutional way'.[47] Only when confronted with official union support for unilateral action did the EEF revive the lock-out threat, as in the case of the electricians' strike for the closed shop for foremen at Cammell-Laird's Penistone works in 1920.[48]

The central focus of Federation strategy, by contrast, was directed to protracted negotiations with union executives – above all the ASE (renamed the Amalgamated Engineering Union in July 1920) – for a comprehensive national agreement on wages procedure and working conditions which would resolve the full range of disputed issues. Smith was prepared to offer far-reaching concessions such as recognized bargaining rights for apprentices, a national grading system for semi-skilled labour, and an industry-based unemployment scheme in return for union acceptance of payment by results and greater flexibility in machine manning. Within the AEU executive, influential figures such as J. T. Brownlie, the union's president, were sympathetic to these proposals, and even those who remained more sceptical were attracted by the prospect of regulating working conditions on a national basis.[49] In 1919, for example, the EEF and the ASE concluded a national piece-work agreement enabling a worker of average ability to earn one-third above time rates, as well as a new agreement incorporating shop stewards and works committees into the disputes procedure.[50] But the high-water mark of the EEF's campaign for the 'national programme' was the Overtime and Night Shift Agreement of September 1920 which levelled up rates and conditions across districts, an agreement pushed through by Smith in hopes of unlocking negotiations on wider issues and putting an end to local embargoes on overtime.[51]

But the Federation's conciliatory strategy ran into growing opposition from disgruntled regional associations experiencing little relief from localized militancy and concerned about the costs of proposed concessions. These grievances sharpened during 1920 as the postwar boom burst and recession spread unevenly across engineering. The worst-hit sectors began to clamour for immediate wage cuts, while the Overtime and Night Shift Agreement in particular sparked bitter resentment from regions facing sharply increased rates. All of Smith's authority and diplomatic skills were required to persuade dissident associations such as the Clyde to adopt 'a broad national standpoint' for the moment, but the scope for further compromises with the unions had clearly been narrowed.[52] Under such pressures, the Federation's commitment to a bargained settlement could only be sustained if union leaders demonstrated their ability to deliver the *quid pro quo* of local compliance with national agreements. As unemployment began to bite more deeply, however, the conciliatory faction within the AEU executive itself lost ground to the defenders of local autonomy and unilateral craft restrictions. Thus in December 1920 the union threw its official weight behind the claim that district committees could maintain their overtime embargoes despite the provisions of the Overtime and Night Shift Agreement which fixed a limit of 30 hours per man per month.[53] Given the unpopularity of this agreement among engineering employers, the AEU's position struck at the heart of Smith's attempt to establish a mutually acceptable framework for industrial relations through national negotiations with union officials. In early 1921, therefore, the EEF threatened to dismiss anyone refusing to work overtime up to the agreed limits and lock out the AEU if it struck in their defence.[54]

From that point onwards, Smith and his colleagues appear to have decided that the weakness of central authority within the unions now required a unilateral reassertion of managerial prerogatives. But if the collapse of the postwar boom eliminated gross disparities between different sectors of engineering, the shift in economic circumstances did not automatically swing employer opinion behind a confrontation with the unions over these issues. Recession did, however, galvanize the EEF to press for the speedy roll-back of war bonuses and postwar wage advances, particularly since the AEU had unilaterally withdrawn from the national wage-arbitration procedure in the summer of 1920. Under heavy pressure from the employers, the unions conceded a staged reduction in July 1921, despite an adverse vote of their members, but by autumn the EEF was demanding further cuts of 26*s*. 6*d*. per week. Smith and the Federation leaders used this crucial period to mobilize support among their members for a broad campaign to extract a formal recognition of managerial prerogatives from the unions and impose a new procedural agreement on the industry. For many employers, however, the EEF's focus on questions of abstract principle represented an unwelcome distraction from the burning need for a drastic reduction in wage costs to restore their international competitiveness. Union restrictions in any case had largely evaporated as the recession deepened, and even the AEU's overtime embargoes had become more symbolic than real. Hence the Federation's proposals to extend the threatened lock-out from overtime to managerial prerogatives in April 1921 met with a distinctly ambivalent response in many districts.[55]

But the downward spiral of demand progressively diminished the costs of a lock-out to the employers, while the political constraints were also disappearing as the coalition government sought to extricate itself from active involvement in industrial negotiations. At the same time, too, the strategic immobility of the AEU enhanced the ideological attractiveness of a formal restoration of managerial prerogative. With union funds depleted by heavy unemployment, by November 1921 the AEU executive felt compelled to accept the EEF's interpretation of the overtime agreement and the employers' right to initiate changes in the workplace pending the conclusion of the disputes procedure, but the proposed memorandum on managerial functions was rejected by a ballot of the membership. At this point, employer opinion swung decisively behind the Federation's confrontational stance, and Smith was even able to extend the lock-out threat to all other unions in the industry unless they too signed the disputed memorandum. Although the government had sought to avoid the lock-out, the court of inquiry it appointed ruled in favour of the employers' position on overtime and the contending parties were left to pursue a war of attrition without further external intervention.[56]

From the beginning, the 1922 lock-out was more comprehensive than that of 1897–8. In March all AEU members were barred from federated factories, and 51 additional unions were thrown onto the streets in May for refusing to sign the contentious document. Local resistance within the AEU was fierce and a majority on its executive held out against further concessions. But, as in 1897–8, many firms were able to continue working, and the three-month dispute finally exhausted the unions' finances and morale. The AEU was a spent force and it would be many years before it could again challenge the employers even at a local level.[57]

AMBIGUOUS VICTORY, 1922–39

The EEF's victory in 1922 was much more complete than in 1898. The full range of engineering unions had been brought within the ambit of a uniform national bargaining system and forced to acknowledge the legitimacy of managerial prerogatives. The AEU itself had been reduced to bankruptcy and its capacity for national action decisively shattered; union membership fell by 45 per cent between 1920 and 1923 and workplace organization was decimated by unemployment and victimization. Demand for skilled engineering workers remained depressed for more than a decade, offering the unions little opportunity to rebuild their organization, and the government had become increasingly reluctant to intervene in industrial relations, whatever the balance of power between the parties. On the shop floor as in the wider labour market, engineering employers had won a free hand in practice as well as in principle.

In this environment, the EEF experienced little direct challenge to its dominance and its leaders were able to impose tough terms on the unions in national bargaining over wages and working conditions. But at the local level engineering employers and their associations were pursuing policies that would prove dangerous for the future. In the older sectors of the industry, firms sought cost reductions through the multiplication of apprentices and downgrading of skilled workers rather than rationalization and re-equipment. Even in newer sectors such as motors, management relied on the manipulation of payment systems rather than machine pacing and tight supervision to drive production processes that remained flexible and labour-intensive.[58] The associations attempted without much success to establish common standards for payment systems, control labour mobility and encourage genuine training; as the economy began to recover in the mid-1930s, growing skill shortages gave rise to competition for labour, wage drift and the resurgence of workplace militancy. The EEF was divided between depressed and booming sections, inhibiting its ability to formulate a common policy, while the Federation's authority over the associations had atrophied during the long period of industrial quiescence. The demands of rearmament also brought the government back into industrial relations in engineering, and the EEF was again forced to negotiate with the unions for the relaxation of restrictive practices.

The EEF moved quickly to exploit its victory in the 1922 lock-out. Sweeping wage cuts were imposed without further delay and unions such as the Foundry Workers which had previously held out against payment by results were now forced to sign agreements for its introduction. In 1921 the Federation leadership had opposed any move away from national bargaining in negotiations over wage reductions, and when trade began to revive in 1923 it successfully resisted claims for advances from AEU district committees in the more prosperous areas. At national level the Federation held out against any wage increase until 1928, demanding off-setting concessions over working hours and conditions; and in exchange for avoiding further wage cuts in 1931, Allan Smith and the EEF leaders persuaded the AEU to accept significant reductions in overtime, night-shift and piece-work rates. The triumph of national bargaining appeared complete, and by the late 1920s the AEU had even agreed to participate alongside the other unions in an Engineering Joint Trades Movement responsible for national pay negotiations.[59]

But beneath the surface the situation was less reassuring. The depression heightened differences in the economic position of individual firms, while the weakness of the unions made solidarity appear less vital to many employers. The number of firms affiliated to the EEF fell from 2690 in 1922 to 1968 in 1931 and 1806 in 1935, and in 1932 the Federation was obliged to grant a rebate on contributions to its strike indemnity fund to assist the local associations and stem the decline of its membership.[60] Throughout this period, Smith and other EEF officials sought to instil a greater strategic awareness among its members, but without the external threats of union power and state intervention their leverage was sharply diminished. Federation initiatives on key issues such as training and grading therefore foundered on the limited time-horizons imposed on manufacturers by depressed trade and their ability to cut production costs without recourse to industry-wide measures. As Smith warned, however, this strategic 'short-sightedness' would have serious consequences for labour supply and industrial relations when trade eventually improved.[61]

More serious still was the position in individual associations. As the Federation Board observed in 1931,[62]

> In several districts, practices or customs agreed or recognised have been allowed to remain in operation notwithstanding the fact that they have since become the subject of national agreements. In other cases objectionable practices have been allowed to grow up unknown to local associations.

The worst offender in this regard was Coventry, centre of the expanding motor industry and one of the most buoyant engineering districts in the country between the wars. After the 1922 lockout, AEU membership in Coventry effectively collapsed and victimization of shop stewards was widespread. In 1927 the Federation admonished the Coventry association that no works committees were functioning in the area; the association was openly reluctant to refer cases to the disputes procedure and local firms were also contravening the provisions of the Overtime and Nightshift Agreement. The Coventry association sought to prevent competition for labour among its members by enforcing the use of the enquiry note, preventing firms from paying above the district rate and ensuring that systems of payment by results were constructed on a solid basis. But the EEF refused to allow expulsions for failure to observe the enquiry note, and poaching of labour became a recurrent problem whenever demand was strong. Under these circumstances, piece-work systems were difficult to police and by 1930 the Federation was complaining that earnings and costs of production in Coventry were well above those in neighbouring districts such as Birmingham.[63]

Conditions in the older sectors of engineering presented distinct but related problems for employer solidarity. On Clydeside, employers moved to stamp out shop-steward organization after the lock-out, but weak demand for heavy engineering products provided little incentive for new investment, and as in the past firms concentrated on cutting costs by cheapening and intensifying skilled labour. The north-west association launched a determined campaign to encourage the diffusion of payment by results, employing an expert adviser to popularize more systematic forms of management, but the poor response from local firms drove him to resign within a year. Even where incentive-payment systems were in operation, rate-fixing was often left to craft-trained foremen, while their central attraction for many firms lay in the possibility of revising rates at will in the absence of workplace organization. Only the best-trained and most versatile craftsmen continued to receive the skilled men's rate, while the majority of AEU members were downgraded to tasks rated as 'semi-skilled', depending on payment by results to make up their earnings. Firms multiplied the use of apprentices and boys whose wages were not subject to collective bargaining, subverting the process of skill acquisition by assigning them to simple, repetitive operations wherever possible. By the early 1930s the north-west association was predicting that 'an improvement in our economic fortunes' would create 'a serious shortage of experienced operatives', but in the circumstances of the depression the association was unable to mobilize support for any form of collective training.[64]

Wage drift had already begun to appear during the upturn of 1924–8, but with the onset of rearmament and the quickening of recovery from 1935 it soon reached epidemic proportions. In old and new sectors alike, engineering employers had run down training during the depression, while their associations had failed to develop the enquiry note into an effective system for controlling the local labour market. Existing reservoirs of skilled labour had largely been drained and few of the unemployed could meet the standards of precision required in the toolrooms of the expanding aircraft factories and other military contractors. To restrain earnings on payments by results, employers had relied on their unilateral ability to cut rates as workers moved up the learning curve, a practice which became increasingly problematic as unemployment diminished, and payment systems degenerated as firms offered *ad hoc* bonuses to attract workers from their neighbours.[65]

Workplace organization began to revive in established centres of trade unionism such as Glasgow and Manchester, while shop stewards reappeared even in largely non-union Coventry, making particular headway in the shadow aircraft factories run by the motor manufacturers. Initially, shop-floor activists won symbolic victories such as the right to smoke at work, but the challenge to managerial authority soon encompassed the collective regulation of payment systems, the allocation of short time and the demand for the closed shop.[66] The challenge to employer authority at factory level in turn placed an intolerable burden on the industry's cumbersome disputes procedure, compelling the EEF to adopt a more flexible, conciliatory stance. By 1934 the Federation was once again advising its members to use 'the greatest discretion . . . before making any serious change in working conditions', including prior consultation with unions whose members might be affected.[67] But the most dramatic reversal suffered by employers was the success of the 1937 apprentices' strikes, which forced the EEF to accept trade-union negotiation of apprentices' rates for the first time in its history.[68]

The Federation likewise experienced mounting difficulty in reconciling the needs of expanding and contracting sectors within a national bargaining framework, as tight labour markets forced it to grant periodic wage advances to the unions from 1934 onwards. Anomalies had crept into wage rates in adjacent districts which were exacerbating local labour shortages, but adjustments could not easily be made without touching off claims in other areas. Any concession to national wage claims was often too much for firms in depressed sectors, while booming districts might prefer more generous advances; alternatively, firms which had already granted high levels of remuneration informally might resent additions to their costs imposed by national agreements. By the late 1930s, for example, a growing number of firms were conceding paid holidays to their workforce, and the EEF included a week's holiday in the 1937 wage agreement to retain control over this movement. But this departure provoked widespread opposition in regions such as Lancashire, while the Coventry association, which had long been divided on the question, ignored the agreement entirely. In Lancashire generally, there were sharp divisions over wages policy between the depressed textile machinery manufacturers and the beneficiaries of rearmament, who were largely concentrated in Manchester; in 1938, after fruitless negotiations with neighbouring associations over increases in labourers' rates, the Manchester association granted a unilateral advance. Employer solidarity was breaking down at the regional as well as the district level, and the new system of national bargaining looked increasingly shaky in the face of its first real test.[69]

In the national political arena as in the workplace and the labour market, the Federation found itself thrust onto the defensive by the eve of the Second World War. After the 1922 lock-out, two cardinal precepts came to define the central thrust of Federation policy: no bargaining with unions over questions of workshop management, and no intervention by the government in the detailed conduct of industrial relations.[70] Hence when shortages of skilled labour began to obstruct the rearmament programme from 1936, EEF leaders sought at any cost to avoid being drawn into tripartite negotiations over dilution with the unions and the government. The Federation fought valiantly to convince the government that the best method to increase the supply of skilled labour was to make individual factory agreements and extend subcontracting networks to a wider range of engineering firms, while national negotiations with the unions 'would make the various forms of dilution more difficult by allowing the AEU to insist on all its preconditions'. Since the AEU itself was desperate to avoid negotiations on dilution, which the executive believed would benefit the general unions at its expense, and the government too anxious to avoid becoming 'a milch-cow for employers and Trade Unionists alike', this policy proved successful for several years. But by 1939 the AEU executive had come round to the view that a formal dilution agreement was vital if the union was to keep control of industrial change, while ever greater labour shortages made it impossible for the EEF to hold aloof from negotiations. The resulting agreement allowed other workers to be employed on skilled men's work where existing supplies of craftsmen were inadequate, but the AEU's approval was required for any changes and pre-existing practices were to be restored as soon as the emergency had ended.[71] The untrammelled freedom of management established in 1922 was now officially suspended without any parallel guarantee of the restoration of prewar practices. As Allan Smith had foreseen, without a comprehensive agreement with the unions to define the scope of managerial prerogative, the employers' historical claim for untrammelled authority proved impossible to sustain over the longer term.

CONCLUSIONS

Why were British engineering employers unable to build on their national victories to institutionalize their solidarity on a more durable and effective basis? No definitive explanation can be given for what remains a highly contingent historical outcome, but partial answers can be identified at the level of the firm, of the local labour market, and of the national industrial and political environment. Despite considerable variations among individual firms and sectors, British engineering employers, like their shipbuilding counterparts, were generally reluctant to assume full control over the production process through the introduction of deskilling technology and more systematic forms of management. Hence employers remained structurally dependent on the skill and discretion of their workforce, and there was an inherent tendency for the re-emergence of a craft challenge to managerial prerogatives when the labour market and the political climate turned once again in a favourable direction. The limited elaboration of managerial hierarchies and heavy reliance on the external labour market meant too that even quite large British firms were unable to follow the 'internalizing' strategies of union avoidance pioneered by their American and German counterparts.[72]

Greater mystery surrounds the failure of British engineering employers to develop more effective mechanisms to control the recruitment and reproduction of skilled labour at the local level. As Howell Harris has shown in the case of Philadelphia, it was eminently possible for small and medium-sized engineering firms manufacturing diverse products to free their supplies of skilled workers from union control, regulate labour mobility and even provide training on a collective basis.[73] Perhaps the answer lies in the greater inclusiveness of the Philadelphia association than its British counterparts, which were dominated by larger firms; perhaps in the greater cohesion attainable in a strictly local organization; or perhaps in the wider industrial and political context of the United States, which weakened union organization at the national level and made an employer-dominated labour market a more realistic objective. But, whatever the reasons, British engineering employers' inability to collaborate in regulating the local labour market reinforced their individual dependence on refractory craftsmen and ensured that national solidarity would prove difficult to maintain when supplies of skilled workers became scarcer.

What, finally, of the institutionalization of solidarity at the national level? Could the EEF have developed into a cohesive, centralized organization negotiating genuinely binding agreements with national unions on the German or Scandinavian model? One possible route might have been the creation of a wider employers' front sufficiently powerful to force the unions into a commensurate degree of centralization, and alliances of this type were occasionally mooted in the headiest moments of industrial unrest during and after the First World War. But by 1920–1 it had become clear that no real revolutionary threat could be expected from the British labour movement, and employers' organizations decisively rejected proposals to invest the NCEO with executive powers over their labour policies and establish a system of mutual support in industrial disputes.[74] A second route, favoured by the engineering employers before 1922 and again during the 1960s, might have been through changes in the legal status of collective bargaining, which would have given public support to the industry's disputes procedure and strengthened the hand of 'responsible' union leaders. A statutory framework for industrial relations involving compulsory arbitration was perhaps a more plausible possibility in the first two decades of this century than it subsequently came to appear during the heyday of British voluntarism. But, as engineering employers themselves recognized, such an arrangement would have been unlikely to exempt managerial prerogatives from external interference and it would also have required a measure of tacit consent from the labour movement.[75]

Paradoxically, therefore, the most plausible route to greater cohesion among engineering employers at the national level would have been through an agreed framework of joint determination with the unions themselves, and this appears to have been the aim of Allan Smith and the EEF leadership during and immediately after the First World War. At first glance, rank-and-file employers' attachment to managerial prerogatives might appear to have posed an insuperable obstacle to this possibility. But as I have sought to show, an abstract commitment to managerial prerogatives was compatible with significant concessions to joint determination in practical matters, and Smith was often able to lead the Federation in directions opposed by sections of its membership. The crucial barrier came rather from the other key actors, the unions and the state. The ASE and its successor the AEU were federal-democratic bodies with little capacity for centralized decision-making, and at key moments their leaders proved unable to win the membership's support for agreed compromises with employers, even in the face of organizational disaster. The state, too, proved incapable of pursuing coherent labour policies or giving effective legislative support to industrial peace, particularly during the crucial years of the Lloyd George coalition, and it retreated into a largely passive voluntarist stance after 1922. As Allan Smith observed during the First World War, British engineering employers needed external assistance to protect themselves from themselves, and this their interlocutors proved neither strong nor singleminded enough to provide.

NOTES

I am pleased to acknowledge the EEF and the Amalgamated Engineering Union for access to their archives, which are held at the Modern Records Centre (MRC), University of Warwick, as well as the Scottish Engineering Employers' Association, which holds the records of the North-West Engineering Trades Employers' Association (NWETEA). I am also grateful to the British Academy for research support, and to Alan McKinlay and Terry Rodgers for help with archival materials. For convenience, I will refer to the Engineering Employers' Federation throughout this chapter although the organization changed its name several times between 1896 and 1939.

 1 See, for example, H. Phelps Brown, *The Origins of Trade Union Power* (Oxford, 1983), ch. 7; and J. Zeitlin, 'From Labour History to the History of Industrial Relations', *Economic History Review*, 2nd ser., 51 (1987). For a fuller discussion, see the concluding chapter in this volume.
 2 The standard account is E. Wigham, *The Power to Manage: A History of the Engineering Employers' Federation* (London, 1973).
 3 For general overviews, see S. B. Saul, 'The Engineering Industry', in D. H. Aldcroft (ed.), *The Development of British Industry and Foreign Competition, 1875–1914* (Glasgow, 1968); T. R. Gourvish, 'Mechanical Engineering', in N. K. Buxton and D. H. Aldcroft (eds), *British Industry between the Wars*, (London, 1979); J. Zeitlin, 'Between Flexibility and Mass Production: Product, Production and Labour Strategies in British Engineering, 1840–1955', in C. F. Sabel and J. Zeitlin (eds), *Worlds of Possibility: Flexibility and Mass Production in Western Industrialization* (forthcoming).
 4 Wigham, *Power to Manage*, ch. 2; K. Burgess, *The Origins of British Industrial Relations* (London, 1975), pp. 21–47; J. B. Jefferys, *The Story of the Engineers,*

1800–1945 (London, 1946), pts I–II; Iron Trades Employers' Association, *Record, 1872–1900* (London, 1900).

5 J. Zeitlin, 'The Labour Strategies of British Engineering Employers, 1890–1922', in H. F. Gospel and C. R. Littler (eds), *Managerial Strategies and Industrial Relations* (London, 1983), pp. 26–30; B. C. M. Weekes, 'The Amalgamated Society of Engineers, 1880–1914' (Ph.D. thesis, University of Warwick, 1970), ch. 3.

6 Wigham, *Power to Manage*, pp. 18–24; J. Zeitlin, 'Col. Henry Clement Swinerton Dyer', in D. Jeremy (ed.), *Dictionary of British Business Biography*, vol. II (London, 1984).

7 'Objects of the Employers' Federation of Engineering Associations, 1896', reprinted in Wigham, *Power to Manage*, pp. 280–1.

8 Zeitlin, 'Labour Strategies', pp. 29–33; *Conference between the ASE and the EEF on the Machine Question, April 1897*.

9 Wigham, *Power to Manage*, pp. 39–43; EEF *Executive Board Minutes* 20 May–1 July 1897.

10 EEF, *Executive Board Minutes 1896–8; passim; List of the Federated Engineering and Shipbuilding Employers who Resisted the Demand for a 48 Hours Working Week, 1897–8*; 'Returns from Districts, 1897–8', EEF F(1)5 (microfilmed case files); Wigham, *Power to Manage*, pp. 43–62; J. F. Clarke, *Power on Land and Sea: A History of R. & W. Hawthorn Leslie and Co. Ltd.* (Newcastle, 1978), p. 59; A. J. McIvor, 'Employers' Associations and Industrial Relations in Lancashire, 1890–1939' (Ph.D. thesis, University of Manchester, 1983), pp. 216–18.

11 Jefferys, *Engineers*, pp. 144–8, 292; Burgess, *British Industrial Relations*, pp. 47, 60–8; Weekes, 'ASE', ch. 4; ASE, *Notes on the Engineering Trades Lockout* (London, 1898).

12 'Terms of Settlement, 1898', reprinted in Wigham, *Power to Manage*, pp. 285–9.

13 Zeitlin, 'Labour Strategies', and 'Between Flexibility'.

14 *Verbatim Report of Conferences between the EEF and the ASE, SEMS and UMWA, Dec.–May 1900*; transcripts of further conferences on the amendment of the terms of settlement, 1906–7, EEF A(2)5–9.

15 Transcript of a special meeting of the Executive Board, 10 July 1906, EEF H(4)4.

16 EEF P(11)5.

17 EEF H(4)4; Weekes, 'ASE', pp. 146–50.

18 Weekes, 'ASE', ch. 6; R. Croucher, 'The ASE and Local Autonomy, 1889–1914' (MA thesis, University of Warwick, 1971); EEF *Emergency Committee Minutes* 8 May, 17 Aug., 8–9 Sept. 1908; *Executive Board Minutes* 18 Aug. 1908.

19 EEF F(5)3 and 5; McIvor, 'Employers' Associations', pp. 56–7, 72.

20 EEF S(3)3; NWETEA, *Minutes*, 13 May, 1–2 June 1910.

21 Memoranda, minutes and circulars in EEF C(4)11 and W(2)1.

22 Zeitlin, 'Labour Strategies', pp. 43–4.

23 EEF M(4)1–2 (Livesey & Sons, Blackburn), P(2)19 (Bow, McLoughlin & Co., Paisley); NWETEA *Minutes* 2 Feb. 1912, 5 June 1914.

24 For the broader development of government labour policy before 1914, see R. Davidson, 'Government Administration', and C. J. Wrigley, 'Government and Industrial Relations' in C. J. Wrigley (ed.), *A History of British Industrial Relations, 1875–1914* (Brighton, 1982).

25 SEF to EEF, 28 Sept. 1911, EEF C(4)4.

26 Circulars and memoranda in EEF W(2)2.

27 EEF I(4)2 and W(2)2; *Emergency Committee Minutes* 29 Nov. 1912; Wigham, *Power to Manage*, p. 303.

28 EEF A(4)1 and 7 (Terms of Settlement and disputes procedure); E(1)29–30 (closed shop); H(1)1 (hours of work).

29 For useful overviews see A. Reid, 'Dilution, Trade Unionism and the State in Britain during the First World War', in S. Tolliday and J. Zeitlin (eds), *Shop Floor Bargaining and the State* (Cambridge, 1985); and J. Turner, 'The Politics of "Organized Business" during the First World War', in J. Turner (ed.), *Businessmen and Politics: Studies of Business Activity in British Politics, 1900–1945* (London, 1984).

30 EEF D(2)9; NWETEA *Minutes* 13 Oct. 1908, 3 Aug. 1909, 15 and 28 Feb. and 3 May 1912; McIvor, 'Employers' Associations', p. 99; and A. Smith's comments to the Armament Output Committee, 20 Apr. 1915, Public Record Office (PRO) MUN5/7/171/1.

31 NWETEA *Minutes* 15 and 28 Dec. 1914, 10 and 15 Feb., 30 Mar. 7–16 Apr. and 31 May 1915; J. F. Clarke, 'Labour in World War One: Some Experiences in Engineering and Shipbuilding on the North East Coast, 1914–18', *North East Coast Labour History Society Bulletin* 14 (1980), pp. 20–1; McIvor, 'Employers' Associations', pp. 361–6; EEF *Emergency Committee Minutes* 30 June and 28 July 1916.

32 NWETEA *Minutes* 30 Mar., 7 Apr. and 31 May 1915; minutes of meeting with Birmingham employers, 20 Apr. 1915, PRO MUN5/7/171/1; C. J. Wrigley, *Lloyd George and the British Labour Movement* (Brighton, 1976), chs 6 and 12; G. R. Rubin, *War, Law and Labour: The Munitions Acts, State Regulation and the Unions, 1915–21* (Oxford, 1987); and Reid, 'Dilution', pp. 53–9.

33 'Minutes of Proceedings at a Deputation from the EEF to the Ministry of Munitions, 8 June 1917', EEF W(4)8; Employers' Consultative Committee meeting, 17 July 1917, PRO MUN5/53/300/92; EEF E(3)3, M(20)12, W(4)11 (unsuccessful local schemes to control labour mobility); *Management Committee Minutes* 22 Mar. 1918; 'Minutes of Evidence before the 'Embargo Committee of Enquiry, August 1918', MUN5/57/320/33; *History of the Ministry of Munitions* (printed but not published, London, 1920–4), vol. VI, pt II, chs 1 and 4.

34 See, for example, Smith's letters to H. Lawton 22 Dec. 1914, and J. R. Richmond, 2 Feb. 1915, EEF W(4)3.

35 EEF W(9)3 (negotiations leading to Shell and Fuses Agreement, 3 Mar. 1915); 'The Organisation of Labour for an Increased Output of Munitions', EEF memorandum submitted to the Committee on Production, 11 Feb. 1915, PRO MUN5/10/180/30; Wigham, *Power to Manage*, p. 91.

36 NWETEA *Minutes* 20 February, 31 May, 11, 18 and 22 June 1915; EEF W(4)5–6; *Emergency Committee Minutes* 16 June 1915.

37 Richmond to A. P. Henderson, 12 Aug. 1916, and J. E. Thorneycroft to Smith, 17 Aug. 1916, EEF C(2)5; *Emergency Committee Minutes*, 25 Aug., 15 and 29 Sept. 1916.

38 EEF *Emergency Committee Minutes* 20 Oct. 1916; *Executive Board Minutes* 27 Oct. and 24 Nov. 1916.

39 For Smith's activities on the EAC and its successor body the Employers' Consultative Committee, see EEF C(1)4, C(2)2 and 5, M(17)3, M(20)6–7 and 11–12, and W(4)9; PRO MUN5/53/300/84, 88 and 92; MUN5/71/324/30 and 32; MUN5/79/340.1/7; MUN5/81/342/14; and LAB 2/243/MWLR 142/84.

40 W(25)1 (National Wages Agreement, 1916); EEF I(1)8–9 (reactions to the Whitley Report); EEF S(4)8 and 12 (Shop Stewards Agreement, 1917); exchange of letters between V. Caillard (Vickers) and Smith, 17 and 24 Sept. 1918, S(4)14.

41 'Memorandum *re* Post-War Industrial Problems', Sept. 1916, and 'Tabulation of Replies from Local Associations', EEF I(1)7.

42 'Report of Sub-Committee on Post-War Industrial Problems', 21 Jan. 1918, EEF I(1)12.

43 EEF *Management Committee Minutes* 31 Aug. 1917; McIvor, 'Employers'

Associations', pp. 372–6.
44 EEF H(3)1 and 9, S(3)6; EEF *Management Committee Minutes* 17 May 1918.
45 EEF C(8)1; Turner, ' "Organized Business" '; T. Rodgers, 'Work and Welfare: The NCEO and the Unemployment Problem, 1919–36' (Ph.D. thesis, University of Edinburgh, 1981), ch. 1.
46 Transcripts of negotiations in EEF H(3)17.
47 'Industrial Unrest', EEF circular letter to local associations, 11 Aug. 1919.
48 Wigham, *Power to Manage*, pp. 114–15; J. Melling, 'Employers and the Rise of Supervisory Unionism', in C. J. Wrigley (ed.), *A History of British Industrial Relations, volume 2. 1914–39* (Brighton, 1986), pp. 254–6.
49 The evolution of the Federation's bargaining position can be followed in the multi-volume transcripts of the national negotiations on working conditions 1919–24, MRC MSS. 237/1/13/1 and 237/1/12/4–13. The clearest statements of Smith's overall strategy appear in his speeches to the London and north-west associations, 17 Dec. 1918 and 25 Jan. 1921, EEF G(1)7–8. For a fuller analysis, see J. Zeitlin, *The Triumph of Adversarial Bargaining: Industrial Relations in British Engineering, 1880–1939* (Oxford, forthcoming).
50 EEF H(3)17 (Piecework Agreement, 1 Apr. 1919; S(4)19 (Shop Stewards and Works Committees Agreement, 3 May 1919).
51 Transcript of a special conference between the EEF and engineering trade unions, 29–30 Sept. 1920, MRC MSS. 237/1/12/5.
52 Birmingham association to EEF, 16 Aug. 1919, EEF C(8)2; 'Replies from Associations to Circular Letter of 1 Oct. 1920 *re* Overtime and Night Shift Agreement', EEF W(9)4, App. 26; letters to Smith from Sir H. Spencer (2 and 31 Dec. 1920), P. W. Robson (15 and 23 Dec. 1920), J. R. Richmond (21 Dec. 1920), all in EEF C(6)1920; and transcript of a general meeting of the NWETEA, 21 Jan. 1921, EEF G(1)8.
53 AEU *Executive Council Minutes*, 31 Aug., 6 and 28 Sept., 9–10 Oct., 22 and 24 Nov., 21–3 Dec. 1920.
54 Transcript of a special conference between the EEF and the AEU, 12–13 Jan. 1921, MRC MSS. 237/1/12/6; EEF *Management Committee Minutes*, 17 and 25 Feb. 1921.
55 NWETEA *Minutes* 19 April 1921; letters to Smith from F. Robson (22 May and 15 Sept. 1921), A. M. Bellamy (24 Nov. 1921) and A. Herbert (25 Mar. 1922), EEF C(6)1921 and M(19)2; 'Replies by Associations to Questionnaire dated 30 January 1922', EEF M(19), App. 2.
56 For the role of the government in the dispute, see PRO LAB2/881/1; and *Minutes of a Court of Inquiry into a Dispute in the Engineering Trade, April–May 1922*, MRC MSS 237/1/14/4. For the broader evolution of state labour policy, see R. Lowe, *Adjusting to Democracy: The Role of the Ministry of Labour in British Politics, 1916–1939* (Oxford, 1986), ch. 4.
57 Wigham, *Power to Manage*, pp. 119–27; H. A. Clegg, *A History of British Trade Unions since 1889, volume II. 1911–1933* (Oxford, 1985), pp. 336–45. For local accounts of the dispute and its impact, see A. McKinlay, 'Employers and Skilled Workers in the Inter-War Depression: Engineering and Shipbuilding on Clydeside, 1919–39' (D.Phil. thesis, University of Oxford, 1986), pp. 97–111; and F. W. Carr, 'Engineering Workers and the Rise of Labour in Coventry, 1914–39' (Ph.D. thesis, University of Warwick, 1978), pp. 278–80.
58 S. Tolliday, 'Management and Labour in Britain, 1896–1939', in Tolliday and Zeitlin (eds), *The Automobile Industry and Its Workers: Between Fordism and Flexibility* (Cambridge, 1986); W. Lewchuk, *American Technology and the British Vehicle Industry* (Oxford, 1987).
59 Wigham, *Power to Manage*, pp. 127–35; Clegg, *British Trade Unions*, pp. 432–4, 495–6, 528–9.

60 Wigham, *Power to Manage*, pp. 125–7, 134–5.
61 Special Committee in Regard to the Supply, Selection and Training of Apprentices, 1927–9, EEF A(7)91; Sub-Committee on Apprentices and Young Persons, 1933–6, EEF A(7)111; meetings, memoranda and correspondence on grading of machine operations, 1923–30, EEF M(22)1; P. Ryan, 'Apprenticeship and Industrial Relations in British Engineering: The Early Interwar Period' (unpublished paper presented to the Workshop on Child Labour and Apprenticeship, University of Essex, May 1986); A. McKinlay, ' "A Certain Short-Sightedness": Metalworking, Innovation and Apprenticeship, 1897–1939', in H. F. Gospel (ed.), *Industrial Training and Technological Innovation* (London).
62 Quoted in Wigham, *Power to Manage*, p. 134.
63 S. A. Vertigan, 'The Coventry and District Engineering Employers' Association during the Inter-War Period' (MA thesis, Birkbeck College, University of London, 1986); Carr, 'Engineering Workers'.
64 McKinlay, 'Employers and Skilled Workers', pp. 120–43.
65 ibid., pp. 120–43, 163–87; Vertigan, 'CDEEA', pp. 24, 48–9; McIvor, 'Employers' Associations', pp. 596–608; R. A. Hart and D. I. MacKay, 'Engineering Earnings in Britain, 1914–68', *Journal of the Royal Statistical Society A* 138 (1975), p. 39.
66 McKinlay, 'Employers and Skilled Workers', pp. 164–88; R. Croucher, *Engineers at War, 1939–45* (London, 1982), pp. 24–9.
67 EEF *Management Board Minutes* 19 Dec. 1934, quoted in H. F. Gospel, 'Employers Organisations: Their Growth and Function in the British System of Industrial Relations in the Period 1918–39' (Ph.D. thesis, London School of Economics, 1973), p. 189.
68 A. McKinlay, 'From Industrial Serf to Wage Labourer: The 1937 Apprentices' Revolt in Britain', *International Review of Social History* 31 (1986).
69 Wigham, *Power to Manage*, pp. 142–6; McIvor, 'Employers' Associations', pp. 602–8; Vertigan, 'CDEEA', pp. 25–6, 42.
70 It was on this basis, for example, that Sir Allan Smith opposed participation in the Mond–Turner talks: see Wigham, *Power to Manage*, pp. 131–3; G. W. MacDonald and H. F. Gospel, 'The Mond–Turner Talks, 1927–33: A Study in Industrial Co-Operation', *Historical Journal* 16 (1973).
71 R. A. C. Parker, 'British Rearmament, 1936–39: Treasury, Trade Unions and Skilled Labour', *English Historical Review* 96 (1981).
72 Zeitlin, 'Labour Strategies' and 'Between Flexibility'.
73 See his chapter 4 in this volume.
74 Rodgers, 'Work and Welfare', pp. 23–6; McKinlay, 'Employers and Skilled Workers', p. 104.
75 For Federation views on labour law and compulsory arbitration from the 1900s through the 1920s, see EEF C(4)4 and 11, T(5)1–4, W(2)1–2.

3 Ford and 'Fordism' in postwar Britain

Enterprise management and the control of labour 1937–1987

Steven Tolliday

INTRODUCTION

From 1945 to 1990 Ford of Britain was highly distinctive in comparison with its major British competitors.[1] Beyond being a subsidiary of an American multinational, it was also exceptional in its compact and rationalized model range, its centralized and professional management structures, its long-range product development, its use of day-rates rather than piece-work payment systems, and its location away from the Midlands engineering heartland. It was also the most successful British motor manufacturer in terms of profits, sales and market share.[2] From the time that the other British companies began to enter crisis in the 1970s, Ford has also consistently been the template against which these companies judged themselves and were judged by others (notably the government and its agencies) and which they have sought to emulate.[3]

Paul Willman has argued that its industrial relations system also possessed a 'comparative innovative advantage' against its competitors in these years, and Wayne Lewchuk has maintained that the failure of its British-owned rivals can be explained by their belated adoption of the Fordist system of production. This absence resulted in a conflict between the requirements of new American technology for greater direct management control of the production process and the constraints resulting from shopfloor 'production institutions based on earlier craft technology'. This contradiction was only resolved by the reassertion of managerial control in the 1980s and the 'belated' introduction of Fordist techniques of labour management.[4]

This chapter analyses the changing structure and dynamics of Ford's industrial relations and labour-management systems in order to account for and evaluate their distinctiveness. As in the case of its British competitors, Ford management strategy interacted crucially with the politics of trade unions and the state. Yet the outcomes of these parallel interactions were strikingly different. Neither the technology nor the national environment determined the outcomes: rather, they were the result of strategic choices in specific historical conjunctures. Against this background, the chapter also considers the limits of Ford's strategy of direct control and argues that there was no technological logic that 'required' a Fordist system of direct control. This in turn casts doubt on any simple notion of inherent efficiency advantages in the Ford system and suggests, contrary to other accounts, that it was something of an irony that in the 1980s the British-owned companies moved towards 'Fordism' with disastrous consequences, just as Ford itself was beginning to realize the underlying weaknesses of its own model and to start to modify it.

ORIGINS OF FORD'S EXCEPTIONALISM: THE NON-UNION ERA 1911–1946

From the time that Ford established manufacturing operations at Manchester in 1911 its methods of labour management were distinctive. They drove out unions at an early date and established a high level of direct managerial control over production that was sustained throughout the inter-war years. Most British car firms shared Ford's commitment to high levels of unilateral management authority and also generally kept unions out of their plants. They exercised control through tight control of piece-rates which ensured high levels of work effort, but Ford, obliged to follow the model of its American parent, eschewed incentives and operated fixed day-rates combined with close supervision to ensure task performance. Driving supervision, unilateral work standards and speed-up were the characteristic style of labour management. The work-force bore the brunt of irregularities of production through layoffs or intensified work and compulsory overtime (demanded without notice and paid at straight time rather than premium rates). The notorious Ford 'spy system' operated and workers who joined unions risked instant dismissal. Wages were cut during the recession of the early 1930s but rose later on, partly to forestall unionization.[5]

Ford's methods of labour management were matched by its attempts to transpose its American production methods and product strategy to Britain in the inter-war years. Ford's refusal to adapt its product to changing conditions brought it close to failure. In the 1920s, Ford stuck rigidly to the production of a single model (the 'Model T') even while the market moved away from such a basic and rugged form of transportation towards the smaller, lighter and better-equipped cars that British firms like Austin and Morris were producing. Consequently, between 1913 and 1929 Ford's share of the British market fell from 24 to 4 per cent. After 1928, in the face of these developments, there was a partial retreat from dogma and the introduction of new models designed specifically with the European market in mind. Nevertheless, the construction of the giant Dagenham works (modelled on the River Rouge Plant in Detroit), which was never able to run at more than half its capacity before the war, showed a continuing commitment to highly standardized volume output that did not suit well the conditions of the British market in the 1930s. The resultant cash-flow strains produced an unrelenting pressure to minimize labour costs in the plant, and the scale of Dagenham's operations only began to pay off in the conditions of expanded demand after the Second World War.[6]

At most of the other companies wartime conditions, tight labour markets and sympathetic state policies made it possible for the unions to organize, at least for the duration of the war. But Ford again remained an exception. The limited involvement of their main Dagenham plant in military contracts kept them outside the ambit of direct pressures from the Ministry of Aircraft Production (MAP). Nevertheless, the national significance of the company and its notoriety had made it a target for a Trades Union Congress (TUC)-led organization drive since 1935, and from 1938 to 1944 the TUC continued to press for union recognition through intermittent private talks with a relentlessly procrastinating Ford management. The TUC felt that their lack of progress was a blot on their prestige and they also shared the MAP's fears that frustration and incipient workplace conflict could explode and disrupt war production.[7]

Despite these pressures, the TUC remained unwilling to support industrial action or use plant grievances to build up organization during the war and confined themselves to informal talks and 'pressure'. Inside the plant, the war had given shopfloor workers the confidence to begin to develop some organization, and by 1943 a considerable number of departments had elected shop stewards. Direct actions in the workplace over shopfloor grievances proliferated, but they were isolated from either union or political leadership. This build-up of workplace grievances and militancy precipitated a crisis in December 1943, when, following yet another interruption of negotiations, 43 stewards occupied the works manager's office at Dagenham in a sit-down protest.[8]

The TUC persuaded the stewards to call off the protest, but it was by now apparent to Ford that they could no longer fend off pressure for union recognition indefinitely. Three years earlier in the United States, under intense pressure from cases at the National Labor Relations Board (NLRB), Ford also sensed the inevitability of union recognition. Their first response had been a rather sordid backstage attempt to engineer a recognition deal with the moderate American Federation of Labor (AFL) rather than the more militant Congress of Industrial Organizations (CIO). When this miscarried and the CIO gained clear majority support in an NLRB-sponsored ballot, Ford, facing serious losses of government war contracts if they did not act, carried through a strategic volte-face. From outright resistance, they moved to a path-breaking contract that included 100 per cent union membership and check-off, an elaborate grievance procedure and a large wage increase. In effect, once they recognized that unilateral management control was no longer feasible, Ford preferred to attempt to establish the United Automobile Workers (UAW) as a 'responsible partner' in control of its workplace membership.[9]

Though there is no evidence of direction by Detroit, the American model was clearly influential on Ford's British management. Yet the different context meant that the system could not simply be transplanted. Ford's notion was that if they had to deal with unions then it was best to deal with them on a highly centralized basis and involve them in the responsibility of imposing agreements on their membership. In November 1943, therefore, Percival Perry, the Managing Director of British Ford, privately indicated to Walter Citrine, the General Secretary of the TUC, a willingness to negotiate a recognition agreement. But he was prepared to negotiate *only* with the general secretaries of the ten unions with members at Ford, and not with their local officials. Ford were keenly aware that leading Communist party members held many of the key negotiating positions in the London regional and district structures of the Amalgamated Engineering Union (AEU).[10]

The fact that there were ten unions with which to deal instead of one undercut any possibility of a monolithic deal similar to that signed in the United States. Moreover, in the British case, Ford already faced an emergent steward organization that had sprung into being on the basis of day-to-day grievances on plant-level issues. A recognition deal along the lines of the national engineering procedure, which applied in all engineering firms affiliated to the Engineering Employers' Federation (EEF), would inevitably give these rather heterogeneous and unruly stewards a place in the bargaining arrangements that the company was not prepared to tolerate. As Rowland Smith, the Dagenham works manager noted, he 'had the impression that not only were the unions unable to handle the shop stewards, but the shop stewards themselves were endeavoring to gain control and defy their unions in every direction'.[11]

Ford accordingly bargained for, and eventually won, the exclusion of shopfloor representatives from any role in the bargaining process. Under the Agreement of April 1944 all major negotiations on wages and conditions were to be in the hands of the union general secretaries sitting with the company on a Joint Negotiating Committee (JNC, later National Joint Negotiating Committee (NJNC)). Shop stewards and local officials had no role in the bargaining process, and workloads, mobility of labour and the necessary steps for 'the achievement of efficiency' were treated as matters exclusively for managerial determination.[12]

Ford were able to conclude such a deal despite the fact that they were under serious pressure from workplace discontent and certain government departments largely because the TUC acted as a willing ally in their campaign to suppress steward militancy in the plant. This had deep roots in the antipathy of the TUC and its Organization Department to local Communist Party influence in the local trades councils in the prewar period. Vic Feather of the Organization Department, who played a key role in these talks, made no secret of his reluctance to support the stewards' cause (a reluctance tinged with hostility towards many of the latter)[13] and the TUC largely accepted Ford's case about the dangers of allowing stewards bargaining rights. As Patrick Hennessy put it, 'the procedure agreement they [Ford] were suggesting would provide proper channels for proper discussions with responsible people instead of providing a breeding ground for the type of Communist troublemaker whom neither they, nor the unions found to be helpful'.[14] The TUC broadly concurred. As Feather put it to Citrine, 'even from a union's point of view, the suggestion of Ford that there might need to be stricter control over shop stewards may not be unhelpful'.[15]

The April 1944 Agreement demonstrated Ford's determination to retain the widest possible managerial prerogatives at workplace level within the context of collective bargaining. The TUC broadly accepted the legitimacy of management's claims in these respects and their anxiety for union 'control' over their membership inhibited them from taking advantage of Ford's weaknesses at the time of the negotiation of the agreement. Citrine was not convinced that the shop stewards could be excluded from the procedure in the long run, but for the time being he was prepared to accept Ford's proposal, hoping to forestall a major dispute. The Ministry of Labour, on the other hand, was very worried about the deal and believed that the exclusion of the stewards would store up a legacy of trouble for the future.[16]

Over the next two years the deficiencies of the initial agreement were quickly exposed. The plant shop stewards, at times in alliance with unionists and non-unionists alike, showed themselves to be capable of calling wildcat stoppages and were erratic and unpredictable in their behaviour. The AEU pressed consistently for the principle of steward recognition, and gradually even those most dubious about allowing stewards a role in the procedure came to believe that it would be better to have shop stewards inside the agreement than outside it. After a strike in 1946 Ford found it prudent to backtrack a little on its original position. While still rejecting shop stewards (who would have rights to negotiate on shopfloor issues), they agreed with the NJNC to amend the agreement to provide a limited role for 'Shop Representatives' in a Joint Works Committee (JWC) who would be 'consulted' on day-to-day problems. The distinction between negotiation at JNC and consultation at JWC was firmly underlined in the agreement.[17]

The union structures that emerged at this period were unique to Ford. Ford's strategic aspirations and the TUC's propensity to compromise left the regulation of workplace matters unclear and produced a system with a poor fit between procedures and union structures. Ford continued to insist that Shop Representatives should be elected as representatives of departments or geographical areas in the works, *not* as representatives of the members of a particular union. In the long run this was to prove seriously counterproductive. The geographical structure meant that Shop Representatives were not directly responsible to any single union. Consequently union control was much less effective and inter-union collaboration at plant level was much easier. As Turner *et al.* described it, Ford's attitude committed them to a 'singularly clumsy bargaining and conciliation agreement . . . and a system of workplace representation which was exceptionally divorced from union control and guidance'.[18]

SHOPFLOOR MANAGEMENT UNDER THE FORD SYSTEM 1946–1968

Ford's product and labour strategies after the war were a marked contrast with those of the British-owned companies. The largest of these was the British Motor Corporation (BMC), which incorporated Austin and Morris after 1952. BMC made a wide variety of models in medium volumes using labour-intensive methods and minimal fixed investment. These methods enabled them to expand and contract output quickly with fluctuations arising from model changes and cyclical shifts in the market. Between 1954 and 1962, for example, BMC introduced five new models, including five new body shells and two new power-trains, and doubled their production capacity, yet spent only £78 million on capital investment, development costs and tooling. They did not build any new factories but concentrated on reorganizing and re-equipping the existing ones, incrementally adding new machines or lines alongside the old rather than scrapping and building new ones. Manual work remained relatively extensive and laborious, and job cycle-times much longer than at Ford. Automated equipment in welding, painting and test sections came only slowly, usually only where it could be added on relatively easily to existing plant layouts. BMC's labour-intensive system did not achieve major economies of scale and, in the absence of extensive machine pacing, it increased considerably the complexity of managing production processes at shopfloor level and threw much of the burden of managing production on to their incentive payments systems.[19]

   These systems were established before the war when the British companies, like Ford, had driven the union out of their factories and achieved high levels of management authority in the workplace. Unlike Ford, however, they used this power to establish payment-by-results systems which became their primary mechanism for controlling the organization of work. Tight control over the setting of piece-rates enabled them to operate a highly effective incentive system, and to offer high wages for intense and continuous effort. There was a direct incentive for workers to maintain continuous production because their earnings directly depended on it. Since unions remained weak in the major British car factories until the late 1950s the bonus effectively substituted for direct supervision of work performance. Individual workers and work gangs would chase up stocks and supplies to ensure continuous work, improvise better ways of performing tasks to increase bonus earnings, devise improvised tools to facilitate tasks at their work station and frequently try to reduce manning levels on their lines so that fewer workers could share the pool of bonus earnings. On the negative side, however, the pursuit of bonuses might result in poor-quality work as workers took short-cuts to increase output which might, for example, lead to greater wear and tear on machines or result in quality problems at later stages of the manufacturing process, or neglect preventive maintenance because it might reduce the time available for earning bonus.[20]

Ford's outlook was very different. Before the war the massive integrated Dagenham plant had suffered from costly problems of overcapacity. But as postwar demand surged, it became possible to utilize the plant fully and to maximize economies of scale for the first time. Ford concentrated on the production of large volumes of a narrow range of standardized value-for-money cars, including, until 1959, the cheapest mass-produced car on the market (the Popular).[21] Ford also invested heavily. While BMC invested only £78 m on capital investment, development costs and tooling at all their plants between 1954 and 1962, in the same period Ford spent £79 m on investment in the new Paint, Trim and Assembly (PTA) plant opened at Dagenham in 1959, invested heavily in facilities for its new Consul/Zephyr series in the early 1950s, and opened a wholly new plant at Halewood. Moreover, Ford's research and development were well known to be generously funded in comparison with BMC.[22] Its investment spending must be conservatively estimated at double that of BMC in the 1950s.[23] Ford's fixed assets per worker and output per worker were correspondingly higher. By 1972 while BMC had fixed assets per worker of only £920, Ford had £2,657 at Dagenham and £3,608 at Halewood;[24] and from the late 1950s until the early 1970s, while BMC (later British Leyland Motor Corporation (BLMC)) produced 7 or 8 vehicles per employee per annum, Ford produced approximately 12.[25] The other side of this picture for Ford, however, was that by 1958 Ford were producing less than 300,000 vehicles with the same value of net assets that BMC were using to produce 500,000.

Ford's pattern of high-volume standardized production of a limited range of models supported by high levels of fixed capital investment in at first one and later two plants contrasted with BMC's production of a diverse range of models, often in low volumes, in several plants, many of which were archaic and suffering from continuing under-investment. It was also a putatively ideal environment for the company to pursue its chosen strategy of direct control of labour through close supervision of measured, fragmented and repetitive tasks. As Ford saw it, the main problem was to maintain managerial prerogatives in the workplace and to resist or contain any challenge from worker organization.

In the late 1940s and early 1950s Ford found their new system basically satisfactory. Moderates dominated the Works Committee in the 1940s, although they were periodically swept aside by surges of direct action involving unionized and non-unionized workers on local grievances such as overtime, tea-breaks and similar issues. Ford was able to resist any concessions to custom and practice, insist on its rights under Procedure and maintain the status quo while the matter crawled its way through the NJNC. As Joe Scott, one of the officials on the NJNC put it in 1949,

Of all the slow drawn-out machinery that I know about with our union
. . . this one just caps it from that angle . . . we cannot encourage or
inculcate the ideas of discipline upon people when we are dealing with
some sort of internal organization of the firm which is foreign to the way
the union functions.[26]

In the late 1940s and early 1950s these frustrations were beginning to pull
forward more militant stewards, and management was becoming perturbed
that the existing Shop Representative structure was too volatile. Ford began
to consider reforms that would make the Shop Representatives more
amenable to union control. The individual unions in the NJNC were
separately sympathetic to such a project. Nevertheless, they were collectively
unable to reach any agreement on the redivision of shop-steward constituencies in such a reorganization and the proposals languished.[27]

After 1952 these reform proposals were overtaken by wider industrial-
relations problems following Ford's take-over of its neighbouring body
supplier, Briggs Bodies. Ford wanted to bring the whole united Dagenham
site under a common agreement but Briggs had a very different shopfloor
history from Ford. Shop stewards had become established at an early stage
in the war, and Briggs stewards had gone on to develop their own distinctive
pattern of shopfloor bargaining including *de facto* negotiating rights on job
standards, certain restrictions on labour mobility, the abolition of compulsory overtime, and recognized tea-breaks and relief times. In addition,
their different payment system with a larger number of grades and
differentials posed an obvious problem in integrating Briggs workers with
Ford conditions.[28]

Ford's stewards at once took up Briggs' conditions as their bargaining
goal while Briggs workers refused to give up their superior conditions. A
number of resulting disputes came to a head in the 'Bell Ringer' dispute of
1956. Ford refused to compromise and took the issue of their right to
manage to a Ministry of Labour Court of Inquiry where they won a decisive
victory. Lord Cameron, the chairman of the court started out from the
premiss of the illegitimacy of workplace-based steward organizations that
did not operate as tributaries of official union structures. He also accepted
Ford's thinly based allegations of malign political motivations. His
characterization of the Briggs stewards as 'a private union within a union
enjoying immediate and continuous contact with the men in the shop,
answerable to no superiors and in no way officially or constitutionally
linked with the union hierarchy' became notorious.[29] The dismissal of the
Briggs convenor was upheld, and following its victory Ford was able to
standardize conditions gradually on its own terms until the NJNC
recognized its *de facto* completion in August 1958.

Thus Ford beat off a potential challenge to the integrity of its system and
remained effectively free of plant-level negotiations on day-to-day issues.
Nevertheless, 'standardization' created problems for its system. Ford's

supervision system relied significantly on the use of merit payments as individual rewards for performance. The incorporation of Briggs tended to distort the system. The old Briggs wage system had contained far more occupational differentials and allowances than had Ford's. Supervisors now tended to use merit payments as a way to ease standardization, and in the late 1950s, the Briggs stewards, having failed to gain the acceptance of the Briggs system in national negotiations, concentrated on winning their demands at departmental level. As Ford Labour Relations director, Leslie Blakeman, described the situation:

> The strain on the lower echelons of management who carry a large share of the responsibility for the application of the merit system had been considerable. Not surprisingly, peace had been bought at the price of merit money and, as some supervisors would say, this has become a system of blackmail.[30]

Second, the integration of two work-forces with such contrasting traditions created a new range of problems. These were particularly concentrated in the new Paint, Trim and Assembly (PTA) building, built in 1958 and staffed roughly half-and-half with Ford and Briggs workers. From 1959–62, against a background of retooling for new models and the consequent wholesale revision of work standards on a non-negotiable basis, the PTA became a centre of frequent disputes. There were 59 strikes and 114 overtime bans between 1959 and 1962. Shopfloor organization began to emerge around the issue of new work standards. Blakeman, the labour director, described the situation as one where 'the whole plant has become a jungle of restrictive practices, inefficiencies and unconstitutional behavior in defense of them'. This overstated the rather limited accumulation of custom and practice on issues such as tea-breaks, overtime allocations and the stewards' rights to hold meetings on company premises. Nevertheless, as Ford tried to rein back these practices the stewards resisted. As Turner *et al.* described it: 'A situation of immanent conflict, combined with a general frustration of the steward organization provided the basis for militants to assume leadership.'[31]

After 1960 some activists began to try to contest manning levels and take highly aggressive attitudes in face-to-face conflicts with their foremen. The prominence of Communist Party members and militants among these activists enabled Ford to represent this as politically motivated disruption. It gave them added leverage with leading right-wingers like Carron on the NJNC to renew their attempts to draw the unions into a joint policing role in disciplining their members. The NJNC unions were sympathetic but confused and ineffectual in their response to Ford's approaches, but they explicitly conceded Ford's right to manage its plants. When the disputes culminated in the crisis of the 1962 strike, their defence of the 17 sacked activists against victimization was confused and hesitant. The 17 stayed sacked after a Court of Inquiry upheld Ford's right to re-employ workers selectively after lay-offs, ignoring 'first-in, last-out' rules. The confusion and major demoralization of the work-force that followed meant the disappearance for most of the 1960s at Dagenham of the sort of shopfloor organization that had begun to emerge before 1962.

After the defeat of the unions at Dagenham in 1962 and with the opening of their new plant at Halewood near Liverpool, Ford had a powerful position from which to recuperate the authority and control of work that had begun to be tested by union and steward pressure in the late 1950s. During the 1960s Ford were able to prevent the emergence of effective shopfloor union organization in their plants. Yet, despite the strength of their position, Ford remained unable to develop and consolidate the direct control they aspired to. Why? In part they were unable to define and elaborate mechanisms by which management could accomplish these goals; in part there were problems inherent in their notion of 'control' itself. Moreover, as key features of their system decayed or ceased to fulfil their intended functions, Ford was unable to get the sort of sympathetic assistance from government and other employers that it hoped for and felt it needed to implement fully its desired labour policies.

Union strength, steward organization and incipient job controls were growing through this period, but they were growing from a very low starting-point.[32] At Dagenham, following the defeat of the unions in 1962, the company implemented its 'firm line' curtailing shop-steward facilities and restoring to supervision a freer hand than they had enjoyed since the early 1950s. The opening of Halewood in 1963 also provided Ford with an opportunity to get away from Dagenham and 'Dagenham ways' and to try to recreate the Ford system in pristine form. Their attempt to circumvent the multi-union problems of the NJNC through a local deal with the more compliant AEU and General and Municipal Workers Union (GMWU) in Liverpool quickly miscarried. But they set out to establish a very tight managerial regime and a very high pace of work from the outset. They aimed to block the emergence of a shop-steward organization at Halewood by meticulous control on the freedom of movement and role of shop stewards (the so-called 'ball and chain' system), tying shop stewards to their sections and operating very tight work standards.[33]

The Halewood strategy broke down in two respects. First, the rigour of the regime provoked intense though disorganized shopfloor conflict. In the absence of shop stewards to articulate them, grievances often became exacerbated and labour-turnover rates were high and rising from 36 per cent in 1966 to 50 per cent in 1969 in the Halewood PTA. Second, the anti-union strategy was not wholly successful. Attempts at selective recruitment broke down under the tide of labour turnover, and union recruitment proceeded rapidly. In contrast to Dagenham, from the start there were close links between plant stewards and local and regional officials and plants like the PTA became a virtually 100 per cent Transport and General Workers' Union (TGWU) shop. Hence in contrast to Dagenham there was not the same gap between geographical, multi-union shopfloor representation and official union structures, and it made possible the emergence of what Beynon has described as Halewood's distinctive pattern of 'unofficial-ism'.[34]

The extent of inroads into managerial prerogatives and the establishment of union job controls was varied and sectional in each plant. At Halewood the early days of the plant witnessed a raw battle for control, often resolved by severe face-to-face conflict. It had been common for management to vary the speed of the lines during shifts to cope with erratic production schedules and this had been a major cause of spontaneous walk-outs, naked resistance or occasional sabotage. To avoid this, management had conceded to shop stewards the right to hold the key that locked the speed of the assembly line during shifts. Nevertheless, the overall speed of the line for each shift remained a matter for management to determine exclusively and workloads continued to be varied. With a change in the model mix a less-than-proportionate increase in manning might be allowed and the new reduced manning ratio retained when lower workloads were resumed. By the late 1960s supervisors at Halewood often allowed overtime rotas or delegated the allocation of tasks to shop stewards as the simplest and most trouble-free way of coping with issues of labour deployment. Thus Halewood stewards had some rudimentary controls over manning levels and the pace of work, though these were more common in the Body Plant than in the PTA and varied widely according to the personality and capability of section stewards. At Dagenham it was rare for stewards to exert such informal controls. Shop stewards, for example, were generally unable to prevent virtually obligatory overtime over long periods and concentrated instead on trying to win the right to get adequate notice of overtime.[35]

Thus shop stewards were able to introduce certain elements of equity and job control, but all these gains were precarious and did not present a very radical challenge to management. Any gains that stewards might make in controlling workloads or allocations of labour were quickly eroded with changes in the organization of work.[36]

There was, therefore, wide-ranging scope for effective management discretion in work organization, yet Ford were unable to translate this into comprehensive control. One reason for this was that, despite Ford's public preoccupation with shopfloor turmoil, the company only slowly gave industrial relations importance in its managerial hierarchy, largely under prodding from Detroit who wanted to see a shift from 'fire-fighting to fire prevention'. An Industrial Relations director was only appointed for the first time in 1962 as part of the 'Americanization' of Ford UK by the parent company who used 'visitations' and reporting procedures to monitor and catalyse local management.[37]

These weaknesses in the structure of labour management had serious implications for line management on the shop floor. Ford's desire for tight administrative control of the workplace put intense pressures on shopfloor supervision who often feared to make decisions. When rules began to bend in face of worker resistance supervisors had insufficient authority to make concessions; yet often they also lacked the power to take a stand. It began to be common practice for production management to use supervisors as 'fall guys', pressing them to resist shop stewards' demands, only to cut the ground from under their feet by themselves making concessions to the stewards in order to keep production going. At Halewood in the late 1960s most section stewards had direct access to the convener who, in turn, was in day-to-day contact with plant management, thus creating the possibility of undercutting line supervision by 'upstaging' them.[38]

Even where there was a negligible steward presence there appeared to be inherent limits to direct control. Management could unilaterally set work-loads but they were still reliant on the foreman and work groups (with or without stewards) to cooperate to solve problems. For example, a sudden change in the product mix could result in a need for a rapid adjustment in manning or for men to 'work down the line'. Uncooperative workers could prove highly obstructive in such circumstances. Moreover, with relatively full employment and high levels of labour turnover young, restless and alienated workers created serious problems for control and discipline. Beynon has described 'the lads' throwing Bostic bombs in skips, pulling the safety wire on the lines to get a break, or refusing to work without iced lime-juice in the hot summer of 1969. If the sack did not sufficiently intimidate them, the front-line supervisors badly needed shop stewards to 'control the lads'. The stewards could control and pacify a section or make them listen to warnings where the foreman could not. In sections where direct monitoring of production was difficult and responsibility for defects hard to pinpoint, such as the paint-spray decks, 'spoiling' of products was hard to trace and it was only a relationship with the steward that could ensure the quality of production.[39] Thus high levels of relatively arbitrary control by manage-ment, in the context of weak supervision, poorly elaborated management structures and disorganized uncooperativeness by workers created difficulties for production.

Payment-by-results systems attempted to resolve similar problems by the use of incentive payments to induce workers to cooperate in the achieve-ment of production and efficiency. But the Ford system turned its back in principle on incentives. It followed that weaknesses in the apparatus of management control that could be disguised under piece-work became much more transparent in the Ford system. Moreover, they created still more problems as the Ford wage system began to show signs of strain and slackness.

By the mid 1960s Ford's wage structure was coming under strain. Despite the company's policy to resist custom and practice demands, special payments and allowances had inevitably crept into a system that had been in continuous operation over twenty years, and anomalies were beginning to appear more and more frequently. In addition the merit system continued to degenerate. The system had provided a carefully dispensed element of incentive linked to management control, but it also made it possible for the company to use it to 'lubricate' their rigid grading system. Since the merger with Briggs merits had come to be expected as a matter of course and rather freely given (annually or across the board in certain departments). It was not easy to restore control to such a system once it had been eroded.[40]

The problem of the merit system was also linked with Ford's growing labour-market problems. By 1965, contrary to the theory of flat-rate payment, continuous rises in merit pay had opened up a wage gap of 4s. per hour between the lowest-paid new starter and workers with seven years' or more service. In the 1960s this brought two further problems. The opening of the new Halewood plant meant that *all* Halewood workers were 'new starters'. After long negotiations and stoppages, the NJNC had agreed on the phased introduction over several years of parity of basic rates between the two plants. But even when this process was completed, the merit situation meant that a wage gap would remain as a source of invidious comparisons. If Ford tried to close this gap via enhanced merits to Halewood they would risk further leap-frogging merit claims at Dagenham. If they did nothing they risked increased strife at Halewood.[41]

At the same time, Ford were becoming victims of their own past successes in wage bargaining. Until the mid-1960s Ford had kept their wages very low in comparison with other car firms by gaining acceptance of modest offers at the NJNC. Low wages, especially for new starters, were beginning to make it difficult for Ford to recruit new workers. High proportions of new recruits were low-skilled immigrants and Ford was finding it hard to get the more skilled or experienced workers that they needed. By the late 1960s some Ford managers believed that Ford needed a substantial hike in basic rates simply to maintain its supply of labour. But the Labour government's successive pay freezes were an obstacle to this.

The legal and political environment proved unfavourable for the re-trenchment of the system. A crucial test case was Ford's failure to get solid support from the government or from other motor employers in the Motor Industry Joint Council (an employers' liaison committee under the sponsor-ship of the Ministry of Labour) for their attempts to restore backbone to their payments systems through an insistence on rigid adherence to procedures and formalized work rules in the mid-1960s. Public calls by the Labour Government for productivity, rationalization and restraint gave them some cause to hope for such support. But their hopes were torpedoed when they took a dispute with their paint-sprayers to a Court of Inquiry. The paint-sprayers walked out on unofficial strike against the imposition of new working conditions and the TGWU subsequently made the dispute official. Ford went to an Inquiry, confident that they would win on the procedural case. But the Inquiry side-stepped these issues, treated the case essentially as one of arbitration, and split the difference.[42] This left Ford feeling let down by the Ministry of Labour, and the Joint Labour Council and vulnerable to further similar claims where their options would be either continuous piecemeal concessions or resistance which might lead to further Courts of Inquiry with similar unsatisfactory results.[43]

THE FORD SYSTEM IN TRANSITION? 1968–1978

These pressures triggered a process of change in the Ford system after 1968. Simultaneously, related changes were altering the face of industrial relations and labour management in the other British car companies. The emergence of effective shop-steward organization in these companies for the first time in the early 1960s had two rather contradictory effects on their systems. On the one hand, shop stewards often operated in quasi-managerial roles in order to keep production and earnings running at high levels.[44] On the other hand, the stewards also began to engage more and more effectively in opportunistic shopfloor wage bargaining. As a result, during the 1960s incentive pay was coming to have an increasingly tenuous relationship to effort. The frequency and effectiveness of sectional bargaining, rather than productivity, increasingly determined earnings. Management's capability to control and direct the piece-work system and to orchestrate the factory through it was eroded. The loss of managerial control on the shop floor was not, however, the same thing as the existence of union control. The results of constant, fragmented sectional bargaining were often unsatisfactory to both management and labour, and the spread of differential earnings within plants became anomalous and chaotic. The wide scope and frequency of sectional bargaining resulted in a regime of high friction between line management, workers and stewards. Each decision could be a dangerous precedent or stepping-off point for further bargaining, and both sides were liable to give ground unwittingly since the implications of particular decisions were often not immediately clear. By the late 1960s this proliferation of bargaining had resulted in an endemic pattern of short stoppages and go-slows.

In many senses management were losing effective control of their piece-work systems in the mid-1960s and felt that the traditional wage system no longer served its purpose. It is important to note, however, that the evidence of the deleterious effects of these payment systems on company performance is inconclusive. As I have argued elsewhere, there is no clear evidence that the increase in shopfloor bargaining resulted in any sharp rise in earnings levels or labour costs, and the prevalence of short local strikes was probably less damaging than has often been argued. Major studies by Turner *et al.* in the 1960s and by Durcan *et al.* and Marsden *et al.* in the 1980s all suggest that small dispersed stoppages had little impact on overall production levels while larger stoppages tended to be associated with recessions.[45] Until 1968 strikes were not a major problem for output. Given the product market situation which Williams *et al.* have described elsewhere, uninterrupted production would often have left BMC/BLMC simply with larger stocks of unsaleable cars. In addition, steward bargaining-horizons remained very narrowly focused on wages and stewards continued to respect surprisingly large areas of unilateral management control and 'the right to manage', especially over issues such as hire and fire, plant closures and information disclosure, labour mobility, and the use of overtime and short-time to cover fluctuations in production. Moreover, both Streeck and Willman have recently demonstrated that shopfloor bargaining posed no major constraints for the introduction of automation or new technology.[46]

Nevertheless, by the late 1960s the management of British Leyland (BL, the renamed BLMC) had come to identify the continued existence of the piece-work system as the principal cause of their production problems and both stewards and management shared the belief that its replacement by a system of Measured Day Work (MDW) based on the Ford model would destroy the bargaining power of the shop floor. They envisaged plant and group negotiations becoming centralized in the hands of management and union officials, thus curbing sectional activities. But they lacked any clear perception either of the difficulties of running such a system that Ford experienced or the enlarged scope of management responsibilities in the organization of production that it would entail.

These problems were compounded when, as MDW was introduced on a plant by plant basis, stewards reorientated their bargaining strategies and set out to 'capture' the new system. Since earnings levels were now fixed, they shifted their focus from an almost exclusive attention to pay and the maximization of earnings to the minimization of effort, better job conditions and security of earnings. The intensity of effort and the pacing role of piece-work fell away. Stewards ceased to attempt to correct production problems as they occurred or chase up materials. Extra labour was now welcomed on to the sections to ease effort rather than shunned because it reduced earnings. Where workers had formerly improvised to keep aged machines running they now let them break down and waited for the repairmen to come. As one commentator has put it, 'effort drift' replaced 'wage drift'.[47]

MDW was hastily established with little method- or time-study and no thorough reform of supervisory systems. It put the responsibility for maintaining the continuity and quality of production and the flow of materials squarely on to management's shoulders; but management was not equipped for these new tasks. Over the next ten years BL struggled to integrate its new payment system with restructured work organization and managerial systems, and to follow through the extensive implications that the new system had for stock and quality control, buying and production programming, and production engineering and job design.

But while other companies were seeking to solve problems by moving towards the Ford model, Ford were seeking new ways to renovate their system and hold it together in face of disruptive pressures. Their first escape-route from the problems described above was a decision in 1967 to restabilize their wage structure and preserve its logic by relaunching it on the basis of job evaluation. The consequent new wage structure was to reestablish the importance of centrally negotiated wage deals against the creeping emergence of local bargaining by stewards, centred on merits and special allowances. By reasserting a rule-bound system they hoped to clear out anomalies and start afresh with a new 'tight' version of their system.

Despite the elaborate and quasi-scientific process of job evaluation, Ford retained tight control of the shape of the final outcome through their control of the 'factor weightings' which they refused to disclose even under pressure from a Court of Inquiry.[48] Despite the complexity of the mechanisms by which the structure was rejigged, the basic change was from a four-grade to a five-grade structure. The hourly rate for each grade continued to be negotiated at NJNC, and earnings thereafter varied only with hours worked or with premiums for overtime, shift and weekend working. No incentives were admitted and merits were eliminated and replaced by a simple scale of service increments.[49]

In fact, however, the new wage structure did not prevent more fundamental changes in Ford's postwar industrial-relations system emerging under the pressure of nascent shopfloor bargaining and its interaction with a shift in the national politics of the trade unions. The new structure made Ford vulnerable to a host of grading grievances some of which, like the strike by female sewing-machinists at Dagenham, threatened to undermine the whole edifice. The logic of the women's case for upgrading was strong, but rectifying their grade could fundamentally disturb the entire male-grading hierarchy and unleash a stream of leap-frogging comparability claims. One result was the paradoxical outcome of the strike noted by Friedman and Meredeen. The women were able to win the apparently broad principle of equal pay for equal work which had significant national political and economic implications for women workers and the Labour Government. But they failed to force the company to concede their apparently narrow and local grading grievance. As Friedman noted: 'In response to a grading claim for five (old) pence per hour confined to 400 sewing machinists, Ford was conceding a pay increase 50% higher than that, to all Ford women workers.' Ford effectively negotiated a settlement on a claim which had never been presented.[50]

The wider developments in the car industry in the late 1960s which we have already described, were also creating new pressures. In particular, costly exercises to buy out old piece-work systems and replace them with MDW pay structures stimulated upward pressure on wages[51] and, in combination with issues of national pay policy and supplier strikes, thrust the issue of layoffs and wage security into the foreground. Alongside these developments shopfloor organization and confidence began to rise again after the demoralization of the defeats of 1956 and 1962. These developments were stimulated by the sewing machinists' strike and symbolized by the formation of the National Conveners Committee and the National Delegate Committee at Ford.

The consolidation of union organization created serious tensions within Ford's policies. On the one hand, Leslie Blakeman, Ford's Industrial Relations director, and his associates were strongly influenced by the ideas of leading academics such as Allan Flanders about 'regaining control by sharing it',[52] and the grading package deal had been singled out for praise by the Wilson government as an exemplary case of 'the Donovan creed of reforming pluralism'.[53] But such overtures towards a new business-like relationship with the unions existed alongside older goals of shopfloor discipline and management prerogatives.[54] For a while in the late 1960s Ford hoped to reconcile the two through wider support for its policies from the state or the law. The Donovan Commission (1965–8) and the Labour Government's openness to legal change in the field of industrial relations gave some hope that the legal system might be fluid and helpful in this respect. Ford argued strongly to the Donovan Commission in favour of laws to curb unions and for the legal enforceability of collective bargaining. Subsequently, their 1969 pay deal, which linked a pay rise and new layoff payments to obligatory adherence to a streamlined Procedure Agreement backed up by 'penalty clauses' against unconstitutional action coincided with the launch of *In Place of Strife* (December 1968) by the Labour Government. Ford's deal was at once labelled 'a private enterprise Industrial Relations Act',[55] and the Department of Employment and Productivity accepted the trade-off of increased pay in return for disciplinary clauses under the government's current incomes policy. But under wider political pressures the government was soon shying away from further legal measures to control unions, and in the absence of broader government backing Ford had to turn independently and rather desperately to the courts in an unsuccessful attempt to have their negotiated agreement with the NJNC declared legally enforceable.[56] If the Labour Government had not backed off, Ford might have had a context in which to move towards structures more akin to their US practices, notably the combination of strict contract language and a powerful interlocutor like the UAW capable of making deals stick at shopfloor level.

The 1969 deal was in fact accepted by the NJNC but the retributional clauses provoked a strong reaction at shopfloor level and, for the first time since the war, the plant conveners were able to hold mass meetings in the plants, reject the package and call a viable national strike repudiating the NJNC's acceptance of a national agreement.[57] A few years earlier this would have been unthinkable, but, partly as effect and partly as cause of the rising confidence of the shopfloor representatives, the attitude of the two biggest unions (the TGWU and the AEF – the Amalgamated Engineering Federation) to the NJNC was undergoing a sea change. An era of slow radicalization in their ranks culminated in 1969 in the accession of the more radical leaderships of Jones and Scanlon. This significantly strengthened the hand of the unions at plant level and established new active relations between the unions and the plant convenors. The response to the strike call at plant level was patchy and it was only saved from collapse by the AEF and TGWU making the strike official. The precarious shopfloor organization required a significant degree of nurturing by supportive national union institutions. Although the settlement of the strike by Jones and Scanlon after nine weeks following government mediation did not wholly eliminate the 'penalty clauses', they were in practice neutralized.[58]

It also provided the occasion for a comprehensive restructuring of the NJNC.[59] The dominance of the TGWU and AUEW (Amalgamated Union of Engineering Workers – the renamed AEF) over decision-making on the union side was insitutionalized and, for the first time, shopfloor representatives in the shape of five conveners were admitted. Shifts in the locus of power at both national and shop-floor levels had changed the rules of the game and undermined Ford's old 'industrial creed'. Until 1969 Ford had always had confidence that the company plus the national officials in the NJNC could control any challenge from the shop floor. Changes in union policy and shopfloor organization now undercut that.

During the 1970s Ford abandoned their old 'industrial creed' and moved towards a new relationship with the shop floor, accepting the legitimacy of negotiation with shopfloor representatives while attempting to keep their managerial prerogatives fundamentally intact. Beynon has described this as one of the most elaborate processes of industrial-relations reform attempted by any company in Britain.[60] But while it is true that major changes took place at the level of collective bargaining, Ford gave almost no ground on their traditional *exclusion* of large areas of workplace regulation from negotiation.

According to two of Ford's leading managers, Bob Ramsey and Terence Beckett, in their evidence to the House of Commons Expenditure Committee in 1975, the company had turned its back on the old ideology of paternalism and direct control and was seeking to modernize its procedures, acknowledging that it must manage by consent with the 'willing concurrence' and 'complete involvement' of the work-force. This change had been much delayed because for too long the company had waited in hope that the government would breathe new life into the old institutions by legal and political changes. Now, however, the company had recognized that it had to sort things out for itself.[61]

This view has subsequently been endorsed by academic commentators,[62] and major changes in Ford's industrial relations policies did indeed occur. During the 1970s, under the powerful leadership of Bob Ramsey and Paul Roots, the management of industrial relations assumed a much greater prominence and strategic role in the Ford hierarchy. Their policies, marking a sharp break with the past, were to expand and institutionalize the role of shopfloor representatives. Until this time Ford had sought to marginalize shop stewards and had regarded them as subversive of company-wide bargaining. But, after 1971, there was a trend towards an accommodation with elected shopfloor representatives.[63] Ford began to give shop stewards an enhanced status and facilities and encouraged the old rank-and-file organizations, notably the plant-conveners committee, to integrate themselves more closely into the official union networks. A layer of conveners and stewards became effectively full-time negotiators in daily touch with management. The pattern of plant negotiations was increasingly dominated by conveners and senior stewards while sectional stewards had a more limited negotiating role, acting primarily as channels of communication about grievances.[64] Finally, the company agreed to a 100 per cent post-entry closed shop and collection of union dues by check-off from the payroll. Again, this was a major departure from Ford's hallowed policy that union membership was a 'domestic matter' for the unions. It explicitly recognized that if the company wished the unions to police agreements on their side, then the company too had an interest in its employees being union members.[65]

Subsequently in 1978 Ford took a further step with a major reform of the NJNC. Whereas in 1969 Ford had reluctantly accepted reform of the NJNC, they now played an active role in initiating the changes. Ford were aware of a growing lack of reality in the bargaining at the NJNC. According to Les Moore, a convener at Halewood, 'They were no longer bargaining with the trade unions as representatives of the workers, but through them with the conveners' committee. Their best arguments, presented by highly professional negotiators, were being wasted on messengers.'[66] To get away from this sort of two-tier negotiations, Ford brought all 23 plant conveners on to the NJNC, giving lay representatives a majority on the committee for the first time. These policies ran in parallel with and were reinforced by the national strategies of the AUEW and the TGWU. Both organizations were seeking to base themselves more solidly on the shop floor, partly because of the programmatic positions of their leaderships and partly because of the strategic needs of their rivalry for dominance of recruitment in the car industry which meant that neither union could afford to distance itself too far from the lay organizations.[67]

The combined effect of shifts in union policies and company orientation to collective bargaining made the 1970s appear to be what Henry Friedman has called a 'decade of continuous shift of power to the shop floor'.[68] There was a definite strategic attempt by the company to realign its formal procedures and to integrate union organization into its collective bargaining. Yet procedural reform and the partial integration of the unions also overlay intense continuing conflict at the workplace level.

The worst conflicts centred on layoffs and shopfloor working practices. Blunt disciplinary instruments at plant level contrasted sharply with the apparently more accommodating and integrative policies of the company at national level, and plant-level conflict actually rose in intensity as the broader policies of 'accommodation' developed. The company's practice of laying off related work groups as retribution after unofficial stoppages caused violent clashes, occupations or protests on several occasions (notably at Dagenham in September 1973, October 1974, April 1975, September 1976 and September 1977) and some 'rioters' were subsequently dismissed with the tacit consent of the unions.[69]

At Halewood working practices were generally the central issue especially after November 1976 when management 'declared war' on informal practices like 'welt' working. Local managers recognized the gulf between their relations with the union and the chaotic day-to-day conflict of the shop floor.

> The unions did not really declare war in retaliation [in 1976] but the workers did. It turned into a nightmare. We enforced discipline, they would walk out. We would again enforce discipline, win some battles, lose others, we would take discipline, they would walk out. It was hell to work here. Nobody wanted to come to work in the morning, because everyone knew we would move right into a battle.[70]

Ford's strategy at plant level in no way matched the seeming coherence of its national-level initiatives. At national level they were pursuing a relationship with responsible and accountable shopfloor representatives with whom they could negotiate. But at plant level there were no gestures towards any real 'partnership in control'. Ford's only concession to the demands of the work-force on job-related issues was a Work Standards Agreement of June 1975 which was significant in that for the first time it committed the company to *consultation* with stewards on work standards and committed the company to ensuring that the standards were 'fair and equitable', but this fell far short of any real negotiating rights.[71]

Ford was prepared to consider reforms of collective bargaining but it maintained its traditional insistence on unilateral work standards, procedure and discipline and it was these issues that were the most prone to trigger plant-level direct action, vandalism and stoppages. By the end of the 1970s Ford were becoming concerned, as they had never been before, that their doggedly maintained control of the labour process was no longer delivering the goods. Constant labour disputes, off-standard performance, inflexible skills, loss of productive time and lack of right-first-time production were becoming real competitive handicaps that their traditional insistence on managerial prerogatives and direct control could not remedy. Punitive weapons such as penalty clauses were proving almost wholly counterproductive and hours lost to strikes rose sharply again in 1977–8.[72]

'AFTER JAPAN' 1978–1987

It was developments in the wider competitive environment in the 1980s that provoked Ford's most fundamental rethinking of its labour strategies. Automakers' perceptions of markets and technology underwent a radical shift in the 1980s. In particular, the new orthodoxy recognized that growing requirements for more flexible production and innovation made repetitive standardized production problematic.[73] In tune with this, Ford began to question their traditional approaches in marketing and manufacturing,[74] centring on a new emphasis on rapid product and technology innovation, a new role for quality in marketing strategy and a recognition of the costs of quality and the need for prevention of defects rather than cure.[75]

These shifts directed attention towards the adequacy of existing labour-management methods and stimulated change, even though the new strategic direction remained unclear and ambiguous. Events at the end of the 1970s made it clear that, although unions and workers did not have the power to challenge management prerogatives broadly, they were able to frustrate managerial designs and impede the translation of formal controls into effective control on the shop floor. The lack of motivation among workers caused the costs of quality and control systems to escalate, and the rigid separation of plan and implementation and the removal of responsibility from workers were becoming counterproductive. Sub-optimal utilization of human resources produced both a poor quality of work-life and spiralling control costs.[76]

The changes that occurred at Ford in the 1980s were not revolutionary but they did mark a watershed in company practices. There were no radical innovations in work organization, the primacy of the assembly line and a highly managed labour process remained intact. But significant reversals in the logic of the system emerged, which, according to some commentators 'seem to mark a change in the old Fordist paradigm of decomposition and fragmentation of tasks'.[77] Alongside these changes more traditional features persisted. Continuous rationalization and the reduction of head-count; the use of international sourcing in Europe; the intensification of work effort (by greater continuity if not greater pace of work); the emphasis on the 'right to manage'; and tight payment systems – all remained in place. By the late 1980s workplace harmony might still be limited, but the old 'aggravation' of workplace relations had been significantly reduced. The extent to which Ford's conversion to 'participative management' went beyond catchwords remained unclear.

The initial impetus to a rethinking of management methods came from a growing awareness of the sources of Japanese success. A trip to Japan in 1978 by Bill Hayden, the head of Ford of Europe, stimulated a first 'shock response'. Hayden was shaken by the size of Japan's efficiency-lead and initiated an 'After Japan' programme to try to close the gap. Until this time Ford of Europe had been relatively uninformed on the nature of the Japanese challenge. They believed that it was based primarily on government support and cheap docile labour. But, following Hayden's visit, Ford's study of Japanese practices in the early 1980s revealed that their greatest productivity shortfall in relation to Japan was not labour productivity but the result of the interaction of design, build complexity, schedule instability and the consequent low level of mechanization and automation.[78] Studies of their allied Japanese company, Mazda, showed that while Ford matched Japanese practice in 'hard automation' they lagged in the effectiveness of its application. In particular, their engineers noted the added inventory costs arising from Ford's use of produce-and-store rather than kanban methods, and an under-utilization of organizational resources resulting from 'organizational chimneys' dividing related departments which particularly raised design and development costs. Still more important, however, were the combined effect of models that were unduly complex to build ('build complexity') and unstable production schedules. Responding to the fluctuating demands of the sales departments, Ford had 'evolved a capability to cope daily, weekly and monthly with dramatic changes in the number and mix of vehicles to be built'. While Mazda or Toyota with systematized option packages were able to stabilize their monthly schedules, Ford were 'unable to set a firm schedule for the number and the detailed mix of options for any period in advance'. This increased costs at the assembly stage by limiting automation, shortening runs and excessively complicating work tasks. At the same time it placed a heavy cost-burden on upstream supplier operations who had to cope with unstable production schedules.[79]

One response to these observations was calls from the engineering side aggressively to reduce build complexity and improve schedule stability, and subsequent rationalization, computerization and reform of relations with suppliers tackled some of these issues. Nevertheless, marketing demands continued to emphasize diversity and market segmentation and this limited the scope of these developments. Instead, the organization had to learn to cope with the implications of ongoing complexity and design innovation. While seeking commonality across its European product range Ford in the 1980s also accelerated product innovation (anti-lock brakes, electronic engine management, fuel-efficient engines and so on), shortened its product cycle and begun to proliferate high-margin versions of its standard products.[80]

The lessons of 'After Japan' were therefore complex and could be interpreted in a variety of ways.[81] At first it changed more in engineering and accountancy than in production management and industrial relations.[82] There were, for example, actions to reduce inventories and build complexity, reform supplier relations, introduce quick tool changes and to emphasize the role of quality. But the implications for labour emerged more erratically. Until 1983 the emphasis continued to be, in rather traditional fashion, on discipline and the control of work through technology. From 1983, however, novel features began to be more prominent, notably a new emphasis on Employee Involvement and participative management and certain elements of job redesign.

Hayden's initial interpretation of the lessons of Japan was that an essential complement of organizational reform was a restoration of discipline and increased shopfloor effort. Thus he stressed that, 'We need plain, tough discipline', and the early 1980s saw a frontal offensive on this issue, particularly at Halewood.[83] The New Disciplinary Code, introduced in November 1980, built on the old tradition of penalty clauses and in particular on a punitive retaliatory layoff system. The code itself was arbitrary and inconsistent and even cut across other elements of agreed procedures. Ford imposed it unilaterally and for six months, notably at Halewood, the code became the focus of bitter battles. A relay of small sectional disputes led to a succession of plant-wide layoffs and a spiral of retaliation. The situation was exacerbated by the timing of the code's introduction along with the launch of the new Escort in 1980. The launch brought with it the teething problems of a new model, a great deal of new technology, a massive introduction of new work allocations and timings and considerable interruptions to production resulting from problems with the new robots. The plant was close to chaos, and threats of the imminent closure of Halewood were flying round before Ford rescinded the code in May 1981 in return for a union undertaking 'to improve self-discipline on the shop floor'.[84]

The code lay squarely in the old tradition of Ford collective bargaining and labour management – a blunt instrument to rectify the company's perceived 'productivity problem' at Halewood.[85] During 1980–3 Ford pursued with little success the forcible imposition of self-certification of work, on-line maintenance and the removal of demarcations. A 1981 'efficiency package' was resisted fiercely at plant level, culminating in the Kelly dispute of March–April 1983. The Kelly dispute was seen by management at Halewood as the culmination of years of 'using the baseball bat': the penalties of confrontation were so great that 'we had to recognize that we had come to a point where force did not pay any more'.[86]

The second axis of Ford's pursuit of control between 1978 and 1983 was to attempt to build-in control through its new technology. This was most effective in eliminating whole areas of labour-intensive and conflict-prone tasks, notably in bodywelding and paint shops. As Derek Waeland, manufacturing engineering manager, Halewood, put it, 'We haven't got control of the labour force, we can't force each man to put each weld in the right place. So we've tried to build in quality through machines.'[87] In other respects, the new technology itself often controlled labour more tightly and eliminated scope for discretion in the labour process in, for instance, practices such as banking up work, building stocks ahead of schedule or 'spelling' colleagues (working more intensively for a while to enable a co-worker to take a break – known as 'welt working' at Halewood). Certain technological changes considerably diminished the scope for argument on certain job-related issues and there was some truth in the notion that new technology and greater order in engineering tended to reinforce managerial control.

Perfecting control via a 'technological fix' remained a tantalizing but illusory goal. The persistence or increase of variants on the line in the 1980s kept issues of labour deployment central. Computer scheduling was unable to overcome all line-balancing and deployment problems arising from model-mix fluctuations (a Sierra Ghia required some 15–20 per cent more work on the line than a base model), problems with supply or delivery, or rearrangements when defective work had to be taken out of the line. Despite extensive computerization daily schedules remained constantly subject to last-minute changes and required work by foremen and industrial engineers to juggle and improvise to balance out under- or over-utilization of labour capacity. In the 1970s at Halewood these needs had been covered by informal flexibility and custom and practice whereby work groups of 8–10 would allocate tasks among themselves flexibly and allow temporary 'overcycle work' to be made up by 'undercycle work' on an hourly basis. The squeeze on this 'welt working' in the early 1980s not only increased tension and conflict but also created additional rigidities.[88]

The continuing weakness of worker organization nationally in the context of recession and redundancy and the Thatcher government's political and legal offensive against the unions provided Ford with a position of strength to explore labour management options. Employment at Ford was cut heavily between 1979 and 1985, with the hourly head-count falling from 58,561 to 37,027, a cut of 36 per cent.[89] This provided the background for the strategies of discipline and technical control of the early 1980s. But it also provided the conditions for the development of a second and increasingly powerful stream of management strategy under the more subtle banner of Employee Involvement (EI). EI dated back to a declaration of intent by Philip Caldwell in 1979, but at that time its implementation was left up to the discretion of local management and it remained mainly a 'communications exercise' or public-relations programme until it slowly moved to centre-stage by around 1983.

In the early 1980s attempts to extend worker responsibility for quality and to minimize process inefficiencies, reducing buffer stocks, wastage and rectification, were largely ineffectual. Tactics that were a mixture of bullying, manipulation and exhortation were counterproductive. A mishandled attempt to introduce Quality Circles foundered on a deep distrust of management and the justifiable union perception that it was in part a deliberate effort to cut across union jurisdiction, bargaining arenas and negotiating structures.

Following this, Ford management shifted their ground and began to focus on negotiated flexibility through reforms to the job and wage structure. The new approach began to develop at Halewood following the nadir of the Kelly dispute. Between 1983 and 1985 seek-and-repair and self-certification were slowly edged in at certain departments at Halewood. Shop stewards fought a tough rearguard action but ultimately had to give way. Management's tactics were to win the hearts and minds of the work-force and 'bring on board' the shop stewards – backed by the threat of large redundancies or closure if the plant did not perform competitively. Stewards and workers were wooed with training courses, discussions and visits to other plants, notably Saarlouis in Germany, using inter-plant productivity comparisons ('the Saarlouis Gap') to spur cooperation.

In 1985 the new approach moved to the centre of national negotiations with an agreement on flexibility at the NJNC which provided a basis for the gradual extension of self-inspection, self-rectification and elements of team work, broader job classifications or new jobs such as 'lead operatives' (where the distinction between production and supervision is blurred).[90] The new 'production operator' title replaced 86 old job titles, and production workers were henceforth expected to handle minor maintenance, self-certification, stock-handling and cleaning their own work stations. At the skilled-worker level a key aim was to increase productivity by increasing the flexibility of deployment of craft workers through the elimination of demarcations and the establishment of two-trades maintenance.[91] At all levels the shift from 'quality control' to 'quality assurance' signalled an intention to increase individual worker responsibility for performance and to change the motivational orientation of the shop floor.[92]

Such changes were partial but potentially significant. They represented a reduction in the fragmentation of tasks, steps towards a restoration of responsibility to operatives and a quest for co-operation and bargained adherence rather than imposition. Top management in the late 1980s began to emphasize their perception of a need for high-trust relations, or what they termed 'participative management'. Their internal organizational goals prioritized the need to change their embedded managerial culture to become 'customer-driven' rather than 'numbers-oriented' in marketing and manufacturing and to develop participative labour management. All these changes represented significant reversals in the logic of Ford's system, though it is still too early to assess how thoroughgoing these changes have been. There are enormous difficulties in reversing the habits of fifty years of direct control in the field of worker responsibility.

Even as Ford began to modify their system in the 1980s, BL was moving to emulate many of the features that Ford was abandoning. When Michael Edwardes became Managing Director of BL in 1978, ten years after implementation of MDW had begun, production organization at factory level was still, in his opinion, 'a shambles'.[93] He initiated numerous reforms of the technical side of management at BL and also conducted a vigorous managerial purge of the 'old guard'. But the key to Edwardes' strategy was to solve what he called 'the labour problem'. His 'recovery plan' was based on four elements. A massive programme of plant closures and redundancies would cut the company back to a viable core operation. At the same time a range of new modern cars would spearhead 'product-led' recovery. This new generation of cars would be manufactured by the most modern automation systems, and the production system would be regenerated by a thorough-going reform of working practices.[94]

Of all these elements, Edwardes prioritized the reform of work practices, arguing that this was a prerequisite for the efficient use of new technology and the production of competitive models. The 'labour question' was seen as being so important that it was worth taking the company 'to the brink' – and possibly over it – in order to resolve it. During 1980–1 the company used the threat of the closure of the company as their principal weapon, and ultimately imposed the new practices unilaterally in the 'Blue Newspaper' of April 1980. This document swept away the old practices of 'mutuality' and established that henceforth the organization of work would be the sole prerogative of management, notably in respect of changes in performance standards, manning levels, relief times and the deployment of labour. The previous 500 hourly paid job classifications were swept away and replaced with five company-wide grades and non-negotiable plant-wide incentive schemes. In a period of three years shop-steward authority on the shop floor was effectively destroyed. The number of full-time shop stewards at BL was cut from 20 to 6 and those that remained had their facilities and mobility restricted and were strictly confined to procedural roles in dealing with job grievances. By 1983 the weakening of shop stewards had gone so far that, at Cowley, over half of the shop-steward constituencies had no representative. Indeed, Paul Willman has suggested that the company had probably gone so far that it was in danger of breaking down the structures of 'orderly' trade unionism.[95] Nevertheless, the crackdown on the unions did reduce the rate of strikes. In the late 1970s BL had lost an average of 5 per cent of working hours per year to strikes but in 1980–5 it lost only 1.5 per cent.

Edwardes claimed that the reform of working practices and the re-establishment of management's right to manage was one of his principal achievements and the foundation for what he called the 'productivity miracle' at BL (subsequently renamed Austin Rover) – a claim that was to achieve almost iconic status in subsequent pronouncements by the Thatcher government. But, as Williams *et al.* have demonstrated, the 'productivity miracle' is a myth.[96] Improvements in output per man had almost nothing to do with changes in working practices. Productivity had plunged between 1972 and 1980 when output collapsed much faster than employment. In 1980–3 Edwardes slashed the work-force from 80,000 to 41,000 and thus brought the work-force into line with the decreased output levels. The main sources of these cuts in labour were not changes in manning levels but the closure of plants and labour-displacing investments in certain key facilities such as highly automated body shops. Apart from mass sackings, the gains from reformed work practices were insignificant. Closures failed to eliminate overcapacity, and the attention to managerial rights was probably dysfunctional in terms of costs and productivity. In particular, Willman and Winch have shown that an obsessive concern with displacing direct labour from the production process was responsible for serious errors in the configuration of automation for the Metro. The Metro facility was 'the line manager's revenge' reducing direct labour to a minimum, but this was only possible by opting for extremely rigid multi-weld systems dedicated to the production of a single model instead of using other more flexible systems that were available. The result was that the company saddled itself with an enormous fixed cost-burden when, as proved to be the case, the Metro lines could only be used at 60 per cent capacity.[97] In the mid-1980s Austin Rover (AR) typically produced only 450,000 cars per year in facilities designed to produce 750,000 cars. Thus any savings on variable costs were more than offset by soaring fixed costs, and the new sophisticated plant remained under-utilized.

Management attention was obsessively focused on 'the labour question' and managerial prerogatives. BL top management, government and wider industrial circles all concurred that the humbling of labour was essential for effective management in the company. Starting from this point of view, the Labour Government in the late 1970s had started the practice of making continued government support for the company dependent on industrial-relations performance, and the Thatcher government made it clear that unless the company demonstrated its ability to control labour it could hope for no further subsidies. Whatever their rationale in terms of the efficiency of production, aggressive policies towards labour were a political *sine qua non* for survival. The moves were given an added political edge by Edwardes's belief that the plants were being kept in 'a continuing state of master-minded anarchy' primarily through the activity of Communist-led militants.[98]

This unbalanced strategy meant that much less effort was directed towards improving supplier relationships, training, quality control or renovation of marketing and distribution networks. Moreover, the strategy of confrontation, discipline and managerial unilateralism fitted uncomfortably with the emergent needs of high-quality manufacturing processes in the 1980s. Austin Rover's attempts to involve employees in concern for product quality or cooperative working practices fitted ill with their coercive managerial style. Moreover, automation did not dispense with the need for continued responsible and attentive work on the part of the work-force.

CONCLUSION

Ford has emphasized and obtained more direct managerial control of work standards, labour mobility, working time, discipline and work organization than any other British car company. But, as we have seen, there are grounds to doubt any simple picture of the superior efficiency or technological rationality of Ford's system of direct control. Ford's experience reveals some important inherent limits to the operation of direct control. First, despite continuing high levels of management authority in the plants, it has never become possible to dispense with the need to generate consent and legitimacy within the system: as Terry and Edwards have noted, 'labour independence' may prove as much of a problem for companies as shopfloor union organization. Second, Ford has found it difficult to develop managerial and supervisory structures adequate to the task of applying control consistently. Third, in the absence of any simple technological logic of deskilling, the need for worker responsibility has remained inescapable. Given the importance of the 'mix problem' and the variability of work on the line, Ford's notion of 'normal' performance to be enforced by direct supervision becomes problematic. Toyota, for example, recognized this by abandoning the idea of a 'normal' task and built the existence of fluctuating work tasks into workers' job standards.[99] Contrary to the industrial orthodoxies of the 1970s or the more recent comments of Lewchuk and others, there is no immanent logic of bringing 'production institutions' into line with the needs of technology. The pursuit of control for its own sake may prove very costly. Similarly, comparisons between the merits of incentive-based or direct-control systems are difficult. Clearly, BL had serious problems with the loss of control of its incentive systems. Nevertheless, for much of the postwar period, piece-work systems proved flexible and adaptable and were much more capable than direct control of blurring lines between supervision and production. The problems arising from labour-management issues at BL need to be carefully balanced against the problems arising from broader product strategies, marketing and management.

Beyond problems inherent in the strategy of direct control, it is also necessary to question its presumed degree of success. Ford's share of UK new car registrations has been fairly consistent though not expansive. It rose from 27 per cent in 1955 to almost 30 per cent by 1965 but then fell to 23 per cent by 1974. Since then it has risen again to 25 per cent in 1978 and 30.5 per cent in 1982. In contrast, BL's market share in the 1980s collapsed from 33 per cent in 1974 to less than 18 per cent by 1982. However, Ford's share of UK *production* has been less impressive, particularly in comparison with BMC/BL/Austin Rover over the crucial period of BL's decline, 1954–78. In 1954 BL's predecessor companies produced 52 per cent of British output and Ford 27 per cent; in 1978 BL still held 50 per cent against Ford's 26.5 per cent. Only after that, as BL's share of UK output fell sharply to 40 per cent by 1986 did Ford's share of output increase significantly to 34 per cent. The key to Ford's strong market share and profitability lay not so much in its superior performance as a British producer but in its capacity as a multinational to bring large quantities of imports into Britain. It may be that the Ford system has been no better than the BL system at manufacturing cars competitively in Britain. However, unlike BL/AR, they have been able to take advantage of their multinational organization. BL's attempt to hold close to 50 per cent of the UK market over time required them to produce a proliferation of low-volume models which could not generate economies of scale and which generated low profits per car. Ford, in contrast, with a more restricted strategy of controlling some 30 per cent of the market with three models were able to use more dedicated investment and economies of scale and achieve higher output per worker and higher profits per car.

Nevertheless, Ford's undoubted distinctiveness clearly demonstrated the scope for managerial strategic choice within a given national context. The extent to which union responses and strategies offered Ford scope for its policies suggests that the British firms may not have been constrained by the unions to the extent that is often argued. Ford was successful in preventing the effective consolidation of shopfloor organization over long periods. One reason for this was its shared aim with national union organizations in the 1940s and 1950s preventing the development of independent shopfloor organization. One result was that the unions only consolidated their position at Ford's from the late 1960s when shifts in both management policy and union strategy enabled shopfloor organization to become more durable. The absence of union support for shopfloor organization in the earlier years meant that the shopfloor organization that existed was much *less* integrated into national union structures than it might have been and was much more unruly and unpredictable. Paradoxically, therefore, the lack of more developed union structures meant that the unions could not control their membership in the ways that Ford often called on them to do. At the same time, the prolonged weakness of local union organization meant that Ford may have ultimately been *too successful* in its collective bargaining for too long. Its wages dropped out of line below other car companies, resulting in problems in the recruitment of suitable labour in the 1960s and painful clashes with national incomes policies in the 1970s when management recognized the imperative to catch up. It was only in the 1970s that Ford began to recognize unions as possible interlocutors at shopfloor level, but their continuing demand for 'discipline' and the historical weaknesses of links between national and shopfloor organization made this a difficult transition to achieve.

Ford might have been able to consolidate its policies more effectively if the context of state policies and the legal framework had shifted. Ford wanted a highly regulated private regime, but as problems grew it increasingly sought sympathetic public assistance from the state or the law to enable the company to hold its system together, notably the resort to Courts of Inquiry in the 1950s and 1960s, Ford's campaign for the legal enforceability of agreements and its 'private enterprise' analogy to the Industrial Relations Act in 1969. At times it seemed as if the sorts of shifts in law and government policy that Ford desired might indeed come to pass. However, even if the company had obtained such institutionalization problems would have remained. In the United States Ford's similar quest for a high-control system within a legalistic and contractual shopfloor framework was indeed institutionalized from the 1940s. It initially legitimated and enforced managerial power. Yet there too, over time, the rigidities of the system came to impose significant and unexpected constraints on management action, ultimately precipitating a quest for reform in the 1980s.[100]

NOTES

1 The other main US-owned company in Britain in this period, Vauxhall, had some similarities to Ford. A comparison would be interesting, but Vauxhall is ignored here because of its relatively minor importance in the British industry for most of this time.

2 See Jonathan Wood, *Wheels of Misfortune: The Rise and Fall of the British Motor Industry* (London, 1988), pp. 145–52, 199–202, 238–47; Krish Bhaskar, *The UK and European Motor Industry* (London, 1984), esp. vol. 2.

3 Ford was a central model for the reorganization at BL in the 1970s studied by Paul Willman and Graham Winch, *Innovation and Management Control. Labour Relations at BL Cars* (Cambridge, 1987) esp. pp. 150–2 and 187; and Paul Willman, 'Labour Relations Strategies at BL Cars', in Steven Tolliday and Jonathan Zeitlin (eds), *The Automobile Industry and Its Workers: Between Fordism and Flexibility* (Cambridge, 1987). For the attitude of governments see the Ryder Report and Central Policy Review Staff, *The Future of the British Motor Industry* (London, 1975).

4 Paul Willman, *Technological Change, Collective Bargaining and Industrial Efficiency* (Oxford, 1986), ch. 7 and esp. pp. 149 and 161; Wayne Lewchuk, *American Technology and the British Vehicle Industry* (Cambridge, 1986); W. Lewchuk, 'The Motor Vehicle Industry: Roots of Decline', in B. Elbaum and W. Lazonick (eds), *The Decline of the British Economy* (Oxford, 1986), p. 150.

5 Steven Tolliday, 'Management and Labour in Britain, 1896–1939', in Tolliday and Zeitlin, *The Automobile Industry and Its Workers*.

6 Tolliday, 'Management and Labour', pp. 33–7.

7 For the MAP's fears see Memorandum by Sir Frederick Leggett, 16th June 1943, PRO LAB 10/274; for the TUC's organizing campaign in the 1930s see TUC Organisation Committee Files, esp. Boxes 602 and 603.

8 On the sit-in see esp. Vic Feather, 'Memorandum: 4.20 p.m. to 7.15 p.m., 6th December 1943', TUC Organisation Committee, Box 602. On the background see Steven Tolliday, 'Government, Employers and Shop-Floor Organization in the British Motor Industry, 1939–69' in Steven Tolliday and Jonathan Zeitlin (eds), *Shop-Floor Bargaining and the State* (Cambridge, 1985).

9 Allan Nevins and Frank E. Hill, *Ford: Decline and Rebirth, 1933–1962* (New York, 1963), pp. 158–66; Robert Lacey, *Ford. The Men and the Machine* (New York, 1986), pp. 393–6.

10 Walter Citrine, 'Verbatim notes on meeting with Perry, 9th November 1943', TUC Organisation Committee Box 602.

11 Minutes of a Conference between representatives of the trade unions and representatives of Ford, 31 Jan. 1944, TUC Organisation Committee Box 602.

12 Report of a conference of trade union representatives, 6 Apr. 1944, TUC Organisation Committee Box 603.

13 He reported to the Trade Union side of the joint committee that was engaged in negotiating an agreement that: 'Among the shop stewards are five or six people of whom I have personal experience who *I think* are totally unsuitable from any point of view, either the unions or the management, for appointment as shop stewards. Every issue they raise is a political one, or inspired by political motives, and they appear to be satisfied not to get things put right but to be able to point to the further iniquities of Ford. The remainder of the stewards are good chaps, sound trade unionists, and who themselves are of the opinion that the proper way to deal with Ford is as trade unionists and not as politicians.' Victor Feather, 'Memorandum to trade union side of JNC, 31st January 1944', TUC Organisation Committee Box 603.

14 As reported by Feather, 'Memorandum, 22nd March 1944', TUC Organisation Committee, Box 603.

15 Letter from Feather to Citrine, 21 Feb. 1944, TUC Organisation Committee Box 602.

16 Comments by the Ministry of Labour on Industrial Relations Department Memorandum, 21 Apr. 1944, PRO LAB 10/274.

17 For the developments of 1944–6 see JNC Minutes and Conference reports in TUC Organisation Committee, Box 603.

18 H. A. Turner, G. Clack and G. Roberts, *Labour Relations in the Motor Industry. A Study of Industrial Unrest and an International Comparison* (London, 1967), p. 215.

19 Karel Williams, John Williams and Denis Thomas, *Why Are The British Bad At Manufacturing?* (London, 1983), pp. 220–4.

20 Steven Tolliday, 'High Tide and After: Coventry Engineering Workers and Shopfloor Bargaining, 1945–80', in Bill Lancaster and Tony Mason (eds), *Life and Labour in a Twentieth Century City: The Experience of Coventry* (Coventry, 1986); Tolliday, 'Management and Labour'; W. Brown, *Piecework Bargaining* (London, 1973); G. Clack, *Industrial Relations in a British Car Factory* (Cambridge, 1967).

21 Jonathan Wood, *Ford Cortina Mk. 1, 1962–66: 1200, 1500 GT, Lotus* (London, 1984), pp. 10–17; Mira Wilkins and Frank Hill, *American Business Abroad: Ford on Five Continents* (Detroit, 1964), p. 384.

22 Wood, *Wheels of Misfortune*, pp. 112–17.

23 Lewchuk, *American Technology*, p. 186. Unlike its British competitors Ford had a conservative dividend policy and concentrated on reinvestment: see Nevins and Hill, *Ford*, p. 400.

24 House of Commons Expenditure Committee, *Fourteenth Report. The Motor Vehicle Industry* (London, 1975), Table 14.

25 Williams *et al.*, *Why Are the British . . .?*, p. 222; D. G. Rhys, *The Motor Industry: An Economic Survey* (London, 1972).

26 Minutes of a Special Sub-Committee of the Joint Negotiating Committee, 15 June 1949, TUC Organisation Committee, Box 605.

27 Minutes of the Joint Negotiating Committee, esp. 11 Apr. 1949 and *passim*, TUC Organisation Committee, Box 604.

28 'Report of a Court of Inquiry into the causes and circumstances of a dispute at Briggs Motor Bodies Ltd., Dagenham, existing between the Ford Motor Co., Ltd. and members of the Trade Unions represented on the Trade Union side of the Ford National Joint Negotiating Committee.' (Cmd 131, Apr. 1957) (= the Cameron Inquiry).

29 Cameron Inquiry, p. 26.

30 Minutes of Proceedings of a Court of Inquiry, 4 Mar. 1963, Ford NJNC Trade Union side papers.

31 Turner *et al.*, *Labour Relations*, p. 215.

32 The following pages draw heavily on Huw Beynon, *Working For Ford* (Harmondsworth, 1973; 2nd edn, 1984), and Henry Friedman and Sander Meredeen, *The Dynamics of Industrial Conflict: Lessons From Ford* (London, 1980), which give massive amounts of detail, for the Halewood and Dagenham plants respectively, in this period.

33 Beynon, *Ford*, pp. 76–7, 90–2.

34 ibid., pp. 77–102.

35 ibid., pp. 149–63.

36 As one steward told Beynon, 'They set a line speed and they get things sorted out and then they change the speed and he's back where he started'. Beynon, *Ford*, p. 161.

37 Robert C. Copp, *Locus of Management Decisions in Industrial Relations in Multinationals*, (East Lansing, Mich., 1974).
38 Beynon, *Ford*, pp. 106–37.
39 See Beynon's description, ibid., pp. 145–1.
40 Friedman and Meredeen, *Dynamics*, pp. 41–2, 64–5.
41 ibid., pp. 64–7.
42 *Report of a Court of Inquiry* (the Scamp Report) Cmd 3749 (London, 1968).
43 Friedman and Meredeen, *Dynamics*, pp. 43–4.
44 This is explored in detail in Tolliday, 'High Tide'; see also Michael Terry and P. K. Edwards (eds), *Shopfloor Politics and Job Controls: The Post-War Engineering Industry* (Oxford, 1988).
45 Turner, *et al. Labour Relations*; J. W. Durcan, W. E. J. McCarthy and G. P. Redman, *Strikes in Post-War Britain: A Study of Stoppages of Work Due to Industrial Disputes, 1946–73* (London, 1983); David Marsden, Timothy Morris, Paul Willman and Stephen Wood, *The Car Industry: Labour Relations and Industrial Adjustment* (London, 1985), ch. 6.
46 Wolfgang Streeck (ed.), *Industrial Relations and Technical Change in the British, Italian and German Automobile Industries. Three Case Studies* (Berlin, 1985): Willman, *Technological Change*, chs 7 and 8.
47 J. Sutherland, 'The Impact of Measured Daywork on Company Industrial Relations' (MA thesis, Warwick University, 1974).
48 Friedman and Meredeen, *Dynamics*, pp. 93–4.
49 The new wage structure is covered in great detail, ibid., esp. pp. 44–6, 68–76, 88–9.
50 ibid., pp. 79–85, 117–20, 166–8; the National Union of Vehicle Builders strike strategy consciously took advantage of this paradox, ibid. pp. 139–41.
51 John Mathews, *Ford Strike, the Workers' Story* (London, 1972), pp. 73–95.
52 The phrase is from Allan Flanders, *Management and Unions* (London, 1972), p. 172. Blakeman was a personal friend of Allan Flanders and married Joan Woodward, professor of Industrial Sociology at Imperial College (Friedman and Meredeen, *Dynamics*, p. 123).
53 Friedman and Meredeen, *Dynamics*, p. 77.
54 ibid., p. 229.
55 ibid., p. 226; Beynon, *Ford*, p. 274.
56 Roy Lewis, 'The Legal Enforceability of Collective Agreements', *British Journal of Industrial Relations* 8 (1970).
57 Friedman and Meredeen, *Dynamics*, pp. 226–7.
58 ibid., pp. 228–30, 263; Beynon, *Ford*, pp. 268–74.
59 Under the old ground rules of the NJNC 10 small unions, representing only 4 per cent of union membership at Ford, could outvote the big battalions of the TGWU and AEF. In 1969 the TGWU and AUEW had 32,000 members at Ford, while the other 14 unions had only 12,000 between them.
60 Beynon, *Ford*, p. 349.
61 Minutes of Evidence of the 14th Report of the Expenditure Committee of the House of Commons (HMSO, London, 1975), paras 921–6, pp. 249–50; see also FMC evidence to Bullock Committee.
62 Friedman and Meredeen, *Dynamics*, pp. 247, 253, 340–8.
63 Ford's attempt to impose the 'firm line' and 'ball and chain' on Halewood stewards in 1971 failed when the company made an unsuccessful attempt to sack Halewood steward John Dillon after the so-called Parity Strike (Mathews, *Ford Strike*, p. 117–44; Beynon, *Ford*, pp. 310–44).
64 Important procedural reforms in 1975/6 abbreviated and decentralized the machinery for grievance settlement giving plant managers and shop stewards new authority to reach settlements on plant level issues without reference to the

NJNC (Friedman and Merdeen, *Dynamics*, pp. 237–46; Beynon, *Ford*, p. 348).

65 Friedman and Meredeen, *Dynamics*, pp. 237–46, 268.

66 Beynon, *Ford*, p. 346.

67 Friedman and Meredeen, *Dynamics*, pp. 260–6; Beynon, *Ford*, pp. 268–74.

68 Friedman and Meredeen, *Dynamics*, p. 270.

69 ibid., pp. 267–8.

70 Private information from FMC plant manager, Halewood.

71 Friedman and Meredeen, *Dynamics*, pp. 244–7.

72 Marsden *et al.*, *The Car Industry*, pp. 115–6, gives strike figures.

73 The rise of the new orthodoxy can be conveniently followed in the documents of the two International Motor Vehicle Projects conducted at the Massachusetts Institute of Technology (MIT) over the decade. The report of the first project was published as: Alan Altshuler, Martin Anderson, Daniel Jones, Daniel Roos and James Womack, *The Future of the Automobile. The Report of MIT's International Automobile Program* (London, 1985); the report of the second project as: James P. Womack et al., *The Machine That Changed the World* (New York, 1990).

74 On the transformation of their marketing philosophy see Christopher Lorenz, *The Design Dimension. Product Strategy and the Challenge of Global Marketing* (Oxford, 1982), pp. 3, 91, who argues that Ford underwent 'a conversion of Galileo-like proportions' in breaking away from their concept of an amorphous mass market.

75 T. J. Pettigrew, 'Process Quality Control: The New Approach to the Management of Quality in Ford', *Quality Assurance* 11/3 (1985).

76 For the managerialist debate in the 1970s and 1980s about whether high control costs are outweighed by efficiency gains in direct control systems see E. E. Lawler, *High Involvement Management* (San Francisco, 1986); T. G. Cummings and E. S. Molloy, *Improving Productivity and the Quality of Working Life* (New York, 1977); E. M. Glaser, *Productivity Gains through Worklife Improvement* (New York, 1976).

77 Ken Starkey and Alan McKinlay, *Organizational Innovation: Competitive Strategy and the Management of Change in Four Major Companies* (Avebury, 1988), p. 29.

78 Ford of Europe Manufacturing Planning and Plan Engineering: J. J. Baumhardt, R. Jedermann and P. Simpson, 'Report on Spring 1983 Japan Visit, March 22nd to April 1st 1983'.

79 The major Japanese producers generally offered 'series-packs' with few freely available options. In contrast, the 1984 Escort offered 15 different main wiring assemblies, 8 engine compartment wiring assemblies, 88 door-trim sidewalls, 32 door mirrors, 9 wheel and tyre assemblies, 40 instrument clusters, 3 steering wheels and 6 car-locks. Ford engineers calculated that a European Escort had a build complexity 50 times as great as a comparable Mazda Familia (461,264 versus 9,984 permutations). See Baumhardt, Jederman and Simpson, 'Report'.

80 In the 1980s European and US companies have generally been attempting to reduce complexity while the Japanese have been seeking competitive advantage by increasing it. But while the Europeans have been reducing mainly 'meaningless' differentiation in the form of huge varieties of option combinations, the Japanese have been increasing 'complex variation' in the form of distinctive product attributes. The overall result is increasing complexity in the assembly process, especially involving line balancing, product sequencing and quality control problems. See John Krafcik, 'Comparative Analysis of Performance Indicators at World Auto Assembly Plants' (M.Sc. thesis, Sloan School of Management, MIT, 1987), and Anthony Sheriff, 'The Competitive Product Position of Automobile Manufacturers: Performance and Strategies' (paper for

the IMVP International Policy Forum, Lake Como, Italy, May 1988).

81 For similar problems in interpreting the 'lessons of Japan' in other US and European companies see Ulrich Jurgens, 'The Transfer of Japanese Management Concepts in the International Automobile Industry', in Stephen Wood (ed.), *The Transformation of Work?* (London, 1989).

82 Marsden *et al., Car Industry*, pp. 115–16.

83 Beynon, *Ford*, p. 356.

84 ibid., pp. 358–64.

85 In 1981–3 the plant was consistently failing to achieve more than 80 per cent of the standard production volumes scheduled by the industrial engineering department.

86 Private information from Halewood plant manager. This thinking was echoed at corporate level. As one senior manager put it: 'there were more effective ways of getting the best out of people than telling them what to do and having them do it' (quoted in Starkey and McKinlay, *Organizational Innovation*, p. 24).

87 Interviewed in 1980 by Harry Scarborough, 'The Politics of Technological Change at British Leyland', in Otto Jacobi, Bob Jessop, Hans Kastendiek and Marino Regini (eds), *Technological Change, Rationalization and Industrial Relations* (London, 1985).

88 Interviews with Halewood shop stewards.

89 Ford–Britain, Manpower Statistics.

90 For a description of the state of play at Dagenham in 1985–6 see Elizabeth Bortolaia Silva, 'Labour and Technology in the Car Industry: Ford Strategies in Britain and Brazil' (Ph.D., University of London, 1988), pp. 356–69.

91 Jurgens *et al.* have argued, by comparing work practices in German auto plants where skilled union demarcations are negligible, that the inflexibility of the UK skilled trades has often been overestimated. Certain 'demarcations' remain irreducible because of competence and safety barriers even in Germany where much broader worker-skill training exists than in the UK: Ulrich Jurgens, Thomas Malsch and Knuth Dohse, *Moderne Zeiten in der Automobilfabrik. Strategien der Produktionsmodernisierung im Länder- und Konzernvergleich* (Berlin, 1989). I am grateful to the authors for allowing me to see a typescript translation of this book.

92 Pettigrew, 'Process Quality Control'.

93 Michael Edwardes, *Back from the Brink* (London, 1984), p. 52.

94 Willman and Winch, *Innovation*, pp. 17–43.

95 Willman, 'Labour Relations at BL Cars', pp. 319, 325.

96 Karel Williams, John Williams and Colin Haslam, *The Breakdown of Austin Rover. A Case Study in the Failure of Business Strategy and Industrial Policy* (Leamington Spa, 1987), pp. 14–34.

97 Willman and Winch, *Innovation*, pp. 129–90.

98 Edwardes, *Back from the Brink*, p. 110.

99 Taichi Ohno, *Toyota Production System: Beyond Large-Scale Production* (Cambridge, Mass., 1988).

100 For a comparative study see Steven Tolliday and Jonathan Zeitlin, 'Shop-Floor Bargaining, Contract Unionism and Job Control: An Anglo-American Comparison', in Tolliday and Zeitlin, *Automobile Industry and Its Workers*; for the problems of the more regulated system in the 1970s and 1980s see Harry Katz, *Shifting Gears. Changing Labor Relations in the U.S. Automobile Industry* (Cambridge, Mass., 1987).

Part II
National models, historical contrasts

4 Employers' collective action in the open-shop era

The Metal Manufacturers' Association of Philadelphia, c. 1903–1933

Howell Harris

INTRODUCTION

Historians have recently argued that much of the 'exceptionalism' of the American industrial-relations system results from the attitudes, behaviour and characteristics of the employing class and business community. Much of their work concentrates on large firms. Given that their principal concern is the development of bureaucratic methods of production and personnel management, this emphasis has been understandable; but perhaps it has also been a little misleading.[1] One cannot safely assume that trends observed in the core economy give an accurate idea of what was happening in smaller firms. This chapter offers a complementary account of the history of employment relations in America's emerging industrial periphery. It examines a group of small and middle-sized metalworking firms through the open-shop era. Historians tell us that their industry was a storm-centre of managerially induced transformations in technology, the labour process and the experience of work. It was certainly one of the most important bastions of employer opposition to unionism.[2] The American labour movement's weakness in the metal trades resulted only in part from the well-publicized resistance of 'center firms' like US Steel, International Harvester or National Cash Register. Failure to expand or preserve membership in middle-sized firms was also crucial to the stagnation of metal-trades unionism in the 1900s and its decay in the 1920s.

National and local employers' associations made a vital contribution to keeping unions out of their member-firms' workshops. Middle-sized and smaller firms formed the bulk of their membership. Such firms employed a large proportion of the industry's labour-force and were comparatively soft targets for craftsmen's organizing drives and bargaining pressures. Big firms could rely on their own resources to meet this challenge. Most metal-trades employers had no such power and confidence. To prevail over their skilled workers' unions they had to adopt strategies of mutual support.[3]

Employer solidarity, or entrepreneurial collectivism, was a general phenomenon of the open-shop era. But we lack detailed accounts of the local and sectoral associations that mobilized the resistance of big capital's lesser brethren and made it effective. This is a case study of one of them, the Metal Manufacturers' Association of Philadelphia (MMA), founded at the outset of the first great nationwide 'open shop' drive in 1903. It flourished throughout the period, its membership increasing from 50 to over 100 firms, their combined work-forces rising from less than 3,000 to almost 30,000 men and women.[4]

THE MMA: ORIGINS AND CONTEXT

The MMA was established in December 1903 by a group of middle-sized foundry operators, local members of the National Founders' Association (NFA). The foundry trade was the most heavily unionized branch of the Philadelphia metalworking industry. Only the very largest local firms had had the strength to keep the Iron Molders' Union (IMU) out of their shops during the great boom of 1898–1902.[5]

Union recognition came with costly strings attached. The IMU pressed for district-wide organization, shorter hours and levelling up of wages and working conditions. It aimed to eliminate scab moulders from the neighbourhood, and to reduce the ability of local founders to contract work out to nearby lower-cost, non-union shops. To further these objectives and protect its members' standards and job security, the IMU tried to throttle the labour supply through strict control of apprenticeship and entry to the trade. Working conditions could then be determined largely by custom and practice and shop-level negotiation. These local developments mirrored what was happening across the nation in other cities, and between employers and other metal-trades unions.[6]

Even the most conservative and respectable union, like the Molders, threatened the profitability of the employers it dealt with. Labour-intensive, seasonal and cyclical industries of small units and often marginal firms were particularly unattracted by the prospect of higher and stickier labour costs and lower productivity. But that was what common American Federation of Labor bargaining objectives threatened to bring about.

Employers met this challenge head on, building on their long history of collective organization. Philadelphia founders had formed unstable local alliances to confront or bargain with their moulders since the 1860s. They established a durable local Foundrymen's Club for the discussion of technical papers and business matters in 1891. In its early years the Club also coordinated its members' resistance to their skilled men's demands, notably for a limit on the number of apprentices and the introduction of moulding machines. It encouraged foundrymen in other production centres to organize too.

In 1896 over 200 firms, most of them members of local associations on the Philadelphia model, met there to form the American Foundrymen's Association. The association concentrated on promoting technical and managerial improvements in this notoriously backward branch of the metalworking industry. But under the leadership of William Pfahler, a Philadelphia stovemaker, it also organized a 'Committee on Defense' to look into the labour problem. This resulted in the setting up in 1898 of the NFA, which was dedicated singlemindedly to protecting its members' interests as employers.[7]

The NFA was patterned after one of America's first nationwide employers' associations, the Stove Founders' National Defense Association, which operated in the most heavily and longest unionized branch of the iron trade. The Defense Association had started out in 1886 as a strikebreaking body, but after five years of costly and indecisive battles with the IMU it abandoned its belligerent approach. It settled down instead to annual national collective bargaining over wages, hours and working conditions, and established permanent joint machinery to settle disputes without strikes. By 1898 this relationship had survived America's worst depression, and seemed to offer employers in the other main branch of the foundry trade – 'gray iron', most of which went into machinery parts – a model to follow.[8]

Defensive employer associations like these existed first and foremost to protect member-firms against strong pressure to accept union demands rather than struggle on alone when they were subjected to the union strategy of the 'strike in detail'. There were two ways of doing this.

The first was by association-wide collective bargaining: all unionized firms in the same labour or product market would then operate under the same basic terms and conditions; the most vulnerable or heavily unionized firms should not be forced to accept worse. And unions would have to organize and finance much larger strikes if they did not settle peaceably, rather than being able to parlay a few victories achieved one at a time into a market-wide advance. So, ideally, the terms resulting from such a settlement would be more moderate, more 'fair' and both sides' behaviour would be modified by their knowledge of the potential scale of industrial conflict if they failed to agree.

Unions had much to gain from this system. They could not win long, large strikes: their members simply would not hold out. Unions were best adapted to sustaining isolated strikes, which they did by giving strike pay, or assisting strikers in finding alternative employment. This support-mechanism broke down very rapidly in the face of widespread and determined employer resistance. Collective bargaining with an employers' association therefore seemed the least risky way of securing a general improvement in members' conditions of employment.[9]

But employer organization also made such resistance more feasible, and therefore more likely. And this was the second, and as things turned out more durable, sort of protection employers' associations gave their members. If all, or even most, of its competitors were struck, a firm would feel less compelled to give in to preserve market share, though perhaps more tempted to do so to steal a march on them. If only one firm or a few were struck, their organization could help them stick it out – especially by providing replacement labour. Employers' associations relied on this strategy and found it quite satisfactory in dealing with sectional strikes by skilled workers whose unions never managed to control the whole labour supply, however hard they tried.

Employers' associations that formed in response to the rise of national craft unions were willing to experiment with union recognition and collective bargaining as ways of protecting their members' interests. In 1899 NFA and IMU negotiators drew up a procedural agreement for the gray-iron trade establishing national recognition for the union and centralized conciliation machinery. Moulders and foundrymen should attempt to settle their differences by direct negotiation, but if they failed there should be no strike or lock-out pending intervention by officers of both organizations.

This 'New York Agreement' covered none of the substantive issues dividing masters and men in the foundry business. Shorter hours, annual national wage bargaining and progress towards national wage uniformity, limitations on piece-work, and the maintenance of apprenticeship, were the IMU's demands. The NFA sought union acceptance of employer sovereignty in the crucial areas of control of entry to the trade via hiring and apprenticeship, the extension of piece-work, the setting of wage rates, and the introduction and manning of moulding machines. These objectives were clearly going to be hard to reconcile.

Nevertheless, the New York Agreement served as the framework for labour relations between the NFA and the approximately 30,000 foundry workers they employed – roughly a quarter of their total labour force – for the next five years. IMU membership increased from 22,000 in 1899 to 52,000, a prewar peak, in 1903. However, from the employers' point of view the New York Agreement had many drawbacks. Its central feature, the conciliation mechanism, did not live up to their expectations. Its failure to provide adequately for local and shop-level bargaining helps account for this. There were 150 local strikes against NFA members while it lasted, a third of them unauthorized, a handful protracted, bloody, costly to both sides, and involving precisely those questions of principle that the national negotiators could not resolve. And the NFA's roughly 500 member-firms generated enough disputes to require about 2,500 joint conciliation meetings. Still, there was no all-out national dispute, and the commitment of both parties to the relationship was sufficiently strong for their leaders to continue trying to compromise their differences until 1904. Meanwhile, agreements were made in a number of important foundry centres which did address the very issues on which no national settlement was reached.[10]

Philadelphia members of the NFA were pioneers in this process, reaching comprehensive one-year written agreements on wages, hours and working conditions with their moulders in 1900 and in each of the next three years. Having to bargain with the IMU brought together local members of the

NFA and non-members who also employed moulders. Their experience with *ad hoc* cooperation persuaded them of the need to complement the NFA's weak system of district organization with a permanent body for the local coordination of employers' interests.[11]

Philadelphia foundrymen followed the lead of another national employers' association, of which a number of them were also members, as they pursued this objective. In 1899 'machinery foundrymen', who operated integrated enterprises with both foundries and machine shops, established the National Metal Trades Association (NMTA) to extend the benefits of association to employers throughout the machine-building and engineering industries, and to contain pressures from the other metalworking craftsmen they employed.

The NMTA's attempt to settle its differences with the International Association of Machinists (IAM) by national collective bargaining was even less successful than the New York Agreement: the 'Murray Hill Agreement' of 1900, concluded after a bitter national strike centred on Chicago, only lasted for one year. It collapsed in good measure because control issues were even more prominent and intractable in the country's machine shops than in its foundries. Machine shops were in the midst of a revolution in technique, while the IAM attempted to limit the impact of change by requiring its members to refuse to operate more than one machine, accept piece-work systems, or instruct 'handymen' – specialized and semi-skilled machine tenders. The NMTA came out of its experiment in negotiation committed to the defence of its members' sovereignty within their own workshops. It drew up a Declaration of Principles that amounted to a wholesale repudiation of collective bargaining and a claim to an unrestricted right to manage.[12]

The NMTA was differently structured than the NFA. The NFA was highly centralized and had a single purpose – dealing with the IMU. The NMTA's union adversaries were more numerous and varied; it grew in part by absorbing local associations; so it devolved much more responsibility to those semi-autonomous bodies, particularly the local recruitment of the diverse skilled strikebreakers they required.

By late 1903 the NMTA was engaged in a national crusade within the employer community for the 'open' (non-union) shop and the right to manage. It had won over the National Association of Manufacturers (NAM) and was campaigning within other employers' associations, like the NFA, to get them to follow the same line. Its national and local officers visited metal-trades employers throughout the industrial north-east, encouraging them to establish new local branches to work with the NMTA and the network of 'Citizens' Alliances' formed by the business classes of small midwestern cities to resist the challenge of labour. Meanwhile NFA and IMU negotiators pursued one another around the country in yet more fruitless efforts to settle their differences.[13]

This was the context in which the NFA's Philadelphia members began to think about abandoning the conciliatory course they had followed for four years. Their own and other local firms' relations with the IMU and less powerful metal-trades unions were increasingly difficult. And when they looked outside their industry they could see the results of strong unionism in other local businesses – the textile industry, Philadelphia's largest, afflicted by a city-wide general strike in 1903; the building trades, large consumers of metal products, riven by jurisdictional disputes between crafts and boycotts of non-union materials; or the Pennsylvania anthracite coalfield, scene of a large and bitter strike in 1902 which shut off Philadelphia metal manufacturers' normal fuel supply.[14]

So they had every reason to conclude 'that a closer relationship of the manufacturing interests [of Philadelphia] was a necessity in order to protect their mutual interests in labor troubles'. But those interests were 'too extensive and diversified to make it practicable to have one association of employers of all industries', along the lines of the burgeoning open-shop associations in smaller, simpler communities. Philadelphia was America's third-largest metropolis. Whether judged by the importance of its manufacturing economy or of its fabricated metal products sector, only New York and Chicago exceeded it.[15]

THE CHARACTER OF MEMBER-FIRMS

The Philadelphia MMA was similar to an NMTA branch in membership, structure and function, but it did not affiliate with the national organization. This was largely because it included foundrymen and machine-shop operators in the same body, and dealt with both the moulders, machinists and other metalworking craftsmen in their employ, thereby ignoring jurisdictional boundaries between the major national employers' associations. This peculiarity resulted from the IMU's prominence in Philadelphia, and the IAM's weakness, which was reflected in the local strength of the NFA and NMTA respectively. The NFA had no branch system to meet its Philadelphia members' desire for local organization; the NMTA had insufficient members to sustain a branch themselves. And the leaders of the MMA included the larger 'machinery foundrymen' who had a foot in both camps. When they established the MMA the fusion of the NFA and NMTA was being actively debated in both bodies. But it did not come to pass: the two associations cooperated closely, but jealously guarded their overlapping pieces of the common turf. The MMA remained as a would-be branch of a kind of united metal-trades employers' association which never emerged.

The MMA was founded at a critical period in the history of American employers' efforts at self-organization. Its development thereafter was further conditioned by the particular character of Philadelphia's industrial economy and business class which provided it with its context and constituency. Philadelphia metal-trades employers had many points of contact with one another. Some had trained in others' firms; many had received their engineering education at the University of Pennsylvania; in maturity they joined the Engineers', Foundrymen's, or Manufacturers' Clubs, or the Union League; and many were active members of the same religious denominations. Philadelphia's was a very homegrown employing community whose members enjoyed many overlapping social connections.

Their firms were tied together by a multitude of business relationships. Metal manufacturers typically did not produce completed goods for a consumer market, but instead supplied raw materials, semi-finished goods, and services to other businesses. The Philadelphia metalworking industry was a metropolis-wide complex of specialized, interrelated firms. Its factories were located in the same neighbourhoods of a sprawling city, particularly along the railway corridors which determined where firms using large quantities of heavy raw materials and fuel could be operated profitably.[16]

But what these manufacturers had most in common was their dependence on the same troublesome skilled labour supply. Businessmen were not all of one mind on religion or politics; they were competitors at the same time as being united by ties of mutual dependence and subcontracting; but MMA members saw a common interest in establishing a dominant position in the labour market. The MMA was to be, and it remained, strictly an employers' association: it eschewed its members' other commercial interests, as these were either so diverse that they offered no basis for common action, or so uncomfortably close as to set them at one another's throats.

The MMA's original members included gray-iron, brass and steel founders, machine-tool makers, and machine-shop operators, making products as diverse as boilers, plumbers' supplies and steam fittings, pumps and valves, industrial power-transmission machinery, gas and electric fixtures, electrical goods, testing machines, and professional and scientific instruments. To manufacture this range of goods, they relied on '[m]achinists, millwrights, blacksmiths, boilermakers, patternmakers, carpenters, structural iron workers, iron shipbuilders, platers, polishers and buffers, brass workers, molders, coremakers, electrical workers, pipe fitters, machine operators, and members of kindred trades, handling iron, brass, steel, or other metals.' Employment of men from those skilled trades was the essential membership criterion.[17]

MMA members were also characterized by their size. None of the original forty members had more than 400 blue-collar employees, and most had considerably fewer (median 52, mean 72 as of 1 January 1905). The foundrymen among them who had the longest tradition of organization were, similarly, small-to-middling enterprises: in 1902, none had employed more than 100 moulders (mean and median: 27). Member-firms were mostly one-factory operations. They were owned and controlled by the same man or men who had established them, and whose name they often bore, or by their descendants. Even if they were incorporated, they were closely held enterprises, prime examples of 'proprietary capitalism'. Management within them was personal, simple and direct. Even in the larger enterprises proprietors and officers were assisted by no more than a few secretaries and clerks, salesmen, designers, superintendents and foremen. There were no elaborate hierarchies. These firms were not well endowed with managerial resources for handling their labour relations or other problems – which was why they saw the advantage in getting together.[18]

Within the Association, firms paid dues, and had votes, in proportion to the number of their blue-collar employees. Membership cost money, but not very much: dues were stable at 10 cents a month per operative for more than twenty years; in real terms, they declined. MMA officers believed in running a lean organization: they kept a close watch on even the smallest expenditures and cut overheads to a minimum.

It was not until the 1920s that fundamental change occurred in the character or size of MMA member-firms. Few branch plants of out-of-town enterprises were members before then, and none of the large local firms which were well able to maintain their non-union status and manage their own employment relations singlehandedly. The latter were also probably deterred from joining by the *per capita* dues. They would have found themselves paying the bulk of the Association's costs, in return for services they did not need because they provided them for themselves already, under their own sole control.

FUNCTIONS AND BEHAVIOUR

> We should not regard the Association as a strike insurance agency, a strike breaking agency, a labor bureau only, nor simply as a body to guard [against] labor legislation. It is all of these combined.
>
> (President Edward L. Langworthy, 1910)[19]

The social and business contacts binding MMA members to one another and the Association should not be undervalued. But their more important reason for joining the Association was their mutual interests, commonly perceived and defended. Proprietors and managers weighed up the costs, risks, difficulties and rewards of membership for their own firms. Joining was a strategic choice which no more than a substantial minority of firms eligible for membership ever took. Membership was conditional, and active membership even more problematical. The organization was sustained because, and only so long as, it delivered worthwhile services not otherwise obtainable. In the Association's first two decades, routine employment management functions were its bread and butter. Members sustained the organization in quiet times to partake of them, and also to keep their strike insurance policy in good condition. In seasons of difficulty it enabled them to tip the scales decisively in their favour in their running conflict with skilled trade unionism.

Member-firms had to coexist with customers and suppliers, as well as with non-local competitors, some of which were notably larger and enjoyed considerable market power. To survive in such an environment, they depended on traditional bulwarks – the tariff, if their products were subject to import pressure; product differentiation; and most of all on a production regime dedicated to cutting labour costs and maximizing its productivity and flexibility without high fixed investment.

Member-firms hoped and discovered that by acting together they could acquire the sort of power in setting the terms of the employment relationship otherwise available only to their larger brethren. For the Philadelphia metalworking industry did include a handful of very large companies – J. G. Brill (streetcars), William Cramp (ships), Niles-Bement-Pond (heavy machine tools), Midvale Steel (ordnance), Henry Disston (saws), all of them counting their work-forces by the thousand; and, at the top of the tree, Baldwin Locomotive, which employed between two and three times as many workmen as all MMA firms put together throughout the prewar years. Their proprietors and executives were leaders in the local business community. They were probably MMA firms' most important local customers. They were 'open shops' before, during, and after the great boom in union membership in 1898–1902. They offered an attractive model for their lesser neighbours to emulate. And their success had set limits on the IMU's and IAM's local strength which meant there was already a significant non-union craft work-force on which the MMA could build and capitalize.

FIGHTING UNIONS

Strikebreaking was not the Association's most expensive or regular activity, but it was undoubtedly the reason why the MMA was formed, and its basic *raison d'être* for its first two decades. Firms which joined it were protected against the strike-in-detail. The Association swiftly became strong enough to be able to boast about never losing a strike for any member with the guts for a fight to the finish. But it did not use the full range of tactics commonly employed by belligerent employers at the time. It did not deal with commercial strikebreaking agencies or private detective firms. It only paid for information once, but it received some free, from dissident union members, and perhaps from friendly national employers' associations. MMA members did not seek injunctions against strikers. Only once did the MMA hire guards to protect strikebreakers at its members' shops, and even then nothing dramatic occurred. Three guards were recruited openly and locally to cover eleven chandelier manufacturers whose 400 workers struck for thirteen weeks in 1910–11 in one of the two largest strikes the Association fought before the war. Metal manufacturers normally relied on the city police to maintain order during strikes, protection which the Association's lobbying helped secure from successive Republican local administrations.[20]

This strangely pacific picture is, in part, a distortion, the result of this case study's focus. For the MMA operated in the protective shadow of the big local open shops; and they showed no such restraint. Philadelphia's metalworking unions were weakened and broken by the opposition of the big employers; the MMA's smaller-scale victories ensured that unions were crippled in their dealings with middle-size employers too, and left with no sure hold on anything much larger than the small jobbing shops right at the periphery of the local industry.

In three pivotal struggles, large local firms broke the unions' repeated attempts to get established or keep a footing within their plants, and cleared a path for MMA members to follow. Bement-Miles (as it then was) wrecked the IMU's ability to sustain a major strike in 1906 by using an injunction to prevent the union's vice-presidents from entering Philadelphia or giving their locals any other assistance. MMA firms fighting the Molders at the same time took advantage of this. In the great Baldwin strikes of 1910, Samuel Vauclain used fair means and foul to prevail, and all that MMA members had to face were comparatively small-scale sympathetic walk-outs. In 1920–1 the IAM concentrated its fire on fighting a mass lock-out at Cramp's shipyard. That battle was lost, and the local Machinists' organization too – the Cramp's strike having the same devastating effect on the membership, funds and morale of the Philadelphia IAM as the great railroad shopcrafts strike of 1922 had on the national union.

These crucial defeats for the IMU and the IAM established the framework within which the MMA operated. MMA members never faced well-resourced strikes from unions controlling the great majority of the local craft labour market. Against their enfeebled opponents they never had to mobilize for open warfare. Other means were adequate.[21] In six of its first ten years the MMA had to deal with strikes involving up to a quarter of its members, and up to a fifth of their operatives, in any one year. Successful labour replacement was essential to winning strikes, and maintaining the loyal resolve of the member firm or firms affected. It could do this far more effectively than the NFA, whose flying squad of scab moulders was simply not large enough for all eventualities. Locally recruited scabs did not have to be transported, housed or paid bonuses. They were no more expensive than ordinary workers, and might even be more productive, as they did not abide by restrictive union practices. They were quite happy to operate moulding machines and to make as much money on straight piece-work as they could.

The MMA's success in strikes depended on its ability to recruit these 'independent workmen'; and this, in turn, depended on the Association's routine work in times of labour peace, which consumed the greatest part of its income even in strike-ridden years. The MMA believed both that the best defence is a good offence, and that in time of peace one should prepare for war. The price of entrepreneurial liberty was eternal vigilance, and the Labor Bureau, with its Secretary, for a long time the MMA's only salaried employee, was the watchman.

MANAGING THE LABOUR MARKET

The labour bureau, an institution Philadelphia copied from other local metal-trades associations, and which it hired an NMTA organizer to establish, played an important role in this and other communities for at least thirty years. And yet these agencies are scarcely noticed in the secondary literature. Published data about labour bureaux consists, for the most part, of the revelations of congressional committees of inquiry into industrial relations in the 1910s and 1930s concentrating on the work of these agencies in overt union-busting. There are few mentions of labour bureaux's less dramatic role, the attempted management of local labour markets.[22]

However, many contemporaries recognized the needs to which labour bureaux were one response. They knew only too well the problems of the chaotic, unregulated American labour market. How could employers find workers? By personal contact, personal recommendation by existing workers, personal application at the plant doorway. These were the informal mechanisms by which most workers found jobs, and employers found 'hands' or 'help'. Large-scale employers of immigrant or common labour used fee-for-service private employment bureaux; employers of domestic and white-collar labour turned to other specialized agencies or put advertisements in the press. The state played a minimal role. The Commonwealth of Pennsylvania's free public employment office in Philadelphia was under-funded, inconveniently located, run by ill-paid political hacks and labour-union has-beens, ignored by employers and workers alike. In this respect as in others, Philadelphia's experience was representative.[23]

In the middle of this mess, how were small-to-middling metal manufacturing plants, located in an industrial metropolis with an inadequate and expensive public transport system, supposed to get in touch with workers who lived a comparatively long way from their work? And not just with any sort of common labour they could recruit at the gate, but with men of proven competence and particular skills? This was one of the special and enduring features of the Philadelphia labour market: there was a rather large proportion of such small plants and of skilled labour well into the twentieth century. The two depended on one another.[24]

Throughout the open-shop era, MMA strategy and behaviour were powerfully affected by the nature of member-firms' product and labour markets and labour processes. In the 1920s, even with workers disorganized, and considerable general unemployment, shortages of skilled men gave MMA members a continuing reason for common action to solve manpower problems. Even much larger companies such as General Electric and Westinghouse depended on skilled labour to build heavy capital goods at their Philadelphia plants. MMA member-firms' labour policies were dedicated, not to deskilling in any meaningful sense, but to trying to maintain an ample supply of skilled workers, while rigging the market, cheapening their price and increasing their flexibility by destroying workers' collective attempts to share in determining the rules under which they worked.[25]

Firms producing small batches or specially commissioned single units of relatively expensive capital goods for customers more sensitive to quality, design and prompt delivery than to price *per se*, faced with widely fluctuating overall demand and highly specific customer requirements, had little choice other than to maintain production processes relying on skilled, flexible labour. The skilled man could be a substitute for the capital and management resources such firms often lacked: an all-round machinist could turn a general-purpose machine tool to a variety of tasks; a trained moulder could produce almost anything in cast metal weighing from ounces to tons; and you could hire the man when you needed, and let him go when you did not.

But when there was work pouring into the shops, as in 1898–1902, or the first part of 1907, or 1916–19, you had to be able to find your man, on pain of losing business. Where could you go? You could poach skilled men from other local firms, thereby increasing wage rates and turnover; you could rely on your foreman – generally a skilled man himself – with his contacts in the craft community; or you could turn to the unions' business agents and their offices, which served as informal employment exchanges, telling unemployed local skilled men, or sojourners and tramping artisans, where they could find work in 'fair' shops (i.e., under union conditions). This placement service was a valued one – a selling-point of a union like the IMU to the employers with whom it dealt, and even more of an advantage to skilled men over their unskilled brethren, who had no such assistance in the task of finding their way around the labour market.

If the MMA was to break the union stranglehold on the loyalties of its skilled workers – an essential precondition to being able successfully to withdraw recognition from their unions and cease bargaining with them – it had to offer member firms an alternative, and better, source of 'help', and skilled workers a better way of getting in touch with job opportunities. This was what the Labor Bureau provided – a centrally located office for one-stop job shopping for skilled metal tradesmen; a courteous reception; no fees to either side – firms got the service as part of their return on their MMA dues; no obligation – the bureau only recommended a man to a firm, the foreman, superintendent or proprietor still did the actual hiring; and no discrimination.

Or at least, not much. Other labour bureaux might maintain a black list, but in a formal sense Philadelphia's never did. This was because the MMA included both non-union shops, where no activist was tolerated, and shops granting unions informal recognition. The IMU was by no means eliminated from the Philadelphia foundry trade, the core of the MMA's membership, even after the Association won the upper hand as a result of large strikes in 1904 and 1905–6.[26]

Accordingly, the MMA had to cater for a membership diverse not just in the range of skilled men they employed, but in their ability to minimize or ignore the union presence in their work-forces. It would warn firms who wanted to maintain non-union conditions not to hire too many 'card men' – i.e., passive unionists who retained their membership even though they were willing to accept work in non-union shops; it would attempt to send 'card men' to union shops, and 'independent workmen' to the rest; it would warn firms not to hire named activists and make it clear that if they found themselves in trouble because of ignoring the warning, they would have to look after themselves. But this warning would not guarantee that the 'agitator' would be fired.

Thus the MMA was not absolutely anti-union. It aimed to maintain its members' independence in labour-relations matters, and that degree of employer autonomy could result in a pragmatic decision to get along with the union at the workshop level. What the MMA would not tolerate was its members' entering into any formal agreement and accepting 'union dictation'; and it was equally determined to atomize labour relations and get away from the era of centralized recognition and bargaining.

Its ideal was the individual employer dealing with independent workmen, but if he chose to deal with them through a shop committee or business agent that was more or less his affair. However, despite repeated union approaches and entreaties, it would neither recognize nor negotiate with unions itself. It was very careful, in encouraging its members to make coordinated wage-movements in line with market pressures, to avoid even the appearance of a concerted response to union demands.

So in the case of the Philadelphia MMA, it seems that the common rhetoric of the open-shop employer – that his workers were free to join, or not to join a union, as they saw fit, but he would take no notice of that decision when he hired them and would not let his employment practices be governed by them – better reflected reality than in other contemporary settings. Indeed, the larger Philadelphia metal-trades firms which claimed to be open shops better fit the realistic contemporary definition – they were open only to non- or undiscovered and inactive unionists. The MMA's membership's behaviour was more moderate than that. Their aim was to alter the balance in their relations with skilled workers, not necessarily to eliminate unions entirely.[27]

The Labor Bureau's usefulness went beyond its undermining of unions. Association members were protected, to some degree, even against the harmful consequences of the resulting 'free' labour market. To the extent that they hired through the Bureau, they were inhibited from hiring skilled men from one another, a practice which, in rush times, gave scarce manpower a real advantage. When they let a man go – as an adjustment to changing demand, rather than as a disciplinary measure – they had somewhere to send him, some hope that his skills would not be lost to the local labour market. When they needed men, they could call both on informal enterprise-specific labour pools and, if that failed, on the Association's central register. They were creating an Association-wide approximation to an internal labour market for the benefit of members who could not possibly have built their own at the level of the individual firm.

With the breakdown of traditional apprenticeship, and given the inadequacy of formal training provision, this imperfect labour market for skilled men even served as a way of organizing the process of 'picking up a trade'. Foremen encouraged purposeful movement from one shop to another, until men acquired the all-around experience local metal-trades employers valued. A man's employment record with the MMA turned into a sort of certificate of competence, or at least proof of experience. An employer did not have to rely entirely on trying the man out – an expensive, chancy business.

The MMA's open-shop campaign was neither a crusade nor a conspiracy. It was a very deliberate defensive strategy, conceived during a boom, but only introduced once the return of significant unemployment made it practicable. Its success depended, not on crude belligerency, but on the Labor Bureau's routine activity of compiling an ever-growing card-file with details of men who worked, or had at any time worked, for its member firms. It knew their track-record; knew what work they could do; cultivated their goodwill by helping them to find regular jobs, and so could turn to them when an emergency occurred. On occasion scabs had to be recruited from out of town, but there were usually ample local supplies. And once Philadelphia acquired the reputation of being a predominantly non-union town, it became a 'refuge for no-card men from other troubled cities'.[28]

The Labor Bureau's ability to recruit local 'independent workmen' as strikebreakers depended on its success in helping make the MMA's rhetoric of the mutuality of interests between masters and men credible to the latter. All that skilled men were offered by the Bureau was some reduction in the costs and hassle of job search, and perhaps in frictional unemployment too, but in early twentieth-century Philadelphia no other institution, public or private, offered anything better.

Philadelphia's skilled workmen had it demonstrated to them that the costs of union membership were high, and might include local unemployability for activists; and that the benefits were few. They seem to have become reconciled, to would-be organizers' distress, to the new regime of employer sovereignty.

That sovereignty did not necessarily entail revolutions in the experience of labour within the workshop. Philadelphia was the home of Frederick W. Taylor, and there were some notable 'scientifically managed' firms within the MMA's membership; but for the most part they were traditional, undynamic enterprises, content or constrained to continue to depend on skilled men paid by day-work or simple piece-work, and paid rather less than their fellows in other large cities, well into the 1920s.[29]

Why did skilled men put up with this? Any explanation must be speculative, but Philadelphia was also a city with low living costs. It had cheaper and better working-class housing, more of it owner-occupied, than any other manufacturing metropolis. It offered skilled workers a large choice of workplaces, which meant some security against prolonged un-employment. And the behaviour of its employers, while authoritarian, was also somewhat paternalistic. Most firms contained cores of long-service skilled workers; some encouraged father-to-son succession. Social stability within the working class neighbourhood and within the proprietary firm perhaps helps to explain the quiescence of the skilled work-force, and perhaps the Labor Bureau, by organizing the labour market, helped achieve this result.[30]

Year in, year out, the Bureau continued its work. Member-firms supplied data on their work-forces when they joined, and were required to keep it updated, whether they hired through the Association or not. When a man was laid off, discharged or quit, they were required to report the fact and the reasons. Non-members cooperated by providing data on men who left their employ and registered with the Bureau. So the card-file grew: after ten years, for example, even though MMA firms only employed about 7,000 men, the Association had details of 35,000, more than half the local metal-trades work-force. Men who applied for work at the Bureau themselves were another source of data, which could be cross-checked with the card-file or with their previous employer.

When a member-firm wanted to hire workers, it could send a requisition to the Secretary for so many men with such-and-such skills, and be reasonably confident of receiving what it wanted. In the Bureau's first nine months of operation, more than 5,000 men registered for work, almost 3,000 references were investigated (unskilled men, revealingly, were not checked on), nearly 2,000 were sent for member-firms to look over, and roughly 1,000 hired, about three-quarters of them skilled men, especially machinists, moulders, polishers and buffers.[31]

The only real obstacle to the Bureau's work came, not from the official union boycott, which was predictable, long-lasting, and ineffective, but from the non-cooperation of MMA members themselves. Given that they paid dues in proportion to the size of their work-forces, they had an interest in under-reporting, and there was no way of checking up on them; given that few had even the rudiments of bureaucratized employment records and procedures themselves, they were understandably reluctant to work with the Association's. Most hiring was still done direct, at the shop door; it was the foremen's responsibility, and it was the devil's own job to get them to report the details to the Bureau. The Secretary had an official commitment to building up his dossiers, a strategic vision of their purpose and practical experience of their usefulness. To members' foremen it was all a lot of unecessary paperwork – until, that is, they needed strike replacements, or were short of workmen to cope with a boom, at which time they became insistent customers critical of any delay in meeting their needs.

So the commonest items in the MMA's annual reports to members were two themes in discordant counterpoint, the upbeat statistics on the Labor Bureau's operations and the plea to members to get their foremen to behave. This problem was aired almost annually, but never solved, because it was the very nature of the Association and of its member-firms that made it insoluble.

For the Association was a voluntary body. If its members did not cooperate, there was no disciplinary sanction short of expulsion, which was reserved for the heinous crime of accepting a 'closed-shop contract' as the price of ending a strike they did not have the funds or the stomach to continue. And their firms were small-to-middling, informally managed affairs. That was why they were members in the first place, and also why it could never be more than partly successful in its constant efforts to get them to accept some bureaucratic controls over their employment procedures.

Nevertheless, the Bureau did a good enough job of meeting members' particular needs for skilled men to persuade firms of the value of Association membership, even in years of high unemployment and labour peace; and it developed sufficiently close and wide contacts with Philadelphia's skilled metal-tradesmen to be able to recruit strikebreakers from among them in times of trouble. It built up reserves of goodwill in both camps on which it could draw.

THE MMA: ESTABLISHMENT AND CONSOLIDATION

The MMA began its work in the early Spring of 1904. It met its first big challenge that summer when the IMU struck the works of its president. That strike was won, with some help from the NFA's flying squad. The moulders were beaten, and piece-work established, but this was only the opening round in a decade-long struggle between the two organizations. Business conditions improved in 1905, and again the MMA's major foundry operators – all NFA members – had to confront their skilled men's demands for wage increases. A bitter strike, lasting almost a year, was fought to a successful conclusion: no MMA firms conceded. The NFA assisted once more, and the Labor Bureau on this occasion had to go out of town to look for replacement workers, as well as to encourage struck firms to hire more 'handymen' and apprentices. The much less well organized Machinists struck two firms in 1905 and 1906, and were similarly defeated.

However, what really enabled the MMA to win and keep the upper hand was not so much its success in these early encounters – though it claimed they had a considerable 'moral effect' on other craftsmen in the city – but the recession which struck in the late summer of 1907. Member-firms' markets slumped, and unemployment soared. MMA firms laid off almost half their men, but they did not withdraw from membership. Unemployed union members turned to the Labor Bureau in their search for jobs. Resistance to the MMA crumbled. It enjoyed three strike-free years, and never again had to use the services of national employers' associations or recruit strike-breakers beyond the locality.

The MMA did not drop its guard even after the immediate union threat its members faced receded. Philadelphia remained, in some respects, a 'union town', to which the AFL devoted limited organizational resources. And the AFL increased its political activity at the state and federal levels to compensate for its general bargaining weakness. The Pennsylvania labour movement, strengthened by the ability of its most numerous and geographically concentrated bloc, coalminers, to return sympathetic state legislators, looked to Harrisburg for tighter employers' liability laws, child-labour laws, control over women's working hours, and stricter factory inspection; and the Commonwealth government responded.

So too did the MMA and other employers' associations within the state: these measures threatened to increase their labour costs, decrease labour supply and reduce their managerial freedom. Foundry operators, for example, would no longer be able to employ boys on dangerous operations. This threat of legislation in workers' interests was sufficient stimulus to get the MMA to coordinate employers' resistance to a tougher employers' liability law in 1907, and to affiliate *en bloc* with the Pennsylvania Manufacturers' Association (PMA) in 1911, two years after the latter's founding.

The MMA heartily endorsed the PMA's object of 'prevent[ing], as far as possible, vicious, unfair, and unwarranted legislation . . . affecting the employment of labour'. It made up one-eighth of the PMA's membership, and shared in its lobbying which helped ensure that Pennsylvania remained a state with rather weak labour laws, and that the new Department of Labor and Industry accommodated employers' interests in drafting and enforcing occupational health and safety legislation. The MMA bought its members their share of this political protection at a reduced group rate, just as it arranged their liability insurance at a discount, at first with a commercial firm, and later with the insurance offshoot of the PMA itself.[32]

In the years before the First World War the MMA was looking cautiously beyond the boundaries of the Philadelphia labour market, but only because what happened outside threatened to raise its members' labour costs and restrict their freedom as employers. In political action as in other fields, the MMA, like its members, was self-interested and tight-fisted. There was little that was enlightened about its conservatism as it resisted the high tide of 'Progressivism'.

Between 1904 and 1916 the MMA operated largely as its founders had originally envisaged, with little change or development. Its membership hovered around the 50 mark, employing more than 6000 blue-collar workers at the peak of the boom in 1907, and about half that number at the end of the 1904–5, 1907–8, and 1914–15 contractions. More firms joined than left on the upswing of the business cycle, and more firms quit than joined –

because of bankruptcy, retrenchment, or a simple realization that unemployment was sufficient strike insurance – during the downswing.

The Labor Bureau's pattern of operation became settled, its strike-breaking techniques refined to a humdrum routine occasionally deployed. The MMA looked after its own, and contacts with the NFA and NMTA atrophied. New functions, like lobbying, were only added when change in the outside environment required. The MMA took no initiatives: it confined itself to responding to threats to its members' freedom to govern their relations with their work-people.

And it was very successful. It helped its members with their problems, and they sustained it. It had difficulty winning their full cooperation with its work, and it had its 'free rider' problem like any voluntary organization: other manufacturers benefited by its opposition to local skilled metal-trades' unions, and its aggressive lobbying, without having to pay their share of the costs. But the MMA had become 'the largest, strongest and most valuable association of metal manufacturers in any city'. For the lowest dues in the country it had helped turn Philadelphia into 'scab city', the paradise of the 'independent workman'.[33]

1916–1920: RIDING THE STORM

The First World War brought the MMA its greatest challenge: after the 1914–15 recession, employment in the local metal trades soared, as Philadelphia turned into America's most important munitions and shipbuilding centre. Small local firms shared in this boom as subcontractors, but they had to compete for scarce labour with new and expanding shipyards and munitions plants, some of them run by out-of-town companies willing to pay top dollar for labour and unconcerned about the effect on their new neighbours with shallower pockets.[34]

The increasing volume of government work further disturbed established local employment practices. Statutory provisions in federal contracts required firms to introduce the eight-hour day, which did not mean cutting hours, at least in the short term, but paying overtime, and further increasing labour costs. The war would not last long, but employers feared its legacy might prove more enduring, and hinder their return to competitiveness thereafter.

The war also threatened the area's metalworking industry's open-shop status. In 1917–19 firms came under pressure from the armaments-procurement agencies and federal dispute adjusters – the permanent representatives of the Department of Labor's Conciliation Service, established 1913, and the temporary, but much more powerful, National War Labor Board of 1918–19 – to recognize unions as one way of stabilizing industrial relations in war industries.[35]

The challenge of the eight-hour day came to a head in 1916, and the threat came not from the familiar quarter – the IMU – but from a newly important adversary, the IAM. Moulders' numbers, like their trade, were in decline. Machinists' numbers, in contrast, were booming, and the broadly based IAM was a formidable foe. It determined to use the war boom as a chance in a lifetime of organizing Philadelphia, and the drive for the eight-hour day as its rallying-cry.[36]

The MMA fought back. It coordinated the opposition of all large metalworking employers of the lower Delaware Valley. Its tactics were straightforward: an oversupply of labour was attracted to Philadelphia by the advertisements and recruiting agents of the large firms; and the MMA provided its members with the usual strike replacements, as well as telling employees through advertisements in the local papers that their employers would not, and could not, give in on the principle of shorter hours. Non-members joined with the MMA to pay for that campaign.

Not all MMA firms held out for the nine-hour day. By 1917 those holding federal contracts found it hard to resist government pressure, and in any case, why should they bother, if the contract was cost-plus? Still, the IAM's hopes of winning an eight-hour standard with its own strength, and turning victories into a golden organizational opportunity, were disappointed.

The MMA, instead, went from strength to strength: firms experiencing difficulties turned to it for aid, were sometimes helped 'for the good of the cause' even if non-members, and were persuaded to join. Meanwhile existing members' payrolls grew. So the MMA's membership list rose from 45 in 1915 to 77 in 1920, and their blue-collar work-force from 3,200 at the pit of the depression to 11,500 at the peak of the postwar boom.

In these years the MMA experienced growth without much change – in the character of its membership, in the personnel of its leadership, in the range or purposes of its activities. 1916 was its busiest strikebreaking year ever: two-thirds of members, employing two-thirds of the total MMA work-force, were affected by strikes, and given help. The next four years were much quieter, but the MMA found other uses for its growing income and resources.

The professional staff was increased, and their salaries raised to compensate for inflation. Their duties changed too. The Labor Bureau was made temporarily redundant by the policies of the wartime state, which established the United States Employment Service as an aid to labour mobilization, and finally as a curb on job mobility. By 1918 the Service legally monopolized the business of hiring common labour, and filling employers' requisitions; it offered skilled men another way of finding jobs; and it would not supply replacements in a strike situation. The Labor Bureau, in any case, thrived when labour was in surplus; from 1916 to 1920 the shoe was on the other foot.

The MMA's Secretary and Labor Bureau did new things rather than shut up shop. They began collecting data, regularly and systematically, from members and cooperative non-members alike, about rates of pay for the many categories of labour in the Philadelphia market. Their aim was to give members an advantage by being able to compare their rates with their competitors'. This would give members the opportunity to bring their wages into line with market norms as a way of minimizing organizational opportunities for trades unions or, more significantly, reducing the impact of skill shortages and turnover upon themselves. If MMA members still had difficulty recruiting or holding labour, at least they would know why, even if they could not afford, or were disinclined, to take remedial action.

The surprising thing about the war period is how little it altered the MMA and its members, not how much. This is despite the fact that in 1918–19 they had to face an even greater challenge than the IAM. National War Labor Board (NWLB) investigators and mediators intervened in local strikes at the unions' behest whether the employers agreed or not. The MMA's strategy of dealing with the NWLB was simple – stonewalling delay. The war, and the NWLB's powers, would not last forever; and of course, they did not, departing in the fall of 1918 without having compelled a single MMA firm to recognize and bargain with the unions they confronted.

There is one exception to this picture of strange changelessness. What the war did bring to the Philadelphia metal trades were new firms, and within them new kinds of manager. Major electrical manufacturers General Electric and Westinghouse, leaders in all the new techniques of man-management, located giant factories in Philadelphia. And some large local firms began to acquire 'employment' or 'personnel' managers, to bureaucratize their internal employment procedures, and to form associations of their own for comparing experience of how the new systems worked, with which the MMA cooperated.[37]

These progressive firms wanted more information about the metropolitan labour market than they could supply just by themselves, and had a more sophisticated strategy than most MMA members. They wanted more than just an oversupplied market full of skilled but relatively cheap workers prepared to work long hours under conditions employers dictated.

They were not much interested in securing strike replacements – especially after the local metal-trades unions were emasculated by the 1920–1 recession and employer offensives from which they did not recover. They were preoccupied instead with new problems – turnover, its definition, measurement, and reduction; morale; and how to gauge the effectiveness of the new personnel programmes they operated. Larger firms were creating their own internal labour markets, which involved paying the best rates in the Philadelphia area for the classes of labour they wanted to recruit, in order to give themselves the pick of the bunch. To operate such a community wage policy, one had to know the going rate. And the war had stimulated the MMA to turn itself into a provider of exactly this information.

As a result, if the war period was one of growth without substantial immediate change for the MMA, the 1920s saw a transformation in the size and character of the organization's member-firms, in the personnel and outlook of its leadership, and in the functions it discharged. This transformation was a response both to the opportunity provided by changes in the Association's actual and potential constituency, and to a crisis within the organization itself.

CHANGE AND GROWTH

The crisis occurred for several reasons. Philadelphia's traditional businesses, especially transportation equipment and steam-engine manufacture, and their associated machine-tool builders and suppliers, missed out on the prosperity of the 1920s. The city had specialized for too long in industries with a great past but no future; its firms were well adapted for custom and batch production, not the increasingly standardized and mass production which better suited the American market of the 1920s; and it was not directly involved in automobile manufacturing, the big growth area.

MMA firms went bankrupt or, on their principals' death or retirement, just folded up. Firms that lingered on, particularly in the declining foundry sector, could not see the point of investing in new equipment or in the creation of another generation of skilled workers. Officers who had led the MMA since its foundation withdrew.[38]

The MMA's *raison d'être* became less compelling. If there is no labour-union threat, why maintain a strikebreaking agency? With no progressive legislation emanating from Harrisburg, why maintain political vigilance?

The MMA could have succumbed to these challenges, as well as to the more obvious problems posed by a decline in revenues as its members' work-forces fell from 11,500 to just 7,000 in the 1920–1 recession. At the same time, operating expenditures remained high. The MMA had emerged from the fat years of 1916–19 with a larger professional and office staff, better paid and equipped, than ever. Through the early 1920s the MMA operated at a loss. In the short term, it survived by liquidating surpluses invested in the good years; but in the long run it needed new leaders, new purposes and new members.

The new leaders were recruited largely from a particular group within the MMA, entrepreneurial members of the Quaker subculture. They were well-educated men with a mass of business and personal contacts among themselves, ideally placed to mount a coup within a voluntary association with a largely passive membership. They volunteered for office, supported one another in packing committees and had some notion of what their association could do that would be relevant to members' changing needs.

These entrepreneurs' firms, while small, were dynamic and innovative, making products with high added value to occupy market niches secured, often by patent, against competition. They operated with long time-horizons, as research-and-development-intensive firms must. They had comparatively large white-collar staffs. And they were in the forefront of the personnel-management movement. This was not just because they realized their dependence on highly skilled workers whom they wished to attract, and hold – the president of one firm reported a fifteen-year learning curve for instrument mechanics – but because they responded to other than strictly economic imperatives.

These Friends were members of a religious denomination with strong commitments to egalitarian and non-coercive interpersonal relations. They lived their beliefs, so they did not treat their workers just as 'hands', subordinates, or costly, troublesome factors of production. The Society of Friends was an international religious community, so these men were not just parochial Philadelphians like most MMA firms' executives – they were instead personally acquainted with the British Quaker entrepreneurs, notably the Rowntrees and Cadburys, whose pioneering activities entitle the early twentieth century to be called the Chocolate Age of British personnel management. Their opposition to the war effort in 1916–19 had forced them to re-examine, and confirm, their convictions, and to strengthen the bonds between themselves by establishing and running Quaker war-relief charities. So they were ideally suited to the task of working together to give their employers' association new life.[39]

These were the men who took over an MMA in the doldrums of the early 1920s. They were prepared to give it their time; they had the respect of the local business community; and they had valuable connections outside of it. They had the assistance of the MMA's full-time staff, in particular its secretary, whose career was tied up with the organization's survival and success. They decided, rather than retrenching, to maintain and even add to its range of activities, in order to attract new members; and they got rid of the last vestiges of crude anti-unionism in the MMA's behaviour. In any case, they had no strikes to fight, which made it easier for them to keep their hands clean and still provide useful member-services.

What did the revamped MMA do? It improved and extended the Labor Bureau's work as a job-filling agency, useful to members and their employees alike in a time of increasing short-term fluctuations in demand for labour against a background of chronic decline in some traditional metalworking sectors while others boomed. It added to the wage data surveys. And it entered new fields, particularly training.

The end of large-scale European immigration in the 1920s dried up a traditionally important source of skilled men. Small-to-middling-sized firms were hardly capable of recreating their own skilled labour force. But the Association could try, and not be bothered by the calculation that time and money spent on training might be wasted as men migrated from firm to firm once trained. Instead, the MMA was resupplying the whole local labour market on which all its members depended; and as a lobbying group it was sufficiently influential to transfer some of the burdens of training from the individual industrialist to the taxpayer, in the shape of the City and State (and even Federal) education budgets. Machinists and foremen were the chief products of this exercise.

Finally, the MMA coordinated joint research into the effectiveness of personnel programmes and the workings of the local labour market, which the University of Pennsylvania's Department of Industrial Research carried out for participating firms. MMA firms supplied researchers with access and data, the University and the Rockefeller Foundation paid the bills.[40]

What all these activities had in common was that they looked towards the more rational management of individual firms' industrial relations, the creation of data bases for improved decision-making, and the development of an association-wide personnel management and human-resources programme in which small firms could participate without even having to pay a proportionate share of the cost.

The revitalized MMA suited the needs and style of the new firms locating and growing in the Philadelphia area in the war and postwar years. The MMA's progressive officers and small but competent staff spoke the language of their personnel managers and shared their commitment to the bureaucratization of employment management. The only obstacle to persuading those larger firms to take up membership in the Association was the old problem of the Association's dues. This was solved by offering reduced rates to employers of over 500, over 1000 and female labour, thus inducing General Electric, Westinghouse, the Atwater Kent radio manufacturing company and other big firms to join. The MMA was transformed: by 1925 less than one-tenth of the 86 member-firms employed more than half the total blue-collar work-force, which at almost 11,000 was not far short of the pre-recession peak; and Quaker activists and professional executives dominated the organization.

For the new members, the MMA was mostly a research and data collection agency. For the traditional type of member-firm, still numerically predominant, the MMA was little more than a highly-effective employment agent, a supplier of skilled men and a meeting-place. But both parties seemed content with the deal. And the MMA prospered, until in the last quarter of 1929 its 113 member-firms reported 28,472 operatives, an increase of 28 per cent over the previous year, four times more than in 1921, and the largest proportion of the whole local metal-trades labour force ever.

But pride comes before a fall. The oceans of self-congratulation at the Association's 25th Anniversary dinner soon turned sour. The non-union employment system the MMA had so carefully constructed and maintained could not withstand the Great Depression.

Bankruptcy and retrenchment reduced its list of members. The economic whirlwind blew two-thirds of their fall 1929 work-force into the ranks of the jobless by 1932, while many of the others only worked short time. The MMA shed staff, curtailed activities, adapted to a new environment and survived. As late as 1935 no member-firms had formal union agreements, but the resurrection of the labour movement and the intervention of the New Deal state soon changed all that. The Labor Bureau closed its doors in 1937. And the MMA concentrated instead on supplying individual members with the information, counsel and labour-market data they needed to operate effectively in the collective bargaining era. Though they bargained with unions as separate plants or firms – normal in the organized sector of the American metalworking industry since the New Deal – they were not on their own.

The MMA adapted once again to changing needs, changing times. Its successor organization, the Manufacturers' Association of the Delaware Valley, formed in the 1950s from a merger of the MMA with an equally old employers' association active in the Philadelphia suburbs, carries on the same activities to this day.[41]

CONCLUSION

The greatest accomplishment of organized labor as I see it is the part it has unwittingly played in forcing into being many organizations of employers. Born primarily of the need for self-defense, and concerned in their earlier years mainly with this, these associations, of which ours is typical, have been the real pioneers and are to-day the most active agents in furthering in every direction those things which make for Industrial Peace.[42]

One does not have to go all the way with Staunton Bloodgood Peck, MMA president in 1921, to accept the essential historical truth of his remarks. To get employers of labour to advance beyond Adam Smith's 'tacit, but constant and uniform combination' took some external stimulus.

The challenge of labour was the necessary stimulus to the MMA's formation, and the cement that held it together for twenty years, but in its last decade before the Depression and New Deal altered for good the ground-rules under which it worked, it developed in new directions, and for different reasons. We do not know enough about other open-shop associations in the 'New Era' of the 1920s to be able to speak with confidence about whether or to what extent they may have followed the same path. The coincidence in Philadelphia of the University of Pennsylvania's social scientists, the progressive homegrown leadership of the MMA and innovative giant incoming firms, would be hard to replicate elsewhere. But the activities these groups grafted onto the MMA, particularly in the area of training, were nothing more than local applications of programmes developed first in other metal-trades cities, notably Cincinnati, Ohio, under employer association, and particularly NMTA, sponsorship.[43]

What these developments of the 1920s, when trades unionism seemed well down the road to extinction, should tell us, is this; that there could be much more to a union-free employment relations policy, even in the open-shop era, than just strikebreaking.

Moreover, this case study of an employers' association which also covers its period of most active strikebreaking should lead us at least to question received impressions about how typical, and how important to the success of the open-shop movement, employer belligerency, bolstered by state repression, actually was. If the Philadelphia case is at all representative, we should de-emphasize coercion and examine more carefully the contributions to employers' power made by their dominant position in the labour market – a 'natural' dominance on which their organizations capitalized. Labour replacement, not the labour spy or the labour injunction, was the most important way to win strikes.

We should also question recent scholarship which has stressed conflict for control of the 'labour process' as *the* fundamental fact of employment relations in early twentieth-century manufacturing. In Philadelphia, at least, struggles between proprietors and employees were much more obviously about control of the labour market. Victory in that arena had to precede an employer's ability to revolutionize the labour process within his firm, but, paradoxically, by reducing the costs of maintaining an *existing* labour process, it also permitted continuing managerial conservatism. Most Philadelphia firms seem to have pursued this line of least resistance, with the result that, even in the 1930s, their work-forces were anything but homogeneous, their tasks anything but 'de-skilled'.[44]

This close examination of the behaviour of a group of firms of a sort usually neglected, in one industry, in one city, in war and peace, prosperity and depression, and through 'progressive' and 'reactionary' periods in American national politics, challenges the conventional wisdom about the open-shop era. But to account for that era, when American businessmen became able and willing to assert their unilateral authority in the employment relationship, we need to go beyond the bounds of a case study and examine the American experience in a comparative context.

The pattern of American employer behaviour in the nineteenth century which Bonnett detailed was very little different from that which McIvor identifies in his studies of Victorian Britain. This is not surprising – the two economies relied on the same sorts of labour and forms of business organization well into the late nineteenth century; and entrepreneurs and labour leaders on both sides of the Atlantic were well aware of one another's problems and 'solutions'. American employers' experimentation with organization for the purpose of collective bargaining in 1898–1900 resulted to some degree from their imitation of what seemed to be a successful labour relations system in the first industrial nation.[45]

But what the open-shop era, of which Philadelphia's experience is representative, emphasizes, is how rapidly and completely American labour relations diverged from this bargaining model. Around 1900 one can begin to speak of the 'exceptionalism' of the American industrial relations system. In the metal trades, the most successful employer organizations were not those that remained committed to bargaining, but those that turned towards warfare. There was nothing to parallel the decline in the use of strike-breakers McIvor charts; no teleological progress from 'defensive', by way of 'procedural-political', to 'market model' collective relations between employers and unions.

This was not because the idea of collective bargaining lacked influential friends in the United States. The National Civic Federation, representing Labor, Capital and the 'Public Interest', gave it strong support in the early 1900s. The US Industrial Commission of 1900, the Department of Labor after 1913, the US Commission on Industrial Relations of 1913–16 and other bodies of worthies all favoured it. The Wisconsin and Johns Hopkins schools of labour economists were propagandists for it. Progressive journalists supported them. And, of course, the American Federation of Labor itself was officially wedded to the extension of organized relations between unions and businesses. But this weak current of opinion in favour of the 'trade agreement system' among some of the great and the good was not translated into coherent or effective policies designed to foster its growth.

So what was missing in the American context was that subtle but powerful state intervention which, in late Victorian and Edwardian Britain, set limits on employers' conflictual behaviour. In the United States, statute and judge-made law legitimized the free market or contractual models of the wage bargain and employment relationship that underpinned the open-shop movement.

What was also missing was that very moderation in the pursuit or exercise of practical control by managers over workers that Zeitlin and others have found characteristic of British firms in a variety of trades. Haydu has attempted to explain this divergence between the two countries' mechanical-engineering industries chiefly in terms of the comparatively shallow roots and recent growth of craft unionism in the United States, and of the different product markets and technological options American employers confronted.[46]

In general terms, such an explanation is quite plausible. But how can it account for the sharp turn towards the open shop which foundry and machine-shop operators took in Philadelphia at the same time as the perhaps more typically American firms, with their narrow product lines and semi-skilled machine-tending work-forces, of which Haydu writes? The Philadelphia case does not answer the question why American employers' behaviour was so different. Instead, it highlights it, because we are dealing with the same sorts of firms, in similar labour and product markets, that in Britain at the same time were behaving so very differently. So an account that goes no further than a sort of economic and technological determinism cannot be wholly satisfying.

What a study of the American metal trades at the turn of the century – or of other industries which maintained distinctive bargaining regimes there-after – also shows, is that a particular pattern of employer behaviour is not something given, something which can be attributed in any unproblematic way to the peculiarities of a nation's 'culture' or 'history'. For there is no single 'American' pattern: comparisons between regions, industries and firms, or even between the same firms, in the same industries and local contexts, across quite brief spans of time, reveal this quite clearly.

What we are looking at here is the range of business strategies which can result from *choice* – from a decision-making process which is, however, neither wholly 'rational' nor unconstrained. The turn of the century was a moment of openness in the American metal trades: employers were genuinely undecided as to how best to meet unprecedented labour-relations difficulties. They made their decisions in the light of an accumulation of immediate experience, but also within a context of constraints and opportunities. Some of these were the material forces Haydu has identified. But by no means all.

Employers in the metal trades and other industries made their critical choices within a uniquely supportive cultural and political framework. They felt no legal or political inhibitions; their ethos of cost-cutting, maintaining managerial prerogatives, protecting or enforcing the 'independence' of the workman in the labour market, minimizing 'outside' or state intervention, found powerful support well outside their own particular class or interest. American open-shop employers' behaviour was sanctioned by most of the institutions of *the national polity*. The course they chose seemed much more than merely sensible or practicable. It was safe, it was profitable, but it was also right.

NOTES

1 See Sanford M. Jacoby, 'American Exceptionalism Revisited: the Importance of Management', in S. M. Jacoby (ed.), *From Masters to Managers: Historical and Comparative Perspectives on American Employers* (New York, 1991); cf. Jonathan Zeitlin, 'From Labour History to the History of Industrial Relations', *Economic History Review* 40 (1987).
2 e.g. Chris McGuffie, *Working in Metal: Management and Labour in the Metal Industries of Europe and the U.S.A., 1890–1914* (London, 1986); David Montgomery, *The Fall of the House of Labor: The Workplace, the State, and American Labor Activism, 1865–1925* (Cambridge, 1987), esp. chs 4–5.
3 Clarence E. Bonnett, *Employers' Associations in the United States* (New York, 1922) and *History of Employers' Associations in the United States* (New York, 1956); Allen M. Wakstein, 'The Open-Shop Movement, 1919–1933' (Ph.D. thesis, University of Illinois, Urbana, 1963).
4 Unless otherwise indicated, primary sources for this and other statements about the MMA are its surviving papers, hereafter referred to as MMAP, accession no. 44, Urban Archives, Temple University, Philadelphia. These consist of minutes of the executive committee, presidents' and secretaries' reports, financial statements and miscellaneous documents – copies of collective-bargaining agreements, wage data surveys *et al*. They will not be cited in this chapter except where directly quoted.
5 'Your Association – What It Has Done to Improve Industrial Conditions', President's Banquet Address, 9 Mar. 1908, p. 2, MMAP, Ser(ies) II, F(older), 5.
6 Report of business agent George D. Kemp to John P. Frey, *International Molders Journal* 40 (1904), pp. 103–4; 'The Conference Board of Philadelphia

and Vicinity', *International Molders' Journal* 41 (1905), p. 512; manuscript 'History of a Strike June 20 1899' and subsequent shop agreement, North Bros Mfg Co. papers, Hagley Museum and Library, Wilmington, Del.

7　Bonnett, *History of Employers' Associations*, pp. 344, 357, 375, 389, 398, 405–6.

8　John P. Frey and John R. Commons, 'Conciliation in the Stove Industry', *Bulletin of the Bureau of Labor* 12/62 (Jan. 1906), pp. 124–96.

9　Cf. Gerald Friedman, 'Strike Success and Union Ideology: The United States and France, 1880–1914', *Journal of Economic History* 48 (1988), pp. 1–25.

10　See especially Russell Bauder, 'National Collective Bargaining in the Foundry Industry', *American Economic Review* 24 (1934), pp. 462–76; F. W. Hilbert, 'Trade Union Agreements in the Iron Molders' Union', in Jacob H. Hollander and George E. Barnett (eds), *Studies in American Trade Unionism* (London, 1906), pp. 185–220; Margaret L. Stecker, 'The National Founders' Association', *Quarterly Journal of Economics* 30 (1916), pp. 352–86, and 'The Founders, the Molders, and the Molding Machine', *Quarterly Journal of Economics* 32 (1918), pp. 278–308; William Huston Chartener, 'The Molders' and Foundry Workers' Union: A Study of Union Development' (Ph.D. thesis, Harvard University, 1952); Frank T. Stockton, *The International Molders Union of North America* (Baltimore, 1921).

11　National Founders' Association, *Food for Thought* (Detroit, [1903]), pp. 3, 56–60.

12　William Franklin Willoughby, 'Employers' Associations for Dealing with Labor in the United States', *Quarterly Journal of Economics* 20 (1905), pp. 110–50; Bonnett, *Employers' Associations*, ch. 4; Jeffrey Haydu, 'Employers, Unions and American Exceptionalism: A Comparative View', *International Review of Social History* 33 (1988), pp. 25–41; Mark Perlman, *The Machinists: A New Study in American Trade Unionism* (Cambridge, Mass., 1961), pp. 25–7; David Montgomery, 'The Machinists, the Civic Federation, and the Socialist Party', in his *Workers Control in America* (Cambridge, 1979).

13　J. Kirby, Jr, *What Should be the Attitude of Employers and Associations of Employers Toward Labor Unions? Address at the Annual Convention of the NAM* (Dayton, Ohio, Employers' Association, 1 May 1903), for the message; 'Manufacturers' Association of Pittsburgh', *Iron Age* 72/15 (15 Oct. 1903), pp. 25–6, for its conveyance to local associations; 'National Conference With the National Founders' Association', *Iron Molders Union Journal* 39/9 (Sept. 1903), p. 714.

14　'The Philadelphia Machinery Market in 1902', *Iron Age* 71/1 (1 Jan. 1903), pp. 71–2; 'President Plumb's Address', *Iron Age* 72/3 (16 July 1903), pp. 50–1.

15　Secretary's Report, 1907, p. 1, Ser. I, F. 12; Circular Letter, 4 Dec. 1903, Ser. II, F. 11, both in MMAP; US Department of the Interior, Bureau of the Census, *Twelfth Census Reports Vol. VII* (Washington, DC, 1902), pp. ccxxx, ccxxxix.

16　Gladys L. Palmer, *Philadelphia Workers in a Changing Economy* (Philadelphia, 1956), esp. pp. 20, 23–6, 50–1.

17　Article III, Constitution, Ser. I, F. 1, MMAP.

18　Assessment for Quarter Beginning January 1st 1905, Ser. II, F. 30; William S. Hallowell to Philadelphia members of NFA, 12 June 1902, Ser. II, F. 41, both MMAP; 'Factory Cost System of Enterprise Mfg. Company', *Iron Age* 2/11 (17 Sept. 1903), pp. 55–8 and 72/13 (1 Oct. 1903), pp. 45–6, for a description of management at a notable Philadelphia metalworking plant. For the long predominance of 'proprietary capitalism' in another major sector of the Philadelphia economy, see Philip Scranton, *Proprietary Capitalism: The Textile Manufacture at Philadelphia, 1800–1885* (Cambridge 1983), and *Figured Tapestry: Production, Markets and Power in Philadelphia Textiles, 1885–1941* (Cambridge, 1989).

19 President's Report 1910, p. 2. Ser. I, F, 7, MMAP.

20 Secretary's Reports, 1910 and 1911, Ser. I, F. 15 b and c, MMAP.

21 'The Chronicler', *IMJ* 42 (Mar.–June 1906); Fred Fones Wolf, 'Mass Strikes, Corporate Strategies: The Baldwin Locomotive Works and the Philadelphia General Strike of 1910', *Pennsylvania Magazine of History and Biography* 110 (1986), pp. 447–57; *Machinists' Monthly Journal* 33 (February–December 1921).

22 Cf. Thomas Klug, 'Employers' Strategies in the Detroit Labor Market 1900–1929' in Nelson Lichtenstein and Stephen Meyer (eds) *On the Line: Essays in the History of Auto Work* (Champaign-Urbana, Ill. 1989); US Commission on Industrial Relations, *Industrial Relations: Final Report and Testimony, Submitted to Congress by the Commission on Industrial Relations . . .* 64th Congress 1st Session (Washington, DC, 1916), esp. Vols I, III, IV; and US Senate, *Hearings before a Subcommittee of the Committee on Education and Labor*, 75th Congress, 1st Session, Pursuant to S. Res. 266 (74th Congress). A Resolution to Investigate Violations of the Right of Free Speech and Assembly and Interference with the Right of Labor to Organize and Bargain Collectively (Washington, DC, 1937), Pt 3.

23 Dorothea De Schweinitz, *How Workers Find Jobs: A Study of Four Thousand Hosiery Workers in Philadelphia* (Philadelphia, 1932); Joseph H. Willits, *Philadelphia Unemployment: With Special Reference to the Textile Industries* (Philadelphia, 1915). On the national context, see Frances A. Kellor, *Out of Work: A Study of Unemployment* (New York, 1915), and Don D. Lescohier, *The Labor Market* (New York, 1919).

24 Palmer, *Philadelphia Workers in a Changing Economy*; William M. Hench, *Trends in the Size of Industrial Companies in Philadelphia From 1915 through 1930* (Univ. of Pennsylvania Ph.D. thesis, 1938), and Eugene P. Ericksen and William C. Yancey, 'Work and Residence in Industrial Philadelphia', *Journal of Urban History* 5 (1979), pp. 147–78.

25 Mildred Fairchild, 'Skill and Specialization: A Study in the Metal Trades', *Journal of Personnel Research* 9 (1930), pp. 28–71, 128–75.

26 See Ser. II, F. 14–19, MMAP, esp. 'Philadelphia Foundries', typescript, Apr. 1913, F. 14, and 'Foundries Employing Union Men', typescript, 19 Feb. 1918, F. 18.

27 US Commission on Industrial Relations, *Final Report*, Vol. III, pp. 2913 (testimony of Mr Henry Morgan, secretary, MMA), 2891 (testimony of Justus William Schwacke, President, MMA).

28 Report of the Secretary, 1915, p. 1, in Ser. I, F. 17, MMAP.

29 H. Larue Frain, *An Examination of Earnings in Certain Standard Machine-Tool Occupations in Philadelphia* (Philadelphia, 1929).

30 Palmer, *Philadelphia Workers in a Changing Economy*, esp. pp. 12, 29, 53–4; for insights into the local metal-trades work-force particularly, see interview schedules, Philadelphia Labor Market Studies, in the Palmer Papers, Accession no. 585, Urban Archives, Temple University. Box 1 includes occupational histories and comments collected from a sample of some 700 millwrights and machinists in May 1936 – the raw data for Helen Herrmann, *Ten Years of Work Experience of Philadelphia Machinists* (Philadelphia, National Research Project in cooperation with Industrial Research Department, University of Pennsylvania, Report no. P-5, Sept. 1938).

31 Report of the Secretary, Jan. 1905, in Ser. I, F. 13, MMAP.

32 J. Roffe Wike, *The Pennyslvania Manufacturers' Association* (Philadelphia, 1960), p. 29.

33 Report of the President, 15 Dec. 1908, in Ser. I, F 6, MMAP.

34 Philadelphia War History Committee, *Philadelphia in the World War 1914–1919* (New York, 1922), supplemented by records of the US Housing Corporation,

Record Group 3, National Archives of the United States, Washington, DC, especially Box 26, 'Project Books, 1918–1919'.

35 Records of the Federal Mediation and Conciliation Service, Record Group 280, and of the National War Labor Board, 1918–19, Record Group 2, both in the Federal Record Center, Suitland, MD, are invaluable guides to industrial disputes – 1916–21 in particular.

36 *Machinists' Monthly Journal* 28 (1916), reports of business agent Wilson, esp. pp. 496–7, 607.

37 US Bureau of Labor Statistics, 'Proceedings of the Employment Managers Conference, Philadelphia, Pa., April 2d. and 3d., 1917'. *Bulletin* No. 227 (Washington, 1917); Willits, *Philadelphia Unemployment*, pp. 169–70.

38 Anne Bezanson and Robert Gray, *Trends in Foundry Production in the Philadelphia Area* (Philadelphia, 1929), Alfred H. Williams, *Study of the Adequacy of Existing Programs for the Training of Journeymen Molders in the Iron and Steel Foundries of Philadelphia* (Ph.D. thesis, Univ. of Pennsylvania, 1924), and David B. Tyler, *The American Clyde: A History of Iron and Steel Shipbuilding on the Delaware from 1840 to World War I* (Wilmington, 1958), illustrate the process of decline.

39 See my 'War and the Social Order: The First World War and the Liberalisation of American Quakerism' (Wilson Center seminar paper, May 1986), and histories of two leading MMA Quaker companies – C. Elliott Barb, *The Yarway Story: An Adventure in Serving* (Philadelphia, 1958), and William P. Vogel, *Precision, People and Progress: A Business Philosophy at Work* (Philadelphia, 1949).

40 Steven A. Sass, *The Pragmatic Imagination: A History of the Wharton School 1881–1981* (Philadelphia, 1982), chs 6–7, for the Department of Industrial Research.

41 Manufacturers' Association of the Delaware Valley, *Staff Services Activities Member Companies 1985* (Valley Forge, Pa.: The Association, 1985). Wage, salary and benefit surveys, assistance with 'Human Resources Management', a placement service, and manager development training are the chief areas of service – in the 1980s as in the 1920s. Significantly, assistance with labour relations – a relatively minor concern – is confined to the collection and dissemination of data on union contract settlements.

42 Report of the President, 14 Dec. 1921, in Ser. I, F. 9, MMAP.

43 'Training Activities of a Great Industrial Association', *Industry* (15 July 1921), pp. 9–10.

44 Irving L. Horowitz, *The Metal Machining Trades in Philadelphia: An Occupational Study* (Ph.D. thesis, Univ. of Pennsylvania, 1939).

45 Bonnett, *History of Employers' Associations*; Arthur J. McIvor, 'Employers' Organizations and Strikebreaking in Britain, 1880–1914', *International Review of Social History* 29 (1984), pp. 1–33.

46 Haydu, 'Employers, Unions and American Exceptionalism'; Zeitlin, 'Labour History'; Friedman, 'Strike Success and Union Ideology'; L. Griffin, M. E. Wallace and B. E. Rubin, 'Capitalist Resistance to the Organization of Labor Before the New Deal: Why? How? Success?', *American Sociological Review* 51 (1986), pp. 146–67.

5 The 'human factor' and the limits of rationalization
Personnel-management strategies and the rationalization movement in German industry between the wars

Heidrun Homburg

INTRODUCTION

Recent scholarly endeavours to explain the 'peculiarities' of German history, in particular the National Socialist state system have recognized the shortcomings of earlier approaches that stopped historical enquiry at the factory gates. Scholars like George L. Mosse, Michael Geyer, Tim Mason and the East German Jürgen John point to competition, struggle and social darwinism as essential and formative principles of Nazi rule and stress the need for a materialist history that, according to Tim Mason, 'sees that subject in terms of economic forces and institutional power, in terms of social and economic practice and individual behavior (intentions)'.[1] This urge for a materialist history that combines a structural approach with historical analysis of ideas and the decision-making processes of individuals in the realm of 'low' and 'high' politics opens up a new and challenging approach to business history that concentrates on economic practice and social interests, on everyday life experiences and their repercussions on the shaping of macro-politics.

The development and implementation of sophisticated personnel management techniques are particularly appropriate for such an approach. In the final decades of the nineteenth century the full force of the Industrial Revolution struck Germany.[2] The growth of industrial firms, enhanced mechanization and the transformation of work and authority were perceived by contemporaries as dramatic economic changes and social challenges that involved managers and workers alike. On the one hand, expansion of firms, increased competition and protracted mechanization made new and greater demands on managers' professional skills. On the other hand, changes of scale and new and innovative manufacturing and management techniques provoked workers' protest and paved the way for strong socialist trade unions that challenged both the autocratic rule of management and the existing political power-structure. By 1890 legal repression had failed to curtail the socialist labour movement or reduce the workers' orientation towards Marxist concepts of class struggle. Accordingly, the elaboration and implementation of personnel management techniques became a focus for management's economic needs and broader socio-political expectations. These practices reflected management's vision of an 'ideal' worker, and its efforts to obtain social control inside the firm and an adequate societal order outside.

In the following chapter I shall first outline some influential concepts of personnel management and the complex societal functions attributed to it, and show how these guided management's expectations and professional endeavours in this field from the 1890s to the 1930s. I shall then turn to the implementation of these concepts, in particular time studies and psycho-technical aptitude tests in the inter-war period, and analyse the difficulties and obstacles management encountered when it ventured to rationalize the 'human factor' in industry. The study concentrates on a core group of metalworking firms in Berlin and in particular on the Siemens company whose managers had already developed sophisticated personnel management techniques in the first decade of the twentieth century and who pioneered the German rationalization movement after the First World War. Finally, I shall discuss management's reactions to the emerging limits of its power to manage the 'human factor' in industry and society.

CONCEPTS OF PERSONNEL MANAGEMENT: VISIONS AND INTENTIONS

In the 1870s the economist Gustav Schmoller (1838–1917) was the most prominent German intellectual who pointed to management's capacity for social engineering and its social responsibility to restructure industrial and labour relations for the common good. From the 1860s Schmoller was the generally recognized leader of the so-called younger historical school, an organic approach that predominated in German economic reasoning from the late nineteenth to the early twentieth centuries, and he became the most influential academic teacher in Wilhelmine Germany. Schmoller gained an even wider audience and direct political influence as organizer and later president of the *Verein für Socialpolitik*, an association founded in 1872 which dedicated itself to the promotion of social reform as a means of preventing social upheaval through the integration of workers into the existing order.[3]

As Schmoller observed in 1889 general welfare, social peace and economic progress depended to a high degree on the inner structure or constitution, industrial relations and personnel-management strategies of big business. The general aim was to turn the enterprise into a *sittliche Gemeinschaft* (moral community). Schmoller suggested that the means were the creation of well-defined career patterns, internal hierarchies of positions, salaries and wages, and social welfare and workers' councils or other limited forms of worker co-determination.[4]

Schmoller's basic argument, his appeal for enlightened management as a last resort against the spectre of a revolutionary overthrow originated by the modernizing, capitalist enterprise, as well as his optimistic vision of the self-healing capacity of large ever-growing industrial firms, had subsequent parallels. Twenty to thirty years later, Taylorism and Fordism contained essentially the same message.

The American gospel of social engineering through technical and organizational means stressed once again and even more explicitly management's power to manage the 'human factor' in industry and thereby its capacity to establish a new 'harmonious' social order. In Taylor's and Ford's visions, however, management's escape from class confrontation was closely linked to the social possibilities of mechanization and applied engineering sciences.[5] Productivity, expertise and optimization were the declared prerequisites for the materialization of their visions of social harmony inside and outside of the factory. Managers and engineers were summoned to do away with antiquated customs and devote themselves to a new, scientifically based approach to all aspects of production and factory organization. Workers, on the other hand, were urged to rely on management's enlightened techniques as best serving their own ends. The prescribed new mutual relationship of friendly cooperation and the combined innovative efforts of management and labour were to pay off economically for both sides and to change the nature of authority from power over men to the administration of things, thus removing – in the last analysis – the objective basis for class formation and class conflict.

German employers needed no instructions about the positive function of friendly relations between employers and employees for enhanced productivity. Without doubt, they preferred the stable, grateful and submissive worker to the mobile, class-conscious and rebellious one. However, Schmoller's and – particularly after the First World War – Taylor's and Ford's visions that the means to induce industrial as well as social consent were at management's own disposal, were eagerly picked up by important sections of the German business community. Their previous objections to any schematic approach and to the implementation of American concepts of efficiency engineering through improved plant logistics, with its risks of increased unproductive time and overhead costs, persisted. They believed that this ran counter to the particular economic needs of German industry. Nevertheless, they turned to these promising visions as a last resort when confronted with the sobering fact of Germany's defeat and its revolutionary repercussions.[6] Schmoller had paved the way for managerial fantasies of omnipotence. Their later reliance on the American version of social engineering through the pursuit of efficiency represented an updated approach to management's old aims. Their common denominator was the utopian vision that management had unrestrained power to manage (and to rationalize) the 'human factor' on the shop floor and even beyond and that it could create a new harmonious social order. This played an important role in shaping managers' collective expectations, guiding their economic actions, stimulating their professional activities and forming their political attitudes. Certainly, self-delusion is always part of such utopian visions. And it is this tension, the gap between vision and reality as well as its broader impact on management's political attitudes, that is central to the discussion in the following sections of this chapter.

VISION VERSUS REALITY: AN ILLUSION DESTROYED

The extent to which enterprise management could achieve the tasks ascribed to it by Schmoller, Taylorism and Fordism depended on many variables. Not all of them were under the direct control of the firm or could easily be influenced by it. One of these variables was the firm's environment. A case in point from the 1890s was the labour market of the Berlin metalworking firms including the Siemens company, Germany's oldest and one of the world's largest electrical engineering firms.

Environmental challenges and constraints

The Siemens company, founded in 1847, had its headquarters in Berlin until 1945. Siemens was one of many metalworking firms that chose Berlin as a location, attracted by its abundant supply of labour, in particular of skilled and experienced workers. It was preceded by Borsig, Louis Schartzkopff and other locomotive and machine-building firms and followed not only by several highly specialized engineering firms, like Ludwig Loewe & Co., but also – especially from the 1880s – by a number of newcomers in electrical engineering like Allegemeine Elektrizitats Gesellschaft (AEG) and Bergmann. In the course of the nineteenth century Berlin thus developed into one of the most important and dynamic industrial regions in Germany. The local concentration of metalworking firms and their economic growth were reflected in their share in the local labour market. In the late nineteenth century they absorbed one-fifth of the city's industrial labour force, amounting to about 250,000 blue- and white-collar workers in 1882, and to about half a million in 1895. After the turn of the century, the metalworking industries outranked clothing and textiles as the dominant employer. In 1907 metalworking employed 227,000, in 1925 374,000 and in 1939 529,000 persons (including both blue- and white-collar workers), comprising 28, 38 and 45 per cent respectively of Berlin's industrial labour force.[7]

The vast majority of those employed in the metalworking industries – about 80 per cent at the end of the nineteenth century, and roughly 70 per cent in the 1920s and 1930s – were blue-collar workers. Despite the mechanization and standardization of work male workers continued to predominate, and *skilled* male workers formed the backbone of the production process throughout the nineteenth century and the first four decades of the twentieth century (Table 1).

This was equally true for the impressive number of 'giant' enterprises that employed more than a thousand or – in the case of Siemens – even tens of

Table 1 The composition of the labour force in the Berlin metalworking industries 1925–1939[8]

	All Workers	Female	(%)	Male unskilled	(%)	Male skilled and semi-skilled	(%)
1925	310980	68059	(21.9)	70990	(22.8)	171931	(55.3)
1933	119814	29133	(24.3)	8316	(6.9)	82365	(68.7)
1933	122571	30583	(24.9)	15771	(12.9)	76217	(62.2)
1939	401587	107778	(26.8)	78566	(19.6)	215243	(53.6)

Sources: 1925, 1933 and 1939 *Vocational Census*; 1933 *Industrial Census*

thousands of employees. According to the industrial census, there were 53 Berlin metalworking firms in 1925 and 85 firms in 1939 that belonged to this category of 'giants'.[9] Siemens had by this time turned into the most important single employer amongst the 'giants'. At the company's plants in Berlin, Siemens employed 4,400 in 1895, 32,000 in 1907, 40,000 in 1914, 68,000 in 1929 and 80,000 in 1939. AEG, its most serious competitor, employed 42,000 in its Berlin plants in 1914, rising to 60,000 in 1929. In all its German plants it employed 72,000 people in 1939.[10]

The continuing dependence on skilled male workers was partly due to the highly diversified production programme of these 'giants'. Siemens, for instance, was a general contractor for the construction of power stations, planning, coordinating and supervising the work. In addition the company manufactured in its several Berlin plants a wide variety of high- and low-voltage electric appliances. The range of manufactured goods included small and rather standardized items like plugs, switches, wires, cords, cables, and light-bulbs as well as technically more complex goods which because of their complexity or because of changing patterns of demand defied standardization, such as electric motors of various outputs and sizes, transformers, generators, electric fans, pumps, hammers, drills, heaters, telegraphs, telephones, electric watches and electrometers. In the 1920s production became even more diversified as Siemens began to manufacture a growing variety of electric household appliances such as vacuum cleaners, irons, refrigerators, stoves, hair-dryers, washing machines, razors, toasters and so on. This diversification reflected both technological innovations and the company's quest for new customers and markets. Thus the firm's most important clients before the 1880s – the public authorities, the German Post and the German Railways – were supplemented first by industrial clients, and from the 1920s also by individual consumers. Stimulating the demand for production goods as well as for consumer durables became part of the company's marketing strategy.

Technological and product innovation, the scope of the company's production programme and its marketing strategies had important repercussions on the company's structure and its production facilities. Technological breakthroughs in high-voltage engineering, notably in the generation, long-distance transportation and applicability of electric power, from the 1880s pushed the Siemens & Halske Company to expand its production facilities. In 1903 the Nuremberg electrical company Schuckert and Co. was successfully merged with Siemens. The merger was followed by structural innovations. Henceforth the Siemens company comprised two major divisions: Siemens & Halske and Siemens-Schuckert, producing and marketing low- and high-voltage electric appliances, respectively. Following the diversification of the product line and technological innovations in the respective fields of electrical engineering, manufacturing was organized and managed in several plants, the majority of which were located in Berlin. The factory layout and the organization of the work process varied according to the product manufactured, its technical 'maturity' and its prospective sales. Products were continuously subject to fundamental or minor changes arising from the novelty of a particular line, design innovations, changing patterns of demand, changing scale of production, or improvements in the production process. Each plant was shaped by its main products. In the Siemens-Schuckert division: cables and wires, large electric motors, medium-to-small electric motors, large generators and transformers, small switches and insulating materials, high-voltage current switches and control panels and meters predominated. In the Siemens & Halske division the main lines were electric light-bulbs, telegraphs and telephones, all kind of electric measuring and signal devices, broadcasting equipment and radios. The corresponding production technologies ranged from quasi-artisanal to standardized mass manufacturing, while there could be a combination of differently structured shops for each of the components of a given item. Each plant's production programme defined its internal organization.

In varying degrees this pattern was also typical for the other 'giants'. AEG, Bergmann, Ludwig Loewe & Co, Borsig – to name only some of the more prominent Berlin metalworking firms – were also composed of a variety of differently organized workshops, each of them reflecting the changing technical and commercial features of a product and the correspondingly varied manufacturing processes.

The ongoing diversification of the product line, the quest for innovations and the competition for new markets that was typical of the 'giant' metalworking firms in Berlin from the 1890s and in particular after the First World War seems to be the key variable in explaining the gender composition of the blue-collar labour force with its remarkably high proportion of male workers who generally had greater skills than their female colleagues. Innovation, continuous change and experimentation with new products or manufacturing techniques required – at least in the initial stages – an experienced, highly flexible, supportive, and motivated work-force. These features required the sort of skills traditionally confined to the male workers who dominated the metal trades since access to public as well as company vocational training was largely restricted to men. Thus the combination of industry's actual needs for an intelligent worker and the traditional gender-bias of the vocational training system preserved traditional male pre-dominance of the blue-collar work-force (Table 2).

Even the Siemens company, which was seen by contemporaries as a prime example of a modern firm with advanced management techniques con-formed to this rule. In early August 1914 male workers represented roughly two-thirds (66.7 per cent) of its blue-collar workforce, in July 1928 they accounted for 69.3 per cent, and in July 1938 this proportion still reached 65 per cent. This occurred despite the fact that the company's total blue-collar work-force in its Berlin plants had increased remarkably in absolute numbers. In comparison to 1 August 1914 it expanded by 64 per cent by July 1928 and by 72 per cent by July 1938.[12]

Though the data are rather scattered, the statistical material available underlines that the continuing dominance of male workers went along with a preponderance of experienced skilled and semi-skilled workers.[13] In the first half of 1928 41.5 per cent of the Siemens company's male blue-collar work-force employed in Berlin belonged to the category of *Facharbeiter mit höchstwertiger Leistung* (vocationally trained workers with qualitatively highest performance). Accordingly, they were paid the highest wage-grade (class I) out of five categories laid down in the collective agreements on wage and working conditions for the Berlin metalworking industries of 1919/21 which still defined wage-grades within the company (though there had not been a binding collective agreement on the actual wage rates between spring 1924 and summer 1928). In the second half of 1928 – that is, after the trade unions and employers had settled a new general collective agreement for the Berlin metalworking industries – 40 per cent of the Siemens company's male workers were paid the highest hourly wage-grade (class A). Their work was classified under the terms of the new collective agreement as *hoch-qualifizierte Facharbeiten* (highly qualified tasks that require skills). A further 20–30 per cent of the male workers were eligible for the second grade (class II, renamed class B during 1928). Only a minority of 30–40 per cent of the male workers and of the available tasks were rated in classes III and IV (C and D from 1928). A census organized by the trade association of German electrical manufacturers produced comparable data for this branch of industry in general. According to its investigation, the proportion of skilled and semi-skilled workers was 78.5 per cent of the male blue-collar work-force in early summer 1933, and 78.7 per cent in May 1940, of which almost half (45.6 per cent) were classified as skilled workers.[14]

One reason that had attracted metalworking, and in particular electrical engineering firms, to Berlin in the nineteenth century was the supply of skilled and experienced labour offered by the capital's labour market. Their particular labour demand locked them into Berlin in the 1920s and 1930s. The local concentration of metalworking industries in Berlin, their dependence on skilled male workers, the existence of several 'giant' enterprises and of numerous small and medium-sized firms, all of them

Table 2 Distribution of the labour force by industrial branch and percentage of female workers in the Berlin metalworking industry 1925–1939[11]

	Electrical engineering		Machine-building		Metal/iron goods		Mechanical optical industry		Iron-/steel-producing	
	All workers	Female %	All workers	Female %	All workers	Female %	All workers	Female %	All workers	Female %
1925	126220	35	101363	9	58261	20	10197	15	14939	9
1933[1]	103097	35	74491	8	61121	16	9062	15	7855	8
1933[2]	54763	37	31989	9	24727	19	5066	17	3269	10
1939	171908	41	141092	11	61276	27	16032	22	11279	15

Sources: 1925, 1933 and 1939 *Vocational Census*
[1] Employed and unemployed workers   [2] only employed workers

characterized by similar patterns of labour demand, thus created a situation of structural competition for labour, and in particular for experienced male skilled or semi-skilled workers. Inside the greater Berlin area whose highly developed transport infrastructure of commuter trains facilitated labour mobility, the worker did not depend on a single employer. Under 'normal' economic and political conditions he could always hope to find better working conditions when he changed places and employers. Workers could leave one company for better pay or improved conditions in the next. Freedom of movement under these conditions was not only a theoretical notion, but a practical possibility the worker could and did make use of.

The firms' location in Berlin implied further challenges for management. The Berlin workers were not only mobile, intelligent and quick-witted, but also radical. From the 1890s Berlin developed into a stronghold of socialist trade unions. During and after the First World War it became in addition a centre of Communist and other leftist opposition groups. The metalworking industries belonged to the best organized trades. From the beginning of the twentieth century over 60 per cent of the skilled workers adhered to the socialist *Deutscher Metallarbeiter-Verband* (German Union of Metalworkers), an industrial union which was the most powerful German union before and after the First World War.[15] Management's quest for social control thus did not remain uncontested. It had to reckon with a strong political and ideological competitor that pitted the concept of class struggle against visions of social peace through extended managerial prerogatives.

Approaches to modern forms of personnel management: Siemens's dual strategy

The environmental challenges that management confronted in Berlin were structural and political. What strategies did the Siemens managers develop to cope with these challenges and how did these strategies affect the firm's environment? Like the challenges, management's strategies were twofold. On the one hand, it tried to promote the workers' identification with the company; on the other hand, it engaged in an ever-increasing effort to organize employers in the industry and develop a collective response to the workers' demands. In the following discussion, I shall call the first 'internal', the latter the 'external' or 'collectivist' approach.

The first time that the Siemens management consciously adopted this dual strategy was between 1904 and 1906.[16] In 1904 Siemens joined the Berlin metalworking employers' association. The association was founded in 1890 and had tried to impose employer control over the labour market and the individual worker by a compulsory employers' labour exchange and by black lists. The association decided to defend the employers' autocratic position and autonomy inside the firm against the trade unions by general lock-outs as well as by publicity and political channels. Two years later, after a series of important strikes that directly or indirectly involved the company's plants in Berlin through either workers' or employers' collective action, Siemens founded a company union, the so-called *Unterstützungsverein von Arbeitern und Arbeiterinnen der Siemens-Schuckertwerke GmbH und der Siemens & Halske AG Berlin*. The members of this 'yellow union' were to enjoy distinct privileges. They were not laid off in case of strikes or lock-outs and were promised different social benefits if they stayed for several years at the company.

This policy of promoting workers' identification with the company, while aiming at the same time at the fragmentation of labour, proved to be quite successful. Unorganized, unskilled, and semi-skilled male as well as female workers in particular joined the company union, though skilled male workers, the backbone of the production process and of the socialist union, stood apart. Nevertheless, membership reached the quota of 40 per cent of the labour force employed that the employers' association had set as a requirement to exempt a member-firm from its obligation to participate in employers' collective action in cases of labour conflicts or strikes. In spite of these promising early years, however, the company union did not survive the First World War. During the war membership declined rapidly. Because of this development and the changing political environment, its underlying anti-socialist and anti-trade-union attitude became obsolete and the company union became more and more anachronistic. Finally, in November 1918, the Siemens management decided to dissolve it in silence.

Though new means were needed after the war, the company's dual strategy persisted; indeed, both its components became even more elaborate. The process of reorientation was accompanied by a remarkable shift in emphasis. In contrast to the prewar period, the 'collectivist' approach gained in importance, and the firm's individual response declined in importance, although the 'internal' approaches became much more refined than before. The reasons for this paradox were both 'technical' and political.

Discussion of scientific management techniques had started before 1914 but they gathered momentum in the immediate postwar period. Germany's defeat and its economic repercussions increased the general cost-awareness and stressed the importance of personnel policies as a central element for systematic management. As a consequence, management tried for the first time to evaluate precisely the costs of the high rate of labour turnover and to scrutinize its causes and possible remedies. Hence the strategy of promoting workers' identification with the company became part of a general endeavour to adopt and implement the principles of scientific management. Immediately after the war the most significant organizational innovation or structural change (to use the categories developed by Alfred Chandler)[17] in the administration of the Siemens company which indicated the new approach was the establishment of a social-policy department and of an adviser to the board of directors on personnel policy, which were to administer centrally all general questions of personnel management. The practical outcome of this department's endeavour to promote workers' identification with the company was a wide range of new methods to achieve the old aims. The measures that were introduced in the immediate postwar period were: vocational-training scholarships for highly qualified apprentices, preferably sons of the company's blue-collar employees; the publication of a monthly company journal that was mailed to every blue- and white-collar worker; the opening of a sanatorium for workers (another one for salaried employees had existed before the war); the construction of company dwellings; and a variety of other social benefits. In the mid-1920s management launched a formal selection procedure for suggested improvements with monetary rewards for the best suggestions in order to increase work motivation, while company-sponsored social activities after work were promoted and service bonuses were introduced to foster workers' active cooperation. Finally, the company tried to improve the recruitment of foremen by new screening procedures and to promote workers' career aspirations by establishing an internal labour exchange for blue-collar workers.

In contrast to the prewar period, when Siemens had been one of the few large Berlin metalworking enterprises that had founded a company union, these measures – though impressive – were not unusual. The professionalization of management, including personnel management, was a general phenomenon. All the larger metalworking firms in Berlin, including Siemens's main competitors for skilled and experienced male workers like AEG, Bergmann, Telefunken, Ludwig Loewe & Co, Borsig and so on, engaged in the same kind of policies and introduced identical measures. As a result though these measures probably promoted a certain 'company spirit' among the workers, they lost their power of differentiation. They made only a limited contribution to Siemens's need to prevent worker turnover and to promote 'friendly cooperation' with management.

As 'internal' policies did not fully achieve these ends, employers' collective action became more important. For example, in periods of high labour turnover the Berlin metalworking employers' association (*Verband Berliner Metallindustrieller*) used binding agreements not to hire workers for a certain period of time unless they could present a written leaving certificate from their former employer.[18] Three other factors increased the importance of employers' collective action. First, collective bargaining was accepted for the first time by the Berlin metalworking employers' association immediately after the war and later legally enforced by the Reich government as the common institutionalized procedure for the settlement of wage and labour disputes. This demanded a higher level of coherence among the employers in order to resist trade-union demands for better pay and improved working conditions. Second, the adoption and implementation of 'scientific' management techniques demanded closer employer cooperation. The methods of time studies, for example, had to be standardized between enterprises if workers were to be convinced of the claimed 'objectivity' of this procedure of wage determination and if wage differentials between different firms for the same task and consequently labour turnover in pursuit of better pay and disorganized competition between firms were to be avoided. Last but not least, class conflict did not disappear as a result either of elaborate company strategies to promote workers' identification with the company, or of the application of sophisticated techniques of efficiency and social engineering. On the contrary, it can be argued that the war and its aftermath fostered a rise of class tensions that prevailed until the fatal end of the Weimar Republic in 1933.

Siemens's management realized the urgent need for a more sophisticated 'collective' strategy among employers immediately after the war. Siemens's top managers, including the head of the company, Carl Friedrich von Siemens, played a very active part in the Berlin employers' association and in the collective-bargaining process. The company's social-policy department, with a staff numbering between 190 and 326[19], was heavily involved in preparing the statistical data and the drafts for the sessions and in analysing collective agreements on wage and working conditions in other German industrial regions that might serve the Berlin employers' association as reference material.

In addition, Carl Friedrich von Siemens and several other high-ranking Siemens managers and senior engineers argued strongly for a collectivist approach by the German business community to efficiency and social engineering. At the end of and immediately after the war they were actively engaged in the formation of different organizations, first on a regional, then on a national level, that were to promote the ideas and techniques of rationalization. Siemens managers thus played a prominent role in shaping the German rationalization movement and the actual work of its most important branches like the National Board of Industrial Standards (founded in 1917/18), the National Efficiency Board (founded in 1921) and the National Committee for Time Studies and Time Rate Setting (founded in 1924).

The foundation of these national committees, which were all preceded by similar joint ventures among the outstanding Berlin metalworking firms in the immediate aftermath of the war, suggests that these calls for industry co-operation were not totally in vain. But a large gap remained between the far-reaching goals that motivated these top managers to take the lead in the German rationalization movement and the actual work of these committees. A case in point was the approach to time studies and to psychotechnical aptitude tests, two areas that aimed to achieve social goals through efficiency engineering.

Testing the vision of cooperation in industry: time studies and the setting of time rates

At the end of the war, preparation for future economic and social battles was an urgent matter for German industry.[20] As this conviction gained ground amongst representatives of the most prominent Berlin engineering firms from 1917 onwards, they began to look to industry cooperation (*Gemeinschaftsarbeit*) as the best means to disseminate new ideas and techniques of efficiency and social engineering which seemed essential for the survival of managerial prerogatives and economic success under adverse conditions. They proclaimed that what German industry needed was not only collective study of the available literature and experience of the new management techniques, but also the filtering out of the most promising techniques so as to define the one best method that could be promptly implemented in German industry.

Suiting the action to the word, the Berlin propagandists of industry cooperation were themselves the first to arrange common study groups and to delegate their representatives to the different committees that were to take care of particularly important issues. Thus by June 1919 managers of the Berlin metalworking firms Siemens, Borsig, Schwartzkopff, Reichswerke Spandau and others who had tackled the problem of time studies in preceding inter-firm meetings presented the first results of their discussions to the interested public: a common and agreed concept of time studies. After this basic step to establish mutual understanding they took the initiative to form a working party called the Committee for Time Studies.[21]

By early 1920 this Committee published a programme for future industry cooperation in this field.[22] It distinguished between time studies and work psychology. The former were defined as a means to evaluate quantitatively the performance that could be attained with given workers, machines or tools and work processes. This was neatly separated from 'work psychology' which was seen as a supplementary means by which one could grasp the 'essence of work' and analyse the psycho-physical preconditions of the required vocational aptitudes in qualitative terms. Scrutiny of the worker's possible performance was seen as an important managerial tool. It would enable factory management to demand a certain, quantitatively well-defined performance from the worker by means of time rates. Time studies were declared absolutely necessary since they were the only way to determine time rates in a reliable way and to calculate the results in advance. Time studies, the programme stated, always had to consist of two steps. First, each work process or task had to be broken down into its individual elements of machine and manual time. Next, these elements had to be put together into a new 'synthesis', the so-called 'rationalization'. The committee expected time studies to facilitate the prior calculation of prices, to guarantee fair wage rates based on objective criteria that could be checked by the workers so that disputes over tasks and wage rates would diminish. Furthermore, time studies were also emphasized as a valuable tool that would help management to improve production planning, work processes and the quality of products, machines and handling devices. In the last analysis and above all, time studies would contribute to lowering production costs.

In view of the manifold resistance by workers, their unions and the business community to time studies, the committee emphasized the necessity for German industry to proceed 'in a methodical, correct, and systematic manner, in short in a scientific way' and it recommended a detailed programme for further investigation in order to make time studies palatable to the workers and to secure optimum results for industry. It proposed to take into account and to analyse carefully all time components that might influence the speed and the completion of a certain task or working process. The methods of time studies and time-rate setting developed by the pioneering Americans Taylor, Gilbreth and Merrick were accordingly to be supplemented and improved. Finally, the programme proposed to fix a single method for time studies and their interpretation, and to train carefully time-clerks in these methods. Only thus would German industry fully enjoy the benefits of time studies without being plagued by the 'teething troubles' experienced in America.

The ultimate result of this collective endeavour was also spelt out. On the basis of this unique method it would be possible, the committee expected, to list time standards for different tasks, handling operations and their individual components. These would be valid for all factories. Their elaboration would thus serve two ends at once. Their general applicability for the same given task in different factories would relieve the individual enterprise of the complex preparatory measures and expenditures that time studies required, thus lowering costs and improving the international competitiveness of German industry. At the same time, binding standardized times and wage rates for the same tasks would also regulate inter-firm competition. Unfair price competition would become less likely as an important element of cost calculation would become more transparent; competition for labour would be reduced as local or even regional wage differentials for the same task, a major cause of labour turnover, would be eliminated.

Although the cooperative endeavours of the big Berlin metalworking firms continued, the results were far from satisfying the heightened expectations. Inter-firm cooperation, the exchange of calculation sheets and the communication of management techniques and experiences proved to be difficult, given the firms' traditional secrecy and the tough competition for market shares. Not until 1921/2 did some Berlin engineering firms start to exchange their advance-calculations and wage-rate settings.[23] The first inter-firm training courses for time-clerks were organized in Berlin in 1922.[24] And the establishment of a 'one best method' for time studies as well as the ensuing list of standard job times encountered more obstacles the more concrete work and energy were invested to tackle the problem.

By 1924 the former radiant optimism was replaced by relativism. In this year, Kurt Hegner, a director of the Berlin engineering firm Ludwig Loewe & Co., published the first extensive German manual on time studies and time rates based upon the practice, experiences and discussions of the small group of Berlin firms that had founded the Committee for Time Studies. Hegner's account, like all manuals that were published later in the 1920s and 1930s,[25] listed four methods for the determination of correct time rates. These were: estimates in the form of a rough calculation; comparisons that made use of tables and graphs; empirical data based on systematic observations; and 'exact' measurements by means of time studies.

This rather wide variety of methods reflected the practical difficulties encountered by engineers and time-clerks when they engaged in running time studies. Even the most fundamental steps were not always easy, given the multitude of different work processes and tasks in an engineering plant as well as the lack of familiarity of the engineer with the work process under scrutiny that contrasted sharply with worker's familiarity with the routine of doing his job. First of all, the engineer had to figure out the exact beginning and end of the task or work process he was observing. He had then to be able to determine precisely its individual components and the time needed for each of them. Only afterwards could he proceed to his proper job of time rate-fixing, which implied (at least in the ideal case) that he had found ways to improve the individual operations and to rearrange their sequence in a more 'rational' way to save time and money. The preparatory steps, however, proved to be more difficult the greater the proportion of manual work involved in the accomplishment of a certain task. The complexity of the 'human factor' – even in cases of seemingly simple manual operations whose individual components could not, however, be exactly discerned – reduced the applicability of time studies, as Hegner and subsequent manuals were forced to concede. The call for a 'one best way' of rate-fixing through time studies proved to be illusory, when confronted with a more prosaic reality. If time studies were to play a role at all, their area of application was limited to those jobs or work processes that were predominantly composed of machine time. The machines, their performance per unit of time, and their operative speed seemed to be a more secure point of departure for time studies and time rate-fixing as it was easy to discern when and how long the machine was in operation and then to determine what kind of manual operations were needed in order to start the machine, to feed it, to keep it going, to remove the finished piece and to assess how much time this manual work required.[26]

As a result the calculation and standardization of machine performance was proclaimed the most important focus of industry cooperation. In 1920 the pioneering group of Berlin managers and engineers had believed that these tasks were comparatively simple and could be easily solved.[27] A wave of optimism arose that industry would soon have at its disposal reliable time standards for machine operations that could serve as a point of reference and an industry-wide basis for the calculation of job times and wage rates. However, these assumptions, too, were soon disappointed. To standardize the performance of machine tools proved to be a lengthy process as it required a voluntary consensus among industrial producers and consumers.

Thus the preparatory intra-industry discussions to standardize the number of revolutions required for machine tools took several years, and it was not before 1929/30 that the first recommendations for industry standards were issued.[28] Industry was forced to realize the gap that existed between theory and practice due to differences in size, layout, organization of the production process and skills, even between firms in the same industrial branch, located in the same industrial region. The calculated maximum or average performance of a machine tool was not universally applicable. These performances, gathered and published by Hegner in lengthy lists, were dependent on the given conditions in a workshop, and soon warnings appeared that calculated machine-tool standards and hence operator-performance standards could not be transferred from one place to the next, unless *all* the conditions that had entered into these graphs and tables were thoroughly checked and 'normalized'.[29]

These far-reaching plans to establish generally applicable and binding standard job times through collective industry efforts failed, not only for technical reasons. It was not so much structural differences between firms or technical difficulties, but differing economic interests and intellectual allegiances that prevented the few Berlin engineering firms that pioneered these practices from agreeing upon the 'one best method' for analysing time studies and filtering out correct times for each operation. In fact, the German manuals of the 1920s and 1930s that were primarily based on their experience continued to juxtapose two methods that led to different results. One method consisted of summing up the mean values established by several time studies for each individual component of a work task, the other one established the job time by combining the mean values of machine operation times, the shortest times taken for the manual work, and precalculated supplementary time units.[30]

This methodological heterogeneity compounded the technical deficiencies and contradicted the original hopes and intentions that had stimulated the pioneering work of the Berlin business community. Nevertheless, the latter continued its activities and relentlessly promoted industry's further co-operation. Their aims remained to promote managerial prerogatives, control workers and increase their performance, lower wage and production costs, and prevent cut-throat competition between German firms through incorrectly calculated prices.

The latter goal had already been important in the discussions of 1918–19 but it became the prevailing concern during the inflation.[31] In 1921–2, when any exact basis for calculating costs and prices seemed to be vanishing, representatives of the leading Berlin metalworking firms began promoting time rates as the only available objective yardstick that could substitute for money and serve industry's need for a standard that was stable in value. And, indeed, they did not only pay lip-service to this new insight. On 1 August 1923 they met in order to discuss whether and how wage rates based on time standards should be introduced in their Berlin workshops. The idea found general support, and two proposals were agreed upon for reconciling wage rates based on time standards with the existing collective agreement on wages and working conditions for the Berlin metalworking industry.[32]

The excitement of the final stages of hyperinflation prevented industry from pursuing this plan fully. However, after the stabilization of the German currency in November 1923, the zeal to make industry switch collectively from piece- to time rates revived, this time fed by new and different challenges. Managers now perceived German industry to be facing at least three problems simultaneously. After the distortions wrought by inflation, adequate or 'normal' terms of competition had to be re-established; wage costs per unit produced needed to be kept low for the sake of Germany's international competitiveness; and industry needed a unified strategy in order to resist the trade unions' push for pay rises to compensate labour for losses during the last hyperinflationary stages. Time rates and their unified introduction by German industry seemed best to serve these ends. Consequently, Berlin's most prominent engineering firms put forward new initiatives to organize and promote a German (standardized) method of time-rate setting. They themselves became the core members of the National Committee for Time Studies and Time Rate Setting that was founded in September 1924.[33]

As the Berlin pioneers had already been forced to realize, the setting of adequate time rates contained many problems. One was the computation of standard times or – as it was called – the lowest average operative times for a certain task, and it was this aspect that had been their primary concern in the earlier discussions. Another problem was now attracting their interest. In practice, supplementary times were – and indeed had to be – added to the elementary standard times before the final time rate was handed out to the workers. These supplementary times were needed either to motivate workers to accept piece-work by guaranteeing them a comparatively higher income than on an hourly-wage payment scheme or to account for so-called 'loss-times' or unproductive times during which the worker could not continue his productive efforts due to personal needs or objective circumstances. The ensuing spectre now haunting the time-study experts was that these supplementary times, unless thoroughly regulated, might call into question the proclaimed objectivity of standard time rates for certain operations established through time studies or other computing methods and thus undermine the inter-firm validity and comparability of wage rates.

The new call for unity and standards failed just like the earlier ones. First of all, though the methodology of time studies and the techniques of time-rate setting were certainly improved, this 'technical' progress was not sufficient to counterbalance the fundamental deficiency of a purely quantitative and mechanical approach to worker performance, namely the worker's willingness to do his best, to cooperate with his colleagues and to integrate himself into a given organizational structure of the production process. Nevertheless, it was not only the workers and their unions that cast a critical eye over management's latest efforts at efficiency and social engineering through time studies and the switch from piece- to time rates. There always remained a big gap between the proclaimed ideals and goals of industry cooperation and the effective results.

In 1928, Kurt Hegner, the doyen of the National Committee for Time Studies and Time Rate Setting, commented critically on the state of the art.[34] With reference to the setting of time rates in the Berlin metalworking firms, he revealed the inadequacies of industry practice as well as some of the underlying causes. The time rate for a certain task was composed of different constituent elements – the operative times and supplementary times. The set time rate for a certain task (expressed in minutes) was multiplied by the money value for a minute of piece-work according to the wage scale union and management had agreed upon or, as was the case in the Berlin metalworking industry from 1924 to 1928, according to the unilaterally fixed wage scale. The product of 60 minutes of piece-work multiplied by the money value of one minute of piece work was defined as the hourly money wage that 'allows the average worker to earn an average income, i.e. the amount of money that equals the fixed hourly rate for piece work'. As Hegner pointed out, the job of the time-clerk was composed of two tasks: on the one hand, he had to compute the 'exact amount of time' a worker needed for a certain task in such a way that an average worker was able to complete the task in the set time. On the other hand, he had to convert the set time into a money wage. As Hegner emphasized, however, it was not part of the time-clerk's business to figure out if the money value for a minute of piece-work or the set time rate guaranteed the worker an adequate income. In fact, it was assumed that separating the merely 'technical' question from the decision on wage scales would at least relieve the strain of conflicts over piece-work from the shop floor and neutralize them, since, by definition, wage questions were relegated from the shop floor to the collective bargaining process.

This vision of a new industrial peace did not materialize. The struggle for better wages re-entered the shop floor, transformed into a struggle over adequate time rates for a given task. In addition, the strict application of the new wage system proved to be counterproductive if labour was scarce. A case in point was the Berlin metalworking industry, where – given the limited supply – the individual firm's dependance on skilled and experienced workers fostered competition for labour. Analysing the industry's reactions, Hegner was apprehensive about the new wage system's 'purity' and future.[35] As the worker was used 'to earning more money than the collectively agreed upon minimum hourly wage rate for piece work', the time-clerk was forced, Hegner noted, 'to include into his calculation of time rates this "plus", that definitely had to be conceded to the workers as it corresponded to the economic circumstances'. This implied, however, that the time-clerk, being himself unable to change the money value per minute of piece work, was forced to change the time rate he had exactly computed, i.e., he consciously falsifies the result of his former calculation and sets a higher time rate than effectively needed for the completion of a certain task. . . . The worker was pretty much aware of such manipulations. He knew that the set time rate was not correct, that it was too generous, and indeed had to be higher than the time that was effectively necessary: because I (the worker) have to earn more money.[35]

As a result, haggling over 'how much more' returned to the shop floor. Hegner did not doubt the negative impact of these manipulations. They would discredit the system of time studies and time rates altogether, and would thus produce the contrary of what had been originally intended. The causes for this highly undesirable development were not difficult to discern. They refer to the inadequacy of the collective wage agreements as well as to the indispensable variability of wage rates to serve the particular economic ends of individual firms competing for skilled labour in the market-place.

The technocratic vision of curtailing the challenges of the market and of superseding them with a well-organized network of friendly cooperation did not materialize. The expectations of 1918–19 were frustrated. Though the Berlin promoters of time studies were not idle, their plans had largely failed by 1928. Many reasons accounted for this sobering development: under-estimates of the inherent difficulties of time studies and time rates, worker dissatisfaction, union influence on wage levels and wage differentials through collective bargaining, and last, but not least, economic competition for market shares and labour between firms which prevailed over the common, but nevertheless more remote, interests of all employers. The prominence of these structural challenges in Berlin led the top managers of its outstanding engineering firms to take the lead in industry-wide co-operation on time studies. In spite of their experience of the limits of management's power to manage over several years of serious effort but debatable progress, they continued and even intensified their calls for industry cooperation in the area of time studies and time-rate setting. They continued to believe that it was not the deficiencies of the tool, but the insufficiencies of the industry's cooperative and standardizing efforts that thwarted employers from harvesting the promised crop in full.

PSYCHO-TECHNICAL APTITUDE TESTS

This pattern of high and rising enthusiasm, followed by calls for collective efforts, disappointments and renewed calls for cooperation to overcome disappointments, was repeated in other areas. The inner core of Berlin engineering firms also became enthusiastic about industrial psychology and its promise to advance the rationalization of the 'human factor' in industry and to improve industrial relations.

Following an invitation by the Berlin section of the Association of

German Engineers, Walther Moede, a psychologist who had developed aptitude tests for the German army's truck and car drivers, lectured in March 1918 on experimental psychology and the multiple pay-offs of its application in industry.[36] Moede's analysis and his seemingly simple and all-encompassing solutions to the problems of recruitment and integration of the work-force in a highly specialized and mechanized industry fostered considerable interest in industrial quarters.

In September 1918 the Berlin section of the Association of German Engineers formed a special committee to study the possible use of psycho-technical aptitude tests. The membership was composed of engineers in leading positions, psychologists and directors of vocational training schools. The committee was commissioned to act on behalf of the general interests of industry. It was to review various proposals, in particular those of Moede, to formulate guidelines and to recommend a selection procedure (aptitude tests) in order to guarantee that workers' abilities would match the requirements of rationalized industry. The leading Berlin metalworking companies financed the first research institute for industrial psychology, founded in October 1918. It was attached to the professorial chair at the Technical University in Charlottenburg (later Berlin) of Georg Schlesinger, the leading German authority on scientific approaches to industrial management. Moede was appointed to the directorship of the institute. The committee and the institute worked hand in hand. Guidelines for testing unskilled labour and apprentices were produced by the end of 1918.[37] Moede specified which machines could be used for testing metalworkers' abilities by October 1919. At the same time Moede claimed that the test programme for apprentices, which involved 32 separate items, had already been proved to be efficient. The institute had tested twenty apprentices from AEG. The grading scale arrived at in these tests in the majority of cases matched the separate evaluation of AEG, which had been arrived at through grades given by foremen and teachers.[38] The guidelines and this first success seem to have accelerated the introduction of tests in industry. Between 1918 and 1920 they were introduced by AEG, Osram, Ludwig Loewe & Co, Siemens and later by some other firms. Tests were not used uniformly. They were introduced step by step. The first groups tested were apprentices and unskilled women employed for special tasks.

However, with the publication of Moede's report in 1919 on the successful use of the so-called 'psycho-technical aptitude test for industrial apprentices' a controversy was unleashed. The opponents, beginning with the professor of psychology at the University of Berlin, Hans Rupp, held a variety of opinions but all attacked the tests on scientific grounds. One of them doubted the efficiency of the apparatus used, another claimed the testing on the machine was invalid in principle because you could not test in this manner the qualities which really mattered, such as character, responsibility and loyalty to the company. A third called into question the validity of integrating test scores because the criteria were partly objective (tests performed on machines), partly subjective (evaluation by foremen and teachers). No unity among professional psychologists was ever reached. The *Reichssparkommissar*, a civil servant who in 1931 investigated the various possibilities for economizing in the public sector, found that though there were now many institutes for applied industrial psychology, none could be closed because each had a very different means of testing, and a different set of clients, and there was no way to decide which approach was the best.[39]

Apart from the controversy among psychologists, doubts arose in industrial quarters. The tests required first an investment of considerable sums for buying the machines for the tests and second the use of paid company time. The personnel needed for testing involved hiring qualified psychologists or the training of supervisors. In addition, the usefulness of the tests was questioned. For example, it was company practice at Siemens to give preference to apprentices who were sons of company employees or who had other connections with the firm. This ran counter to the idea of an objective selection-procedure based on tests. Even after introducing a general revised testing programme for apprentices in 1923 Siemens discovered that the firm was more interested in the character of the potential employee than in his objective skills. Management therefore again placed more emphasis on school and personal interviews. Aptitude tests on machines were entirely eliminated.[40]

Osram was the first company to develop a general testing programme for unskilled workers immediately after the war. Even after several years of testing practice, the firm admitted in 1923 and 1925 that it could not evaluate the efficiency of the testing programme adequately. First of all, after eight weeks' employment the majority of women tested and hired had already left the company. Both workers who had tested well and those less good had left, vitiating Moede's vision of continuity; this was primarily because of better pay in similar firms or other industries. Of those that stayed, many were no longer working at the machine for which they had been tested. Then there was the problematic role in the testing procedure of foremen who did not possess the criteria for evaluating new workers and lacked sufficient contact with the workers to say much about their performance.[41] These difficulties were not limited to this particular case. Other Berlin engineering firms went through similar experiences and disappointments. Their reactions differed: some firms continued experimenting in order to improve their testing techniques, others decided to give them up or, like Siemens, ceased testing some parts of their work-force.

Though the pioneering Berlin engineering firms experienced the manifold limits of psycho-technical aptitude tests in attempting to apply them, they continued to support the basic concept or even initiated calls for its more sophisticated extension. Such calls proliferated in the late 1920s and early 1930s. Under the presidency of Carl Friedrich von Siemens (the head of Siemens) the German National Board for Efficiency Engineering pressed industry in 1929 for further sustained collective efforts in order to improve the techniques of industrial psychology and to promote their implementation. The Board argued that 'a truly perfect rationalization' could not be achieved by exclusively technical means. It also required the 'rationalization of man'.[42]

The latter was declared an essential interest of German industry. Though German industry had made considerable progress with efficiency engineering, as could be seen from the development of standardized mass production, the elaboration of industry technical standards and time rates, there still existed a 'diversity of results achieved by different workers' that, in the Board's view, resulted from the individual worker's varying aptitude for a particular job or work process. As a consequence, according to the Board's analysis, those workers who were less suited to perform a particular job and who considered themselves overtaxed by the time rates set would become uninterested in their job and, exhausted, would deliver low-quality work, start arguing about their effective wage income and show an insufficient identification both with their work and their company. Under these conditions 'the man having lost any inner relationship to his work' would start 'to see himself as a slave of the machine, of technical rationalization' and henceforth would become 'unable to be a valuable member of human society'. Indeed, it could not be ruled out that 'his disinterest or his hatred of the violation of his personality experienced on the job' would result in his 'disinterest or his hatred of the society that allowed this mutilation'. After having painted this rather dark picture, the Board reminded the business community of the remedy that already existed. The recruitment and placement of workers by means of a psycho-technical aptitude test emerged as a quasi-wonder weapon and was recommended as 'the most important means . . . to rationalize the factor "man" ', allowing management to overcome all remaining problems:

> It will be possible to standardize the result per unit of time not because of any instruction as to how a job should be done, but because of the selection and placement of individual workers in view of their particular aptitude for certain tasks.[43]

Given the difficulties in establishing a convincing or even practically useful 'one best method' of aptitude tests and in view of the many problems, corrections and partial withdrawals of those Berlin engineering firms that had pioneered in the area of industrial psychology from its very beginning, the new efforts to sell psycho-technical aptitude tests and selection schemes as a general remedy for industry's malaise sounded anachronistic. Despite contradictory experiences and countervailing evidence, the Berlin promoters of the German rationalization movement continued to nourish the illusion that they would be able to solve 'the human problem' in modernized factories, if only management would unite its efforts, improve its methods and agree upon unified standards of implementing and handling psycho-technical aptitude tests. This was an ideological position. In contrast to 1918–19 it was no longer stimulated by naïve enthusiasm for a scientific utopia, but propelled by management's quest for social control. It presumptuously maintained that industry would finally succeed in forming the 'transparent' worker who, without even the slightest inner resistance, would put his energy, his performance and intelligence at management's disposal, the worker who would accept management's rule and would consent to being 'used' and employed by management like the other factors of production.

In fact, Siemens and the other prominent Berlin metalworking firms, confronted with the challenges of the market and tough economic competition, had started comparatively early to defend and enlarge management's power to manage through sustained investments into better techniques of personnel management. However, the results of management's combined 'internal' and 'collectivist' approach to efficiency and social engineering did not meet expectations. The utopian vision of management power to rationalize the 'human factor' in industry, to neutralize the challenges of the labour and product markets and to create a new harmonious social order beyond class conflict, but not beyond capitalism, did not materialize. Not the power to manage, but its multifaceted constraints became evident the more management engaged in rationalizing the 'human factor in industry' and the more it seriously tested the scope and the effects of those techniques that claimed to offer an integral, straightforward solution to management's struggle for social control and the individual firm's economic survival.

CONCLUSIONS

Since the late nineteenth century concepts stressing management's power to manage the 'human factor' inside the factory and beyond its gates entered debates on economic and social policies. Many of the techniques and methods of 'enlightened' management – organizational and technological innovations, welfarism, time studies, industrial psychology and the like – were presented by German scholars like Schmoller or Muensterberg and by American engineers/entrepreneurs like Taylor, Gantt, Merrick and Ford before 1914. Though German managers, in particular those of metalworking firms, had already experimented with these new techniques, it was only after the war and in order to cope with the new challenges of its aftermath that they started fully to endorse these inherently technocratic visions and to promote a unified industry approach towards their implementation. In fact, rationalization proved to be a lengthy experimental process, characterized by repeated trial and error as well as by the simultaneity and novelty of different approaches. The gap that opened between the vision and reality, and the fact that German managers could not achieve their goal of curtailing the trade unions and controlling the workers in the expected way, helps perhaps to explain later political options. Confronted with a more prosaic reality, German managers did not renounce their technocratic utopia, but superseded it with wishful, ideological thinking. And it was perhaps this ideologized perception of management's need for unlimited power to manage and its obstacles that induced the majority of German managers in the final years of the Weimar Republic (1930–3) to vote openly or secretly for the destruction of the trade unions and to accept willingly or, as in the case of Siemens, at least silently the shift towards an autocratic and even a dictatorial regime that promised to abolish class struggle and the challenges of the market-place by political means and state terrorism.

This hypothesis certainly requires further investigation of how German managers themselves established a balance-sheet of their efforts to solve 'the human problem' in industry under the given political circumstances and in view of a seriously depressed economy. The argument advanced here does not, however, imply that the German business community or parts of it had the capability to 'produce' a National Socialist mass movement, nor that they directed Hitler and his party's quest for totalitarian rule or profited from its outcome in every respect. On the contrary, German managers, including those of Germany's most outstanding giant corporations, discovered after January 1933 that their own expectations were not matched by the dynamics of the Nazi power system. The proclaimed National Socialist goals were to establish by means of state terrorism a 'popular community' (*Volksgemeinschaft*) based on political and racial homogeneity, and to forge the Germans into an obligatory vast 'plant community' (*Betriebsgemeinschaft*) where workers were expected to cooperate with managers for the common weal as defined by the ruling political elites. These goals were not identical with the ideal of safeguarding managerial prerogatives in order to improve socio-economic conditions for the sake of private capitalism. Indeed, workers' trade unions and their traditional socio-cultural and political organizations were destroyed by law and party and state terrorism after Hitler's 'seizure of power' between February and June 1933, and the labour force was forged into an amorphous and apolitical, but also passive mass. At the same time, however, the quest for totalitarian rule did not stop at the factory gates. Managers themselves were confronted with interventions of the Nazi state and its mass organizations even into those realms that management had always striven to keep under its exclusive control such as strategic economic decision making and the structuring of industrial relations inside the firm. Management's struggle against the trade unions thus came to an end without achieving its primary goal, the autonomy of the private enterprise from external interference. The disillusionment about the 'improvements' achieved under Nazi rule took time to develop, and politically acceptable alternatives were not available after Hitler had completed his 'seizure of power'. Management's struggle against incursions by the National Socialist state system began soon after its establishment.

However, this struggle should not be confused with resistance to the political system and the atrocities of the regime. It was, on the contrary, primarily directed towards safeguarding the autonomy of the firm inside and against the Nazi system. Indeed, it was only after Germany's total defeat, and under the pressure of re-education and of integration into the western bloc that Germany's managerial elites slowly learned to accept the challenges of a pluralistic democratic society, a social order that allowed for powerful unions and that was not a mere extension of the firm's internal organizational needs to society at large.[44]

NOTES

The following notes refer only to the most important or quoted sources, books and articles. For a broader discussion of statistical and other source materials see Heidrun Homburg, *Arbeitsmarkt – Rationalisierung – Management. Der Siemens-Konzern in Berlin 1900–1939* (Berlin, 1989).

Abbreviations:
AwF *Ausschuss für wirtschaftliche Fertigung*
BAK Bundesarchiv Koblenz
IC *Industrial Census*
MBB *Monatsblätter des Berliner Bezirksvereins Deutscher Ingenieure*
RKW Reichskuratorium für Wirtschaftlichkeit (The German National Board for Efficiency Engineering)
SAA Siemens-Archiv-Akte
SPA (Siemens company) Sozialpolitische Abteilung (Social Policy Department)
StDR *Statistik des Deutschen Reiches*
VC *Vocational Census*

1 Tim Mason, 'Intention and Explanation: A Current Controversy about the Interpretation of National Socialism', in Gerhard Hirschfeld and Lothar Kettenacker (eds), *The 'Führer State': Myth and Reality. Studies on the Structure and Politics of the Third Reich*, Publications of the German Historical Institute, London, vol. 8 (Stuttgart, 1978), pp. 23–42, esp. p. 40; cf. Jürgen John, ' "Autoritäre" und "konstitutionelle" Fabriken im Deutschen Kaiserreich', *Zeitschrift für Geschichtswissenschaft* 35 (1987), pp. 589–600; Michael Geyer, 'The Nazi State Reconsidered', in Richard Bessel (ed.), *Life in the Third Reich* (Oxford, 1987), pp. 57–67; George L. Mosse, *The Nationalization of the Masses* (New York, 1975); idem, *Nazi Culture: Intellectual, Cultural and Social Life in the Third Reich* (New York, 1981).

2 Cf. V. R. Berghahn, *Modern Germany: Society, Economy and Politics in the Twentieth Century* (Cambridge, 1982).

3 Cf. Otto Hintze, 'Gedächtnisrede auf Gustav von Schmoller,' *Abhandlungen der Königlich Preussischen Akademie der Wissenschaften* (Jahrgang 1918, Philosophisch-historische Klasse, Berlin 1918), pp. 3–16; Karl Pribram, *A History of Economic Reasoning* (2nd edn, Baltimore, 1986), pp. 36, 216–23, 372; Dieter Lindenlaub, *Richtungskämpfe im Verein für Sozialpolitik, 1890–1914* (Wiesbaden, 1967).

4 Cf. Gustav Schmoller, 'Über Wesen und Verfassung der grossen Unternehmungen' (lecture, 30 Dec. 1889, published in *Allgemeine Zeitung*, 24–31

Jan 1890), reprinted in Gustav Schmoller, *Zur Social- und Gewerbepolitik der Gegenwart* (Leipzig, 1890), pp. 372–440, esp. p. 387.

5 Cf. Charles S. Maier, 'Between Taylorism and Technocracy: European Ideologies and the Vision of Industrial Productivity in the 1920s,' *Journal of Contemporary History* 5 (1970), pp. 27–61.

6 Cf. Charles S. Maier, *Recasting Bourgeois Europe. Stabilization in France, Germany, and Italy in the Decade after World War I* (Princeton, 1975); Lothar Burchardt, 'Technischer Fortschritt und sozialer Wandel. Das Beispiel der Taylorismus Rezeption', in Wolfgang Treue (ed.), *Deutsche Technikgeschichte*, Göttingen, 1977), pp. 52–98; Heidrun Homburg, 'Anfänge des Taylorsystems in Deutschland vor dem Ersten Weltkrieg. Eine Problemskizze unter besonderer Berücksichtigung der Arbeitskämpfe bei Bosch 1913', *Geschichte und Gesellschaft* 4 (1978), pp. 170–94; Jürgen Boenig, 'Technik und Rationalisierung in Deutschland zur Zeit der Weimarer Republik', in Ulrich Troitzsch and Gabriele Wohlauf (eds), *Technik-Geschichte. Historische Beiträge und neuere Ansätze* (Frankfurt-on-Main 1980), pp. 390–419.

7 Cf. Table I in Homburg, *Arbeitsmarkt-Rationalisierung-Management; Berliner Statistik*, special no. 1 (June 1953).

8 Cf. *StDR*, vol. 403/3 (*VC* 1925), pp. 16ff., 8ff.; *StDR*, vol. 454/3 (*VC* 1933), pp. 29ff., 10ff. (the figures represent only the employed workers); *Berliner Wirtschaftsberichte* (1936), supplement to no. 7 (*IC* 1933), pp. 50ff.; *StDR*, vol. 557/3 (*VC* 1939), pp. 30ff.

9 Cf. *StDR*, vol. 415, fasc. 2a, pp. 4ff. (*IC* 1925); *StDR*, vol. 568/3, pp. 2ff. (*IC* 1939). In 1925 the 53 'giants' employed 48.5 per cent of the total work-force in the Berlin metalworking industries (399,961 workers). In 1939 the 85 'giants' employed 59.5 per cent of the total work-force (540,943 workers).

10 Cf. Table 22 in Homburg, *Arbeitsmarkt-Rationalisierung-Management*.

11 Cf. *StDR*, vol. 403/3 (*VC* 1925); *StDR*, vol. 454/3 (*VC* 1933); *StDR*, vol. 557/3 (*VC* 1939).

12 Cf. Table 42 in Homburg, *Arbeitsmarkt-Rationalisierung-Management*.

13 As far as I know there is no English equivalent for the German term *Facharbeiter* which evolved in the 1920s to describe workers who had qualified by apprenticeship or training on the job for more complex and demanding tasks in their respective trades. The term codified a form of dilution. It implied that it was no longer the certificate of a formal vocational training but the nature of the task performed by the worker that decided his classification and wage scale. For the following cf. Siemens company, SPA *Annual Report* 1928/9, appendix; SAA 15/Lc 774.

14 Cf. *Statistisches Reichsamt, Abtlg. VII. Industrielle Produktionsstatistik. Textbericht*, 'Amtliche Produktionserhebung der elektrotechnischen Industrie 1933', MS, pp. 7–8, BAK R 13 V 123; Wirtschaftsgruppe Elektrotechnische Industrie, 'Aufgliederung der beschäftigten Arbeiter in der Elektroindustrie nach Industriezweigen, Stand Mai 1940', 28 May 1941, BAK R 13 V 120. In May 1940 the electrical industry employed 221,012 male, 154,229 female workers and 19,245 apprentices. The percentages in the text refer to the male workers, apprentices excluded.

15 For a detailed discussion of the formative years of the DMV, its membership and policies in Berlin from the 1890s to 1932, see Homburg, *Arbeitsmarkt-Rationalisierung-Management*, ch. III.

16 Cf. Heidrun Homburg, 'Externer und interner Arbeitsmarkt. Zur Entstehung und Funktion des Siemens-Werkvereins 1906–1918', in Toni Pierenkemper and Richard Tilly (eds), *Historische Arbeitsmarktforschung* (Göttingen, 1982), pp. 215–48.

17 Cf. Alfred D. Chandler Jr, *Strategy and Structure: Chapters in the History of the*

American Industrial Enterprise (1962; 8th edn, Cambridge, Mass., 1975); idem, *The Visible Hand: The Managerial Revolution in American Business* (Cambridge, Mass., 1977).

18 This 'remedy' was applied during the war and again between 1920 and 1922 and in 1925, cf. Gerald D. Feldman, *Army, Industry, and Labor in Germany 1914–1918* (Princeton, 1966); Hans Ulrich Lembcke (SPA), 'Das Wesen des Tarifvertrages und dessen Gestaltung in der Berliner Metallindustrie' (unpublished dissertation, Technical University Berlin, 1923), pp. 61–65; SPA, Annual Report 1924/5, fol. 9, SAA 15/Lc 774; W. Bolz (Siemens manager/SPA), 'Produktionsverteuerung – Produktionsverminderung 1914–1923–1924', *Der Arbeitgeber* 16 (1926), pp. 165–8.

19 Cf. SPA, *Annual Reports*, 1918–19ff., SAA 15/Lc 774.

20 Cf. A. Schilling, 'Die Bedeutung neuzeitlicher Ausgestaltung industrieller Betriebe für die Wirtschaft nach dem Krieg,' lecture followed by a discussion, 11 Nov. 1917, in the Berlin section of the Association of German Engineers in *MBB* (1918), pp. 10–29; Friedrich Meyenberg, 'Bericht über die bisherigen Arbeiten und die zukünftigen Ziele des Unterausschusses für Betriebsorganisation . . . in *MBB* (1918), pp. 73–4; 'Was will Taylor?', *AwF* 3 (Berlin, 1919).

21 Cf. Eduard Michel (president), 'Ausschuss für Zeitstudien', report of the meeting, 12 Dec. 1919, in *Mitteilungen des AwF* 5 (1920), pp. 23–4.

22 The following details are drawn from: Geschäftsstelle des AwF, 'Ausschuss für Zeitstudien beim AwF', in *Mitteilungen des AwF* 5 (1920), p. 23; cf. Eduard Michel, 'Ideale Griffzeiten oder mittlere Zeiten', *Mitteilungen des AwF* 10/11 (1920), pp. 45–6; Eduard Michel, 'Warum und wie macht man Zeitstudien', *Mitteilungen des AwF* 15 (1920), pp. 74–6.

23 Cf. Valentin Litz (Borsig manager), 'Maschinen- und Handarbeitszeitbestimmung. Lohn- und Offertkalkulation', in *Der Betrieb* 4 (1921/2), pp. 313–15; Kurt Hegner (L. Loewe & Co. AG manager), *Lehrbuch der Vorkalkulation von Bearbeitungszeiten, vol. 1: Systematische Einführung*, Schriften der Arbeitsgemeinschaft Deutscher Betriebsingenieure 2 (Berlin, 1924), p. VI; Engelbert Penchhold, *50 Jahre REFA*, (Darmstadt, 1974), p. 50.

24 Cf. Hegner, *Lehrbuch* (1924), p. VI; *Mitteilungen für die Mitglieder des Verbandes Berliner Metallindustrieller* 12 (1930), pp. 57–8.

25 Cf. Hegner, *Lehrbuch* (1924), pp. 27ff., 34ff., 38ff., 70ff.; ibid., 2nd edn (Berlin, 1927); Reichsausschuss für Arbeitszeitermittlung (ed.), *REFA-Buch, Einführung in die Arbeitszeitermittlung* (Berlin, 1928), pp. 21–45; idem, *Zweites REFA-Buch. Erweiterte Einführung in die Arbeitszeitermittlung* (Berlin, 1933), pp. 88–107. See also for the following paragraphs the revised second edition of this *Zweites REFA-Buch* (Berlin, 1936, with several reprints, published by the Reichsausschuss für Arbeitsstudien; the consulted edition dates from 1939); Ausschuss für Handarbeit beim AwF (ed.), *Grundlagen für Arbeitsvorbereitung. Zeitstudien* (AwF Bestell-No. 225), (Berlin, 1929).

26 Cf. E. Michel, 'Zeitstudien', *Der Betrieb* 1 (1918/19), pp. 133–42; Hegner, *Lehrbuch* (1924), pp. 15, 171–4; *REFA-Buch*, pp. 15–16, 23; Ausschuss für Handarbeit, *Grundlagen*, p. 109; *Zweites REFA-Buch* (1933), p. 41.

27 Cf. Michel, 'Ausschuss für Zeitstudien', p. 24.

28 Cf. Georg Schlesinger, *Wesen und Auswirkung der Drehzahlnormung* (AwF Bestell-No. 239), (Berlin, 1931), pp. 35–41, 67–75.

29 Cf. Kurt Hegner, 'Richtzeiten für die Kalkulation', in *Der Betrieb* 4 (1921/2), pp. 323–9; Hegner, *Lehrbuch* (1924), pp. 34–70, 129–70; *REFA-Buch* (1928), p. 48; *Zweites REFA-Buch* (1933), pp. 35–6, 41–3; *Zweites REFA-Buch* (1939), p. 7.

30 Cf. Eduard Michel, *Wie macht man Zeitstudien* (Berlin, 1920); C. W. Drescher (Siemens manager) 'Anwendung der Zeitstudie im Grossbetrieb', *Der Betrieb* 3, (1920/1), pp. 128–35; Valentin Litz, 'Unproduktive Arbeiten in der industriellen

Facharbeit,' *Der Betrieb* 3 (1920/1), pp. 565–74; Hegner, *Lehrbuch* (1924), pp. 77–84; *REFA-Buch* (1928), pp. 34–5; Ausschuss für Handarbeit, *Grundlagen*, pp. 109–20; *Zweites REFA-Buch* (1933), pp. 64–75; *Zweites REFA-Buch* (1939), pp. 64, 72.

31 Cf. Hegner, *Lehrbuch* (1924), pp. 1–4; Ausschuss für Handarbeit, *Grundlagen*, pp. 1–6; Pechhold, *50 Jahre REFA*, pp. 48–55.

32 Cf. Litz, 'Maschinen- und Handarbeitszeitbestimmung', p. 313; C. W. Drescher, 'Der Zeitakkord', *Maschinenbau* 3 (1923–4), p. 60.

33 Cf. Kurt Hegner, 'Das Problem der Vorkalkulation', *Maschinenbau* 3 (1923–4), pp. 701–2; Lembcke, 'Das Wesen des Tarifvertrages', p. 92; C. W. Drescher, 'Richtlinien für die Einführung des Zeitakkords ausgearbeitet vom Unterausschuss für Handarbeit beim AwF', *Maschinenbau* 3 (1923–4), pp. 719–21; Ausschuss für Handarbeit, *Grundlagen*, pp. 1–6; *Zweites REFA-Buch* (1933), pp. 5–8, 36–40; Penchhold, *50 Jahre REFA*, pp. 48–57.

34 See also for the following Kurt Hegner, 'Stückzeitberechnung und Tarifvertrag', *Maschinenbau* 7 (1928), pp. 97–103, esp. pp. 97, 99.

35 Quoted ibid., pp. 97–8. See also W. Steinmann, 'Die Stückzeitberechnung in der Praxis', *Maschinenbau* 7 (1928), pp. 617–22.

36 Cf. Walther Moede, 'Die experimentelle Psychologie im Dienste des Wirtschaftslebens' (lecture followed by a discussion on 3 Mar. 1918), *MBB* (1919), pp. 1–14, 19–31; W. Moede, 'Übersicht über die seitherige Entwicklung' *MBB* (1919), pp. 32–3. For a general overview on the evolution of aptitude tests and applied psychology in Germany see Franziska Baumgarten, *Die Berufseignungsprüfungen. Theorie und Praxis* (2nd edn Berne 1943; 1st edn 1928); Ulfried Geuter, *Die Professionalisierung der deutschen Psychologie im Nationalsozialismus* (Frankfurt, 1984).

37 Cf. 'Arbeitsausschuss für industrielle Psychotechnik', *MBB* (1918), pp. 123–7, esp. p. 127; Moede, 'Übersicht', p. 33; August Riebe, 'Die Auswahl der Arbeiter in den Fabriken', *Der Betrieb* 1 (1918–19), p. 57. See also Walther Moede,' 10 Jahre Institut für Industrielle Psychotechnik T. H. Berlin', *Werkstattstechnik* 22 (1928), pp. 587–92; Georg Spur, *Produktionstechnik im Wandel. Georg Schlesinger und das Berliner Institut für Werkzeugmaschinen und Fertigungstechnik 1904–1979* (Munich, 1979), pp. 297–327; Geuter, *Professionalisierung*, pp. 88ff., 576.

38 Cf. Walther Moede, 'Die psychotechnische Eignungsprüfung des industriellen Lehrlings', *Praktische Psychologie* 1 (1919/20), pp. 6–18, 65–81; Georg Schlesinger, 'Praktische Ergebnisse aus der industriellen Psychotechnik' (lecture followed by a discussion, on 1 Oct. 1919), *MBB* (1919), pp. 137–52.

39 Cf. RKW (ed.), *Der Mensch und die Rationalisierung I. Fragen der Arbeits- und Berufsauslese, der Berufsausbildung und Bestgestaltung der Arbeit* (RKW Veröffentlichungen 71), (Jena, 1931), pp. 17–107; RKW (ed.), *Der Mensch und die Rationalisierung III. Eignung und Qualitätsarbeit* (RKW Veröffentlichungen 87), (Jena, 1933), pp. 251–61; Geuter, *Professionalisierung*, pp. 83–100, 132–3. See also Homburg, *Arbeitsmarkt-Rationalisierung-Management*, ch. V.5.b.

40 Cf. Homburg, *Arbeitsmarkt-Rationalisierung-Management*, ch. V.5.c. Practice at the Siemens company is discussed by Hans Rupp, 'Untersuchung zur Lehrlingsprüfung bei Siemens-Schuckert-Berlin', *Psychotechnische Zeitschrift* 1 (1925/6), pp. 11–25, 54–75; Hans Kellner, 'Die Lehrlings-Beschaffung und Auslese in der Berliner Metallindustrie' (unpublished dissertation, Technical University Berlin, 1927), pp. 26, 10.

41 Cf. Walter Levy and Curt Piorkowski, 'Die Anwendung psychotechnischer Verfahren und deren bisherige Ergebnisse im Osram-Konzern', *Werkstattstechnik* 16 (1922), pp. 555–9; W. Ruffer, 'Auswertungsverfahren der Psychotechnischen Prüfstelle der Osram G.m.b.H. KG, Fabrik S', *Praktische Psy-*

chologie 4, (1922/3), pp. 225–36; A. Schneider, 'Eignungsprüfung und Erfolgskontrolle in einem Grossbetriebe der Elektroindustrie (D-Fabrik der Osram GmbH KG)', *Industrielle Psychotechnik* 2 (1925), pp. 108–18; W. Ruffer, 'Über die Organisation und Bewährung der Eignungsprüng der Fabrik S der Osram GmbH KG', *Industrielle Psychotechnik* 3 (1926), pp. 35–46; W. Ruffer, 'Anlern-Erfolgskontrolle bei Osram', *Industrielle Psychotechnik* 5 (1928), pp. 86–94. See also Homburg, *Arbeitsmarkt-Rationalisierung-Management*, ch. V.5.c.

42 Rudolf Schindler, *Das Problem der Berufsauslese in der Industrie*, (study commissioned by the RKW) (Jena, 1929), p. 3.

43 Cf. ibid., for all following quotes, esp. pp. 14, 11, 13, 14.

44 Cf. Tim W. Mason, 'Zur Entstehung des Gesetzes zur Ordnung der nationalen Arbeit vom 20. Januar 1934: Ein Versuch über das Verhältnis "archaischer" und "moderner" Momente in der neuesten deutschen Geschichte', in Hans Mommsen D. Petzina and B. Weisbrod (eds), *Industrielles System und politische Entwicklung in der Weimarer Republik*, (Düsseldorf, 1974), pp. 322–51; Henry A. Turner, *German Big Business and the Rise of Hitler* (New York and Oxford, 1985); Michael Prinz, *Vom neuen Mittelstand zum Volksgenossen. Die Entwicklung des sozialen Status der Angestellten von der Weimarer Republik bis zum Ende der NS-Zeit* (Munich, 1986); Marie-Luise Recker, *Nationalsozialistische Sozialpolitik im Zweiten Weltkrieg* (Munich, 1985); Klaus Wisotzky, *Der Ruhrbergbau im Dritten Reich* (Düsseldorf, 1983); Carola Sachse, 'Betriebe rationalisieren das "Privatleben". Betriebliche Sozialpolitik als Familienpolitik in der Weimarer Republik und im Nationalsozialismus. Mit einer Studie der Firma Siemens' (unpublished dissertation, Technical University of Berlin, 1986); Volker, R. Berghahn, *The Americanisation of West German Industry 1945–1973* (Leamington Spa, 1986).

6 Employers' associations and industrial relations in postwar Germany

The strategies of Ruhr heavy industry

Werner Plumpe

INTRODUCTION

Until recently there has been little dispute that the reshaping of industrial relations after the Second World War played a key role in the so-called 'economic miracle' in the Federal Republic of Germany. After the war, a low strike propensity and shopfloor peace, as well as the largely pacific relations between trade unions and employers' associations within the framework of a legally ordered system of collective bargaining constituted an apparently smooth-running model of industrial relations. In comparison with other West European economies the Federal Republic appeared to be an island of industrial peace. Moreover, Germany also seemed to have made a clean break with its own past of intense conflict between employers' associations and trade unions. Today it is a matter for debate whether this model will continue to work under the less favourable economic conditions of the 1980s and 1990s. But its success in the 1950s and 1960s is nevertheless impressive.

What were the reasons for this fundamental change in industrial relations after the Second World War? The explanations presented in the literature on the subject are contradictory. As far as the role of the trade unions is concerned the analyses largely concur with one another about the trend, although some evaluations are more critical than others. After internal disagreements during the 1950s the unions reached a fundamental consensus among themselves on the acceptability of social partnership.[1] Assessments of the development of the position of the employers, on the other hand, are unclear and contradictory. Some authors emphasize the continuity of employers' views on trade union and company co-determination.[2] Others stress the anti-trade-union attitude of certain parts of industry, notably heavy industry, and focus on employers' claims for social leadership that were not altered either by the war or by the postwar period.[3] Finally, some authors speak of an 'Americanization' of German industry: the adoption of American marketing and production strategies, combined with the simultaneous decline in the influence of heavy industry, eventually led employers to accept the trade unions as equals, at least in principle.[4] Although the thesis of the Americanization of German industry is partially convincing, it overlooks the fact that numerous German traditions, particularly those of heavy industry, played a role in the restructuring of industrial relations after the war. This analysis takes account of these traditions, and their effectiveness, importance and influence in the period following the end of the Second World War.

THE STARTING-POINT 1945–1947

The British role

By the spring of 1945 the British government had completed its own plans for the reshaping of future industrial relations in Germany. These were collated in a directive that was presented to the European Advisory Commission.[5] It stated:

> You should therefore direct that there should be no interference with free associations having the character of Trade Unions or employers' associations so long as the activities of such bodies are not directed against the Allied authorities or detrimental to their control, and so long as they do not produce such disorder as to threaten the security of your forces or the accomplishment of the objects of the occupation.

The wording of this directive and of subsequent additions to it gave the British Military Government in Germany (the Control Commission for Germany/British Element (CCG/BE)) a good deal of scope in regard to the formation of trade unions. Although it provided that wage controls should be replaced by free negotiations between employers' associations and trade unions, the abolition of wage controls was linked to prior requirements that could only be fulfilled by a currency reform and a resolution of the problem of high inflation.

Thus the future relationship between employers' associations and trade unions was not precisely stipulated. On the contrary, the reconstruction of the trade unions was subordinated to British political interests which increasingly centred on conflict with the Soviet Union. The conservative Military Government regarded the trade unions which sprang up after the war as 'fifth columns' of the Soviets. With the consent of the Ministry of War they proceeded to suppress them rigorously.[6] Indeed, in the face of the mutual agreement between the British government and the Military Government in Germany on this matter, reconstruction of trade unions was so restricted 'that at first union work was essentially impossible'.[7] German trade unionists had to build up organizational structures from the local level while subject to constant British control.

An episode of conflict in the autumn of 1945 clarified British trade-union policy. Drawing on the lessons of the failure of the Weimar trade-union movement, the founding circles of the new German unions wanted to build up a comprehensive, economy-wide trade-union federation with a centralized organizational structure. Supported by the British government, the Military Government turned this proposal down, fearing the construction of a large, Communist-influenced power centre. Socialist and other German trade unionists were informed in no uncertain terms that an organizational model of this type would not be permitted under any circumstances. Nevertheless, the German trade unionists stuck to their concept and only gave way under great pressure from all sides, including the TUC, acting more or less as an official arm of the British government, and the Military Government in Germany. Faced with the alternative of either not being able to organize or agreeing to a decentralized federation on the lines of the British TUC, the German unions bowed to British pressure in early 1946. Only after this were they able to begin to construct lasting organizational structures.

British policy was not based on a long-term model of future industrial relations in Germany. Rather, it was subordinated to her social and foreign policy. Although a 'British' organizational model had been imposed upon what became the *Deutsche Gewerkschaftsbund* (DGB/German Trade Union Federation) of the British Zone of Occupation, this did not go beyond general statements concerning future cooperation between trade unions and employers' associations. Right from the start, the Military Government was intent upon getting unions and employers around the conference table to deal more easily with social problems through a 'social partnership'. This policy met with little opposition on the British side. There were divergent opinions in London about the way in which trade unions should be treated in occupied Germany, but both the Ministry of Employment and the TUC subordinated themselves to priorities of foreign policy. With a few exceptions, the Military Government took up an extremely conservative position. One of these exceptions was Wolfgang Friedmann who was in charge of the Organizations Branch of the Economic Subcommission of the CCG/BE and who clearly regarded structural social and economic reforms as prerequisites for the formation of a democratic Germany. On the key issue of the restructuring of employers' organizations, where the unions wanted to impose restraints, Friedman was at least able to hold off a decision in favour of the employers while he was in office. But his return to London at the end of 1946 put an end to his 'leftist' influence.[8]

The British lacked a concept for the reshaping of industrial relations in Germany after 1945 – apart from a fear of strong Communist unions. Accordingly, the Military Government orientated itself pragmatically towards a system of social cooperation as a part of their programme of economic control. The Allied Control Council in Berlin, the common military government of the four occupying powers, was likewise unable to develop or implement an appropriate concept. In 1945 the *Deutsche Arbeitsfront* (DAF), the compulsory organization of capital and labour under fascism, was banned and the Nazi works-constitution law, the *Gesetz zur Ordnung der nationalen Arbeit*, which had introduced openly fascist tendencies in companies, was revoked. On the other hand, due partly to profound internal political differences about the character of 'free trade unions', the Control Council was not able to agree either on a trade-union law or on the basis for legal rulings on relations between capital and labour, industrial disputes, strikes and lock-outs.[9] Its only achievement was the passing of the Works Council Law of April 1946 which made the precise definition of the rights of works councils the object of negotiations between management and the work-force.[10]

No explicit ruling on industrial relations materialized, but other measures did have considerable consequences for the relationship between capital and labour. In 1945 and 1946 the British Military Government confiscated the collieries and iron- and steelworks. In August 1946 the British Foreign Minister Ernest Bevin announced the socialization of the iron and steel industry. At the beginning of 1947 the deconcentration (*Entflechtung*) of the integrated steel companies began and on 1 March, 1947 the establishment of the first demerged plants coincided with an announcement by the British government of the introduction of parity co-determination based on equal rights for both sides. This co-determination model meant that the supervisory boards of the newly established steelworks comprised an equal number of representatives of capital and labour, with one representative of the control authority (the North German Iron and Steel Control) as neutral chairman of the board. Second, on the management boards, a new office of Labour Director (*Arbeitsdirektor*) was created, which became responsible for the social and labour problems of the plant. The rights of the works councils were not regulated by this model of company co-determination.[11]

In most of the literature and in contemporary German statements these measures by the British government and the Military Government are seen as steps towards a comprehensive social-reform policy in Germany, the realization of which would have led to a profound restructuring of the relationship between capital and labour.[12] According to this view it was primarily the United States that, from 1947 onwards, used its powerful financial influence to force socially conservative policies on the British government. The actions of the British government do not appear inconsistent with this interpretation, but it is incorrect in a number of important points. After his return to England in 1947, in a resumé of occupation policy, Wolfgang Friedmann clearly emphasized the conservative character of the Military Government.[13] It prohibited the socialization of the coal-mining industry in Rhineland-Westphalia on its *own* accord in 1948. More recent research has also shown that the British Government's main motives in its occupation policy had very little to do with concepts of structural reform. Their main interest was in keeping the occupation costs as low as possible and in guaranteeing effective control of the German economy. This was the most important explanation of the confiscation of the collieries and steelworks. The British also pursued a strictly anti-Soviet foreign policy which strongly influenced its occupation policy. The announcement of proposals to socialize heavy industry was mainly intended to prevent the internationalization of the Ruhr area which was being championed by the French. The British believed that such a policy would 'bring the Russians to the Rhine' as one of the international control powers. However, they did not wish to snub completely their French Allies and dismiss French security interests. Once the danger of such an internationalization of the Ruhr receded, it was hardly surprising that the idea of socialization was given up by the British with little resistance in the Washington negotiations of autumn 1946 between the United States and Great Britain.[14]

It has long been presumed in the literature that the introduction of parity co-determination in the coal, iron and steel companies (*Montanmitbestimmung*) constituted some sort of compensation to pacify the unions for the retreat on socialization.[15] The co-determination initiative of the British controller of the iron and steel works, Harris-Burland, and his German advisors was rather a result of the specific situation at the turn of the year 1946–7. Until 1946 the British Military Government believed their industrial relations policy to have been successful. The new union bodies were dominated by a Social Democratic majority and company industrial relations were developing as harmoniously as the occupying forces could have wished, facilitating effective control of the German economy. But with the winter crisis of 1946–7 and the outbreak of the dispute about the co-determination rights of the works councils, the situation became unstable. The Works Council Law of April 1946 had made the rights of the works councils the object of company-level agreements. However, since the work-forces as well as the trade unions were demanding economic co-determination for the works councils this led almost automatically to fierce internal conflicts over co-determination with employers strongly resisting these demands. The intransigent position of the employers along with the deteriorating supply situation led to a growing crisis. The British were of the opinion that it was mainly the Communists who were exploiting the situation to push the works-council question. But the leaders of the unions were also put in a difficult position since the demand for economic co-determination constituted an important part of the union program. The union leaders generally tried to de-escalate the disputes, but their model agreement for the completion of the works-council law clearly marked out that position and made conflict with the employers unavoidable.[16]

The British found themselves in an unpleasant situation. On the one hand, they wanted to leave the arrangement of industrial relations up to the Germans themselves, as they had tried to do as far as possible up to this time. On the other hand, the conflict surrounding the co-determination question could have consequences that might affect broad occupation policy and call its aims into question. Moreover, the issues at stake in these conflicts were alien to British experience which was not acquainted with either statutory co-determination rights or the dual system of union and company representation in its German form. Hence their policy conclusions were often confused. The head of the Manpower Division of the CCG/BE, W. R. Luce, suggested increasing the power of moderate trade unions at the expense of the works councils and wanted to vest these unions with greater rights in economic questions at the same time. This was directed, on the one hand, against the German works councils – which the British believed were inspired by the Communists – and represented a rejection of economic co-determination in the company. On the other hand, however, the suggestion also corresponded to the British tradition of channelling company representation through the trade unions.[17]

This was the background against which parity co-determination was introduced in the dismembered plants of the iron and steel industry in 1947. The British did not intend to create permanent new co-determination forms. They saw their establishment rather as a temporary solution until the Germans finally clarified the pattern of internal company relations. The temporary character of this arrangement showed that the British did not have their own industrial-relations concept for Germany but were guided in this matter solely by considerations of security and occupation policy. The apparent exception – parity co-determination – was conceived as a temporary measure and was not a product of a socio-political programme. Nevertheless, the German public perceived part of the British occupation policy as a conscious shift of the balance of power in favour of the trade unions and the labour movement, impressions which seemed all the more plausible as a Labour Government (an apparent ally of the *Sozial Demokratische Partei Deutschlands* (SPD), the German Social Democratic Party and the trade unions) had been in office in London since August 1945.

The German trade unions

Although the political labour movement in Germany began to split into enemy camps again after 1946–7, the founding of a unified trade-union federation with a broadly accepted and comprehensive programme nevertheless represented considerable progress. Union demands for the reconstruction of German society reflected traditions from the Weimar period which had been sustained in exile and from the experience of fascist dictatorship, which many believed had been supported decisively by German industry. A unified trade-union movement appeared essential for the realization of a programme including the socialization of key industries, banks and insurance companies, as well as the legislative anchoring of union rights via company-level co-determination and industry-wide economic control. The leading unionists of the immediate postwar period were well aware that the division of the labour movement had favoured the emergence of fascism.[18]

To achieve this sort of 'economic democracy' (*Wirtschaftsdemokratie*) with legally established co-determination, the trade unions believed that the regulation of labour relations, wages and working conditions should be the object of equal negotiations between capital and labour. The prerequisite of this equality, according to the unions, was the prohibition of the traditional German form of employers' associations, separate and distinct from trade associations. Instead, they favoured their amalgamation into general trade/ employers' associations.[19] But, with few exceptions, this position met with resistance from both the occupying forces and the new employers' and trade associations. The unions needed to exert pressure in order to achieve such demands. The Social Democratic union leaders, under pressure from the British, were considerably less prepared to undertake such measures than the Communists. Thus in relation to the works-council issue in the second half of 1946, although union leaders supported the demands of the work-force for the establishment of rights of economic co-determination within the company and even put them forward in the form of a general model agreement, they shied away from strikes and demonstrations.[20] The Communists, therefore, played a considerable role in the radicalization of the work-force on these issues, even though they only mobilized them for generally accepted union aims.[21]

The introduction of the *Montanmitbestimmung*, the Marshall Plan, the formation of the Federal Republic and finally the Cold War eventually led to the expulsion of the Communists and a consequent split in the unions. It is nevertheless important to note that this expulsion was not primarily the result of diverging ideas on future labour relations. Indeed, in their plans immediately after the war the SPD had shown itself to be more radical than the *Kommunistische Partei Deutschlands* (KPD), the German Communist Party, which had initially only argued for anti-fascist unity and the completion of the bourgeois revolution. The division between the SPD and the KPD which began to re-emerge in the western zones at an early stage was, therefore, only superficially due to differences in political ideas. Indeed, the KPD was initially much less radical than the SPD which in its founding appeal of the summer of 1945 had placed socialism on the agenda and declared the death of capitalism.[22] A major reason for the revived anti-communism of the *Schumacher-Büro* – which claimed a leading role for the SPD in the western zones – was the power struggle within the Berlin party executive for the leadership of the SPD. The Berlin party executive, headed by Otto Grotewohl, decided to cooperate closely with the KPD. Later it also gave its consent to the unification of the labour parties and to the formation in the Soviet zone of the SED (*Sozialistiche Einheitspartei Deutschlands*), a development which in the western zones was seen as a forced unification and self-defamation of the SPD.[23] Then by refusing to cooperate closely with the KPD and by emphasizing his independence Kurt Schumacher was able to expand his leading role in the western zones as the supporters of the policy of unifying the parties in the West were more prepared to accept the authority of the Berlin party executive. The internal power struggle within the SPD thus fitted into the emerging Cold War which first escalated the situation and then decided it in Schumacher's favour. The turn against the KPD was based on pragmatic politics which gave it an intensity that could not be explained by ideological differences.[24]

The unions did not escape the effects of the renewed split in the labour movement, even though the demand for the formation of a non-party unified trade union initially concealed the splits and the programmes of the two sides were not fundamentally divergent. Individual parts of the unions, from Christians to Communists, shared a common programme including nationalization/socialization of large-scale industry and the larger banks, planning and control of the economy, and union co-determination at all levels. These common aims, which amounted to a fundamental change of the inherited social and political structures, were born out of anti-fascist motives, as much as aims to fundamentally improve the position of the labour force.[25] The latent, party-political differences came to the fore over the Marshall Plan question in 1947–8 and thereafter rapidly intensified. Faced by American Occupation policy with the question of whether to stick to a policy of structural reform or to sacrifice this in exchange for generous American economic aid, the Social Democratic wing of the unions – very reluctantly in the British zone – decided to accept the Marshall Plan. Thus they accepted also the division of Germany and the restoration of capitalist relations.[26] This automatically brought with it the beginning of a change in union policy that involved giving up the struggle for structural reforms in favour of a fight for material improvements. Accordingly, the Communist minority increasingly came into conflict with majority union policy. This initially tactical conflict over the Marshall Plan had profound ideological consequences. At the beginning of 1947, as the *Montanmitbestimmung* was introduced, this split was not yet final. The relationship between the trade unions and the employers' associations was also still determined by the focus on the rejection of independent employers' associations and the union demand for equality with employers on all levels. In industry, particularly heavy industry, this programme met with resistance right from the start. The circumstances did not permit an outright rejection of the trade unions, especially since their Social Democratic leadership was openly supported by London and parts of the Military Government. But the more far-reaching co-determination proposals were rejected, along with the institutionalization of a union role in economic planning and control. However, heavy industry's rigid position began gradually to restrict its scope for manoeuvre, which became a serious weakness in face of far-reaching interventions by the occupation authorities.

THE REACTIONS OF HEAVY INDUSTRY 1946–1947

The confiscation of the collieries and their exclusion from the integrated steel companies in the autumn of 1945, the seizure of the plants of the iron and steel industry in the summer of 1946, the announcement of their socialization, the dismemberment of the steel trusts and finally, at the beginning of 1947, the introduction of parity co-determination, seriously threatened the economic and political power of heavy industry. At the same time the iron and steel industry itself admitted that it was in a precarious economic situation. Cut off from the importation of high-quality ores from abroad, subjected to strict production limitations and discriminated against in allocations of coal, they had run up losses of several hundred million Reichsmarks. Despite the support of the British, necessary price increases could not be pushed through the Berlin Control Council. But while little could be done about the poor economic situation in the short term, the industry believed that the seizures and break-ups were destroying its long-term economic viability and undermining the foundations of its power. Under these circumstances the leading representatives of the steel trusts decided on a far-reaching break with tradition and offered the unions extensive rights of co-determination in order to win them over to a common front against the British plans to break up the big firms. In a public declaration, they stated,

> Finally we declare our sincere willingness to allow the work-force and the trade unions full rights of participation. We do not want to shut ourselves off from the demands of a new age, and we give our full consent to the participation of the labour force in planning and control as well as in the supervisory bodies of large companies in the iron and steel industry.[27]

This generally worded offer was reiterated to the unions along with a more precise statement to the effect that they were prepared to accept equal representation on the supervisory boards.[28] Even though these moves by the company representatives represented a break with their previous position they did not go beyond the co-determination model that Harris-Burland was urging at this time. For obvious reasons the trade unions did not agree to this suggestion.[29]

Why did the threat of a break-up of the companies make heavy industry's leading representatives ready to give up their traditional anti-trade-union position? The power-base of heavy industry had developed in the last third of the nineteenth century. The technical economic requirements of large-scale heavy industry resulted in the adoption of positions during the Great Depression of the 1870s and 1880s that cartelization of production and high-protective tariffs were essential for the success of German heavy industry. The trade and employers' associations founded after 1871 became the mouthpiece of this standpoint. They keenly pursued both cartelization and protective tariffs, and the successful implementation of these policies from 1878 onwards in turn strengthened the associations. The policy brought with it a concentration and centralization of capital that accelerated the integration of coal and steelmaking, under the hegemony of the large steel groups. These groups formed the real pillars of the trade associations: the *Verein für die bergbaulichen Interessen* (Association of the Coal Mining Industry), the *Nordwestliche Gruppe des Vereins Deutscher Eisen- und*

Stahlindustrieller (Northwestern Group of the Association of the Iron and Steel Industrialists – VdESI) and the *Verein zur Wahrung der gemeinsamen wirtschaftlichen Interessen in Rheinland und Westfalen* (Association to Protect the Common Economic Interests in Rhineland and Westphalia, the so-called *Langnamverein* or 'Long-Name Association').[30] With the founding of the *Rheinisch-Westfälisches Kohlensyndikat* (Rhenish-Westphalian Coal Syndicate, RWKS) in 1893 – which eventually completely controlled the production and sales of coal, as well as various iron and steel cartels (which were less effective) – this process of the formation of combines, cartels and trade associations was completed around the turn of the century. Despite the objections raised by certain historians, there seems little doubt that these powerful organizations ensured heavy industry a dominant position in the politics of German industry more broadly.[31]

This dominance was particularly noticeable in relations with labour and the trade unions. Heavy industry was traditionally patriarchal, but by the 1890s it was employing increasing numbers of itinerant unskilled workers and reacting harshly to the new challenges of industrial disputes and unions. This reaction corresponded to the quasi-military structure of labour relations in the mines and steelworks, and also expressed a principled rejection of any political claims by the labour movement, claims which not only demanded an 'expensive social policy' but which also questioned the whole imperial political system, the chief guarantor of the policies, which underlay the success of heavy industry. Heavy industry also forced these anti-union and anti-democratic policies on other branches of industry through the employer associations founded in the 1890s and 1900s (*Arbeitnordwest* for the iron and steel industry, the *Zechenverband* for the coalmining industry). Similar practices did not succeed in other areas such as the construction and foodstuff industries where the technical and economic conditions did not allow for outright confrontation with the unions.[32]

The First World War brought about some acceptance of the unions because of their willingness to cooperate in the German war economy. Heavy industry had to recognize unions in the so-called Stinnes–Legien Agreement of 1918, but this did nothing to change heavy industry's fundamental anti-trade-union stance. The War and its aftermath somewhat weakened the organization of heavy industry. Conflicts about export markets and prices, which had begun to emerge during the war, intensified after 1918 and led to government intervention in industrial price setting. But such conflicts did not destroy the unity of the employers on questions of working hours and wage systems; indeed, the employers' role after 1919 in attempting to suppress the achievements of the Revolution enhanced the status of the employers' associations.[33]

This suppression was only partly successful. Under the collectivist system of Weimar labour law, although the eight-hour day was more or less dispensed with by 1923, the trade unions remained party to industrial agreements and compulsory state arbitration was also retained and served to ensure the continuing existence of the unions and maintain workers' living standards. At the same time heavy industry had to come to terms with works councils under union influence, something which until that time they had vigorously rejected because they saw it as a gateway into companies for 'external elements' (i.e., the unions).[34] From 1928 heavy industry actively sought to dismantle the Weimar social system with a view to achieving an 'objective' economic and social policy independent of parliamentary majorities and the unions. This position intensified during the world economic crisis. Leading industrialists called for an open fight against the unions, although only a few initially declared themselves in favour of a take-over by the National Socialists.[35]

After the First World War heavy industry's influence relied on the unity of its organization and the social and political homogeneity of its leading groups which had increased despite economic rivalry and personal disputes. Although heavy industry found itself in a state of permanent economic crisis with its significance in the national economy on the decline and its entrepreneurial performance not always convincing, this sector still managed to maintain what Weisbrod has called a 'veto position' in the representation of German industry, thus making the assertion of an alternative concept of closer cooperation between business and the unions almost unthinkable.[36] Instead, on the basis of a rejection of the unions and the union-influenced works councils, they favoured the *Werksgemeinschaft* (works community), a model in which there was room only for peaceful labour representation on economic issues. Since the revolutionary changes had institutionalized parliamentarism, unions and works councils, heavy industry was forced into a position of fundamental opposition to the Weimar state. From 1929–30 onwards, heavy industry pursued the modification or dissolution of the Weimar state in favour of more authoritarian rule.

Against this background the offer made by heavy industry in 1947 seems at first sight surprising. It is, however, comprehensible if one bears in mind how a comprehensive break-up of the large companies would have weakened heavy industry's scope for political action. Another reason for their willingness to compromise should not be overlooked. After the suppression of the trade unions in 1933 and the replacement of the works councils with pliant and effective *Vertrauensräte*[37] or 'trustees' councils', union influence was effectively eradicated and the manager became 'master in his own house'. Nevertheless from 1936–7 onwards, once full employment had been achieved, the position of individual workers was strengthened. They could now improve their working conditions and wages individually by changing jobs and it became apparent that mechanisms for pacifying internal conflicts and solving wage issues no longer existed. The DAF could not play this role because, swaying backwards and forwards between propagandist swindle and quasi-trade-union activity as it did, it was incapable of quashing unrest.

Occasionally, the DAF even trod on the toes of the employers with their national socialist pathos about *Volks- und Betriebsgemeinschaft* (people's and works community).[38] There is some evidence that under full employment after 1936 leading industrialists began to come to terms with the idea of cooperating with free and economically peaceful trade unions as well as with those works councils aligned with company aims.[39] Whilst this concept represented a retreat from the fascist model involving the deprivation of the rights of the work force, it was reminiscent of the *Werkgsemeinschaft* of the 1920s, despite the different circumstances of the day.

At the end of the war works councils and anti-fascist committees sprang up spontaneously in most mines and steelworks.[40] In addition to taking responsibility for the plants' maintenance and everyday operations, these organizations soon levelled demands at management. They called for the withdrawal of especially incriminated members of plant management and demanded to be included in management themselves. Dinkelbach, Chairman of the *Vereinigte Stahlwerke*, the largest iron and steel company in Germany, reported on 18 January 1946 to the select board meeting of the newly founded *Wirtschaftsvereinigung Eisen- und Stahlindustrie* (Iron and Steel Industry Trade Association) that the works councils of the *Vereinigte Stahlwereke* 'had demanded state ownership of the works, and further, a greater say for the works council in management'. At the same meeting, Karl Jarres, the chairman of the Klöckner Trust supervisory board, described the situation in Duisberg. The local unions there had also demanded the state ownership of heavy industry. Furthermore, the works councils had called for equal representation between capital and labour in both supervisory boards and management boards. Although Klöckner had rejected all such proposals, there remained the view that, in Jarres's words, 'a constructively-minded work-force should be allowed to share responsibility in the larger enterprises . . . to do nothing would be to make the situation worse. Serious consideration was very necessary. Employee participation was not avoidable'. Jarres was ready to accept a limited participation of the work-force in the supervisory boards, along the lines of the Weimar *Betriebsrätegesetz*. He was less willing to consider participation on the management board. The companies belonging to the Iron and Steel Industry Trade Association began to take various initiatives for a dialogue with the newly formed unions. It was agreed that work-force representation on management boards should be rejected. Instead, they hoped to achieve a workable compromise with the unions which would block claims for further rights of company-level co-determination and divert moves towards legal reform.[41]

Negotiations with the unions had been directed by Robert Lehr, the head of the administration in the North Rhine province, since the beginning of 1946. The heavy industrialists involved worked hard to prevent the total breakdown of talks, but they resisted broad concessions on company-level co-determination. Nevertheless, they were prepared to make concrete agreements on work-force participation at shopfloor level 'man to man'.[42] The main aim, however, was to win time and block any settlement that might be forced at company level by pressure from the work-force. The picture changed slightly after mid-1946 when trade unions started to repeat their demands for industry-wide co-determination, the disbanding of separate employers' associations and equal representation of capital and labour in the chambers of trade and industry. Heavy industry was more willing to compromise on the issue of industry-wide co-determination; but any shift in the balance of power within the plant in favour of the works councils and unions was strongly rejected. The aim was to keep their influence as far away as possible from company affairs.

Parallel with the negotiations with the unions, the iron and steel industry started to rebuild separate employers' associations. The Iron and Steel Industry Trade Association was reorganized from its fascist predecessor with British support in September 1945. Subsequently, the *Arbeitgeberverband für die rheinisch-westfalische Eisen- und Metallindustrie* (Employers' Association for the Iron and Metal Industry of North Rhine Westphalia) was formed early in 1946. Though it covered the entire metalworking industry it was clearly led by the Ruhr iron and steel industry and was financed by the trade association. The employers' association secretary participated regularly in the board meetings of the trade association.[43] The calculated promotion of this employers' association indicates the limitations of heavy industry's willingness to compromise on substantive matters.

Conflict over the content of the Allied Control Council's Works Council Law was not surprising in this situation. The employers were not prepared to make concessions. They rejected the equal representation of capital and labour on supervisory and management boards[44] and categorically denied the works councils any rights of co-determination in economic matters. Their rights were to be limited to a tightly defined sphere of social and personnel questions. A veto on information was the only suggestion for economic questions. The iron and steel industry also rejected the union demand for the disbanding of separate employers' associations. Admittedly, this did not entail the same sort of deadlock that characterized the issue of company-level co-determination. The retention of separate employers' associations was pushed through mainly by the metalworking industry. The small scale of factories in this area heightened employers' fear of infiltration by labour organizations. Separate employers' associations were seen as a weapon that could be used to prevent any compromise with unions within these companies, managed predominantly on patriarchal lines.

In the iron and steel industry on the other hand it was possible to imagine a take-over of socio-political functions by the trade association. Similarly a close working relationship between the two types of organization was called for. This was admittedly already the case between the Iron and Steel Industry Trade Association and the employers of the metalworking industry. A clear decision was reached only in the context of the deconcentration in

1947 and the introduction of parity co-determination with labour directors. The latter made union influence possible in the trade association under certain circumstances (namely, representation of a newly established dismembered steel plant by a labour director). All plans for an integrated organization of industrial interests were put into cold storage under increasing pressure from manufacturing industry, even though some plans had already been discussed with the unions. Agreement remained, however, that a close harmonization between employers' and trade associations should continue in the future. Only in public and to the unions should a clear division be apparent.[45]

By the end of 1946 the fundamental lines of Ruhr heavy industry policy were clear. First, rejection of all substantial works-council co-determination rights within the plant, whether in the supervisory or management board. Second, a willingness to compromise in the setting-up of co-determination rights over and above the individual plant in the form of economic councils at county and regional level; these councils were reminiscent of the temporary *Reichswirtschaftsrat* (Reich Economic Council) of the Weimar Republic as one of the solutions discussed after 1936 during the crisis of fascist labour law and regulation. Third, a rejection of union demands for the disbandment of separate employers' associations; this was in particular the result of the pressure from manufacturing industry.

The pressures on heavy industry intensified in 1947. Because of the failure of economic planning in the winter of 1946–7, the material situation of the population deteriorated drastically.[46] Above all in the Ruhr area, strikes and hunger marches, and calls for an improvement in the food situation linked up with more general demands for fundamental social reform, and particularly for the socialization of large-scale industry.[47] At the same time the influence of the Communist Party was growing. This was not confined to the *Landtag* (state parliament) and local elections. In certain coal districts the Communists won more than 50 per cent of the seats in works-council elections.[48] This pressure had political repercussions. In their *Ahlener Programm* in the spring of 1947 even the more conservative *Christlich-Demokratische Union* (CDU), the Christian Democratic Party, queried the continuing existence of large-scale industry and was generally very critical of the capitalist economic system, particularly because of its links with the genesis of National Socialism.[49] Simultaneously in the Landtag of North Rhine-Westphalia there had emerged something of a grand coalition for the socialization of heavy industry.[50]

At the same time the implementation of deconcentration in 1947 created an entirely new situation: it destroyed the power-base of heavy industry and it introduced into the dismembered works the very form of parity co-determination which had been so decidedly rejected by the employers. It also weakened heavy industry's organization because the dismembered plants belonged initially to neither the trade nor the employers' associations. 1948, however, saw their entry into the trade association. This led to a shift in power in favour of heavy industry which had just lost its iron and steel producing works. The newly created companies under trustee administration (*Treuhandverwaltung*) remained consistently at one remove from the employers' association because of the opposition of both the *Treuhandverwaltung* and the management as newly defined by parity co-determination. While the director of the GHH Trust Hilbert continued as chairman of the *Arbeitsgeberverband für der rheinisch-westfälischen Eisen- und Metallindustrie*, the association could in fact no longer represent the socio-political interests of iron and steel. The interests of metal-manufacturing works dominated unmistakeably as a result.[51]

In this context, various Ruhr companies bargained with the unions that they would agree to company-level co-determination in return for the unions supporting the employers' opposition to the deconcentration. Such offers became immaterial with the completion of dismemberment. The representatives of the now-dismembered companies or trusts therefore rapidly returned to their previous positions with an eye to a permanent future settlement of labour relations. This consisted of limited concessions to company-level co-determination and a greater willingness to compromise on the question of industry-wide co-determination rights. This policy was clearly motivated by the hope of delaying the legal settlement of labour relations until a new German government could enforce a solution agreeable to the trusts. For the settlement would involve not only the question of company-level and industry-wide co-determination but the reorganization of the trust structure. The success of this policy and therefore the abolition of parity co-determination seemed only a matter of time. In 1947 and, especially, in 1948, it became clearer that the British socialization plans were not practicable. In fact, an American model of private capitalism was being set in motion by the Marshall Plan and the currency reform of June 1948.

Such an assessment is fully laid out in a paper presented at the end of 1947 by Wilhelm Beutler, later first secretary of the *Bundesverband der Deutschen Industrie* (BDI or Federation of German Industries), and Wilhelm Salewski, secretary of the Iron and Steel Industry Trade Association and the *Arbeitgemeinschaft Eisen und Metal* (Working Group of the Iron and Metal Industry). This paper stressed to the supporters of socialization that the current economic situation would not permit the application of their policies to heavy industry. Production backlogs and a lack of capital meant that the socialization question had to be deferred

> until on the basis of careful and conscientious investigations, and after sufficient clarity has been gained about our political and economic future, it [the socialization question, W.P.] is mature enough to be decided upon freely by the entire German people in accordance with the rules of democracy.[52]

This tactic of postponing socialization and waiting until political conditions were more favourable for heavy industry had been successful once before, after the November Revolution of 1918–19.[53] At the same time, Beutler and

Salewski were aware that the trade unions were not going to be won over easily. They therefore wanted to involve the latter in the responsibility for economic reconstruction and suggested 'legal measures' for 'the construction of an economic democracy', and 'the securing of social peace'.[54] The 'construction of an economic democracy', which was the terminology of a traditional trade-union demand,[55] was to be achieved in two steps. First, the planning necessary to overcome the consequences of the war was to be carried out by self-governing organs comprised of an equal number of representatives from employers' associations and trade unions. Second, the peak organizations of labour and capital would establish a central economic chamber which would represent a sort of economic parliament with wide powers of executive action and rights to take initiatives in relation to parliament. Both suggestions appear at first sight to demonstrate extensive concessions to the trade unions, but they were actually very vague. The proposed 'equal control' of economic policy in the aftermath of the war was of a purely temporary nature and the experiences with the Reich Economic Council during the Weimar period[56] had been anything but positive as far as the trade unions were concerned.

At company level representatives of heavy industry were not prepared to make substantial concessions. In fact, their suggestions were not as advanced as the Works Council Law of the Weimar Republic, which had itself severely restricted the rights of the work force in the company. Employee representatives, according to Beutler and Salewski,

> should be given the possibility: (1) in all questions concerning the efficiency and technical production, (2) in all questions concerning workers' settlement and future security, (3) in the whole social area, to constantly liaise with the employers and thus to gain information from the management and to make suggestions, and also on their own responsibility to take an active part in affairs and to work productively.[57]

The proposals were designed above all to increase productivity by improving internal industrial relations through locking the worker into the interests of the company. As Beutler and Salewski put it, 'The idea of class struggle, bound as it is to the collectivist concept of compulsion, will only be overcome when the individual has a conscious sense of belonging to an order which he believes to be just'.[58] This *Betriebsfrieden* or shopfloor peace was to be achieved by guaranteeing the right to work in return for the cooperation of representatives of the work-force in the company. The guarantee of the right to work did indeed represent a far-reaching concession, but the details as to how this could be achieved remained vague, especially since it was to be the responsibility not of the employer but of the state. Finally, the almost revolutionary-sounding suggestion of investment controls in the producer-goods industry was quickly toned down on the grounds that such a control could only be executed on a European basis. In 1947 such a European solution was not in sight.

This was the frame of reference with which heavy industry faced the conflicts over parity co-determination and the works constitution after the founding of the Federal Republic. It was a model of *Betriebsgemeinschaft* (enterprise community) orientated towards employers and industrial peace in the context of a more formally defined right to industry-wide co-determination. It rejected union demands just as much as it disavowed the strong anti-union stance which had been championed before 1933. Nevertheless the shift in policy was confined to industry level: the plant itself was to remain the exclusive domain of capital.

CONFLICT OVER CO-DETERMINATION AND THE WORKS CONSTITUTION LAW IN THE EARLY FEDERAL REPUBLIC

The results of the first federal election and the formation of a conservative-liberal government were very satisfactory for the industrialists. In August 1949 Hermann Reusch, the chairman of the management board of the GHH Trust who had helped to finance the CDU and *Freie Demokratische Partei* (FDP) election campaigns, wrote privately, 'The results of the election came as a pleasant surprise. I can only hope that the results are assessed in a responsible manner. God save us from a second Weimar coalition' (an allusion to the participation of the SPD in government).[59] These hopes were realized. The government was a conservative one, even though parliamentary support partially rested on those groups within the CDU/CSU (*Christlich-Soziale Union*) faction who were sympathetic to the unions.

Despite their basic approval of the new government, however, the response of industrial interest groups to its proposals speedily to implement a Works Council Law was mixed. The parliamentary debates on the proposal did nothing to allay fears. Even representatives of the CDU spoke of the timeliness of equal representation between capital and labour within enterprises.[60] However, industry was given a chance to delay legislation until the conservative government had firmly established itself because of the government's insistence on the prior agreement of capital and labour on fundamental points.[61]

There was little clarity within industry on how to handle these government-imposed negotiations. There was a divergence of opinion between the *Bundesvereinigung der Deutschen Arbeitgeberverbände* (BDA – the peak organization of all regional and branch employers' associations) and the BDI (the peak organization of all trade associations). The leading group in the BDA around Walter Raymond and its executive manager Gerhard Erdmann, a former secretary of the *Zentralarbeitsgemeinschaft* (ZAG) and subsequently a more or less prominent Nazi, proposed an industry-wide organization of employers and unions, an idea rooted in the tradition of the Stinnes–Legien agreement and subsequent National Socialist proposals after 1936. Many non-metalworking employers also accepted this policy, especially since an all-out confrontation with the unions would not be acceptable to the CDU, the dominant party in the conservative government. Raymond and Erdmann supported only limited compromises at company level, namely one-third union and worker participation in supervisory boards and co-determination for works councils only on social and personnel matters. They believed that, given the internal conflicts between Communist and Christian traditions within the DGB, there was a possibility of winning union consensus on these issues.

The BDI, however, strongly opposed these proposals, rejected any concessions to the unions and proposed the alternative of 'man to man' negotiations at shopfloor level. Heavy industry was not directly represented in the BDI, but it was dominated by the metalworking industries of North Rhine–Westphalia and Bavaria with close links to certain parts of heavy industry such as the GHH Trust. This and other former integrated companies were represented through their manufacturing branches. The GHH Trust, for example, was represented by its manufacturing branch through its participation in various machine-building factories. The group around Fritz Berg, the President of the BDI, and Wilhelm Vorwerk, chairman of the North Rhine–Westphalia employers' association, believed that negotiations with the unions could only be used to delay the decision on the Works Constitution Law until the conservative government was strong enough to stand up to union demands.[62]

In late 1949 and early 1950 the leaders of the BDA were rudely called to heel by the BDI during the first meetings with the DGB and instructed that they were not to offer any concessions without prior reference to the BDI.[63] This veto was largely responsible for the discussions between the DGB and BDA in spring and summer 1950 achieving very little. The employers rejected any form of works-council co-determination on economic matters and equal representation of capital and labour on supervisory boards. They also rejected any union representative on supervisory boards as an element alien to the company. Employee representatives would be confined to one-third of the supervisory board, and should consist of employees from the plant in question over 30 years old and with more than ten years of service in the plant. Company-level co-determination was to be confined to social and personnel matters.[64]

The government shared the fundamentals of this view; nevertheless, its precarious power balance made its actions unpredictable. Following the failure of the talks between the unions and the employers' associations, the CDU/CSU faction put forward its own legislative proposals which went further than the government would have liked. In particular, they provided for economic committees (*Wirtschaftsausschüsse*) with equal representation of capital and labour and for one-third employee representation (possibly including union representatives) on supervisory boards.[65] The background to these proposals was the CDU/CSU faction's desire to anticipate a more radical SPD bill and to conciliate its own labour wing without antagonizing industry. In this it was only partially successful. The BDI and the metalworking employers' associations protested about the bill to Chancellor Adenauer and threatened to withdraw promised financial support from the CDU's election campaign in North Rhine-Westphalia. As a result, Adenauer publicly distanced himself from his own party's proposal and announced his own government proposal.[66]

Heavy industry, as an organized group, did not play a decisive role in this phase, though it was still a strong influence within the BDI and employers' associations. It had itself to accept the operation of co-determination rights in its own dismembered plants and to work together with unions on the control boards of the seized collieries and steelworks.[67] However, it continued to assume that once deconcentration was settled and there was a return to old ownership relations, existing co-determination practices would be revised. Nevertheless, there were differing views on strategy. Some like Robert Lehr, now the Home Secretary, and Gunter Henle, the director of the Klöckner Trust, wanted a political solution based on consensus and an understanding with the unions similar to the CDU/CSU proposals, which made certain concessions but still involved the abolition of existing parity co-determination and were fairly close to most industrialists' demands. Unlike the BDI leaders Berg and Reusch, they wanted to avoid a frontal confrontation with the unions which they did not believe would be acceptable to the CDU. Their ideas differed in style and tone from that of Berg and Reusch; but in substance they were not so far removed.

Other employers were, however, prepared to go further. At the beginning of 1950, Heinrich Kost, director of *Deutsche Kohlenbergbauleitung* (DKBL, the German coal trusteeship), representing the coal companies that were not integrated with the iron and steel industry, proposed to the unions negotiations on extensive co-determination rights in the coalmining industry.[68] While Kost did not want to concede equality to the unions, he did want to involve them in his plans for a new industrial order directed against the domination of the former integrated companies or ex-trusts (*Altkonzerne*). There was a growing difference between the attitude of the iron and steel firms and the coalmining industry, reflecting their conflicting interests in the restructuring of Ruhr heavy industry. Both groups rejected equality of labour and capital within the plant. But they differed on what form agreement with the unions should take, just as they differed on the future form of company structures. The Schuman Plan further entangled the issue of co-determination with dismemberment and the shape of the new industrial order. The question of co-determination therefore became increasingly involved with wider political and economic questions.

COMPROMISE ON THE PARITY CO-DETERMINATION (*MONTANMITBESTIMMUNG*) LAW 1951

These interlinked issues came to the fore at the end of 1950 when the question of the final reorganization of company structures in heavy industry came on to the political agenda. Law no. 27 of the High Commission for Germany made the final restructuring of the iron and steel and mining industries the responsibility of the Allied High Commission in consultation with the Combined Control Group for heavy industry and the trustee administrations (the *Stahltreuhändervereinigung* (Union of Steel Trustees) for steel and the DKBL for coal).

Different interest-groups crystallized very rapidly on these issues and on the issues of the Schuman Plan which was being negotiated simultaneously. American policy was based on an anti-trust stance. The English and French were interested in weakening German competition as much as possible. They therefore argued for a further division of the trusts and rejected the reintegration of coal and steel.[69] The federal government saw in the Schuman Plan a way out of the discriminatory regulations of the Ruhr statute and therefore accepted it. But at the same time it wanted to place German heavy industry in a strong competitive position and therefore wanted scope for the most efficient company structures. The ex-trusts likewise hoped to reintegrate coal and steel and to shake off parity co-determination. They recognized that the creation of new company structures through Law no. 27 would raise the question of co-determination. But it was also clear that the steel trustees, the DKBL and the unions would only agree to the proposed reintegration of coal and steel if the co-determination issue was settled to their satisfaction.

On 20 November 1950 the representatives of Mannesman, Hoesch, *Vereinigte Stahlwerke* and Klöckner agreed to offer five of the eleven positions on the supervisory board to union and employee representatives. The eleventh member would be a neutral appointment.[70] The representative of *Vereinigte Stahlwerke* wrote to the Home Secretary Lehr that,

> I again emphasize that I am thoroughly prepared to reach a reasonable understanding with the unions on the question of the composition of the supervisory boards in the new companies – as I believe most of the gentlemen of the former companies are. However, this assumes that the stubborn demand for the equal representation of capital and labour in the supervisory boards and the general introduction of the labour director is not maintained.[71]

Despite their retention of these fundamental aims, however, the ex-trusts realized that their proposed compromise would go too far for the BDI. They feared that the 'free entrepreneurs . . . might interpret it as a measure with which the Ruhr industry is stabbing them in the back'. The ex-trusts rejected this view.

> It should be recognized that we already have a status quo in the iron and steel industry as a result of dismemberment which is such that the above suggestion represents an improvement at all events. So we would not be

giving the unions a greater platform from which to fight but merely trying to win back that which has been lost. In this way it would be possible to follow this path without being accused of lacking loyalty'.[72]

Among the ex-trusts, only GHH (with its greater production-base in metal manufacturing) and Reusch and Hilbert continued to reject totally the unions' demands for co-determination. By the second half of 1950 this position was isolated in the camp of heavy industry. That very isolation, however, brought it strong support from leading members of the BDI. In the trustee administrations the situation also remained complex. The Union of Steel Trustees welcomed parity co-determination, but also supported a limited reintegration of coal and steel. The DKBL, however, rejected the restoration of integrated coal and steel firms on principle, not least because of the strong representation of mines which had never belonged to steelworks.[73]

Against this background, and in the context of negotiations on the Schuman Plan, the federal government took the initiative. In November 1950 the government, the Union of Steel Trustees, the DKBL and the ex-trusts agreed to a proposal for the reorganization of the iron and steel industry and the mines. It planned a moderate reintegration. 25 per cent of coal production was to be linked to the iron and steel companies. When the newly created companies were transferred from occupation regulation into German law, parity co-determination was automatically removed.[74] IG Metall (the Metalworkers' Union) at once called a strike in defence of parity co-determination, with 95 per cent of both steelworkers and coalminers supporting the strike in their initial ballots. The strike threat disrupted the strategy of the federal government and the ex-trusts by threatening to draw in the Allied High Commission. At the same time the unions made it clear that they would support the reintegration proposals provided that parity co-determination was maintained in iron and steel and extended into coal.

This was Adenauer's moment. Long negotiations in the Chancellor's office resulted in a compromise in January 1951.[75] There was to be equal representation of capital and labour on the supervisory boards (five shareholder representatives plus five union/employee representatives). The neutral eleventh member had to be chosen by agreement between both sides. A Labour Director was also to be appointed, such appointments to be subject to veto by employee representatives on the supervisory board. His duty was 'to work for the protection of the human dignity of every employee . . . [and] to create a good working atmosphere and a warm interest within the plant with the understanding of all employees'. The rights of the works councils were, however, not settled.[76]

Thus the ex-trusts were pressured into compromise, and this precipitated major conflicts on the periphery of the employer camp. Reusch and the GHH, the only ex-trust involved, along with the BDI and some metalworking employers, made great efforts to block the new agreement. Their strategy was to reject negotiation under pressure and take on a strike if necessary. By 6 January 1951, Reusch and the employers' associations of North Rhine-Westphalia had succeeded in again creating a united front against the unions' strike threat. Reusch claimed the support of Adenauer and Erhard and hoped to go on to the offensive: he wrote to Fritz Berg that the 'situation had never been so good. The execution of the strike would signal the collapse of the united trade-union movement'.[77]

Reusch and the BDI, however, under-estimated the unity and readiness to strike of the DGB. The unions refused to withdraw their strike notice in defence of *Montanmitbestimmung* and thereby broke up the employers' united front. The leaders of the ex-trusts, notably Henle and Kost, finally accepted Adenauer's compromise on union involvement combined with reintegration of steel and coal and, under pressure, agreed to the incorporation of *Montanmitbestimmung* under German law. The settlement deeply conflicted with their principles, but it was the price to be paid for their primary goal of the restoration of the old integrated trust structures.

The BDI and the various employers' associations had more or less reluctantly to watch these developments, and they withdrew from negotiations in Bonn. The withdrawal was also motivated by a desire to underline the exceptional character of the negotiations. The BDI and BDA now began to focus primarily on blocking any extension of the model provided by the coal, iron and steel industry and holding the government to its promises not to permit a generalized extension of these rulings. They succeeded in this to a great extent, partly because of government support and partly because the DGB was not well prepared for the ensuing negotiations on the broader Works Constitution Law.[78]

Debate now focused on the rights of works councils and of company-level co-determination in industry as a whole. In response to union demands for equal representation, the stance of industry during 1950 was that the co-determination rights of works councils should be limited to social and personnel matters, along with a 'right to information' in economic questions; employees should be allowed one-third representation on supervisory boards: these representatives would have to work in the plant and only one-half could be chosen by the unions.[79]

After the special ruling on the coal, iron and steel industries in 1951, the employers' attitude hardened. Their position was strengthened by the government's change of heart once it became assured of the support of the CDU/CSU faction's labour wing. This group had come into conflict with IG Metall over the latter's 'illegal threat to strike' and their relationship with the unions had become tense. When the Works Constitution Law was passed in 1952, the unions no longer had the means to exert political pressure that they had enjoyed during the debate on the Schuman Plan, and their strategy in regard to extending *Montanmitbestimmung* was unclear. The unions' failure to exert significant pressure to modify the works-constitution bill during 1952 was striking, even when the repressive attitude of the labour courts is taken into account.[80]

The core of the postwar legal settlement was shaped by the attitudes of the employers and the conservative–liberal government. Their weak point was the destruction of heavy industry's power-base by the occupation policy of deconcentration. In order to reconstruct this base against occupation opposition, heavy industry needed union support. But the unions were only prepared to lend such support if the co-determination introduced in 1947 in the context of deconcentration was maintained. Thus, although the former power-base of the steel trusts and the mines of the Ruhr was restored in 1952, a price had to be paid. On the one hand, the employers' social influence was constrained; on the other hand, they became entangled in international control structures through the European Coal and Steel Community. Moreover, divisions became apparent within heavy industry. Those enterprises more involved in manufacturing took a much more reserved stance on the issue of co-determination and of the ECSC than the ex-trusts who wanted to restore their industrial base, whatever the concessions they made to co-determination. Thus the introduction of *Montanmitbestimmung* was not the result of a concept for the settlement of industrial relations, either when introduced under British auspices in 1947 or when later embodied in German law. It was the outcome of political compromises. Nevertheless, its consequences were to be of great importance, even though private capital's position of power at company level remained substantially intact.

DEVELOPMENTS IN POSTWAR INDUSTRIAL RELATIONS

How was the subsequent development of industrial relations influenced by parity co-determination in coal, iron and steel? The position of the heavy industrialists, as set out in the paper by Beutler and Salewski, reflected the debate and experience of the 1920s and 1930s.[81] The rationalization of the 1920s demonstrated the necessity of improved social and labour structures within the plant.[82] In this context, management had assigned to works councils an important role in the settlement of disputes and the implementation of social legislation, on condition that they did not act as an extended arm of the unions.[83] At the same time there was an expansion in what was called *Soziale Betriebspolitik*, 'personnel policy' or 'human-resource management'. Management increasingly devoted attention to the organization of the social side of the production process, from the recruitment of workers to safety in the workplace, both as an issue in itself and as one related to increasing productivity.[84] These policies continued to expand during the Nazi era, even though there was no longer a dimension of settling internal company disputes.[85] In relation to increased productivity, such policies proved to be more and more necessary.

After the War, enterprises revived these developments. They grew further in importance in 1948–9 in order to integrate foreign unskilled workers or inadequately trained immigrants from East Germany. They were seen as an essential part of the revival of international competitiveness. Revived competitiveness was seen to depend on the restoration of prewar trust structures and the optimal use of plant and on the organization of the social side of the production process. Beutler and Salewski echoed the rising flood of literature on personnel management and on social legislation to secure the well-being of the worker in arguing that it was necessary to integrate workers at plant level to facilitate a smooth organization of the production process.

Heavy industry perceived the unions as a threat to the smooth flow of production. They were also concerned about the difficulty of disciplining the re-created works councils after 1947. Relief came with the introduction of parity co-determination. It reduced the works councils' scope for action to a degree that was functional for the enterprises concerned in the settlement of internal disputes. At the same time the introduction of labour directors forced and allowed a differentiation and specialization of personnel management. The introduction of *Montanmitbestimmung* in 1947 and its defence in 1951 represented a political defeat for the industrialists. But it ultimately resulted in an improvement of industrial relations at company level.[86] It also shackled the unions to the persistance of private capitalism and effectively committed them to social partnership between capital and labour. In short, it led to a modernization of the political debate in heavy industry at company and institutional level after 1951. The Works Constitution Law gave the unions a nominal victory but also restricted the rights of the work-force; at the same time, however, the strong anti-union traditions of the employers were decisively restricted. These twin changes provided the basis for a reconstruction of industrial relations.

NOTES

This chapter was translated by Kirsten Jones and Beverly Locke, Bochum. The German terms *Arbeitgeberverbände* and *Wirtschaftsverbände* are translated as 'employers' associations' and 'trade associations' respectively. The former deal with 'social' issues such as wage negotiations, while the latter deal with questions of economic policy and regulation.

1 See Theo Pirker, *Die Blinde Macht. Die Deutschen Gewerkschaften seit 1945*, 2 vols (Munich, 1961). For a less critical position see, Klaus Schönhoven, *Die Deutschen Gewerkschaften* (Frankfurt, 1988).
2 See Michael Schneider, 'Unternehmer und soziale Demokratie. Zur unternehmerischen Argumentation in der Mitbestimmungsdebatte der sechziger Jahre', *Archiv für Sozialgeschichte* 13 (1973), pp. 243–88; Michael Schneider, *Unternehmer und Demokratie. Die freien Gewerkschaften in der unternehmerischen Ideologie der Jahre 1918 bis 1933* (Bonn, 1975).
3 Oskar Negt, 'Gesellschaftsbild und Geschichtsbewusstsein der wirtschaftlichen und militärischen Führungsschichten. Zur ideologie der autoritären Leistungsgesellschaft', in Gert Schäfer and Carl Nedelmann (eds), *Der CDU-Staat. Analysen zur Verfassungswirklichkeit der Bundesrepublik* (Frankfurt, 1969), vol. 2, pp. 359–424.

4 See Volker R. Berghahn, *Unternehmer und Politik in der Bundesrepublik* (Frankfurt, 1985). English version: *The Americanisation of West German Industry, 1945–1973* (Leamington Spa, 1986).

5 Rolf Steininger, 'England und die deutsche Gewerkschaftsbewegung' *Archiv für Sozialgeschichte* 18 (1978), p. 44. The quotation is from p. 48.

6 Steininger, 'England', p. 48.

7 Richard Detje *et al.*, *Von der Westzone zum Kalten Krieg. Restauration und Gewerkschaftspolitik im Nachkriegsdeutschland* (Hamburg, 1982), pp. 118–21.

8 Werner Plumpe, *Vom Plan zum Markt. Wirtschaftsverwaltung und Unternehmerverbände in der britischen Zone* (Düsseldorf, 1987), pp. 52–7.

9 Steininger, 'England', p. 49.

10 Gloria Müller, *Mitbestimmung in der Nachkriegszeit. Britische Besatzungsmacht, Unternehmer, Gewerkschaften* (Düsseldorf, 1987), pp. 86ff.

11 Eberhard Schmidt, *Die verhinderte Neuordnung 1945–52. Die Auseinandersetzungen um die Demokratisierung der Wirtschaft in den Westzonen und der Bundesrepublik Deutschland* (Frankfurt, 1970), pp. 53ff.

12 Ernst-Ulrich Huster *et al.*, *Determinanten der westdeutschen Restauration* (Frankfurt, 1972), pp. 44ff.

13 Wolfgang Friedmann, *The Allied Military Government in Germany* (London, 1947).

14 Rolf Steininger, *Deutsche Geschichte 1945–61. Darstellung und Dokumente* (Frankfurt, 1983), vol. 1, pp. 167ff; Falk Pingel, 'Die "Russen am Rhein"? Zur Wende der britischen Deutschlandpolitik im Frujahr 1946', *Vierteljahrshefte für Zeitgeschichte* 30 (1982), pp. 98–116.

15 Frank Deppe *et al.*, *Kritik der Mitbestimmung. Eine Studie* (Frankfurt, 1969), pp. 58ff.

16 Müller, *Mitbestimmung in der Nachkriegszeit* pp. 146ff.

17 ibid., pp. 197ff.

18 Schmidt, *Verhinderte Neuordnung*, pp. 25ff.

19 For a general account see Bernd Otto, 'Der Kampf um die Mitbestimmung', in Heinz-Oskar Vetter (ed.), *Vom Sozialistengesetz zur Mitbestimmung* (Cologne, 1975), pp. 399ff.

20 Detje *et al.*, *Von der Westzone zum Kalten Krieg*, pp. 139–42.

21 On Communist influence see Müller, *Mitbestimmung in der Nachkriegszeit*, pp. 163ff.

22 Huster *et al.*, *Determinanten der westdeutschen Restauration* pp. 120ff.

23 Reiner Pommerin, 'Die Zwangsvereinigung von KPD und SPD zur SED. Eine britische Analyse vom April 1946', *Vierteljahrshefte für Zeitgeschichte* 36 (1988), pp. 319–38.

24 Christoph Klessmann, 'Betriebsparteigruppen und Einheitsgewerkschaft. Zur betrieblichen Arbeit der Parteien in der Frühphase der westdeutschen Arbeiterbewegung', *Vierteljahrshefte für Zeitgeschichte* 31 (1983), pp. 272–307.

25 Otto, 'Der Kampf um die Mitbestimmung', *passim.*

26 Schmidt, *Verhinderte Neuordnung*, pp. 114ff.

27 Hermann Reusch (GHH) *et al.* to Viktor Agartz, Chairman of the Bizonal German Economic Administration, 21 Jan. 1947, in Erich Potthoff, *Der Kampf um die Montanmitbestimmung* (Cologne-Deutz, 1957), pp. 45ff.

28 Reusch (GHH) and Jarres (Klöckner) to the DGB of the British Zone, 18 Jan. 1947, in Potthoff, *Der Kampf*, p. 44.

29 Müller, *Mitbestimmung in der Nachkriegszeit*, pp. 125ff.

30 Gerhard Schulze, 'Der Langnamverein', in H. J. Fricke (ed.), *Lexikon zur Parteiengeschichte*, vol. 4 (Cologne, 1986), pp. 379–401.

31 Elaine Glovka Spencer, *Management and Labor in Imperial Germany: Ruhr Industrialists as Employers, 1896–1914* (New Brunswick, NJ, 1984); Gerald D.

Feldman, *Iron and Steel in the German Inflation, 1914–23* (Princeton, 1977), pp. 27–49.

32 Ilse Costas, *Die Auswirkungen der Konzentration das Kapitals auf die Arbeiterklasse* (Frankfurt, 1977).

33 See Gerald D. Feldman and Irmgard Steinisch, *Industrie und Gewerkschaften, 1918–24. Die überforderte Zentralarbeitsgemeinschaft* (Stuttgart, 1985). On the price-setting problem, see Feldman, *Iron and Steel.*

34 Volker Hentschel, *Geschichte der deutschen Sozialpolitik 1880–1980* (Frankfurt, 1983), pp. 71ff.

35 Bernd Weisbrod, 'Die Befreiung von den "Tariffesseln". Deflationspolitik als Krisenstrategie der Unternehmer in der ära Brüning', *Geschichte und Gesellschaft* 11 (1985), pp. 295–325.

36 Bernd Weisbrod, *Schwerindustrie in der Weimarer Republik. Interessenpolitik zwischen Stabilisierung und Krise* (Wuppertal, 1978), pp. 246ff.

37 For the situation after 1933 see Andreas Kranig, *Lockung und Zwang. Zur Arbeitsverfassung im Dritten Reich* (Stuttgart, 1983).

38 For a general account see Timothy W. Mason, *Sozialpolitik im Dritten Reich. Arbeiterklasse und Volksgemeinschaft* (Opladen, 1977): Klaus Wisotzky, *Der Ruhrbergbau im Dritten Reich. Studien zur Sozialpolitik im Ruhrbergbau und zum sozialen Verhalten der Bergleute in den Jahren 1933–39* (Düsseldorf, 1983), pp. 139ff.

39 See Rudiger Hachtmann, 'Von der Klassenharmonie zum regulierten Klassenkampf', in Heinz-Gerhard Haupt (ed.), *Soziale Bewegungen. Geschichte und Theorie. Jahrbuch 1: Arbeiterbewegung und Faschismus* (Frankfurt, 1984), pp. 159–83.

40 Hartmut Pietsch, *Militärregierung, Bürokratie und Sozialisierung. Zur Entwicklung des politischen Systems in den Städten des Ruhrgebietes 1945–48* (Duisberg, 1979).

41 Minutes of a meeting of the *Eisenkreis* (the board of the *Wirtschaftsvereinigung Eisen- und Stahlindustrie)*, 18 Jan. 1946, Historical Archive of the Haniel AG (HA) 400 101 46/115.

42 Note of a meeting of the *Eisenkreis*, 28 Feb. 1946 (Rheinish-Westphalian Business Archive (RWWA) 1/201/5).

43 Minutes of a meeting of the *Eisenkreis*, 31 Jan. 1946 (HA 400 101 46/115); Minutes of a meeting of the *Eisenkreis* 25 Apr. 1946 (HA 300 101 46/72).

44 HA 400 101 46/159.

45 Minutes of a meeting of the trade associations of the metalworking industries, 2 May 1947 (HA 400 101 46/159).

46 Hans Schlange-Schoningen (ed.), *Im Schatten des Hungers. Dokumentarisches zur Ernährungspolitik und Ernährungswirtschaft 1945–49* (revised by Justus Rohrbach) (Hamburg, 1955), pp. 123ff.

47 Christoph Klessmann and Peter Friedemann, *Streiks und Hungermärsche im Ruhrgebiet 1946–48* (Frankfurt, 1977).

48 Works Council election results in Pietsch, *Militärregierung*, p. 312.

49 Franz Focke, *Sozialismus aus christlicher Verantwortung. Die Idee eines christlichen Sozialismus in der katholisch-sozialen Bewegung und in der CDU* (Wuppertal, 1978), pp. 251ff.

50 Ernst-Ulrich Huster, *Die Politik der SPD 1945–50* (Frankfurt 1978), pp. 65ff.

51 Werner Bührer, *Ruhrstahl und Europa. Die Wirtschaftsvereinigung Eisen- und Stahlindustrie und die Anfänge der europaischen Integration* (Munich, 1986), pp. 51–6.

52 Wilhelm Beutler and Wilhelm Salewski, undated paper, probably November 1947 (Hauptstaatarchiv Düsseldorf RWN 96/33, B11. 29–36: here Bl. 31).

53 Feldman and Steinisch, *Industrie und Gewerkschaften, passim.*

54 Beutler/Salewski papers, Bl. 33.
55 For a general account see Rudolf Kuda, 'Das Konzept der Wirtschafts-demokratie' in Heinz-Oskar Vetter (ed.), *Vom Sozialistengesetz zur Mitbestimmung* (Cologne, 1975), pp. 253–74. Playing with 'leftist' terms in order to confuse was common practice in industrial circles after 1945: see the programmatic speech of the Chairman of the *Wirtschaftsvereinigung Chemische Industrie der britischen Zone*, Wilhelm Alexander Menne, Mar. 1947, entitled 'Pflichten eines schopferischen Unternehmertums': DGB Archiv, Ordner Britische Zone/allegemeines 1945–9.
56 For the temporary *Reichswirtschaftsrat* and for the Weimar conception of labour law and co-determination, see Bernd-Jürgen Wendt, 'Mitbestimmung und Sozialpartnerschaft in der Weimar Republik', *Aus Politik und Zeitsgeschichte*, 28 June 1969, pp. 27–46.
57 Beutler/Salewski papers, Bl. 34.
58 ibid., Bl. 35.
59 Hermann Reusch to August Heinrichsbauer, 18 Aug. 1949 (HA 400 101 145/149).
60 Minutes of the Bundestag, 4 Nov. 1949. Gabriele Müller-List, *Montanmitbestimmung. Das Gesetz uber die Mitbestimmung der Arbeitnehmer in den Aufsichtsräten und Vorständen der Unternehmen des Bergbaus und der Eisen und Stahl erzeugenden Industrie* (Düsseldorf, 1984), p. 4.
61 Horst Thum, *Mitbestimmung in der Montanindustrie. Der Mythos vom Sieg der Gewerkschaften* (Stuttgart, 1982), pp. 47ff.
62 ibid.
63 Reusch to Hilbert, 6 Jan. 1950 (HA 400 101 46/160).
64 See Müller-List, *Montanmitbestimmung*, pp. 48ff; Berghahn, *Unternehmer und Politik*, p. 219.
65 Müller-List, *Montanmitbestimmung*, pp. 153–61.
66 Reusch to Berg, 15 May 1950 and 20 May 1950 (HA 400 101 46/30).
67 Thum, *Mitbestimmung in der Montanindustrie*, pp. 51ff.
68 Notice of the French High Commissioner, François-Poncet, about a meeting with representatives of the German coalmining industry, 14 Jan. 1950; Müller-List, *Montanmitbestimmung*, pp. 58ff.
69 Thum, *Mitbestimmung in der Montanindustrie*, pp. 57ff.
70 Müller-List, *Montanmitbestimmung*, pp. 164ff.
71 Letter from Hans Günter Sohl to Robert Lehr, quoted by Müller-List, *Montanmitbestimmung*, p. 177.
72 Müller-List, *Montanmitbestimmung*, p. 165.
73 Thum, *Mitbestimmung in der Montanindustrie*, pp. 55ff.
74 ibid., p. 68.
75 ibid.
76 Rulings about co-determination in the coalmining and iron and steel industries, 26 Jan. 1951, Müller-List, *Montanmitbestimmung*, pp. 268ff.
77 Reusch to Berg, 8 Jan. 1951 (HA 400 101 46/33).
78 Thum, *Mitbestimmung in der Montanindustrie*, pp. 86–93.
79 Berghahn, *Unternehmer und Politik*, pp. 235ff.
80 Thomas Blanke *et al.*, (eds), *Kollektives Arbeitsrecht. Quellentexte zur Geschichte des Arbeitsrechtes in Deutschland. Vol. 2, 1933 bis zur Gegenwart* (Reinbek, 1975), pp. 222–4; B. Wahsner, 'Das Arbeitsrechtskartell – Die Restauration des kapitalistischen Arbeitsrechts in Westdeutschland nach 1945', *Kritische Justiz* 7, (1974), pp. 369ff.
81 Peter Hinrichs and Lothar Peter, *Industrieller Friede? Arbeitswissenschaft und Rationalisierung in der Weimarer Republik* (Cologne, 1976); Peter Hinrichs, *Arbeitspsychologie, Industrie- und Betriebssoziologie in Deutschland* (Cologne,

1981): Rüdiger Hachtmann, *Industriearbeit im Dritten Reich. Untersuchungen zu den Lohn- und Arbeitsbedingungen in Deutschland 1933–1945* (Göttingen, 1989).

82 Rudolf Schwenger, 'Die soziale Frage im Betriebe', *Zeitschrift für die gesamte Staatswissenschaft* (1935), pp. 148–63; Rudolf Schwenger, *Die betriebliche Sozialpolitik im Ruhrkohlenbergbau* (Munich, 1932).

83 Ernest Fraenkel, 'Zehn Jahre Betriebsrategesetz', in Thilo Ramm (ed.), *Arbeitsrecht und Politik. Quellentexte 1918–33* (Neuwied, 1966), pp. 97–112.

84 L. H. Adolph Geck, *Soziale Betriebsführung. Zugleich Einführung in die betriebliche Sozialpolitik* (Essen, 1953; 1st edn, 1938).

85 Hachtmann, *Industriearbeit*, pp. 254–301.

86 Rudolf Judith (ed.), *40 Jahre Montanmitbestimmung. Erfahrungen. Probleme. Perspektiven* (Cologne, 1986); Frank Deppe *et al., Kritik der Mitbestimmung. Partnerschaft oder Klassenkampf* (Frankfurt, 1979), pp. 110–151.

7 Enterprise management and employer organization in Italy

Fiat, public enterprise and *Confindustria* 1922–1990

Giovanni Contini

EMPLOYERS AND FASCISM

During the early years of fascist rule, *Confindustria*, (*Confederazione Generale dell'Industria Italiana*, the General Confederation of Italian Industry), wavered in its relationship with the new regime. A number of leading employers had financially supported Mussolini's seizure of power in 1922, and *Confindustria* itself had collaborated with his government in the first years of its existence.[1] In 1924, however, during the Matteotti crisis, *Confindustria* kept its distance from Mussolini's shaken government.[2] When the fascist regime overcame that crisis and reinforced its policies *Confindustria* fell into line. But in 1926–7 it campaigned against Mussolini's revaluation of the lira, which created an economic crisis in Italy despite world-wide prosperity and expansion, and proved fatal for many small firms.[3] *Confindustria* likewise firmly, and finally victoriously, opposed the proposals put forward by Edmondo Rossoni, the fascist trade unionist, with the support of a few small and medium-sized firms, for 'integral corporativism', a single trade union of workers and employers.[4] But the fluctuating attitude of *Confindustria* towards fascism cannot erase the basic fact that Italian industrialists bowed and conformed to the regime, while from 1925 onwards, the organization itself was integrated into the fascist state, as a result of the Palazzo Vidoni Pact which established the representational monopoly of the new corporations.

As the years passed, the fascist regime was able to exercise growing control over the activities of private firms, which needed state support to obtain tariff protection, import-quota restrictions and public contracts. Giovanni Agnelli, the founder of Fiat, aptly characterized the situation with his tart remark that Italian industrialists were 'governmental by definition'. The turn towards economic autarky was also a result of the fascist regime, developing after the international sanctions which followed Italy's conquest of Ethiopia in 1936. In that year, Gaetano Salvemini, the famous anti-fascist historian who had fled to the United States, maintained that the power of Italian industrialists had been reduced while that of the fascist state had grown. To request the assistance of the state meant having subsequently to submit to the control of state officials and fascist party bosses. The trade unions, too, according to Salvemini, represented a threat to the industrialists from within the fascist regime: 'If the capitalists were to stop favouring the policy of the party, the party could finally move to the left'. But if Salvemini's interpretation captures the growing dependence of industry on the state during the late 1930s, it also over-emphasizes the political pressures on employers and neglects opposing pressures on the regime from the industrialists.[5]

The state and the political system had always played a crucial role in the Italian economy, but the coming of the Fascist regime marked a change of gear in the political role of employers, particularly larger firms such as Fiat (*Fabbrica Italiana Automobili Torino*, Italian Automobile Works of Turin). Recently Sapelli has proposed a model of the relationship between the industrial firms (particularly Fiat) and the fascist state which goes beyond both the one-sided image of industrialists as the true masters of fascism or the opposite image of a fascist government independent of industrial power.[6] According to this interpretation, during the fascist regime, competing interests clashed directly within the fascist party, soon to be absorbed by the state, which was thus 'parcelled out' among the more powerful industrialists. The proliferation of decree laws is the clearest indication of this process. In the one-party state, he argues, it was mostly the larger firms that were able to impose their interests, because their social position and material resources exercised by definition a 'conditioning power' over the regime. When the interests of the large firms were injured, Sapelli suggests, they subsequently obtained some form of compensation. But when the interests of the small and medium-sized firms were sacrificed they received no such compensation in the absence of alternative channels of representation.

Naturally, there were moments in which even large firms, such as Fiat, were unable to defend their interests. At the end of the 1930s, for example, the fascist regime attempted to alleviate the disastrous state of the public finances by imposing a tax of 10 per cent on the capital stock of all firms, a tax on petrol and higher charges on foreign exchange.[7] But this was shortly before the war, when Fiat began to experience growing difficulties in its relations with the regime, difficulties which were to increase during the course of the conflict. In previous years, Fiat had managed to overcome the disadvantages resulting from the revaluation of the lira: its losses in the sphere of exports were made up through adjustments to its fiscal obligations.[8] When in 1929–30, the Ford Motor Company tried to establish itself in Italy, Fiat succeeded in blocking this initiative and had its foreign rival expelled from the Italian market on the grounds of 'national order', in Mussolini's words.[9]

During the fascist era, Fiat was thus able to protect its interests more efficiently than were other firms, and as well as *Confindustria* which represented them. Its vast size ensured that the company's demands were more readily met than those of the multitude of small firms, and its contacts with international finance allowed Fiat to move outside a purely Italian orbit, and therefore partly to escape the regime's totalitarian grip, particularly towards the end of the war.

Fiat developed an ideology of superiority to the rest of the Italian economic world, which remained strong well after the end of the fascist regime. As Agnelli's lieutenant Vittorio Valetta declared:

> Rationalized industry could thus address the rest of the social-economic world: my machines work, my plants are solid, my calculations are infinitesimally exact. . . . But you, my friends, colleagues in other industries, in commerce and finance . . . what are you doing, you who are so obviously incapable of upholding the continuity of my technical effort with your policy, your economy, your finance?[10]

Agnelli's practical proposals in this period demonstrate this sense of superiority in action. For example, in order to overcome the impact of the 1929 crisis on popular purchasing power, the elderly senator suggested a reduction in working hours with no loss of wages.[11] This proposal would have proved fatal for many small and medium-sized firms, and would have triggered a gigantic process of capital concentration and an increase in the mass of wages. As Agnelli intended, however, it would also have resulted in an enormous stimulus to economic recovery. This proposal, which was taken up with some interest by the International Labour Office and the fascist trade unions, was strongly opposed by *Confindustria*, which maintained that if implemented it would provoke a major crisis of authority within the organization. The regime too reacted negatively, judging the proposal to be 'Fordist'. But Fiat managed yet again to obtain some compensation in the crisis, in the form of state export subsidies, quota restrictions and bilateral trade agreements.[12]

POSTWAR: *CONFINDUSTRIA'S* 'GOLDEN AGE'

The organizational structure of *Confindustria* was easily rebuilt after the war. By 1946, with an affiliation of 85 trade associations, 98 territorial associations and 70,000 firms, it was the largest association in Italy.[13] *Confindustria* was, and still is, a 'secondary' association, whose membership includes both territorial and industrial associations. Unlike the workers' unions, who forced their members to join both horizontal and vertical associations, *Confindustria* allowed its members, if they wished, to belong only to one kind of 'primary' association. Small entrepreneurs, in particular, preferred to affiliate only to the territorial association.

Employers' financial contributions to *Confindustria* were based on the number of employees per firm, and voting power in electing the organization's governing bodies was allocated on a similar basis, reinforcing the dominance of large firms within the organization. From the late 1950s, as smaller firms became more numerous and more important, *Confapi*, a new general organization of small entrepreneurs was formed. But the majority of small firms declined to join this organization, preferring instead to maintain their membership in *Confindustria*.

After the war, despite the organizational strength of *Confindustria*, Italian industrialists' history of compromises with the fascist regime weakened their position with the first parliamentary governments, formed by Communists, Socialists, Christian Democrats and members of the Action Party. Even those industrialists most compromised by fascism managed to escape the postwar purge, but the top of the organization clearly had to be renewed. Angelo Costa, a shipbuilding industrialist from Genoa who had held aloof during the fascist period, was called to preside over the association: in politics he was a Catholic integralist and a Christian Democrat; in economics, a vigorous free-trader, as were the economists who worked for the first postwar governments.

The new political class which replaced the fascists had very little administrative experience, and the experts in economic policy who were chosen were all from a liberal background. Concentrated in the Treasury, in the years immediately following the war they devoted their energies to 'demolishing with determination controls on prices, output, and on all forms of financial activities'.[14] Protectionism and the interventionary policies of the previous regime were considered the economic side of fascist authoritarianism; thus for the left and the extreme left, it became extremely difficult to champion state economic intervention, at the risk of appearing nostalgic for fascist economic policies. It was no accident, therefore, that the left only proposed a Keynesian strategy in 1949, two years after the Communist and Socialist parties had been expelled from the government, and after the draconian deflation imposed by Luigi Einaudi, the Chancellor of the first centre-right government, which had socially weakened the working class.[15]

Confindustria accepted deflation as a necessary concomitant of political normalization.[16] This policy damaged small and medium-sized firms, whereas it favoured larger enterprises which had less trouble in raising capital.[17] Divergence of interests thus emerged among the industrialists, and it is in these years that there appeared that ambiguous entrepreneurial type, who 'first requires the state to intervene to protect national industry. Once he has pocketed the grants and obtained the protective tariffs, he denounces the state in the name of free enterprise'.[18] Such 'liberal protectionism' did not correspond solely to a psychological type: it became more and more the model for the behaviour of the state itself in the sphere of trade liberalization. As government practice moved away from the theoretical principles of *laissez-faire*, industrialists were able to exercise pressure on the state through the majority party, the Christian Democratic Party (*Democrazia*

Cristiana or DC), and through *Confindustria*. Economic liberalization was consequently accompanied by growing public support for industry.[19]

This state intervention took place under the aegis of the DC, which used it to consolidate its power by mediating between extremely different interests. When the power of the DC increased, as we shall see, the party was able to become more independent from the industrialists and their organization. There were times when violent disagreements arose between *Confindustria* and the government because the organization demanded the complete abolition of controls over the export of capital and the dismissal of labour, or, in the early 1950s, because *Confindustria* opposed – again in the name of free trade – the Schuman Plan;[20] or, finally, when Ugo La Malfa, the Minister of Foreign Trade, accused *Confindustria* of ambiguity in its attitude to trade liberalization: '. . .The fact that there are conflicting interests among you does not exempt you from giving the government a univocal and not equivocal indication'.[21] It was also the public sector which supported Italy's entry into the European Coal and Steel Community over *Confindustria*'s objections in 1953.[22]

But despite these disagreements between the government and *Confindustria* – well documented by Abrate[23] – and despite the fact that Costa never tired of reproaching the state for seeking to gain an autonomous role, independent of the parties, these were disagreements inside a basic consensus. In the years of Costa's presidency (1944–55), Fiat found itself quite isolated in the world of Italian industry. Already in 1946, when questioned by the Economic Commission of the Ministry for the Promulgation of the Constitution (*Ministro per la Costituente*), Valletta, the managing director of Fiat, had outlined a development plan that included an international marketing strategy based on small and very small automobiles, to be built using new American technology.[24] When questioned by the same Commission, Costa argued that only the small and medium-sized firms would be capable of growth, since larger enterprises in Italy were 'unnatural'; the management of Alfa Romeo had gone so far as to foresee a development, in Italy, confined to the artisanal sector alone.[25]

Fiat's policy, in the succeeding years, consistently followed the plans outlined by Valletta in 1946: loans were successfully requested from a series of American banks, and the importance of the Marshall Plan, which the Americans considered to have been betrayed by Einaudi's deflationary policy, was immediately understood, and the firm was able to appropriate a large proportion of the funds available. Fiat also initiated, against the will of *Confindustria*, that policy of high wages which was to characterize the company until the beginning of the 1960s, while also launching a bitter campaign of victimization against Communist and Socialist union activists.[26] Meanwhile, until the late 1950s, Fiat also continued to enjoy the privilege of protective tariffs, which sheltered it from the competition of foreign firms in the Italian market.[27] Valletta was practically the only industrialist during this period who maintained direct relations with the political parties, breaking the monopoly which Costa had managed to establish over business contributions to the parties, which all passed through *Confindustria*.[28]

The 1950s are remembered by the trade unions as the worst period in their recent history. In those years, particularly from 1955 on, the employers progressively eroded workers' power on the shop floor, left-wing militants were persecuted inside the factories and the unions were severely weakened.[29] *Confindustria* was seen by the unions as the 'number one' enemy; but a Parliamentary Commission of Enquiry discovered that many firms, particularly in the south, declined to join the organization precisely in order to avoid any obligation to implement agreements reached with the unions at the national level.[30] It is noteworthy that in the 1950s even the newly formed Catholic and Social Democratic unions CISL (*Confederazione Italiana dei Sindacati Lavoratori*) and UIL (*Unione Italiana dei Lavoratori*) were unable to play an autonomous bargaining role, despite their more collaborative attitude towards employers. They proposed, for instance, to link workers' wages to the productivity of individual firms. But the employers, in the short run, did not need more collaborative unions, since the working class, as a whole, was extremely weak, and the CISL proposals remained unheeded. As we shall see, the frustration of the CISL and UIL militants would ultimately play an important part in shaping the attitude of the political system towards the employers.

The sections which follow are organized into three parallel narratives covering the period from the mid-1950s through the late 1960s: the emergent conflict between *Confindustria* and the Christian Democratic Party; the developing relationship between Fiat and the political system; and the increasingly autonomous role played by public enterprises in Italian politics and industrial relations.

CONFINDUSTRIA VERSUS CHRISTIAN DEMOCRACY

What Speroni, perhaps exaggeratedly, has called the 'golden age' in the relationship between the DC and *Confindustria* ended in the mid-1950s, when a series of events pushed the Christian Democratic Party progressively to the left.[31] The first major consequence of this movement was the government's decision to detach the state-controlled enterprises from the *Confindustria*. The state holding company IRI (*Istituto per la Ricostruzione Industriale*) had been established by the fascists in the early 1930s. It was originally a rescue operation aimed at saving large firms faced with bankruptcy as a result of the 1929 crash. But both during the fascist period and in the immediate postwar years, state enterprises had been very similar to private firms, not least because of the classical liberal formation of the directors of IRI. During the fascist period, Avagliano has argued, the IRI managers had given the impression that they wanted to oppose both Italian and foreign private trusts, making state industry the warden of the free economic game.[32]

With the crisis of the centrist governments that began in 1953, Amintore Fanfani's Christian Democratic left began to grow in importance, and it reorganized the party efficiently, granting space to many popular elements of the Catholic party that did not identify with the industrial bourgeoisie. At the same time, the Christian Democratic left began to develop its relations with the ENI (*Ente Nazionale Idrocarburi*), the giant public energy holding company run by Enrico Mattei. Immediately after the war, ENI was to have been dismantled, but its president Mattei managed to consolidate the structure of the firm, aiming at a monopoly of all sources of energy in Italy. From the very beginning, ENI polemicized quite vigorously against *Confindustria*'s cautious and conservative policy: Mattei needed, in fact, a good relationship with the political system and very soon financed a specific Christian Democratic faction, the so-called '*corrente di base*'. The ENI was to play an important role in the government's decision to detach public industry from the associations of private industry and would become an ally of Fiat's.

The Catholic trade unionists, another component of the new DC emerging in those years, were disillusioned by the behaviour of Italian industrialists, who had not accepted their offer of responsible negotiation. In their view, it was necessary to weaken the employers' front which behaved in an autocratic way towards the trade unions. The formation of a Ministry of Public Enterprises in 1955 and the legislative decision to form a separate association for enterprises with state participation in 1957 was intended to soften up *Confindustria* and, at the same time, to set a positive example of more modern and democratic industrial relations.

The Christian Democratic left also began to demand the nationalization of the electrical industry. *Confindustria*'s reaction was to move towards the right. This movement in fact preceded the IRI firms' withdrawal from the organization. It began in 1955, more than five years before the passage of the nationalization law, when the *Assolombarda* (Association of the Industrialists of Lombardy) and the electrical groups forced the organization to replace Costa with De Micheli (close to Edison, the leading firm in the electricity sector) and to break its friendly relations with the Christian Democratic governments. De Micheli's presidency (1955–61) transformed the image of *Confindustria*: whereas under Costa's direction political interventions had been cautious, the new president maintained that the organization should 'show its face' and enter directly into politics. *Confindustria* was almost transformed into a party, reflecting in this metamorphosis the highly politicized character of the Italian trade unions.[33]

De Micheli began to finance only the right wing of the DC and, even more, the Liberal Party, which was transformed into a megaphone for *Confindustria*'s point of view. The neo-fascist and monarchical extreme right was also subsidized. *Confindustria* promoted an alliance with *Conf-*

agrocoltura (the organization of Italian landlords) and with *Con-fcommercio* (the organization of traders). During the election, *Confindustria* supported its own candidates from the party lists. In this phase small firms fluctuated between loyalty towards the electrical groups, which could set differentiated electric tariffs, and loyalty towards the DC, the traditional party of the industrialists, which in those years began introducing legislation for special credits to small business.[34]

The effective results of this turn to the right were wholly negative. The *Confindustria* candidates lost the election and *Confagricoltura* and *Confcommercio* proved unpopular organizations, helping to ruin the prestige of the association of industrialists. This destroyed the organization's image in the eyes of the parties. Previously, *Confindustria* had been able to reach the party secretaries; at this point, it was only able to influence specific groups of deputies. The organization was now only able to tackle specific legislative measures, whereas before it had been in a position to promote general policies.[35]

The leftward evolution of the political system was not hindered, but on the contrary accentuated. In 1962 the centre-left experiment began and electricity was nationalized, and during the course of the 1960s there was a growing political and economic mobilization of the working class. In the same period the economy underwent a period of unprecedented growth, especially in the industrial sector. But though *Confindustria* played a role in this process, it had spoiled its relations with the sources of power in the political system. The aggressive behaviour and dark prophecies of the electrical industrialists, in particular, seemed to have pushed them exactly in the direction they were trying to avoid – a case of self-fulfilling prophecy.

After nationalization many of the indemnities paid by the state were squandered,[36] but Edison, the largest of the electrical groups, decided to merge with Montecatini, an important group largely based on chemicals in 1966. The two managements, however, were unable to collaborate effectively. The former Montecatini managers sabotaged operations, as a protest against the fact that the former Edison men had used their financial contribution to appropriate the top positions, and the massive dimensions of the new group allowed for the initiation of uneconomical projects, which the organization was frequently incapable of evaluating properly. By the end of the 1960s Montedison had accumulated an astronomical deficit. At this point, by means of an extremely circumspect round-up of shares, the publicly owned ENI, under Mattei's successor Eugenio Cefis, won control of the company in alliance with the IRI.[37]

Just over ten years after *Confindustria*'s turn to the right, the old electrical companies, which had been the leaders of that policy, found their firms nationalized, a centre-left government in power and leaning towards further left coalitions in the future. Moreover, Montedison, the largest Italian firm and the recipient of Edison's investment capital, was now controlled by the state. At the same time, the *Intersind* (the new organization of public enterprises) and Fiat had begun transforming their industrial relations, accepting a relationship with the trade unions and breaking the employers' front.

FIAT'S HERETICAL RELATIONSHIP WITH THE POLITICAL SYSTEM

Fiat had meanwhile used its large share of American aid for a massive process of technological modernization. From 1953 onwards, moreover, the firm began discreetly to support the Christian Democratic left, currents which were principally responsible for the campaign to detach state enterprises from *Confindustria*, the nationalization of the electricity industry and the creation of the centre-left government.[38] In these same years Fiat formed an alliance with the most dynamic and progressive group in the public sector, Mattei's ENI. Fiat and ENI addressed themselves to the same political issues; the ENI lowered the price of petrol, while Fiat ceded all of its activities in this area to the ENI; and both enterprises, together with Italcementi and Pirelli, participated in the financial consortium that built the Milan–Naples motorway.[39]

But Fiat's progressivism was not applied to the relationship between management and labour: in the 1950s, in fact, the militants of the Socialist–Communist trade union were extensively victimized by Valletta's staff, to the point that the Socialist and Communist parties cited Fiat as a key example of industrialists' anti-democratic behaviour, demanding that the Republican Constitution of 1948 be allowed inside the factories. This contradiction between Fiat's progressive politics and its reactionary industrial relations, which Valletta frankly described as a policy of the 'iron fist at Mirafiori and the velvet glove in Rome', remained characteristic of the company for a long period. It arose from two different logics, which in the medium term were destined to clash. Support for the Christian Democratic left, like the formation of the parliamentary group of 'friends of the automobile', which was supported by representatives from all parties except for the PCI (*Partito Communista Italiana*), had two principal aims: to promote measures in favour of automobiles (rate rebates for motorists, a reduction in the price of petrol, the construction of motorways by public enterprises, low-cost iron and steel production); and to promote the formation of more representative and therefore more stable governments (the centre-left), capable of isolating the Communist extreme left and of assuring social peace.

Valetta managed to achieve the first goal, to the point that even a Communist journalist could maintain that 'in the absence of any national economic planning, the main element of planning in our economy comes from the development of Fiat'.[40] Fiat tried to achieve its second goal of social peace, not only by supporting more representative and stable governments, but also through the 'iron fist at Mirafiori'. Valletta and his managerial staff had an extremely hierarchical conception of production and could not tolerate any form of shopfloor discretion on the part of the unionized work-force. Even its relationship with the Catholic trade union, the CISL (*Confederazione Italiana dei Sindacati Lavoratori*), which would have liked to collaborate with the firm, proved to be difficult, and resulted in an internal split and the formation of a company union, the SIDA (*Società Italiana dell'Automobile*), entirely controlled by Fiat.

At the same time, however, Valletta favoured reductions in working hours and wage increases for Fiat employees; in this way he sought to divide the latter from the rest of the working class organized by the national trade unions. As a result, he clashed both with the trade unions, which accused him of not understanding 'that the relationship between Fiat and its workers had to be identical to that of thousands and thousands of other Italian firms' (with their workers) and with *Confindustria*.[41] The latter, for example, accused Valletta of being 'an enemy of *Confindustria* and a promoter of the dialogue between Catholics and Socialists', when in June 1956 Fiat unilaterally reduced its working hours.[42]

This clash became more acute with the formation of the first centre-left government in 1963 with the participation of the Socialists. At this point Valletta openly supported the new formula and criticized *Confindustria*. But a few days later Fiat workers participated for the first time in many years in the national strike over the renewal of collective contracts for the metalworking industry. As Turone has observed, the resumption of worker protest was also related to 'the firm's need to avoid showing its authoritarian side'.[43] Fiat was torn between its two sides. First, it attempted to impose a lock-out while reaching an agreement with the trade unions which it dominated, UIL and SIDA. Then, faced with the fury of the workers who destroyed the headquarters of the UIL and with it the image of Fiat as an ally of the centre-left, the company together with Olivetti signed a separate protocol with the trade unions as an advance against the future contract renewal. The employers' front was broken a second time when *Intersind*, the association of public sector employers, signed its own contract with the unions. A few months later, after the first comprehensive metalworkers' strike for nine years, *Confindustria* was also obliged to sign an agreement on similar terms.

In the years which followed, the government reacted to rising labour costs with a traditional deflationary policy. The Socialists at first participated actively in government coalitions, but the new formula of the 'organic' centre-left gradually slipped into decline and had become clearly discredited by the end of the decade. The conservative opposition of *Confindustria* helped to undermine the centre-left reforms, but the Christian Democratic Party also contributed to their failure, because the conflicting interests in the party prevented it making clear choices to support reforms which would have favoured some and harmed others. In these years Fiat continued to persecute left-wing militants in its factories, but went on supporting the centre-left, progressively detaching itself from the DC and moving towards the Socialist Party.[44]

In 1965 Gianni Agnelli, grandson of the founder of Fiat, replaced the elderly Valletta at the head of the firm. Between 1965 and 1969, before the strike wave known as the 'hot autumn', the repression inside the factory slackened, though the speed-up of production continued. Agnelli claimed publicly that the large firm was the best interpreter of the general interest and he also began to support a group of 'young industrialists' that resolved to transform the social and political role of *Confindustria* and of industry more broadly. These young industrialists proposed to democratize the structure of *Confindustria*, to abandon its conservative/reactionary political position, to support a policy of economic planning and to promote a better relationship with the democratic parties. Their policies proved particularly successful in the late 1960s and early 1970s as the workers' struggles finally and completely eclipsed *Confindustria*'s established style of behaviour.[45]

THE AUTONOMY OF PUBLIC ENTERPRISE

From the mid-1950s to the late 1960s, the public enterprises represented the most progressive and innovative sector of industry in their relations with the leftward-moving government coalitions and with the trade unions. Whereas Fiat's support for the centre-left formula was the product of strategic calculations based primarily on the specific interests of the automobile sector, that of the state enterprises arose from the fact that its top management themselves were left-wing Christian Democrats and CISL unionists, sharing the ideology, the political loyalties and frequently the militant past of the Christian Democratic politicians who led the centre-left governments.[46] This implied a certain willingness to bargain with trade unions, and the public enterprises systematically superseded *Confindustria* during labour negotiations. The state-controlled firms were much more straightforward in this respect than Fiat. They even went so far as to articulate theoretically a positive role for conflicting interests as the motor of economic growth. Such pluralism was strikingly radical at the time, since the whole of private industry (with the possible exception of Olivetti), considered industrial conflict subversive, sought to avoid it and certainly were not prepared to acknowledge its legitimacy. The public enterprises, on the other hand, began an experiment with 'articulated' bargaining at the level of the firm and the sector, as well as introducing formal systems of job evaluation.[47]

But the very closeness of the management of the state enterprises to the Christian Democratic leadership would gradually sap its economic vitality. In the 1950s even *Confindustria*, which considered state industry its enemy, was forced to recognize the seriousness and professionalism of the IRI managers.[48] As time passed, however, the state-controlled firms resorted more and more to special credits, endowment funds and other privileged methods of finance, thanks to their relations with the Christian Democratic leaders. The bond with the DC, which was originally political and ideological, came to be based on interest: the party guaranteed finance to the firms, and the firms funded the party factions with which they sympathized. Management, too, was chosen and promoted more and more often on political grounds rather than on the basis of professional merit; top managers 'passed from one position to another more frequently according to the rules of political alchemy than according to the needs of the company'.[49] The result was a gradual loss of economic efficiency on the part of public enterprises.

At the same time, the policies of the centre-left were failing, while in the late 1960s a new political alignment began to emerge which would displace the DC. Fearful of this possibility, the public enterprises moved towards the right. Finally, when the workers' struggles exploded in 1969, the state-controlled firms found themselves faced with an extremely aggressive union, which disorientated their management and bore no resemblance to their earlier image of the union as an institutionalized channel for conflict. The good relations between the unions and the public enterprises had already begun to break down during the contract renewals of 1965–6, when *Intersind* formed an alliance with *Confindustria* not to recognize the unions' shopfloor structures as bargaining agents, but rather to treat them as mere representatives of the provincial unions.[50] The decline of the more progressive centre-left played an important role in this *rapprochement* between the two organizations.

By 1973 public enterprise comprised a large and growing part of the industrial sector, accounting for 29.8 per cent of all sales, 39.2 per cent of invested capital and 25.17 per cent of the labour force.[51] The leaders of this sector of the economy, whom Scalfari and Turani called the state bourgeoisie or '*razza padrona*' ('race of bosses'), had lost along the way its Catholic reformism of the 1950s. But it had continued to speak of the supremacy of social interests over purely capitalist interests, whenever it was necessary to resort to special financing by the state to cover budget deficits or to prevent bankruptcy and dismissals. These enterprises consequently gave a powerful impetus to the inflationary spiral, which began to characterize the Italian economy in these years, and they became increasingly discredited in the eyes of the mass media and public opinion.

Montedison provides an anomalous yet extremely important case in this scenario. It was anomalous because, despite the fact that a majority of its voting shares were in public hands, the company was able to continue its membership of *Confindustria* since the state's majority remained ineffective, while private and public shareholders were balanced on the controlling committee.[52] Important because it was Montedison which constituted the most faithful support for the 'integralist' attempt to restore the cultural and political hegemony of Christian Democracy launched by Fanfani, DC party secretary and head of the government from 1973.

A few years after ENI had secured a voting majority of Montedison's shares, its president Eugenio Cefis left to become president of Montedison. Thereafter, although the government tried in several ways without success to secure some control over Montedison through ENI's shares, he was able to restrict the influence of the state's majority voting power. Cefis also clashed with Girotti, the president of ENI, when Montedison reorientated itself towards fine chemicals, directly conflicting with ENI's sphere of interests. Cefis's strategy was to extract massive financial support from the state (whose secret mechanisms he knew all too well as a long-time Christian Democratic public-sector manager) in order to 're-establish' Montedison, despite the fact that its management remained 'private' – denationalization of the profits and nationalization of the losses, as it was described. In fact, not only did the state lavishly finance Montedison, but it went so far as to create a new institution, the EGAM, which took over all the unprofitable firms of which Cefis had decided to dispose.

The relationship between Montedison and the political system resembled that of the state-controlled enterprises, but the 'private' management of the group made it a particular object of dislike for the opposition and a sitting target for the press.[53] At the same time, Montedison remained inside *Confindustria*, appearing to the large private firms as the 'long arm' of the state within the organization, despite the fact that an absolute majority of its shares always remained in private hands, offsetting the state's control of a majority of the voting power. Cefis's Montedison had similar interests to those of the other public enterprises in supporting by all possible means the political power of the Christian Democratic Party. But perhaps the company felt that it needed that kind of protection more urgently because of its greater number of enemies. For this reason Cefis openly supported Fanfani's 'integralist' policy, which beginning in 1973 sought to re-establish the lost harmony between DC and Italian society by violently attacking all the cornerstones of non-Catholic culture. Cefis, in particular, purchased control of an impressive number of newspaper titles, and at the same time managed successfully to block the election of Visentini, the candidate promoted by Agnelli and Pirelli, as the new president of *Confindustria*. Thus Cefis demonstrated the power of Montedison within *Confindustria*, making a clash with Fiat and the Agnellis inevitable.

THE 1970s: FIAT VERSUS MONTEDISON

At the beginning of the 1970s, as we have seen, Gianni Agnelli had become the point of reference for industrialists dissatisfied with *Confindustria*, which had been caught totally unprepared by the strike wave of 1969. In the years which followed Agnelli became the inspiration of those who wished to reorientate *Confindustria* politically, and at the same time to reassert the values of industrial enterprise, proposing it as a model of rationality and efficiency for the reform of the inefficient and corrupt state administration. This attack was motivated not only by high principles, but also by resentment against the state's damage to Fiat's interests during the late 1960s and early 70s. In particular, the state built the Alfa Sud factory to produce 'public' automobiles in the south, as a punishment for Fiat's failure to collaborate in southern industrialization, and froze the price of cars while increasing the price of petrol.

After the crisis of the system of industrial relations precipitated by the strikes of the hot autumn, and as the economy began to deteriorate sharply, the larger firms became more and more interested in *Confindustria*, which underwent a series of reforms, inspired by the 'young industrialists' supported above all by Agnelli and Pirelli. The latter, in particular, lent his name to the reform of *Confindustria*'s constitution in 1970, which created regional federations in parallel to the new regional governments – and flanked its president with a series of vice-presidents responsible for distinct operational functions (public relations, internal relations, economic relations and relations with the unions).[54]

In the years which followed, the intervention of the Agnelli brothers in the affairs of *Confindustria* became more intense, stimulated by the national industrial-relations crisis, which was particularly serious at Fiat, and also by the oil crisis, perhaps even more serious for the firm.[55] On the one hand, they pressed for agreements with the unions, hoping to make them into strong and reliable bargaining agents. Thus in 1972–3, Umberto Agnelli tried to resolve the metalworkers' contract dispute, but the newly established *Federmeccanica*, influenced by the smaller metalworking firms, broke off the negotiations.[56] On that occasion, Gianni Agnelli said that he was worried that the strike at Fiat had not been successful – better a 'strong and firm' union. Again in 1975 Gianni Agnelli strove to reach an agreement establishing a wage-indexation system (the so-called '*scala mobile*'), which was later judged extremely favourable to the workers and was strongly criticized by the small industrialists.[57]

On the other hand, the Agnelli's public stance also became more prominent. In 1972 Umberto took up a proposal by the president of *Confindustria* to establish a common programme between the industrialists and the unions, aimed at presenting a united political front.[58] In the same year, he also proposed – with little success – a second reform of *Confindustria*, demolishing the new vice-presidencies, concentrating power in the territorial associations, and at the top level, in the hands of the president.[59] Gianni, speaking in those same days, maintained that industry had become unprofitable because of the burden of 'rent', understood both in the sense of housing, important for Fiat's workers, and of the financial depredations of public enterprises, important for private employers. This burden had been tolerable so long as labour costs remained low but, as they had risen, profits now tended to disappear altogether. There were only two choices, and Fiat was for the second: either a head-on clash with the unions to lower wages, or an alliance of all the productive classes against unproductive 'rent'.[60]

Gianni Agnelli maintained this stance for a number of years with the support of other important private employers such as Pirelli. A further estrangement from the DC ensued: 'For 30 years the Catholic party with 40 per cent of the vote enjoyed 80 per cent of the power', Agnelli stated, for example, in an interview with *Newsweek* in June 1974. The DC in those years, as we have seen, was allied with Cefis and Montedison and therefore formed part of a strategy that was profoundly different from and opposed to that of Fiat. While the latter proposed to restore the image of the industrial firm and fully to recognize the workers' unions in order to form an alliance against the parasitic rentier state, Montedison aimed at reducing its industrial employment and therefore the unions' strength and, at the same time, at establishing a 'symbiotic relationship with the state' in order to obtain a profusion of privileged credits, and to induce the state to resolve its employment problems by a vast expansion of the public administration.[61] These two entrepreneurial positions were certainly linked with the divergent interests of different industrial sectors, notably between those with a highly capital-intensive development strategy, like Montedison and the chemical firms, and those who still needed a large number of employees, like Fiat.[62] But they also correspond to two different industrial philosophies, whose importance it would be wrong to underrate.

With the election of Gianni Agnelli as president of *Confindustria* in opposition to Cefis's candidate, with the sucess of the left and the failure of the DC during the referendum on divorce and the 1975 and 1976 elections, the Montedison–DC project was defeated. The DC was forced to abandon the idea of an 'integralist' restoration. Montefibre, Montedison's fine-chemical project, failed and Cefis lost the presidency of Montedison, became involved in a financial scandal and left Italy in 1977. At the beginning of the 1980s Montedison was wholly privatized, and a society formed by Agnelli, Pirelli, Orlando and Bolchini bought the ENI's shares. Later Ferruzzi, a financial group specialized in the grain trade became Montedison's major shareholder, controlling more than 40 per cent of the company's stock, an unprecedented achievement. Mediobanca, a public/private investment bank created in 1946 from the banking holdings acquired by IRI during the depression of the 1930s, played a crucial role in the transformation of the Italian industrial landscape during the late 1970s and early 1980s. Despite the fact that the state was formally the major shareholder, Mediobanca's director Enrico Cuccia always managed to protect the interests of private industry, to promote the privatization of public enterprises and to oppose the development of open share issues on the Wall Street model.[63] In the end, even Mediobanca itself was privatized.

THE 1980s: CRISIS AND RENEWAL

Between 1976 and 1979 the Communists participated indirectly in the government, supporting it from the outside, and it appeared as if the 'industrial pact' that Agnelli had proposed in 1972 might now have become possible. But a series of events pushed in the opposite direction. The level of conflict within the factories did not decrease, and the industrialists began to clash head-on with the unions. At first they were encouraged to do so by the Communists' reluctance to defend the unions' interests while they were close to the government, and later by the Communists' weakness when the Christian Democrats, having improved their position, broke the alliance. Gianni Agnelli also disapproved of the PCI's entry into the government, although he would have preferred a strengthening of the secular and Socialist parties at the expense of the DC. His brother, on the other hand, put himself forward as a parliamentary candidate on the DC list as soon as the Catholic party had abandoned its integralist strategy.

Relations between Fiat and the unions have always exercised a decisive importance for the history of Italian industrial relations, and this pivotal role was confirmed once again by the events of 1980. In that year, a new top management assumed control of the Fiat group, reorganized the car firm, abandoned any project for collaboration with the unions and successfully took them on in a head-to-head clash, thereby liquidating one of the labour movement's most important strongholds.[64] In the years that followed, Fiat launched a massive programme of automation and robotization in its plants, significantly reducing its labour requirements, while at the same time a fortunate choice of models and an efficient reorganization of the firm made Fiat highly successful in the European market during the 1980s.

During the same period Fiat took an active part in the privatization of several major firms, former strongholds of the public sector. The first coup was the privatization of Montedison in 1981, whereby the group was taken over by 'Gemina', an investment company formed by Mediobanca, Pirelli, Orlando, Bonomi and Fiat, whose stake was later sold to the Ferruzzi group which became its major shareholder. A second major coup was the purchase of Alfa Romeo, the state-controlled car firm which had once challenged Fiat's monopoly in the national market. By the mid-1980s Alfa Romeo was in crisis, and Ford was negotiating to buy it from the IRI. After months of public manoeuvres, in which Fiat presented itself as the champion of Italian national interests, the company succeeded in blocking the Ford deal and acquiring Alfa for itself in 1986. Since Fiat had already absorbed Lancia and Autobianchi, it thus became the sole producer of automobiles in Italy.[65]

But precisely during the late 1980s Fiat seemed to have lost the support of the political system, and of the Socialist Party in particular, once very friendly with the Turinese firm. Fiat was increasingly accused of being a monopoly, particularly after the absorption of Alfa Romeo, and an anti-trust law was under discussion; by this time, Fiat's empire ran from cars, buses, tractors, aero-engines and trains through machine tools, robots, biomedical equipment, armaments and nuclear-power stations to newspapers, banks, advertising agencies, insurance companies and investment funds.[66] Fiat owed its recent success to the car sector, and to Vittorio Ghidella in particular, the manager who launched the successful new models Uno and Tipo. Yet Ghidella was accused of 'automobile-centrism' and was fired in November 1988, and Cesare Romiti, the winner of the internal power-struggle, remained alone at the top of the firm. This sensational event was seen as a sign of Fiat's shift from an agressive and successful industrial policy toward a more traditional configuration based on financial speculation, spurred by fear of the coming abolition of internal customs-barriers within Europe in 1992.[67]

Unionization in Fiat, according to Marco Revelli, decreased dramatically during the 1980s: by the middle of the decade, it reached only 25 per cent of what it had been five years before, while in the key shops of Mirafiori (Fiat's biggest plant) it had fallen to 12 per cent of the previous figure.[68] During the second half of the decade, Fiat management again began to sign agreements with shopfloor unionists: the growing success of Fiat's models pushed the management to ask for additional working hours, Saturday work and greater internal mobility of the work-force. Although the unions' views were not unanimous, they largely excepted management's demands, obtaining in exchange the return to work of former employees laid off in 1980.[69] While bargaining resumed, the unions' role remained a subordinate one, with little opportunity to pursue a more conflictual line because of the increasingly collaborative behaviour of the workers themselves. An interesting sign of this latter process was the rapid growth of quality circles at Fiat, whose numbers jumped from 100 in the mid-1980s to 450 in 1989 and 700 in 1990.[70] Most recently, Romiti has denounced the negative effects on product quality of the authoritarian shopfloor regime installed in 1980, calling for a 'Total Quality' campaign aimed at meeting Japanese competitive standards, although it remains to be seen how far the firm will be able to mobilize the collaboration of its work-force without the active support of the unions.[71]

The early 1980s saw a sharp change in the strategy of *Confindustria* as well as that of Fiat. Employers had grown increasingly disenchanted with the *scala mobile* established by Gianni Agnelli during his presidency of *Confindustria*, which they judged overly favourable to wage-earners. The moderate coalition which came to power in 1979 likewise saw the reform of the wage-indexation system as a crucial means of reducing inflation and cutting the public sector deficit in the wake of Italy's entry into the European Monetary System. With the encouragement of the Socialist-led Craxi government, *Confindustria* successfully attacked the *scala mobile* in 1983–4, and managed to obtain a new agreement with two of the three union confederations modifying the wage-indexation formula which was then made law by administrative decree. At that point, a referendum opposing the government's wage policy was introduced by the Communist Party, the Radical Party and the extreme-left party *Democrazia Proletaria*, supported by the Communist wing of the CGIL. But the Communists' overtly political stance provoked a clash with the Socialists within the CGIL, as well as with the CISL and the UIL, who supported their parties within the government, thereby undermining the trend towards inter-confederal unity that had characterized the Italian labour movement during the 1970s. The referendum in any case was defeated at the polls, compounding the isolation of the Communists and the political disarray of the unions. A major consequence of this clash over the reform of the wage-indexation system was the break-up of the tripartite model of industrial relations established during the previous years. From this point onwards, 'the state was there, but it could not show itself'.[72] In 1986 the reform of the *scala mobile* was definitively settled by the passage of a law which reduced the average proportion of workers' earnings covered. Although the new *scala mobile* was intended to restore wage differentials which had been compressed under the old formula, 'the differentiation by grade was very modest, and indeed virtually negligible if instead of contract minimums, actual earnings are used'.[73]

During the 1980s the interest of larger firms in *Confindustria* seems to have declined. The organization became more and more involved with the small firms which boomed in the 1970s, but subsequently experienced difficulties in certain sectors and increasingly needed its support, particularly at the regional level. In 1980 *Confindustria* acquired a new president, Vittorio Merloni, a 'Christian' small entrepreneur, who managed to strengthen the links between the employers' association and the government, accepting and promoting a discussion on the duties of the enterprise, and obtaining important concessions from the political system, notably the modification of the *scala mobile*. During the very bitter confrontation between Fiat and the unions in 1980, *Confindustria*'s support was very weak indeed: according to Cesare Romiti, Fiat's top manager since the late 1970s '*Confindustria*'s Board of Directors discussed for half a day whether or not to express its solidarity with Fiat'.[74] The links between *Confindustria* and the socialist governments ruled by Bettino Craxi were further reinforced during the presidency of Luigi Lucchini (1984–8), to the point that one can compare these years to those of the Costa/De Gasperi alliance during the 1940s and early 1950s. After Lucchini, Sergio Pininfarina, a close friend of Agnelli, became president of the organization.[75]

The crisis of the unions at Fiat, following an established historical pattern, seems to have influenced the whole industrial relations system, and in particular the private sector. By the mid-1980s, scholars had already noted that Italian unions were shifting from solidarity to competition, and from general representativeness to free-riding.[76] Unemployment rose dramatically during the 1980s, reaching three million or 12 per cent of the labour force in 1987, while the unions were having increasing difficulties in their relationship with the workers: membership fell by 25 per cent in the industrial sector while strike activity in the period 1984–6 was 22 per cent below that of the previous three years.[77]

Although the Italian unions have lost part of their political and industrial influence, they still retain significant bargaining power. As in the 1960s, for example, the unions' position has been buttressed by the collaborative policies pursued by management in the public sector. In 1986 IRI signed a protocol with the unions on the adoption of an 'active employment policy' whereby both parties would seek alternatives to redundancies through 'part-time work, rotation of workers on special *cassa integrazione guadagni* [the public fund for temporary unemployment compensation], new work schedules and organization of working time, solidarity contracts, internal and external mobility, adequate reallocation of excess manpower and income support for workers not placed in new positions, privileged quotas in new hiring for certain groups, cooperatives and worker self-management, and productivity accords'. Similar protocols were also signed with two other state holding companies, EFIM and GEPI. In the latter case, the protocol was mainly aimed at maintaining employment levels without loss of competiveness: unions were to be fully involved, both nationally and regionally, in decisions aimed at 'regaining economic health, re-employment and job creation, restructuring, divestitures, and industrial promotion'.[78]

In the private sector, too, bilateral bargaining between unions and employers has largely filled the gap left by the collapse of tripartite negotiations during the conflicts over reform of the wage indexation system in 1983–4. Some groups of employers, notably *Federmeccanica*, the metal-working-industry association, have pushed for a rapid transition to decentralized bargaining at the company level, while also seeking to bypass the unions through direct communication with employees. But other important employers' associations such as those in chemicals and textiles have openly opposed this approach, as has the government, and national collective bargaining remained important at both the confederal and the sectoral levels.[79] During the summer of 1990 the leadership of *Confindustria* unilaterally disavowed the revised *scala mobile*, seeking to block the renewal of all sectoral contracts pending a comprehensive reform of pay structure. But after a highly successful stoppage of metal and chemical workers, the coalition government, whose economic ministers had initially encouraged *Confindustria*'s hardline stance as part of their counter-inflationary strategy, then stepped in to avert a threatened general strike by forcing the employers back to the bargaining table. Under pressure from Socialist and Christian Democratic ministers sympathetic to the unions, *Confindustria* eventually agreed to extend the *scala mobile* through December 1991 and remove its veto over sectoral contract renewals in exchange for the unions' commitment to bilateral negotiations for a new wage structure and government funding for cuts in employers' social contributions.[80]

CONCLUSIONS

During the past decade, as in previous periods, the labour policies of Italian employers have been strongly influenced by their ambivalent relationship with the state and the political system, as well as by union strategies and their own internal politics. Since the 1920s successive 'political projects' have failed to establish consistent and dynamic relationships between employers, unions and government. At each stage, internal divisions and problems of coalition building undercut successive strategies pursued by *Confindustria*; yet despite periodic setbacks the organization has always managed to reorientate itself and re-establish its central role in Italian industrial relations. The behaviour of Italian employers, as this chapter shows, did not simply reflect their material or sectoral interests. Instead, political change, state policies and union strategies constantly reshaped their interests and perceptions while also being reshaped by the latter in turn.

In neither the fascist period nor the 'golden age' of postwar collaboration with the Christian Democrats were the relationships between business and government so harmonious as they have often been presented. Before the war, *Confindustria* was only ambiguously integrated into the fascist state: it was the ambitious giant Fiat which came out best in the contest for the parcelling-out of power. After the war the state's role in the economy expanded rapidly and *Confindustria* was one of the most powerful influences within the ruling DC, securing a free hand to move against the unions in the factories. Yet the DC always remained a broader coalition, too autonomous, too ready to constrain managerial freedoms and too wedded to the promotion of state enterprise for *Confindustria*'s liking. As the DC began to shift leftwards in the late 1950s, *Confindustria* attempted to use its political weight to forestall the changes. In particular, it sought to forestall the consolidation of a new public-sector power bloc or model of modern and democratic business enterprise. Yet its strategy of resistance backfired. *Confindustria*'s overt politicization isolated the organization and undercut its grip on key political levers. Instead, the public sector attained new levels of influence within both the economy and the political system.

Fiat had always stayed on the periphery of *Confindustria*, preferring to make its own bargains with political parties and the state in a more aggressive and expansionist mould. In the 1950s and 1960s, while *Confindustria* failed to stem the leftward tide in the DC, Fiat swam with more progressive political currents, finally moving into effective alliance with the Socialist Party. During the 1960s Fiat and the public-sector firms committed themselves to the emergent centre-left project. Representing the most innovative and dynamic sectors of industry, they looked to combine social reforms with the direct use of state power for industrial growth, planning and political stability, though Fiat was much less willing than the public enterprises to match this national approach with 'pluralist' labour relations policies within the firm.

But during the late 1960s and early 1970s this strategy miscarried. The centre-left consensus on a business–government partnership for economic modernization broke down as workers radicalized and inflation rose. Meanwhile the relationship between the public sector and the government deteriorated from a strategic political and ideological alliance for economic reform into an increasingly inefficient nexus of interests based on mutual financial support. In the 1970s these developments gave rise to new divisions among employers as Fiat and Montedison contended for the leadership of *Confindustria*. Agnelli and Pirelli sought to reanimate a 'progressive' coalition by reorientating large firms towards a more active leadership role within *Confindustria*, shifting towards a new 'industrial pact' in the workplace, and allying with the Socialist Party as the DC backed off from its earlier reform commitments. With the reform of *Confindustria* in 1970, Agnelli's elevation to the organization presidency and the DC's set-backs in the 1975–6 elections, this position seemed to have triumphed. Montedison's project, on the other hand, remained more right-wing and allied with the DC. It reflected the degeneration of the public-sector model as it increasingly used the power of the state to promote its own transition into a powerful private-sector grouping.

Once again in the late 1970s, however, broader political shifts precipitated major strategic reorientations among Italian employers. During these years high levels of industrial conflict on the shop floor and the collapse of the Communist-supported government of national unity prompted Fiat's new top management to abandon the firm's earlier project, swinging back towards financial expansionism, privatization of state enterprises and a repressive factory order. As larger firms withdrew to pursue their own projects, small and medium-sized businesses gained the ascendancy within *Confindustria*, and the organization won the support of the government for a major reform of the wage-indexation system during the mid-1980s. But government and unions together have restrained hardline employers from adopting unilateral strategies to bypass collective bargaining (unlike in other countries such as Britain or the United States), while *Confindustria* and its affiliates continue to play an important part in labour negotiations at all levels of the industrial-relations system.

NOTES

1 P. Melograni, *Gli industriali e Mussolini* (Milan, 1980), pp. 43–72; D. Speroni, *Il romanzo della Confindustria* (Milan, 1975), pp. 30–2; and A. Lyttleton, *The Seizure of Power: Fascism in Italy 1919–29*, 2nd edn (Princeton, 1987), pp. 205–13. The enthusiastic message of *Confindustria* on the formation of Mussolini's first government is reproduced in E. Rossi, *Padroni del vapore* (Bari, 1966), p. 50.

2 R. De Felice, *Mussolini il Fascista*, vol. 1, *La conquista del potere 1921–1925* (Turin, 1966), pp. 677–8; Melograni, *Gli industriali*, pp. 73–115; M. Abrate, *La lotta sindacale nella industrializzazione in Italia* (Milan, 1966); Speroni, *Il romanzo della Confindustria*, pp. 31–2. The crisis was caused by the assassin-

ation of the socialist deputy, Giacomo Matteotti. Those responsible for the murder were Fascists belonging to a secret network, as Mussolini was well aware.

3 Melograni, *Gli industriali*, pp. 181–5 and 208–24; De Felice, *Mussolini il Fascista*, vol. 2, *L'organizzazione dello Stato fascista 1925–1929*, pp. 245, 255, 281–4, 563ff; Lyttleton, *Seizure of Power*, pp. 337–43.

4 De Felice, *Mussolini il Fascista*, vol. 2, pp. 315–35; A. Aquarone, *L'organizzazione dello Stato totalitario* (Turin, 1965), p. 146; Melograni, *Gli industriali*, pp. 240–4; and Lyttleton, *Seizure of Power*, pp. 221–31, 308–32. On the support of small and medium-sized firms for Rossoni's proposals, see G. Carocci, *Storia d'Italia dall'unità ad oggi* (Milan, 1975), p. 254.

5 G. Salvemini, *Sotto la scure del fascismo – Lo stato corporativo di Mussolini* (Turin, 1948), pp. 394–6.

6 G. Sapelli, 'FIAT e sistema politico fascista', in G. Sapelli, E. Pugno, R. Gobbi and B. Trentin (eds), *FIAT e Stato* (Savigliano, 1978).

7 V. Castronovo, *Giovanni Agnelli* (Turin, 1977), pp. 427–30; P. Bairati, *Valletta* (Turin, 1983), p. 74.

8 Castronovo, *Agnelli*, pp. 326–30; Sapelli, 'FIAT e sistema politico fascista', pp. 12–13.

9 Castronovo, *Agnelli*, pp. 339–43; Sapelli, 'FIAT e sistema politico fascista', p. 13.

10 Valletta's public statement, quoted in Bairati, *Valletta*, p. 70.

11 Castronovo, *Agnelli*, pp. 374–82; Sapelli, 'FIAT e sistema politico fascista', p. 13.

12 G. Sapelli, *Fascismo, grande industria e sindacato* (Milan, 1975), p. 57.

13 G. Pirzio Ammassari, *La politica della Confindustria* (Napoli, 1976), p. 3.

14 M. De Cecco, 'La politica economica durante la ricostruzione', in S. J. Woolf (ed.), *Italia 1943–1950 – La ricostruzione* (Bari, 1975), p. 291.

15 M. Salvati, *Stato e industria nella ricostruzione* (Milan, 1982).

16 Pirzio Ammassari, *La politica della Confindustria*, pp. 33–4.

17 S. Lombardini, *La programmazione, idee, esperienze, problemi* (Turin, 1967), p. 19.

18 F. Ferrarotti, 'Verso una politica di sindacalismo autonomo', *Communità* 23, (Feb. 1954).

19 G. Amato, *Il governo dell'industria in Italia* (Bologna, 1972).

20 G. Raimondi, 'Soggetti e politiche delle relazioni industriali: La Confederazione Generale dell'Industria Italiana', in F. Peschiera (ed.), *Sindacato, Industria e Stato negli anni del centrismo* (Florence,), vol. 2, p. 7.

21 ibid., pp. 10–11.

22 A. Becchi Collidà, 'Le associazioni imprenditoriali', in G. P. Cella and T. Treu (eds), *Relazioni industriali* (Bologna, 1982).

23 M. Abrate, 'La politica economica e sindacale della Confindustria (1943–1955)', in S. Zaninelli (ed.), *Il sindacato nuovo – Politica e organizzazione del movimento sindacale in Italia negli anni 1943–1955* (Milan, 1981), pp. 445–547.

24 A. Graziani, *L'economia italiana: 1945–1970* (Bologna, 1972), pp. 126–30.

25 Bairati, *Valetta*, p. 163.

26 ibid., pp. 156–222.

27 A. Martinelli, A. M. Chiesi, N. Dalla Chiesa, *I grandi imprenditori italiani* (Milan, 1981), p. 245.

28 ibid., pp. 156–222.

29 G. Contini, 'Politics, Law and Shop Floor Bargaining in Postwar Italy', in S. Tolliday and J. Zeitlin (eds), *Shop Floor Bargaining and the State* (Cambridge, 1985).

30 *Documenti della Commissione parlamentare d'inchiesta sulle condizioni dei lavoratori in Italia* (Rome, 1958–1960).

31 Speroni, *Il romanzo della Confindustria*, p. 66; Contini, 'Politics, Law and Shop Floor Bargaining in Postwar Italy', pp. 201–3.

32 L. Avagliano, *State e imprenditori in Italia – Le origini dell'I.R.I* (Salerno 1980), p. 238.

33 Raimondi, 'Soggetti', pp. 57–64.

34 Martinelli *et al.*, *I grandi imprenditori italiani*, pp. 248, 250, 253; cf. also C. Weiss, *Creating Capitalism: Small Business and the State* (Oxford, 1988), chs 4–6.

35 Speroni, *Il romanzo della Confindustria*, pp. 89–98.

36 E. Scalfari and G. Turani, *Razza Padrona* (Milan, 1974).

37 ibid., pp. 230–49.

38 R. Gobbi, 'FIAT e sistema dei partiti negli anni sessanta', in Sapelli *et al.*, *FIAT e Stato*, p. 45; V. Comito, *La FIAT tra crisi e ristrutturazione* (Rome, 1982); Scalfari and Turani, *Razza Padrona*.

39 Bairati, *Valletta*, pp. 304–8.

40 Comito, *FIAT*, p. 134.

41 The interview with Storti has been reprinted in Bairati, *Valletta*, p. 302.

42 ibid., p. 292.

43 S. Turone, *Storia del sindacato in Italia* (Bari, 1976), p. 350.

44 R. Gianotti, *Lotte e organizzazione di classe alla FIAT (1948–1970)* (Bari, 1970), pp. 245–8; Comito, *FIAT*, p. 137.

45 Speroni, *Il romanzo della Confindustria*, pp. 97–110.

46 Pirzio Ammassari, *La politica della Confindustria*, pp. 109–10.

47 A. Collidà, 'L'Intersind', in A. Collidà, L. De Carlini, G. Mossetto and R. Stefanelli (eds), *La politica del padronato italiano – Dalla ricostruzione all' 'Autunno Caldo'* (Rome, 1978), pp. 100–7.

48 ibid., p. 83.

49 Martinelli *et al.*, *I grandi imprenditori italiani*, p. 253.

50 Pirzio Ammassari, *La politica della Confindustria*, p. 125.

51 A. Graziani (ed.), *Crisi e ristrutturazione dell'economia italiana* (Turin, 1975).

52 Scalfari and Turani, *Razza Padrona*.

53 ibid.

54 Mirella Baglioni, 'L'organizzazione regionale degli interessi economici – Il caso Confindustria' (unpublished paper, Facoltà di Economia e Commercio, Università degli studi di Parma, 1986).

55 G. Contini, 'The Rise and Fall of Shop Floor Bargaining at FIAT, 1945–1980', in S. Tolliday and J. Zeitlin (eds), *The Automobile Industry and its Workers: Between Fordism and Flexibility* (Cambridge, 1986).

56 Pirzio Ammassari, *La politica della Confindustria*, p. 146.

57 ibid., pp. 82–3.

58 ibid., pp. 147–50.

59 L. De Carlini, 'Padroni e padroncini', *Rinascità* 15 Dec. 1972, compares Umberto Agnelli's proposal to that of a 'constitutional monarchy of the Scandinavian type'. The proposal was rejected, mostly because of opposition from the small industrialists: see Pirzio Ammassari, *La politica della Confindustria*, pp. 165–6.

60 See Scalfari's interview with Gianni Agnelli, in *L'Espresso*, 19 Nov. 1972.

61 Martinelli *et al.*, *I grandi imprenditori italiani*.

62 A. Graziani, 'La strategia della divisione', *Quaderni Piacentini* 56 (July 1975).

63 According to A. Friedmann, *Agnelli and the Network of Italian Power* (London, 1988), pp. 234–62, Mediobanca and Fiat worked together in order to squeeze out Montedison's manager, Mario Schimberni, whose aim was to transform the firm into a 'public' company on the Wall Street model with a large base of small investors. Fiat's version of the story can be found in C. Romiti, *Questi anni alla FIAT – intervista di Giampaolo Pansa* (Milan, 1988), pp. 245–64.

64 Comito, *Fiat*, pp. 57–92; Contini, 'The Rise and Fall of Shop Floor Bargaining at FIAT'.
65 Friedmann, *Agnelli*, pp. 155–72.
66 See Friedman, *Agnelli*.
67 On the Ghidella affair see for instance the articles of Gianfranco Modolo, Salvatore Tropea and Giuseppe Turani in *La Repubblica – Affari e Finanza* (2 Dec. 1988).
68 M. Revelli, *Lavorare in FIAT* (Milan, 1989), pp. 107–9.
69 R. Locke and S. Negrelli, 'Il caso FIAT Auto', in M. Regini and C. F. Sabel (eds), *Strategie di riaggiustamento industriale* (Bologna 1989), pp. 79–87.
70 See, respectively, Locke and Negrelli, 'Il caso FIAT Auto', pp. 82–83; Revelli, *Lavorare in FIAT*, p. 126; Antonio Calabrò, 'Date a Cesare quel ch'è di Nissan', in *Republica – Affari e Finanza* (11 May 1990).
71 See the report of his speech to a general meeting of Fiat managers on 21 October 1989 in *Il Manifesto* (25 Apr. 1990), p. 3. For the union response to Fiat's quality campaign, see the report of a national conference on the company organized by the PCI in *La Repubblica* (23 June 1990), p. 5.
72 S. Negrelli and E. Santi, 'Industrial Relations in Italy', in Guido Baglioni and Colin Crouch (eds), *European Industrial Relations: The Challenge of Flexibility* (London, 1990), pp. 184.
73 Ministero del Lavoro e della Previdenza Sociale, *Report '88: Labour and Employment Policies in Italy* (Rome, 1988), p. 164.
74 Romiti, *Questi anni*.
75 Personal communication from Guglielmo Aragozzino; L. Lahzalaco, 'Pinifarina, President of the Confederation of Industry, and the Problems of Business Associations', in R. Y. Nanetti and R. Catanzaro (eds), *Italian Politics: A Review*, vol. 4 (London, 1990).
76 P. Perulli, 'L'evoluzione strategica delle organizzazioni sindacali negli anni '80', in M. Carrieri and P. Perulli (eds), *Il Teorema sindacale: flessibilità e competizione nelle relazioni industriali* (Bologna, 1985), pp. 108–25.
77 Ministero del Lavoro, *Report '88*, pp. 176–8.
78 ibid., pp. 184–5.
79 ibid., pp. 163–92; Negrelli and Santi, 'Industrial Relations in Italy', esp. pp. 181–3, 186–8, 193.
80 For these events, see *La Repubblica* (20 June–12 July 1990); *Confindustria* repudiated the *scala mobile* on 19 June and the tripartite agreement between the employers, the unions and the government was signed on 7 July.

Part III
Against convergence

8 Technological convergence and limits to managerial control: flexible manufacturing systems in Britain, the USA and Japan

Bryn Jones

INTRODUCTION

Contemporary debates about managerial strategy have raised the possibility of a new transnational paradigm for combining and controlling labour and production capital. Technological change, in what are still – at the moment – relatively specialized spheres of production automation, is an important element in descriptions of new control models. What is problematic is whether new practices and policies are sufficiently uniform and coherent to constitute a distinctively new outlook. If there are differences between managerial strategies and enterprise functions both between firms and within the same firm or establishment, it becomes difficult to argue for a new paradigm.

A more specific issue for Britain follows from the implications of the transnationalization proposition. Older styles of management, production methods and forms of labour relations, and enterprise regulation have either declined or broken down in the advanced capitalist economies – notably so in Britain. These changes have led some observers to claim, or at least speculate, that the emergent patterns are being based upon regimes that are more typical of other countries. Keith Sisson focuses on this issue, in his chapter, in relation to changing systems of collective bargaining. The problem addressed here concerns the British particularities in work practices, training, the occupational division of labour and broader management policies for handling labour issues. Are the indigenous practices of enterprise and plant-level systems of work organization and labour control being displaced by the seemingly global trend towards the adoption of new production technologies with a universal design and purpose?

To deal with these questions this chapter examines the introduction of computer-integrating technologies into the automation of batch production processes in the metal-engineering industries. These are principally sectors and sub-sectors engaged in aerospace and marine engineering, and the manufacture of products such as machine tools and other forms of industrial equipment. In relation to these industries and technologies the automobile industry is, strictly speaking, a special case, so only a few comparisons will be made to recent changes in that sector. The framework will be a comparative one drawing principally on case-study evidence from the USA and Japan.

There are three objectives in this account: (1) to sketch out the probable limits to a technology-driven convergence of the control and management of labour; (2) to show that changes in enterprise organization, such as automation, though often having the major impact upon jobs and labour relations, may be the result of managerial aims, policies and decisions that have only a minor direct concern with these effects; (3) to demonstrate that management strategy and policy implementation in British manufacturing in the 1980s continues to be characterized by eclecticism and particularism.

The first step in the analysis is to set these issues in the context of the conflicting evidence and interpretations of the relationship between technical-organizational change in production processes and the enhancement of managerial control over labour. The second section contrasts real and predicted managerial control aims with the actual implementation and operation of so-called 'flexible automation' technologies in Britain. The third part discusses changes and continuities in British industrial structure, industrial politics and business institutions as causes of the differences between technical and work organization in Britain and the Japanese and US patterns.

TECHNOLOGY AND THE CONTROL OF LABOUR

This chapter takes issue with interpretations of manufacturing automation as enhancing managerial control of labour. The bases of these interpretations can be summed up in three points. First, there are increases in managerial surveillance and monitoring of work and workers. Modern computer technologies provide higher levels of management with immediate and more accurate data on the progress of work-tasks and the individual workers in the plant who are responsible or available for the relevant tasks. These forms of control may come as a by-product of the production monitoring involved in computer-controlled machinery such as numerically controlled (NC) machine tools. Alternatively, there are more deliberate Management Information Systems which provide designated managers throughout the company with access to real-time data bases which combine company records with up-to-the-minute changes keyed in by workers or their immediate supervisors.[1]

The second technological improvement to labour control concerns the stabilization of the cost/effort ratio. Computerized automation not only cuts the total wage bill, by reducing the number of workers required for a particular work process, it also eliminates the direct relationship between the amount of human effort and the amout of output. The inputs required from individual workers are less continuous, and variations in required output are no longer met by increasing or decreasing the numbers of workers employed on the process in question. Hence additional uncertainties involved in the management and (re)negotiation of payment for effort, or recruitment and re-allocation of labour can be avoided.[2]

Third, control over labour is enhanced in the indirect sense that it becomes less necessary. Machines with computers that can calculate numbers, angles, tolerances, speeds, feeds and the priority to give to the working of different types of component and product have less and less need of the application of human skills, knowledge and attention at the point of production. This greater control over the planning, methodology and operation of production processes, it is argued, is accompanied by *de facto* enhancement of control over the activities of the remaining technicians and shopfloor workers. Workers' former discretion and skilled judgements are made redundant. Their remaining contributions of labour become more predictable as subjective solutions, and therefore sources of error and departures from designs and plans, are excluded. Work-roles are therefore more closely regulated.[3]

Most aspects of these propositions, but especially the second and third mode of control, have been developed into axioms of the labour-process literature. More interestingly, it is not difficult to find reasonably accurate support for some of these aims coming directly from managerial participants in automation schemes.[4] Reductions in labour costs and greater managerial control over the execution of designs and plans are regularly cited as principal aims of flexible automation projects.[5] Labour control is allegedly the goal of new investments in automation. Yet writers who emphasize the centrality of such aims often also acknowledge the difficulties of achieving them. Both Noble and Wilkinson,[6] for example, point out the effectiveness of rudimentary forms of shopfloor subversion of the methods prescribed for operating new technology. There is moreover a growing body of evidence that the 'tacit knowledge' phenomenon may present an inevit-able and insuperable obstacle to the capacity of contemporary technology to replace many conventional job-skills.[7] More pertinently for the present discussion, there is no shortage of reported cases of managements who are prepared to upgrade skills, and who attempt to plan for increases in some aspects of worker discretion or autonomy.[8]

Observers of such bifurcations between, on the one hand, greater task regulation through deskilling and, on the other, more responsibility and reskilling often adopt Friedman's convenient classification. This dis-tinguishes between managerial strategies aimed at 'direct control' and those that delegate 'responsible autonomy' in order to win the consent of unionized workers.[9] However, this simple dichotomy, like a similar cyclical distinction for levels of general participation by Ramsay,[10] provides only a limited, and somewhat essentialist, specification of the determinants of one outcome rather than the other. Autonomy and responsibility are only ceded, according to these perspectives, when there is a challenge, or risks of resistance, from organized labour to plans for change. This kind of explanation does not take account of the possibility that there may be other determinants of managerial strategy stemming from separate, and possibly conflicting, perceptions and interests within management, and varying external influences upon them.[11]

Evidence of complexity and variability in the managerial decision-making and implementation processes has led to some support for Buchanan and Boddy's distinction between control objectives, aimed at reducing human involvement and resulting uncertainties, and the 'strategic' and 'operational' aims of automation.[12] Strategic objectives are concerned with improving position in external markets. Operational objectives are aimed at improvements in the establishment's internal performance – in terms of cost reductions and quality enhancement. This analytical classification has the advantage of being able to help to locate different kinds of aims in different managerial strata. Thus, Buchanan and Boddy identify strategic aims principally with top managers, operational goals with financial and middle-level line managers and control objectives with lower-level line managers.

However, there is, as with Friedman's and other analytical classifications, obvious overlap, and some confusion, between the categories in substantive cases of change. 'Internal' cost and quality improvements are also gains in 'external' market terms. Most 'control' objectives are also aims that are closely tied to – and may either follow from or contribute to – operational gains. In a later case study of NC machining Buchanan suggests that the dichotomy of skill and control patterns corresponds with two opposed complexes of managerial intentions: *either* a technically based *or* a socio-technically based perspective. The narrow, short-term and internal orientation of the technical view would also favour close control of labour and work-roles, and risk minimization limited only to sections of the organisation. The vague general aims of this outlook are in contrast to the socio-technical paradigm's clearly expressed aims, long-term goals and focus on external strategy. There is also, in the latter, a linked emphasis upon operational rather than labour-control criteria and on organizational rather than a sectional frame of reference.[13]

These refinements, even if they are accurate representations, still explain little of *why* one pattern rather than another should develop. At a more general level it would clearly be desirable to consider broader socio-economic contexts, if only to understand differences between Britain and other countries. Yet historical shifts in Britain's internal political economy, let alone the changing industrial structure of the international economy, remain unanalysed as sources of variation in internal corporate policy. The only partial exceptions to this weakness are Ramsay's association of changing control perspectives with cycles of economic growth and recession, and Friedman's correlation of the shifts between shopfloor autonomy and control with the product cycle within the British motor-car industry. Yet, as we have seen, in these accounts, the dependent variable – that of the forms of control themselves – remains simplistic.

A more influential and ambitious explanation of shifts in labour and job control characterizes these as effects of changes at the supranational level of capitalism – in changes from a 'Fordist' to a more sophisticated 'neo-Fordist' industrial system. From its origins in the so-called 'regulation school', such as the Marxist scholars Aglietta and Palloix, this conception has undergone a number of applications and modifications.[14] However, for present purposes, it should be sufficient to outline the theory's most common themes. It argues that the industrial structure and vitality of the post-World War II boom was based upon the symmetry of mass production and mass consumption. This Fordism involved a Tayloristic system of tight controls over job definitions, in a highly specialized and detailed division of work-tasks. The consequent standardization and thus cheapening of products allowed the maximum number of goods to be sold to the 'mass workers' of many other Fordist industries, thus maintaining a virtuous circle of production and consumption that spread out of its original base in the USA to Western Europe in the 1950s and 1960s. While intensely restrictive and exploitative of labour power at the point of production, Fordist managements eventually accepted, or were pressured into, tolerating plant, company and sometimes even national-level bargaining with unions over pay and conditions.

By contrast, it is argued, neo-Fordism uses the greater systemic controls of programmable automation over the realization of designs and plans at the point of production in order to improve commitment by ceding lower-level responsibilities in task requirements and authority relationships. Individual workers are deskilled of certain conventional manual and craft techniques, which can now be pre-programmed. However, the consequent reduction of uncertainty about the detailed execution of production operations allows for a relaxation of many of the preceding Tayloristic controls. Remaining tasks may now be recombined into 'enlarged' jobs, individual work-roles may be spread amongst new teams of workers, who may have the opportunity to plan for themselves the allocation and execution of work and even to self-supervise/self-police themselves as a unit, rather than submit separately to the conventional hierarchy of authority.

However, the interpreters of these reforms are highly critical of their authenticity. The interpretation is that capitalist enterprises may have changed their spots but they have not changed their basic motives and interests. The autonomy of work-groups, it is argued, is defined within strict limits. Their new-found authority is often restricted to trivial responsibilities and is cynically engineered so as to create an illusory independence and a collective commitment to overall production goals that have been well defined in advance and from above. Worse still: it is also observed that the spread of this pseudo-collectivist identity is often seen by management as an alternative to the Fordist pattern of collective bargaining over well-defined individual rights and grievances, and as a way of regaining control over employee relations from unions.

Despite the coherence of these theories, they do not involve a specific evaluation and characterization of the technological changes. Indeed in some recent commentaries,[15] in which a new post-Fordist harmonization of employment with consumption is attributed to the segmentation of product ranges, a technological shift is alleged that is seemingly infinite in its flexibility. The most common example of the technological aspect of the shift from Fordism to neo-Fordism is the motor-car industry's move away from 'dedicated' technologies, of the fixed purpose transfer-line type, to the systems that gain flexibility by reprogramming the central computers to make a range of parts and models with the same machinery. The theorists of neo-Fordism and flexible capitalism see changes in work-roles and authority patterns as arising more from changes in the scale of production, size of markets and product ranges. Often the technology is treated as a convenient intermediate variable for realizing labour-control outcomes that arise from inevitable system-level shifts in policy. As Scott has pointed out, at least as far as the 'regulationist' writers are concerned, the detailed forms and applications of the technology are either unexamined or misinterpreted.[16]

Leaving aside these detailed reservations, which have been exposed in some detail elsewhere,[17] if the Fordist/neo-Fordist divide were applied to the British evidence then a superficially appropriate explanation could be derived. Those firms that had Buchanan's 'technical' perspective would still be automating within Fordist manufacturing assumptions and its attendant concern with detailed forms of labour control and task regulation. Those with a 'socio-technical' approach, on the other hand, would have a more strategic vision that recognized that the break with mass production and standardized products was best achieved through technological rationalization at the organizational level. To complement this shift greater control at organizational/operational levels would follow from ceding control of work-tasks and their immediate determination to the workers themselves. Buchanan's model ignores collective-bargaining processes, but appropriate changes to industrial relations practices, that are consistent with radical organizational shifts, have been documented and implicitly linked to aspects of the socio-technical pattern.[18]

The relevant restructuring of work organization may be given a benign and liberatory characterization as with proponents of work humanization[19] or a sinister and manipulative interpretation as with the regulationists and most Marxists. But from different directions, and with varying levels of overlap and generalization, there is convergence of opinion about such a plausible new pattern of labour control in manufacturing industry. However, to some extent such interpretations claim, or imply, that a new generalized production paradigm is being constructed from a universally available technology. If they do this then these theories must rely upon an implicit technological convergence that transcends not only particular national economies but also different industrial sectors. Moreover, even if this kind of dualism in manufacturing philosophies and labour-control policies is emerging, we still have no idea of why some managements are not choosing the neo-Fordist option that is, seemingly, generally available to all. A closer assessment of the realism of these models, and their relevance to Britain, can only be gained from more detailed evidence on the adoption and operation of the most advanced of the relevant technologies. The currently most appropriate of these is the Flexible Manufacturing System (FMS).

THE MANAGEMENT AND OPERATION OF COMPUTER-INTEGRATED SYSTEMS IN BRITAIN

FMS is a crucial stage in the advance to Computer-Integrated Manufacturing (CIM) in which different computer-controlled systems are linked together to eliminate repetitive human translation of one set of data and instructions into another. The systems involved include Computer-Aided Design (CAD), Computer-Aided Manufacturing (CAM) planning and parts specification, machine tools and production control and scheduling. At the moment there is only sufficiently advanced software to link together a few of these, such as CAD with CAM, and production scheduling with NC in FMS. Indeed, because fully-fledged FMSs involve automated material- and tool-transfer systems, cells of Computer Numerically Controlled (CNC) machine tools and central computer systems for scheduling the sequence of machining programs and parts-transfer, they are sometimes referred to as rudimentary cases of CIM.[20]

A recent estimate is that there are around 30 fully-fledged FMSs in Britain.[21] These systems are fairly evenly spread between different metal-engineering sectors.[22] By comparison, estimates for the number of FMSs in USA and Japan by 1990 are 220 and 150 respectively.[23] Yet the total pool of potential FMS users in Britain may be only 200–300. Systematic evidence on the pattern of use, and reasons for adoption, of FMS is not available. In Britain the highest sectoral concentrations (outside the marginal technological case of automobiles) are in the aerospace, machine tools, diesel engines and agricultural and earth-moving equipment industries. Existing technological sophistication, as in aerospace, and examples set by foreign competitors and parent companies appear to be the principal stimuli to adoption in these types of company rather than others. The exception to this pattern appears to be mining equipment where both the main British producers appear to have made independent decisions to adopt FMS based upon intrinsic productive criteria.

Research carried out from Bath University by Scott[24] suggests that the managers' rationale and anticipated gains from FMS are varied and often ambiguous. Shortening of the lead time between design and production, reductions in inventory and labour costs, together with higher machine utilization, figure prominently. Flexibility in switching between different product-types either was not sought or proved difficult to achieve in practice. Economic reductions in batch-size also presented problems. The influential Ingersoll consultants[25] recommend adaptation of the FMS to a clearly specified product, and allowance of adequate development time. The study found that these safeguards were often violated. It seems that conventional automation perspectives are obscuring the potential for production flexibility. The dominant management view seeks short-term quantifiable savings in direct costs such as machine utilization and labour costs.[26] Yet pursuit of these goals may obscure more strategic gains of competitiveness in product markets.

The workers operating these FMSs almost all had experience or qualifications in craft skills. Most continued to use some of their previous machining expertise in making tooling and workpiece adjustments, setting-up and loading. In three cases these ex-machinists also did remedial part-programming, and in three firms some of the day-to-day changes to the programmes for scheduling parts through the system. Although in four firms minor tasks had been delegated to FMS operators, most of the maintenance responsibilities remained with the conventional, specialist, electrical and mechanical departments. One aerospace company, pursuing a comprehensive plan for CIM, had attempted to merge its electrical and mechanical maintenance trades in order to respond more effectively to problems with equipment such as FMS. However, trade-union opposition had checked this scheme.

In one of Scott's companies, management had originally established a conscious scheme for an autonomous and polyvalent work-group. The degree of 'vertical' job enlargement was more authentic than the pseudo-reskilling envisaged in the neo-Fordist scenario. The management scheme conformed to that theory, however, in terms of its industrial-relations aspects. The FMS project was implemented in a separate purpose-built shop, from which the rest of the work-force, including the union representatives, were denied access or information. However, problematically for the theory, the eventual transfer of the debugged system to the main production area did not include the flexible work-roles. Personnel managers and union representatives could not agree upon a pay-and-grading scheme that did not upset the hierarchies and differentials for the rest of the factory. After pressure from the personnel managers the production engineers agreed to a traditional technician–operator demarcation within the FMS with a consequent deterioration of work-group flexibility.[27]

In three other firms the job descriptions of the FMS worker exceeded both the conventional task range of the craft machinist and that predicted for neo-Fordism. They resembled genuine polyvalence where 'vertical' tasks such as programming and scheduling were combined with a 'horizontal' expansion of machinist responsibilities such as tool procurement and maintenance and inspection. Haywood and Bessant report a general drift to 'horizontal' job enlargement in the smaller-firm Flexible Manufacturing Cells: smaller units in which control by the central computer system is more limited.[28] Yet it was only in one company, a machinery manufacturer, where operators were clearly being confined to the most minor mechanical remedial work, that there was a substantial deskilling in relation to their previous jobs.

The potential of the computerization of production for enhancing managerial surveillance and hence control of workers stressed by some predictions[29] may also be overstated. Systems such as Direct Numerical Control often require operators to report back to a central computer at each stage of a production cycle. Management Information Systems enable middle and senior managers to carry out 'real time' monitoring of the whereabouts and actions of each individual worker. While such arrangements have been fully utilized in some automobile plants,[30] in some respects over-riding the traditional powers of first-line supervisors, their relevance is limited by other concurrent changes in production priorities, management techniques and the shopfloor balance of power.[31]

Studies of Computerized Production and Information Control Systems, which put production planning, inventory and work-in-progress monitoring into central computer schedules instead of clerical administration, show that there is no universal imperative either for centralizing or decentralizing the responsibility for such systems. They may be run either by a centralized production-control management or the sectional supervisors.[32] It may, indeed, be more suitable to relax supervisory controls at these first-line levels in order to encourage real or contrived perceptions of work-group autonomy, responsibility and commitment. Where managements have successfully displaced union shop stewards as the main channels of information to the shop floor, supervision may, in some cases, have become more concerned with the function of communications rather than direct control.[33] However, Sabel[34] suggests that 'flexible specialization' in product and production versatility will need genuine, 'high-trust',[35] forms of work-group autonomy. If this approach is followed then the conventional exercise of managerial control through first-line supervisors will also be unworkable.[36]

An implication largely unconsidered by prophets of more centralized control of task execution is that automation of many manual effort contributions simultaneously replaces the need for detailed surveillance of workers such as setters and operators. Instead, there is a need for managers and workers to monitor *the machinery* more closely. For output levels and machine techniques are largely independent of the efforts of these direct workers. Generalized commitment and motivation to quality and the proper running of the machinery is now more important than workers' effort contributions. British FMS installations lend some support to this proposition. In four of Scott's case studies line authority for the FMS crews had been combined with the new post of 'system supervisor' or 'system manager', whose main concerns were with software and scheduling rather than with discipline and labour control.[37]

In general, however, no more thought seems to have been given to the systematic recasting of supervision and labour-control issues than was given to comprehensive job redesign. The majority pattern is one of fairly fluid work-roles and varying degrees of FMS operators' involvement in programming aspects. At one pole are a small minority of firms retaining Tayloristic principles of work organization and labour control. At the other pole are a few cases where there is a fairly conscious attempt to expand work-roles and devolve responsibility, although it is far from clear that these innovations are integral parts of the kinds of comprehensive managerial strategy predicted by the neo-Fordist or socio-technical models. The vast majority have retained craft skills and supplemented them on an *ad hoc* basis with varying degrees of additional training or responsibility.

CONTRASTING ASSUMPTIONS IN THE UNITED STATES AND JAPAN

United States

Of the 220 claimed FMSs in the USA many would not qualify as such on strict engineering criteria of flexible manufacturing, such as random assignment of parts to workstations. However, in general, they possess a higher level of technological sophistication than Japanese or European installations in terms of automatic parts-transfer and automatic sensors for tool wear and so on. Also, the US experience is longer than that of Europe; a few of these FMSs have been running successfully for a decade or more. Consistent with this lengthier experience, US firms are more likely to purchase a complete 'turnkey' FMS from automation specialists, or from advanced technology machine-tool companies. In Japan and Britain it is not uncommon for the user firm's engineers to develop at least part of the system rather than risk an inappropriate purchase from an external vendor.

Perhaps as a consequence of the resulting high costs, and more so than in Britain, the users are almost exclusively the larger corporations. A further factor may be that, outside the aerospace and defence industries, FMS costs do not get the specific government subsidies available in Britain. Moreover, whilst UK firms report a variety of reasons for investment, the overwhelming – though not universal – emphasis in the rationale for adopting and operating American FMSs is conventional cost reductions that are easily quantifiable in accounting terms. More 'qualitative' gains in terms of streamlined management controls, product innovation, market responsiveness or better use of employee expertise are much less prominent.[38]

Similarly, FMS operation is based neither on socio-technical forms of devolved authority, nor even on the limited relaxation of direct supervision found in some British cases, but on the continuation of hierarchical organizational principles. Programming functions and process controls tend to be the strict prerogative of managerial grade staff with little officially recognized modification to the original parameters prescribed by system engineers. By and large traditional forms of job classification and work roles are maintained. This is true even where some loosening is possible, because of weak or non-existent unions, or where it is desirable in order to increase the operational flexibility of the systems.

During 1984 I visited eight FMS firms that were traditional small-to medium-batch manufacturers in the machine tool, agricultural and construction equipment, and aerospace sectors. Only one firm satisfied the strict manufacturing flexibility criterion of responsiveness to continuing product variations. Instead, the systems were being applied mainly as singular technological solutions to bottlenecks that could not be dealt with by means of manufacturing techniques in the Fordist mould. The flexible occupational roles and participative management arrangements that are currently popular in other parts of US industry – notably in the form of Quality of Work Life schemes in parts of the US auto industry[39] – were conspicuously absent in these firms. Neo-Fordism, if it was present as an operations strategy, was not being extended to the spheres of labour control and employee relations. Instead, there were conventional forms of line-management, work organization and industrial relations. However, there was limited, though sometimes grudging, recognition of the importance of conventional skills in keeping the FMS running and adjusting machine operations. Yet these jobs were regarded as a strictly defined and sometimes residual sphere of manual input rather than as a core element in the systems' performance potential. Official rotation of jobs was almost non-existent, and a rigid barrier separated computer control and programming tasks from the mechanical operating duties. In some respects operators were treated as (and were capable of acting as) the new bottlenecks, hampering the required levels of FMS utilization on jobs such as pallet and tool loading.

Differences in managerial styles and industrial-relations histories gave no grounds for assuming that the low-trust and adversarial attitudes arose from the specific experiences of the individual companies. Instead, the generalized and unthinking preference for hierarchy, occupational specialization and the demarcation of computer-related tasks from the shop floor could only be attributable to a deeply rooted Tayloristic managerial culture and an institutionalized, and legally buttressed, resistance to any possibility of the extension of trade-union involvement in managerial decisions. Amongst unionized plants, managers were generally only too aware that less direct supervisory authority and more informal individual job responsibilities in the FMS would risk complicating conventional bargaining and work organization arrangements in the rest of the plant. For, despite some commentators' assessments,[40] the arrangements favoured by the unions worked as much, if not more, to the benefit of the managers. By defining computer programming and controlling tasks as a managerial job, and therefore beyond the scope of collective bargaining, managements are conveniently able to avoid union influence over these jobs.

Where more of a socio-technical approach is attempted, the more generalized emphasis on direct financial gains from the automation schemes provides an inhospitable environment. In one of my case studies the FMS had been introduced to improve the quality of the motor frames for diesel-electric locomotives. The main operating objective was reduced machining-time. Despite being designed for only two small 'families' of parts, rather than extensive product variations, considerable debugging and mechanical adjustment was necessary after installation. Management and union worked out a provisional agreement on all-round work-roles for loading, operating, tooling and maintenance tasks. There was also a relatively revolutionary – by US standards – aspiration to involve the operating crew in the computer scheduling of the parts through the system. However, all of these inno-vations broke down amidst recriminations from the union and work-force and a withdrawal of further cooperation when senior management revoked the accompanying payment system. Only a few thousand dollars per week out of a capital cost of several million were at stake. Yet it seemed that management had made a narrow, and somewhat cynical, calculation (the reversal took pace when most of the running-in problems had been resolved) to continue to aim for primary gains on the cost, rather than the performance, side.

FMSs in the US have been purchased and used principally to achieve more conventional Fordist cost economies on fairly restricted product lines. Within these limits the systems exhibit considerable technical sophistication and several users seem committed to seeking additional technological solutions to some of the problems set by human inadequacies. The ideologies behind the traditional adversarial and legal-contractual indus-trial-relations system, rather than any concrete local manifestations of conflictual labour relations, appear to lock both management and unions together in their indifference to or anxiety about more responsible and flexible forms of work organization.

The novel trends, in US sectors such as automobiles, towards 'participa-tion', less narrow collective-bargaining foci and broader work roles have attracted much academic interest. Kochan *et al.* suggest that these and other work-reform measures are especially important in the non-union sector which increasingly acts as a model and threat to practices in unionized plants. These authors, however, provide no indication of the extent to which the new model is spread amongst sectors, let alone US industry as a whole. Moreover, they mistakenly assume that the increasing sophistication of production technologies requires more flexible and expanded work-roles. They do not recognize that managers may see such automation policies as a self-contained solution to labour and productivity problems.[41] For example, one of the FMS firms I studied had a non-union plant on a greenfield site. Yet it had still introduced the narrow occupational division of labour typical of older unionized plants. Radical work-reorganization patterns seem not, so far, to have made much impact upon firms in metalworking manufacturing.

Japan

Most western media attention to Japanese schemes for computer-integrated production lines has focused on the alleged technological virtuosity that has led to 'workerless factories' such as Fujitsu Fanuc's new plant for robot production. A factory visit and interviews there in 1985 revealed that the 'workerless' night-shift is prepared for by generously staffed daytime shifts, processes only a few well-tested components and is continually monitored by the shift supervisor. It is true that Fanuc's plant and some others have some, undoubtedly advanced, forms of automation. More importantly, however, they are not necessarily aimed at substituting human skills and knowledge in the same way as many western applications.

It is generally recognized that large Japanese firms do not seek the same degree of direct management authority and detailed control over shopfloor work-tasks as their Anglo-American counterparts.[42] Japanese industry is also credited with greater internal mobility of workers within the enterprise and plant – with job rotation possibly occurring as frequently as half-day intervals in many plants.[43] Many western experts in CIM have emphasized that such automation schemes will only be effective if the pre-existing organizational framework is sufficiently malleable.[44] The Japanese superiority in this administrative dimension may thus be more useful than sheer technological commitment. However, their organizations' dependence upon collective ingenuity and individual discretion is not likely to appeal to these western technologists.

Like most North American and many British FMSs, Japanese systems rank reductions in operating costs ahead of qualitative gains, such as more product variability. FMS vendors thought that smaller batch-sizes and increasing product-ranges, together with the ubiquitous Japanese concern for further improvements in final product quality, were attractive considerations for purchasing firms. Financial considerations were given most emphasis. Round-the-clock working reduced the length of the pay-back period, and the flexibility of the systems for resetting to different uses reduced or eliminated the need to purchase new or additional machinery. Although quality improvements are seen as an important residual aim, the range of parts that they can machine is sometimes quite rigid. The relative simplicity of technology and the concern with overall production cost (not primarily labour) may follow from the fact that retained profits, rather than external funding (at least in the firms visited), is the principal source of finance. This more circumspect approach affects purchasing policies. Production managers tend to put together the constituent elements of the system themselves rather than buying complete, and more expensive, turnkey systems.

The lack of emphasis upon operating flexibility as a gain from the technology may simply indicate that the human organization already provides this quality. Technological advance and the bias towards cooperative working and work-role flexibility are mutually conditioning. These forms of work organization that have proved so effective in the past discourage the kind of detailed record-keeping found in the more hierarchical and Taylorized factory administrations of the west. This tendency, for decision-making by work-groups and a reliance upon the on-the-job knowledge of all relevant individuals, is in turn made possible and reinforced by employment policies based on the famous 'long service' and 'life-time employment'. As a result, the written data bases from which computerized information controls such as CAD/CAM, must be compiled, are lacking.

Work-role flexibility, and the cooperative character of the detailed production tasks delegated to workers and supervisors, also compensates for the tendency to more rigidity in the design parameters and range of products in some FMSs. The pressure is, on the whole, towards operator involvement in computer programming and controls of FMSs. As in one of the US firms, Sabel's flexible-specialization hypothesis was supported by one of the Japanese case studies. Here greater flexibility of product range corresponded to, and seemed to presuppose, even more polyvalence and autonomy amongst production staff than in the other cases.[45]

Job categories were simply an extension of normal practices in the rest of the plant. So, unlike the American FMSs, job categories were much less specialized, with simple programming tasks, routine repairs and maintenance, tool and workpiece setting and quality inspection being the responsibility of a single class of 'operators'. Most leading Japanese firms have no concept of the Anglo-American craftworker; so questions of specialized qualification, separate from on-the-job training, and occupational redefinition and deskilling of such a status group did not emerge. Paradoxically, this kind of human *kanban*, developing skills only as and where they are needed, enhances managers' dependence upon the existing work-crews. Specific skills are not readily available elsewhere within the firm, or on the external labour market, so labour cannot be redeployed to immediate effect. FMS areas tend to be treated like any others: sometimes relatively 'green' labour is introduced, but is supported by more experienced workers.

In at least one firm there was little movement out of the FMS areas because the extra time taken to develop machining skills limited the numbers of recruits with appropriate experience. The likelihood that a large proportion (perhaps half) of the shop floor are graduate-entry 'career workers' – in transit to eventual management positions – further limits the pool of available experience, because these employees gradually move away from the shops and plants where they gain their production experience.

BRITAIN IN CONTEXT: INDUSTRIAL STRUCTURE AND INSTITUTIONAL INFLUENCES

In terms of the relationship between the purposes and uses of computer-integrated automation and the impact on work-roles and labour control, Britain falls somewhere between Japan and the US. All three countries tend to organize work and recruit for FMSs on much the same basis as in their other conventional production areas. Some British firms may, however, be more adventurous in their expansion of FMS workers' skills and responsibilities than their US counterparts. In this sense there is some movement away from job specialization of the US kind towards a pattern that more resembles Japanese practice. It is more likely, however, that these limited changes are due to the loosening of detailed union controls over job territories and demarcation stemming from the general decline of union power in the 1980s.

In terms of production strategies the British firms' FMS objectives were more similar to the US norm of a preoccupation with financially reinforced cost reductions – although, again, the impulse seems less strong and less pervasive amongst all the firms studied. What then accounts for this seeming eclecticism and 'middle of the road' character in Britain? The broader context of industrial structure, financial culture and government policy clarifies this heterogeneity. It demonstrates the range of pressures that influence British managers away from coherent and equivocal models of labour control and production strategy. In the last decade the most significant of these influences on automation patterns may have been the emergence of a dual industrial structure amongst larger firms in the manufacturing sector.[46]

The spread of programmable automation in Britain has been rapid and extensive enough for the claim to be made that a greater number of British enterprises now have 'some form of automated manufacturing' than other European nations.[47] But the distribution of the particular kinds of system, by sector, region and type of industrial enterprise, is uneven. In the metal-engineering heartland of the West Midlands there is only one fully-fledged FMS.[48] Robots are confined to the automobile and electrical-goods sectors. Freeman argues that another reason for the patchy investment pattern in robotics is the changing industrial structure. Larger plants tend to have more robots; but these kinds of establishment are more typical of firms making simpler metal goods and electro-mechanical products.[49] These are the sectors of British manufacturing that have contracted most severely in the 1970s and 1980s.

According to Freeman, traditional British manufacturing firms may now have settled into product markets of middle value and middling sophistication in international trade terms. But many companies of this type are distinct from another type which is more involved in international markets for more advanced products. The latter may be branches of American, and more recently Japanese, corporations or indigenous competitors in international markets. This second group, which would include aerospace and motor vehicles and the more complex types of industrial machinery, are advancing toward the pursuit of eventual CIM. The senior management of these 'high-tech' automaters understand the latest technologies and want to force through long-term programmes of system integration. Their managerial problems may be more to do with how to embed programmable automation in traditionalistic, indigenous local plant and work-group cultures.

For the more traditional firms and industries, the latter problem permeates entire enterprises. A web of organizational, financial and business policy complexities inhibits strategic programmes of investment. Corporate structure may be fragmented into networks of 'federal firms' with restricted communications and managerial career paths. Investment plans may be piecemeal and initiated from below by the managers of individual plants, or even departmental heads. Line managers rather than unions may be the most sceptical and resistant to advanced automation schemes.[50] Their technological sluggishness is a focus for governmental concern and initiatives.

Amongst the internationalized category are firms such as British Aerospace, the monopoly civil aircraft and aerospace-weapons contractor, and Rolls Royce, the international aero-engine manufacturer. Both have been prominent developers and users of FMS and CAD/CAM and are enthusiastic exponents of CIM. To a certain extent their technological proficiency results from the examples set by their high-technology rivals and cooperators in the intensely competitive international market for civil aerospace vehicles. Participation in joint projects is stimulating their involvement in development of advanced software for the integration of different kinds of automation systems. The European dimension to technology advance is also emphasized by British Aerospace's appointment to be lead contractor in the EEC-funded CIM Project 955, which is aimed at developing standards for inter-systems communications and will also be applied to Airbus production.[51] Another influence is the beneficial effects of long-term Research and Development and investment support gained from the continuing high levels of state spending on military hardware since the advent of the Conservative government in 1979.

Yet, whatever the causes, little of this technological sophistication is matched by higher trust in forms of work organization. The FMSs in the large aerospace firms are often those with minimal expansion of operators' roles. As far as a sophisticated neo-Fordist programme, or a socio-technical philosophy, for work organization and labour control is concerned, defence expenditures and the general retreat of union militancy have provided diversions rather than stimuli. Longer-standing volatility in aerospace-product markets, a highly concentrated enterprise structure and high unionization amongst all grades of employees, are all conditions that have fostered, and seem likely to continue to foster, considerable, though often muted, industrial-relations frictions.[52]

Key groups of technologists and other advisers to the Tory administrations appear to have maintained some continuity of technical goals with the growth-orientated spirit of previous interventionist governments. In that period industrial policy regarded automation as part of a rationalization process to achieve American levels of efficiency, Fordist-type economies of scale and capital intensity. The continuity in manufacturing philosophy underlying these state interventions is best summarized by the Department of Industry working party, the Automated Small Batch Production Committee, set up under the Labour Government in 1976. It proposed support for the establishment of automated cells similar to current FMSs. However, the proposed gains from such systems were conventionally Fordist: reduced inventory and work-in-progress, reductions in direct labour costs, and higher levels of machine utilization. Automation would allow small-batch producers to reduce the prices of their low-technology products relative to foreign competitors. By 1983 the available technologies were more advanced but the message was only slightly modified. A working party of the influential Cabinet-level Advisory Committee on Advanced Research and Development argued that 'New and advanced manufacturing technologies . . . offer even greater scope for improved productivity and product quality.'[53] In similar vein the Advanced Manufacturing Systems Group of the tripartite National Economic Development Office, though recognizing the competitive gains from the flexibility of new systems, presented the 'key results' of Advanced Manufacturing Technology in terms of material costs, total production costs, operating profit, tendering time and delivery time.[54]

The official doctrine is that 'it is for industry to take the initiative' while Government's role 'is to create the right climate for the use of Advanced Manufacturing Technology'.[55] In practice there has been a set of compromise measures, with an implicit double focus. On the one hand, a succession of schemes has aimed at spreading proven technologies, such as CNC and robots, to smaller (or more backward) firms, through financial inducements. On the other hand, large sums have been given to a very small number of bigger firms, to act as demonstrations of the potential of newer systems such as CAD/CAM and FMS for larger firms with the in-house technological expertise to exploit them. The numbers of firms applying under these schemes has often exceeded the funds allocated to them. As far as FMS is concerned, for example, a majority of firms would probably not have been able to justify them financially to their boards of directors without the grants of up to 33 per cent that were made available.[56]

The fact that many of these firms are large and generally profitable suggests that it may be accounting procedures rather than available funds that restrict investment in flexible automation. If these pressures towards a US pattern were able to work themselves out unchecked then they would tend to bias objectives towards the redundancy and marginalization of the workers involved. However, they are often checked by the immediate production perspectives of production management, and by hybrid and nebulous rationales for the automation schemes. Attempts to re-plan the contribution of labour may seem less relevant now that broader political and economic changes have made it less of an organizational problem than it was a decade ago.

Buchanan's argument, described above, also suggests that the different dimensions of automation schemes – the external-strategic, cost-performance and control of production aspects – may sometimes be in conflict with one another. Re-examining these different objectives in the broader structural, institutional and political context indicates that for many British firms, at least those implementing schemes such as FMS, there are almost inevitable conflicts and inconsistencies. Moreover, it is these tensions and incompatibilities in enterprise policy that play the major role in creating pragmatism, uncertainty and heterogeneity in job definitions, work practices and principles of labour control.

Apparent arbitrariness in favouring one kind of objective rather than another may be attributable to practical inconsistencies between different strategic dimensions or managerial levels. An alternative interpretation is that final schemes are compromise arrangements worked out to satisfy competing business objectives and managerial groups, formulated on the basis of a mixture of calculation, conjecture, hunch and imagery. First of all, it must be recognized that different stated aims have different weights for the management groups with most influence over employment and labour issues. In some cases objectives such as reducing certain kinds of operating cost will indeed be features of a systematic plan of change. In other cases they may be, at least partly, after-the-event and cosmetic justifications. (This point is developed with respect to CAD by McLoughlin.)[57] There may be, in other words, a distinction to be made between managers' manifest and latent objectives.

There is considerable evidence that detailed financial analyses of the costs and benefits of automation investments are either limited or speculative.[58] What seems to happen in many cases is that operations managers single out a few demonstrably quantifiable cost savings such as work-in-progress, labour costs or machine-utilization rates. They then use these claims as the basis for securing approval from the financial and senior managements of their firm. This characterization of advantages need not, of course, correspond to the direct gains sought by managers responsible for the operation of the new systems. However, its limited relevance is indicated by the apparently distorted investment priorities that result; where, for example, the actual labour-cost reductions represent less than 20 per cent of the total savings and a less than 1 per cent saving on the total wage-bill.[59]

Underlying the general investment process is the financial constraint noted by Senker for CAD acquisitions.[60] New technology investments have to come out of the particular budgets for designated cost centres which may not correspond to the totality of an enterprise's operations. Often key investments such as CAD, which could form the basis for higher levels of computer integration, are made by relatively low-level and specialist departmental heads. But these departments are defined in terms of specialized cost centres that are separate from other functions such as production shops. So a strategic perspective is precluded. These managers also tend to justify investments to senior managers on the basis of short-term accounting methods such as Discounted Cash Flow or short payback time-limits. Consequently, financial justifications are made on the basis of direct cost advantages such as labour costs. This preoccupation is exacerbated by the sales-pitches of perceptive equipment vendors. This justification constraint means that operations managers in general, whatever efficiency gains they themselves perceive, have to claim a return on investment that can be achieved within a relatively short-term payback period of around two years. The underlying institutional condition here is the conventions of the financial environment. Senior managers see new investments in plant in terms of the length of time they take to make the financial returns that will improve companies' half-yearly statements of profits and share dividends.

Some production managers making a case for investments in flexible automation may therefore describe the benefits in terms of financially quantifiable short-term savings. However, the underlying advantages sought may be of a more qualitative character, such as the capability to respond quickly to certain kinds of orders and customers, or to improve production quality for some types of design. An artificial case of the value of purchasing an FMS on the grounds of direct cost savings may be made to top management. The real aim, however, could be the system's technical proficiency and the improved responsiveness to urgent and special orders. Fieldwork has revealed other cases where production managers and engineers believed the FMS investment would reduce batch-sizes and increase versatility for making different kinds of products. But in these firms the technical staff were subsequently pressured by senior or financial managers to minimize, or eliminate, the necessary experimental time and extra programming needed to make the systems more flexible. The policy, instead, was to maximize machine-utilization times and so reduce the financial payback period. Thus these types of gain get priority, rather than the more qualitative advantages.[61]

So industrial policy, financial controls, industrial context and managers' strategic perspectives constrain production organization. The labour consequences of such limitations on flexible production methods are that the systems are put to uses that are more restricted than their potential or the original plans. Then managers have less need to involve setters, operators and system supervisors in programming and planning adjustments. Less attention need be paid to shopfloor expertise and training. All the companies in Scott's study brought in setters and operators with craft or technician level skills to run their FMSs. However, in the majority of cases, new *training* was limited to familiarization courses by the system suppliers, or on-the-job training as the systems were built up. It was noted above that there were only isolated instances of a move towards autonomous work-groups with a higher 'vertical' level of responsibility; but there is little evidence that this derived from conscious management plans to restrict the workers' skills and decision-making (a finding that parallels Haywood and Bessant's report that over half the firms installing the smaller FMSs had given no advance consideration to re-organizing work-roles).[62]

The majority pattern of eclecticism and pragmatism is partly a result of contingent circumstances. The relative newness of the systems encourages attempts to involve all concerned in order to achieve normal running as quickly as possible. The simple effect of the smaller numbers on the shopfloor means that the numbers of operators and setters is normally well below that in conventional and CNC machine shops. So the individual operators tended, in most cases, to be given tasks that were additional to those that would have been distributed on a more specialized basis where there was a higher number of workers. Paradoxically, the unions' diminished powers of resistance may also be making managers more amenable to some extensions of worker responsibility. Changes in work practices are less likely to become issues of principle for union-management contestation. Coordinated management attention to detailed job designs and control of work-roles comes to be seen as less important.

CONCLUSION

Three propositions were put forward about the changing relationship between work organization and labour control in key sectors of British manufacturing. First, that there are limits to a convergence of labour control and labour-management policies by means of a common technological solution. Second, that the major impact upon jobs and labour relations, arising from changes in production organization through automation, will not stem primarily from specific labour-orientated policies incorporated within the planning and implementation of automation schemes. Instead, a more important factor will be the indirect influence of other business conditions and practices. Third, that British eclecticism and particularism in the management of manufacturing has not been transcended, in the 1980s, by competitive strategies of which the adoption of new technology is thought to be a central feature.

We saw that essentially the same FMS technology was staffed by workers with distinctly different roles and levels of responsibility in the three countries. Each country relied partly on traditional skills of what the British would call a manual-craft type. However, with the partial exception of Britain, the occupational distinctions and boundaries that labour-market or industrial-relations institutions had formed in the traditional production areas survived. Several British plants had adopted FMS work-roles for their operators that were more flexible and responsible than those for conventional processes. But these practices did not seem, on the whole, to stem from any grand designs in comprehensive strategic-level plans for corporate change.

There was not any general pattern in Britain towards more centralized control but neither was there sufficient change in authority systems and work-group accountability to conform either to Buchanan's socio-technical strategic paradigm, or the manipulative pseudo-autonomy predicted for neo-Fordism. Even within the British FMSs there was considerable diversity in managerial attitudes and practices for the work-organization and labour-relations consequences. There are therefore distinct national and local limits on the extent to which technologically based production changes will promote a universal model of work practices and labour control.

It seem likely that many of the current British FMSs would not have been set up without Government financial assistance and the publicity associated with the Department of Trade and Industry schemes. The underlying policy assumptions have favoured 'performance' gains of the familiar direct labour-saving kind. These influences have been complemented by the predisposition to seek performance improvements for direct and short-term profit gains conducive to matching the expectations of the powerful British financial interests. These constraints often circumscribe the purposes to which production managers put flexible technologies such as FMS. But they do not predetermine the outcomes. The most likely response of local managers and engineers is to try to steer a middle course between tangible cost savings that will conform to the initial investment justifications and more qualitative gains such as market responsiveness and product-quality enhancement.[63]

Since these operating objectives also affect the roles and status of the production staff we find that their job definitions and work-tasks fall halfway between the marginalized American operatives and the more responsible Japanese crews. Flexible automation does destroy jobs and potentially limit the importance of manual skills, but such results do not arise from the needs of the technology. To a significant extent they are effects of the broader financial frameworks, governmental influence and different, though overlapping, managerial perspectives and priorities – forces that are also, to a certain extent, modified at the point of implementation.

The only constant characteristics in all the engineering industrial sectors are the common metalworking processes and the associated workers' skills. It might therefore be thought that ideas about a technology-driven convergence of labour affairs are intrinsically naïve. This is true up to a point. Yet it should be borne in mind that current changes amount to more than a narrow set of technological determinants. Government agencies, technocrats and manufacturing consultants are aware that their radical automation schemes presuppose more fundamental reforms of organizational structure and managerial practice. The pressures for a transformed model of the production enterprise, incorporating new hierarchies of skill and decision-making based on a common technological core, do exist.

What is at issue is the strength of the countervailing conditions that have hitherto made for heterogeneity, compromise and pragmatism in the face of previous paradigms such as Taylorism and Fordism. The suggestion here is that the effects of higher-level constraints and controls of financial regulation of production policies, and state targeting of industrial goals through technology support schemes, may promote diverse and partially inconsistent practices by those in charge at plant level. If a technological dualism, between traditionalist and internationalized types of firm, develops then this may constitute another source of particularism. This chapter has deliberately excluded historic and highly localized labour-management contests over shopfloor variations in jobs, tasks, their autonomy or control; but these struggles will also continue to be decisive in particular cases.

NOTES

1 Cf. H. Shaiken, *Work Transformed: Automation and Labour in the Computer Age* (New York, 1985).
2 M. R. Hill, 'FMS Management. The Scope for Further Research', *Journal of Operations and Production Managements* (1985), pp. 5–21; P. Willman, *Technological Change, Collective Bargaining and Industrial Efficiency* (Oxford, 1986).
3 Cf. *inter alia* M. Cooley, *Computer-Aided Design: Its Nature and Applications* (Richmond, 1971); H. Braverman, *Labor and Monopoly Capitalism* (New York, 1974); P. Thompson, *The Nature of Work* 5 (London, 1983); B. Wilkinson, *The Shopfloor Politics of New Production Technology* (London, 1983); D. Noble, *Forces of Production* (New York, 1984).
4 J. Parish, 'A Strategy for Integration', *Engineering* May 1987; P. A. Dempsey, 'New Corporate Perspectives in FMS', in K. Rathmill (ed.), *Proceedings of the Second International Conference on Flexible Manufacturing Systems* (Kempston, 1983).
5 J. Bessant and B. Hayward, 'Experiences with FMS in the UK' in C. Voss (ed.), *Managing Advances Manufacturing Technology* (Berlin, 1986). D. Buchanan and D. Boddy, *Organisations in the Computer Age* (Farnborough, 1983); J. Gerwin and J. C. Tarondeau, 'Uncertainty and the Innovation Process for Computer Integrated Manufacturing Systems: Four Case Studies', in E. Rhodes and D. Wield (eds), *Implementing New Technologies: Choice, Design and Change in Manufacturing* (Oxford, 1985).
6 Noble, *Forces of Production*; Wilkinson, *Shopfloor Politics*.
7 B. Jones, 'Division of Labour and Distribution of Tacit Knowledge in The Automation of Metal Machining' in T. Martin (ed.), *Design of Work in Automated Workshops* (Oxford, 1984); B. Jones and S. Wood, 'Tacit Skills, Division of Labour and New Technology', *Sociologie du Travail* 4 (1984), pp. 4–84; L. Libetta, 'Tacit Knowledge and the Computerisation of Skills' (Ph.D. dissertation, University of Bath, 1987).
8 T. A. H. Wallace and F. B. Whitehall, 'Some Industrial Relations Aspects of New Technology in the Machine Shop Environment', in T. Lupton (ed.), *Human*

Factors: Man, Machine and New Technology (Berlin, 1986); G. Lee, 'The Dynamics of Technological Change – The Case of CAD/CAM' (mimeo., University of Ashton, Management Centre, 1987); B. Jones and P. Scott, 'Working the System: FMS in Britain and the USA', *Work, Employment and Society* 2 (1987).

9 A. L. Friedman, *Industry and Labour: Class Struggle at Work and Monopoly Capitalism* (London, 1977). J. Child, 'Managerial Strategies, New Technology and the Labour Process', in D. Knights, H. Willmott and D. Collinson (eds), *Job Redesign: Organisation and Control of the Labour Process* (Aldershot, 1985).

10 H. Ramsay, 'Cycle of Control', *Sociology* 11/3 (1977), pp. 481–506.

11 K. Thurley and S. Wood (eds), *Industrial Relations and Management Strategy* (London, 1983); M. J. R. Rose and B. Jones, 'Managerial Strategy and Trade Union Responses in Work Reorganization Schemes at Establishment Level', in Knights et al. *Job Redesign*.

12 Buchanan and Boddy, *Organisations*; I. McLoughlin, 'Management Strategies for the Introduction and Control of Interactive Computer Graphics Systems' (paper for Social Science Studies on CAD/CAM in Europe, Kernforschungszentrum, Karlsruhe, 28–30 Oct. 1985); B. Burnes, 'Human Factors in the Introduction and Use of CNC', in Lupton, *Human Factors*.

13 D. Buchanan, 'Canned Cycles and Dancing Tools: Who's Really in Charge of Computer-Aided Manufacturing' (University of Glasgow, Dept of Management Studies, Working Paper 1, 1986).

14 Cf. *inter alia* M. Aglietta, *A Theory of Capitalist Regulation* (London, 1979); C. Palloix, 'The Labour Process: From Fordism to Neo-Fordism', in Conference of Socialist Economists, *The Labour Process and Class Strategies* (London, 1976); A. Gorz (ed.), *The Division of Labour* (Brighton, 1976); C. Sabel, *Work and Politics* (Cambridge, 1982); P. Blackburn, R. Coombs and K. Green, *Technology, Economic Growth and the Labour Process* (London, 1985).

15 e.g. R. Murray, 'Benetton Britain: The New Economic Order', *Marxism Today* 29/11 (1985).

16 P. J. Scott, 'Craft Skills in Flexible Manufacturing Systems' (Ph.D. thesis, University of Bath, 1987).

17 See B. Jones, 'Flexible Automation and Factory Politics: Britain in Comparative Perspective', in P. Hirst and J. Zeitlin (eds), *Reversing Industrial Decline? Industrial Structure and Policy in Britain and Her Competitors* (Oxford, 1989).

18 H. Scarborough and P. Moran, 'Technical Change in an Industrial Relations Context', *Employee Relations* 8 (1986), pp. 17–22; R. Williams, 'Negotiating the Introduction of Advanced Manufacturing Technologies: Union and Management Strategies and Initiatives', in T. Lupton (ed.), *Proceedings of the Third International Conference on Human Factors in Manufacturing* (Berlin, 1986).

19 J. Bailey, *Job Design and Work Organisation* (London, 1983); L. Hirschhorn, *Beyond Mechanisation* (Cambridge, Mass., 1985).

20 J. Bessant, R. Lamming and P. Senker, 'The Challenge of Computer Integrated Manufacturing', *Technovation* 3 (1985), pp. 283–95.

21 A. Kochan, 'European FMS Growth Predicted at 40–50% a Year', *FMS Magazine* 3/1 (1985), pp. 42–4.

22 J. Bessant and B. Haywood 'Experiences with FMS in the UK' in C. Voss *Managing Advanced Manufacturing Technology*.

23 'Survey: The Factory of the Future', *The Economist* (30 May 1987).

24 B. Jones and P. J. Scott, 'Flexible Manufacturing Systems in Britain' (unpublished report, University of Bath, 1985); Scott, 'Craft Skills'.

25 Ingersoll Engineers, *The FMS Report* (Bedford 1982), p. 33.

26 M. Farish, 'The Design Dream Postponed', *Engineering* (March 1987); B.

Haywood and J. Bessant, *Flexible Manufacturing Systems; and the Small to Medium Sized Firm* (Brighton, 1987); Jones and Scott, 'Flexible Manufacturing Systems'.

27 Jones and Scott, 'Working the System'.

28 Haywood and Bessant *Flexible Manufacturing Systems*.

29 e.g. Conference of Socialist Economists, Micro-Electronics Group, *Capitalist Technology and the Working Class* (London, 1980).

30 Rose and Jones, 'Managerial Strategy and Trade Union Responses'.

31 Scarborough and Moran, 'Technical Change'.

32 P. Senker and M. Beesley, 'Computerised Production and Inventory Control Systems: Some Skill and Employment Implications', *Industrial Relations Journal* (Autumn 1985), pp. 52–7.

33 S. Rothwell, 'Supervisors and New Technology', in E. Rhodes and D. Wield (eds), *Implementing New Technologies: Choice, Design and Change in Manufacturing* (Oxford, 1985); B. Jones and M. J. R. Rose, 'Redividing Labour: Factory Politics and Work Reorganisation in the Current Industrial Transition', in S. Allen, K. Purcell, A. Waton and S. Wood (eds), *The Changing Experience of Employment* (London, 1986).

34 Sabel, *Work and Politics*.

35 A. Fox, *Beyond Contract: Work, Power and Trust Relations* (London, 1974).

36 Jones and Scott, 'Working the System'.

37 Scott, 'Craft Skills', pp. 312–83.

38 J. Jaikumar, 'Flexible Manufacturing Systems: A Managerial Perspective' (Harvard Business School, Working Paper 1–74–078, 1984). This whole section of text is based on an earlier report on foreign FMSs in Jones, 'Flexible Automation'.

39 H. Katz, *Shifting Gears: Changing Labor Relations in the US Automobile Industry* (Cambridge, Mass., 1985); S. Wood, 'The Cooperative Labour Strategy in the US Auto Industry', *Economic and Industrial Democracy*, 7 (1986); T. A. Kochan, H. C. Katz and R. B. McKersie, *The Transformation of American Industrial Relations* (New York, 1986).

40 Cf. H. Shaiken, S. Hertzenberg and S. Kuhn, 'The Work Process under More Flexible Production', *Industrial Relations* 25/2 (196), pp. 167–83.

41 Kochan *et al., Transformation*, pp. 96, 235.

42 Cf. C. Littler, *The Development of the Labour Process in Capitalist Societies* (London, 1982); R. Dore, 'Introduction' to S. Kamata, *Japan in the Passing Lane* (London, 1984); K. Koike, 'Internal Labour Markets: Workers in Large Firms', in T. Shirai (ed.), *Contemporary Industrial Relations in Japan* (Madison, 1983).

43 Koike, 'Internal Labour Markets'.

44 Dempsey, 'New Corporate Perspectives'.

45 Sabel, *Work and Politics*; Jones, 'Flexible Automation'.

46 For a fuller account see B. Jones, 'Social Aspects of Flexible Automation: The British Case' (Vienna Centre Conference on Social Problems of Flexible Automation, Turin, 1987).

47 M. Farish, 'Suppliers On Tape', *The Engineer* 23–30 July 1987.

48 K. Mahadeva, 'Advanced Manufacturing Technology in the West Midlands: A Pilot Survey' (Final Report to SERC, City of Birmingham Polytechnic, Dept of Mechanical and Production Engineering, July 1986).

49 C. Freeman (ed.), *Technological Trends and Employment 4. Engineering and Vehicles* (Aldershot, 1985).

50 R. Loveridge, 'Business Strategy and Community Culture', in S. Clegg and D. Dunkerley (eds), *International Yearbook of Organizational Studies* (London, 1981); P. Senker, 'Implications of CAD/CAM for Management', *Omega* 12

(1984); Mahadeva, 'Advanced Manufacturing Technology'.
51 *Metalworking Production* (May 1986).
52 B. Jones; 'Controlling Production Work: Legal Regulation and State Adminis-tration in the US and British Aerospace Industries', in S. Tolliday and J. Zeitlin (eds), *Shopfloor Bargaining and The State* (Cambridge, 1985); C. Smith, *Technical Workers: Class, Labour and Trade Unionism* (London, 1987).
53 Advisory Council for Applied Research and Development (ACARD), *New Opportunities in Manufacturing* (London, 1983), p. 2.
54 Advanced Manufacturing Systems Group (NEDO), *Advanced Manufacturing Technology* (London, 1985), p. 7.
55 ACARD, *New Opportunities*.
56 Jones and Scott, 'Flexible Manufacturing Systems'.
57 McLoughlin, 'Management Strategies'.
58 Gerwin and Tarondeau, 'Uncertainty'; J. Finnie, 'Financial Evaluation of Advanced Manufacturing Systems', in Voss *Manufacturing Advanced Manufacturing Technology*; Haywood and Bessant, *Flexible Manufacturing Systems*.
59 Haywood and Bessant, *Flexible Manufacturing Systems*.
60 Senker, 'Implications of CAD/CAM'.
61 Jones and Scott, 'Flexible Manufacturing Systems'.
62 Haywood and Bessant, *Flexible Manufacturing Systems*.
63 Only two of the FMS managers in Scott, 'Craft Skills', saw labour-cost reductions as a major objective of their FMS schemes.

9 Employers and the structure of collective bargaining
Distinguishing cause and effect

Keith Sisson

As the Introduction to this volume suggests, after years of being virtually ignored, in recent years employers have come to occupy centre stage in the industrial-relations literature. This is above all true of the British literature: the prevailing wisdom seems to be that it is the exceptionalism of British employers that explains a wide range of industrial-relations phenomena. Thus, British employers are compared with their West German or Swedish counterparts – to show how lacking in collective solidarity they have been in dealing with trade unions and how this has made for a disorderly system of pay bargaining; with their US counterparts – to show how weak they have been in protecting the exercise of managerial prerogative in the workplace from the incursions of shop stewards and how this has contributed to a relatively poor productivity record; and, more recently, with their Japanese counterparts – to show how inept they have been in failing to adopt integrated human–resource management strategies and how this has led to a failure to secure comparable levels of employee commitment. At first sight, the case appears pretty strong – especially if the tendency to shift the point of comparison to suit the argument is ignored and it is forgotten that British employers have not always been regarded as so weak or lacking in foresight.

This chapter, which draws on a larger study of the role of employers and their organizations in the development and practice of collective bargaining in Britain, France, Italy, Japan, Sweden, West Germany and the USA[1] suggests that much of the discussion is misplaced. Three main points will be made. First, although the approach of British employers to collective bargaining does appear to differ from that of employers in most other countries in major respects, there is no one dominant model: the approach of employers to collective bargaining and trade unions more generally is far more varied than is normally recognized. Second, the institutions of collective bargaining which implicitly, if not explicitly, most commentators seem to feel are determined by employers, are themselves perhaps the most important single influence on employer behaviour. Third, rather than being determined by employers or, for that matter, by the state, these institutions are deeply rooted in an historical compromise which reflects the pattern of industrialization and the nature of the trade-union challenge.

IS THERE A DOMINANT MODEL?

One of the things that emerges very quickly when a number of countries are compared is that it is not only British employers who are held to be exceptional in their behaviour. Indeed, this tendency to see issues through the eyes of one's own country is perhaps the major problem in distinguishing fact from opinion in comparative research. Thus, Sellier has argued that the individualism of French employers and their lack of organization was a major consideration in the relatively slow development of collective bargaining in France;[2] while Brizay's account of decision-making in the apparently powerful metalworking employers' federation, the *Union des Industries Minières et Métallurgiques*, also suggests that it is not only British employers who have found it difficult to maintain a common line.[3] Similar expressions and comments can be found in the Italian literature about employers in that country.[4]

Clearly, employers everywhere are faced with a common set of problems: how to recruit, to develop and to maintain their authority (especially when faced with organized labour protest) over their workers. It is also true that collective bargaining has proved to be a major – some would say *the* major – method by which employers in capitalist economies have been obliged to legitimize their authority when faced with such protest. But the details of the policies and practices that have been adopted are very different from one country to another. In short, although it will be argued in the following section that the structure of collective bargaining in Britain differs in important respects from that in most other countries, this does not mean that there is a single or dominant model.

Consider the levels at which collective bargaining takes place. A major distinguishing characteristic is whether or not the bargaining is collective on the side of the employers. At first sight, the major difference appears to be between Japan and the USA, where employers would seem to have preferred to deal with trade unions independently, and Britain and the Western European countries, where (at least historically) they have wanted to deal with them collectively. Yet not only does multi-employer bargaining take place in Japan and the USA (in Japan in shipping, the private railways and sectors of printing and textiles, and in the USA in clothing, construction and printing), but there is also very considerable coordination of the single-employer bargaining; in Japan, for example, the employers' confederation, Nikkeiren, plays an important role in coordinating the outcome of the enterprise-level negotiations at the time of the annual *shuntō* or 'spring offensive' mounted by the trade unions.[5] Similarly, in Western Europe multi-employer bargaining can take place at a variety of levels. Thus, in Britain, Italy and Sweden multi-employer bargaining within branches or industries is predominantly national in coverage; in France and West Germany it is national in many industries but predominantly local in metalworking. The multi-employer bargaining can also be single-industry or multi-industry in its coverage; in Britain and the Federal Republic of Germany multi-industry bargaining is noticeable by its absence; in France it takes place on social affairs but not on pay; in Italy and Sweden it takes place on a range of issues including pay.

Similarly – if one sets Britain on one side for a moment – there are major differences in the extent to which employers are constrained by the legal framework in their relationships with trade unions. First, in Sweden and the Federal Republic of Germany the statutes are relatively silent on the procedure to be adopted in negotiations and the substantive content of collective agreements, whereas in France they are extremely detailed on both. Second, there are considerable differences in the treatment of employee representation in the workplace; in France, for example, there are no fewer than three forms of statutory workplace representation, whereas in Sweden there are no such provisions. Third, the details of the contractual status of collective agreements have different implications for the 'peace obligation' which is implicit, if not explicit, in the negotiation of an agreement. In Sweden, the Federal Republic of Germany and the USA the 'peace obligation' is more or less unqualified so far as the signatories to the collective agreement are concerned; a party that breaches the 'peace obligation' lays itself open to a claim for damages. By contrast, in France and Italy the right to strike is enshrined in the constitution and reigns supreme, and the 'peace obligation' is very substantially qualified. Fourth, in Sweden and West Germany the 'sympathetic' lock-out, which has proved to be a major weapon in the employers' armoury, is not only condoned by law but supported by it; in France and Italy it is effectively unlawful and is very rarely, if ever, used.

THE STRUCTURE OF COLLECTIVE BARGAINING AND ITS SIGNIFICANCE

Preliminary remarks

In recent years the institutional approach to the study of industrial relations has come in for considerable criticism and there has been a tendency to down-play, if not totally ignore, the significance of institutions. This is especially unfortunate in the case of international comparisons. Clearly, institutions do not exist in a vacuum and are not fixed and immutable; there is also a need to explain how they come about and how they change. But it is important not to forget either that institutions are important in their own right and that they mediate economic, political and social developments as well as being influenced by them. In short, institutions are relatively autonomous and do exert an independent influence.

This is, above all, true of the institutions of collective bargaining – the level of collective bargaining, the contents and status of collective agreements and so on. The reason for this, as will be argued in more detail below, is that the structure of collective bargaining is deeply rooted in a specific historical compromise that defines the nature and extent of trade-union involvement in the process of making the rules governing the employment relationship. Just as the level of negotiations and the contents and status of collective agreements have a profound effect on the ability of trade unions to mount industrial action, so too they affect the ability of employers and their organizations to resist such action or to respond in kind. The structure of collective bargaining in Britain offers a good illustration of the point.

The 'common law' model and its implications

A great deal has been written about the structure of collective bargaining in Britain and, although it is not always obviously so, the major distinguishing characteristics should be well known. In the final analysis, and following Kahn-Freund and Flanders,[6] there are two characteristics that stand out above all others and they are the contents and status of collective agreements. First, in Britain the relationship between employers and trade unions is based on procedural rules, whereas in most other countries it is mainly built on a code of substantive rules in force for a specific period. In Kahn-Freund's words,

> Here [in Britain] all the emphasis is on institutions such as joint industrial councils and the like, on the machinery, its constitution, above all its procedure. The substantive rules about wages, hours and other conditions are not, as they are in many foreign countries, built up as a series of systematically arranged written contracts between employers and unions. They appear as occasional decisions emanating from permanent boards on which both sides are represented and sometimes they are informal understandings, 'trade practices' never reduced to writing. A very firm procedural framework for a very flexible corpus of substantive rules, rather than a code laid down for a fixed time – such is the institutional aspect of much collective bargaining in this country.[7]

Second, in Britain priority has been given to voluntary rather than compulsory collective bargaining. In other words, the procedural rules are largely made by the parties themselves rather than being imposed by government and, along with any substantive rules they might negotiate, are deemed to be 'gentlemen's agreements' binding in honour only rather than legally enforceable contracts and codes as they are in most other countries. In short, and to draw on Clegg,[8] whereas practice in most other countries conforms to a 'statute law' model of collective bargaining, in Britain it inclines to a 'common law' model.

The neutralization of the workplace

It will be argued here that the distinction between the 'common law' and 'statute law' models of collective bargaining is profoundly important. Above all, the 'common law' model has made it extremely difficult for British employers to neutralize the workplace from trade-union activity. On the face of it, and unlike, say, agreements in the USA, collective agreements in Britain, especially of the multi-employer variety, impose few limitations on the rule-making of the individual employer: the limited coverage and the lack of detail in the agreements mean that he can settle most matters in the workplace as he sees fit. Indeed, this was the logic of the managerial-prerogative clause set out in the 'Terms of Settlement, 1898' in the engineering industry. But – and this is the point which must be emphasized – the price of this freedom is that the trade union and, perhaps more importantly, its members in the workplace also have few limitations imposed upon them. In general, the agreements give the employer few points of reference that can be defended as legitimate in the event of unilateral action by him being challenged: most issues have to be settled in a vacuum or in the light of previous decisions or against the background of custom and practice. Moreover, in the absence of detailed substantive agreements lasting for a fixed period, issues have to be dealt with as and when they arise rather than periodically and collectively with other employers. Other things being equal, then, the individual employer is given little respite from claims and grievances. Also, the disputes procedure may or may not be honoured by the trade union and its members in the event of a failure to agree. Even if it is, they are free to take industrial action against the individual employer as soon as its provisions are exhausted. As Clegg points out,

> the procedure may experience considerable difficulty in resolving disputes over managerial rights unless the matter is specifically reg-ulated by agreement. Once procedure has failed to resolve the issue, however, the union is free to take industrial action against a managerial decision.[9]

By contrast, and paradoxical as it may seem, the more comprehensive and detailed multi-employer agreements of the Western European countries give the individual employer greater control. Three points can be made. First, the limitations which such agreements impose on the employer are not so extensive as might be imagined. Few of the rules in the agreements are standard: most establish minimum conditions only or allow considerable flexibility in their application. Second – and perhaps more importantly in the present context – the comprehensive and detailed coverage of the agreements imposes limitations on the activities of the trade union and its members in the workplace: it tends to exhaust the scope for further negotiations or ensure that these negotiations are largely administrative or supplementary. For example, it is one thing to negotiate over the position of a job in a detailed job-classification system; it is quite different to negotiate an independent and separate rate for a job in a vacuum. Third, com-prehensive and detailed agreements that are fixed-term tend to concentrate workplace bargaining in the period following the negotiation of the multi-employer agreement; and, because of the legal status of the agreement, it is difficult for the trade union or its members to take industrial action during the life of the agreement in support of claims and grievances. In brief, then, the comprehensive and detailed coverage of substantive issues in multi-employer agreements makes a major contribution to the neutralization of the workplace in the Western European countries.

To return to Britain for a moment, in practice a great deal depended on the relative power of the parties. In the 1920s and 1930s the 'common law' model allowed the individual employer a fair measure of autonomy. In the post-World War II period of full employment and buoyant product markets, however, the policy of controlling the workplace through procedures proved to be nowhere near so successful – especially as employers came under pressure to increase the pace of change.

Employer solidarity

Fundamental though they are, the implications of the 'common law' model go far beyond the workplace. Just as Clegg[10] has shown how many features of trade unions can be explained in terms of the structure of collective bargaining – including membership density, the distribution of power and the ability to mount industrial action – so too can many aspects of employers' behaviour. Thus, the relative weakness of employers' organizations in Britain, rather than being a cause of the practice of multi-employer bargaining, is better seen as a consequence of it. The development of multi-employer bargaining along procedural and voluntary lines encouraged British employers to deal with issues in an informal and *ad hoc* way in their workplace; and the more they did so, the more difficult it became not only to develop common policies through their employers' organizations and to maintain the solidarity of their counterparts in other countries but also, even more crucially, to maintain the solidarity of their predecessors. In short, manifest collective action by employers in Britain is largely a thing of the past; the more distant its experience, the more difficult it is to contemplate.

Clearly, the argument on this point cannot be proved conclusively. It is, nevertheless, significant that an analysis of the structure and government of employers' organizations suggests no major differences between Britain and other countries. Strictly speaking, the structure and government of the Confederation of British Industry is different from that of its counterparts. But the CBI was only formed in 1965. The structure and government of its predecessor, the British Employers' Confederation, was no different in major respects. Similarly, there is nothing exceptional about the levels at which multi-employer bargaining takes place within industries or branches in Britain. Significantly, too, a number of employers who in Britain have never been members of their industry or branch employers' organization or who have resigned from membership, are very active members of employers' organizations in other countries – and, what is more, are parties to the multi-employer agreements they negotiate with trade unions largely because of the institutional advantages that a 'statute law' based system of multi-employer bargaining offers.

Ford, which in Britain has always been regarded as a proponent of independence of action, is perhaps the most notable example. Ford decided to join the metalworking employers' organization in North Rhine-Westphalia in 1963 when faced with industrial action by IG Metall in support of demands for a company agreement. In the absence of any collective agreement governing its relationship with Ford, this was something IG Metall was perfectly entitled to do under the law. Once Ford joined the employers' organization, however, it immediately placed itself under the protection of the 'peace obligation' of the regional metalworking agreement to which IG Metall was a party. Had IG Metall persisted with its industrial action, it would not only have laid itself open to the charge of infringing Ford's right of association; it would also have been vulnerable to action for damages for breaching the 'peace obligation' in the multi-employer agreement. In the circumstances, then, it is perhaps not surprising that Ford joined the employers' organization.

The legal framework

It can also be argued that the development of collective bargaining along procedural, as opposed to substantive, lines has also had a profound effect on the nature of the legal framework of collective bargaining. At first sight, this argument appears even more far-fetched than that made in respect of employers' behaviour: surely it is the legal system that has helped to determine the structure of collective bargaining rather than the other way round? The justification for this view is particularly strong in view of the similarities that appear to exist between the legal systems in Britain and the other countries – the common law in Britain and the statute law in the other countries – and the two types or models of collective bargaining referred to earlier.

As Kahn-Freund has said of Britain:

> there is an extraordinary similarity between the spirit of the common law and the spirit of industrial relations in Britain. The common law is permeated by a deep distrust, by an almost obsessional fear of 'tidiness'. So is much of the British system of industrial relations. Both sides have a traditional desire of solving problems ad hoc, as they arise. So does the common law.[11]

By the same token, it can be argued that there are equally striking similarities between the statute law and the 'contractual' method of collective bargaining: in both cases the emphasis is on rights and obligations that are explicitly spelt out.

Once this is said, the temptation to conclude that the differences highlighted in this section are to be explained in terms of the legal system must be resisted. As Kahn-Freund again has pointed out,[12] there is no intrinsic reason why collective agreements should not be regarded as legally enforceable contracts under the common law; and even the famous Section 4(4) of the 1871 Trade Union Act, which forbade agreements between trade unions and employers' organizations from being enforced as legal contracts, was not the problem it has often been supposed to be. Added to which, Australia and the USA have a similar legal system to Britain but the legal framework of collective bargaining is very different. Similarly, not all the countries where the system of statute law prevails regard collective agreements as legally enforceable contracts. Kahn-Freund quotes Belgium as an example.[13] In these and other cases, then, it would seem that the legal framework of collective bargaining reflects wider considerations than the legal system. It is with these considerations that the following section is concerned.

HOW IS THE STRUCTURE OF COLLECTIVE BARGAINING DETERMINED?

Very rarely have attempts been made to account for differences in the collective-bargaining behaviour of employers and when they have – the notable exception being Fox[14] – the results have been far from satisfactory. Thus, attempts to explain employer behaviour in terms of the characteristics of the material structure of infrastructure[15] quickly break down as soon as they are subjected to scrutiny or when other countries are added to the equation. Similarly, explanations which put great store by the type of industrializing elite,[16] while superficially attractive, do not take things very far; the approach of employers in Britain, Sweden and the USA – all of which are supposed to be examples of countries where the 'middle class' elite presided over industrialization – could hardly be more different; and the same goes for Germany and Japan, which are seen as examples of countries where 'dynastic' elites were dominant.

As has already been indicated, any serious attempt to account for the structure of collective bargaining has to adopt an historical perspective in order to capture the significance of the interaction between employers, trade unions and the state. But this does not mean that no generalizations can be made.

The first half of this section will attempt to give an overview of developments in the seven countries. The second will compare developments in Britain and Sweden in an attempt to account for the distinguishing characteristics of the structure of collective bargaining referred to in the previous section.

Overview

It was not simply a question of Britain and other countries following different paths of development from the very beginning. In industries such as printing, building and parts of the clothing industry the origins of collective bargaining were remarkably similar from one country to another, regardless of the many differences between them. Multi-employer bargaining was dominant and the rules on which it was originally based were voluntary with a strong substantive bias; rates of pay or piece-work prices and hours of work figured prominently.

In industries such as printing, for example, the impact of industrialization was very similar from one country to another. There was a growth in the market and in the size of operations, leading to the split between masters and journeymen. But there were no significant changes in technology until the end of the nineteenth century. In these industries, where establishments remained relatively small, labour constituted an important share of total costs and competition was intense, employers were confronted with the challenge of craft trade unions which were able to establish an effective control over the supply of labour. Much as they might find it distasteful, employers were more or less obliged to join forces and to come to some form of accommodation with trade unions. In these industries too multi-employer bargaining not only helped to institutionalize industrial conflict but also to regulate wage competition. Hence the emphasis on substantive rules.

By contrast, in the manufacturing industries, and especially in the metalworking industries, the impact of industrialization was very different from one country to another. In particular, there were significant differences in the timing, the pace and the concentration of industrialization – all of which had a profound effect on the nature of the trade-union challenge and of the employers' response. Here the structure of collective bargaining was rooted in very specific compromises which, due to the size and significance of these industries, were to have a determining influence on the overall structure of collective bargaining in each country.

Although some iron and steel employers had come to an accommodation with trade unions at an earlier date, in Britain the key date so far as the important group of engineering employers was concerned was 1898; so far as employers in many other industries were concerned it was the period 1917–19. In Sweden the key date so far as engineering employers was concerned was 1905, and for employers more generally 1906. In France, Italy and Germany the periods following World War I and, to a lesser extent, World War II were critical. In the USA and Japan the critical periods were 1933–7 and 1945–8 respectively.

The circumstances in which the compromises were struck also reveal a great deal about employers' motives for engaging in collective bargaining. In Britain and Sweden the settlements in engineering in 1898 and 1905 respectively did not involve the state directly and were grounded in voluntary rules. In France, Italy and Germany, the state was involved directly and the compromises were underwritten by governments with compulsory rules. The major reason for this difference is that although the British and Swedish settlements followed major industrial conflicts, in France, Italy and Germany the conflict was on a much wider scale. Indeed, the very fabric of existing society appeared to be threatened by industrial and political unrest. The situation was also very special in the USA in the mid-1930s and in Japan in the late 1940s; governments, faced with major economic and social crises, were anxious to secure the cooperation of the trade unions that employers hitherto had refused to recognize. It can be concluded that employers and governments agreed to recognize trade unions and to allow them to participate in the process of making and administering employment rules first and foremost in order to institutionalize industrial conflict, and that they did so in response to circumstances without any overall plan.

To understand why the structure of collective bargaining emerged in the form it did, it is necessary to appreciate the relationship between employers and trade unions at the time the compromise was struck. Thus, in Britain and Western Europe multi-employer bargaining emerged not because of the employers' desire to regulate the market. In many cases employers were quite capable of settling wages in collusion with one another without the help of trade unions. Indeed, it was the control of the market – partly as a result of government tariffs and partly as a result of the cartels – that was a major consideration in the ability of employers in France, Germany and Italy to withstand the challenge of trade unions until World War I; the large employers especially, who tended to dominate their local communities, had little to fear from competition in the event of industrial action. Put simply, multi-employer bargaining emerged because employers were confronted by the challenge of national trade unions organized along occupational or industrial lines who were anxious to protect their members against the 'devastating and degrading effects of unregulated labour markets'.[17] In these circumstances multi-employer bargaining made it possible for employers and governments to meet trade-union demands for a comprehensive coverage of the substantive issues of collective bargaining with a single act of recognition – an especially important consideration in the crisis years immediately following World War I. Furthermore, and crucially, as well as helping to maximize the bargaining power of employers, multi-employer bargaining made it possible for employers to neutralize the workplace from trade-union activity: that is to say, to exclude the trade union from the workplace or, at the very least, to set limits to the role that it was allowed to play there.

The situation was very different in the USA and Japan. It was not that employers, as has been argued in the case of the USA,[18] were opposed in principle to collective action. Far from it. Employers have been as willing to cooperate with one another to deal with trade unions as they have in Western Europe: witness the defeat of the 'Knights of Labor' in the 1880s and the conduct of the 'Open Shop' campaign at the beginning of the century.[19] By the time legislation was introduced requiring employers to recognize trade unions in the 1930s and 1940s, however, the large individual employers that emerged at a relatively early stage of industrialization had already exerted a profound influence on the trade-union movement. In the USA these large employers had inflicted a major defeat on trade unions at the turn of the century with the success of the 'open shop' campaign; in Japan they had, more or less, prevented the emergence of an independent trade-union movement altogether. In both countries employers used 'welfarism', 'internal job ladders' and 'employee representation plans' or company unions to keep the external trade unions at bay. In the circumstances there was little or no pressure from trade unions for legislation to promote multi-employer bargaining, and single-employer bargaining appeared to be the lesser of two evils for employers. Not only did single-employer bargaining mean that employers did not have to unscramble their own internal systems of job regulation but it also meant they were able to deal with their own employees (even if they were now organized in 'independent' trade unions) rather than the external trade unions that they had struggled to avoid for so long. Paradoxical as it may seem, then, it was single-employer bargaining that served to neutralize the workplace in the USA and Japan.

The degree of compulsion entered into by governments also reflected the relationship between employers and trade unions. In Britain and Sweden, where employers had been obliged to come to terms with trade unions largely because of their competitive product-market positions, there was little need for governments to intervene with compulsory rules. In the case of Sweden – and for reasons explained below – it was enough simply to pass the Collective Agreements Act of 1928 making collective agreements legally enforceable. In the other countries, where employers had been able to take a far tougher line with trade unions either because of their size (USA and Japan) or because of the presence of a small number of large employers and protection (France, Germany and Italy), the government was obliged to intervene with compulsory rules. In the USA and Japan, where the 'SCAP' administration's 1945 Trade Union Law was closely modelled on the 1935 Wagner Act, there seemed no other way of overcoming employers' opposition; in France and Germany both the government and trade unions were anxious lest the large metalworking employers would revert to their previous position once the immediate crisis was over; and in Italy the government was looking for ways and means of containing the revolutionary challenge presented by trade unions during the 'red years' of 1919 and 1920.

It remains to comment on what can only be described as the remarkable permanency of the main dimensions of the structure of collective bargaining. It will be argued here that it is employers – at least in the countries included in this review – who have been primarily responsible for maintaining the structure of collective bargaining in more or less its original form. Collective bargaining involves mutual recognition. In agreeing to make some issues subject to joint regulation, employers implicitly, if not explicitly, were requiring trade unions to recognize the employers' right to make the other rules unilaterally; it did not mean that employers were committed to joint regulation as a matter of general principle or that they were any less anxious to minimize the impact of trade unions. Thus, even if they had little responsibility for it in the first instance, the structure of collective bargaining did help to define – and so limit – trade-union involvement in the rule-making process; and, as in the case of multi-employer bargaining, the structure of collective bargaining could usually be exploited to dent the full impact of trade-union involvement. Perhaps not surprisingly, then, employers have been reluctant to change the structure of collective bargaining, unless there has been an overriding need to reach a new accommodation with trade unions or unless a relatively costless rolling-back of the trade-union position can be achieved. Better the devil they know than the devil they do not.

Britain and Sweden

The contents and status of collective agreements in Britain can perhaps best be explained in comparison with Sweden. In both cases employers were obliged by their market situation, which was much more competitive than that of their counterparts in Western Europe, to seek an accommodation with trade unions on the basis of voluntary rules. In Britain, where industrialization was early and protracted, the challenge to employers came mainly from craft unions, such as the Amalgamated Society of Engineers, which had been able to establish a significant degree of unilateral control over the terms and conditions of employment at local level. In Sweden, where industrialization was later and more rapid, the challenge came from skilled workers, such as the iron and metalworkers' union, who had not yet been able to develop the kind of craft controls of their British counterparts. In Britain, with informal local bargaining involving the district committees of the craft unions already well established, the means to institutionalizing industrial conflict was a national disputes procedure designed to put the district committees, in Wigham's words, in a 'strait jacket of national control'.[20] In Sweden, with little or no history of local bargaining and the iron and metalworkers' union anxious to establish minimum rates of pay and other conditions of employment, employers secured the same objective with a fixed-term national agreement on substantive issues.

A second respect in which Britain and Sweden differ involves the status of collective agreements. In both cases collective agreements began life as voluntary arrangements unregulated by the law. In Britain, with the possible exception of the period of the 1971 Industrial Relations Act, collective agreements have remained 'gentlemen's agreements' binding in honour only. In Sweden collective agreements were made into legally enforceable contracts with the passage of the Collective Agreements Act of 1928. In Britain the practice of collective bargaining was hardly conducive to the development of contractual relations. The voluntary system also appeared to be more than adequate to employer needs – so much so that in the 1920s the engineering employers' opposed greater legal regulation for fear that it would be to the trade unions' advantage. In Sweden employers had been anxious to give contractual effect to their collective agreements from the very beginning in order to reinforce the 'peace obligation' implicit in their fixed-term substantive agreements. Indeed, if the *Svenska Arbetsgivareföreningen* (SAF) had had its way collective agreements would have been made legally enforceable following the unions' defeat in 1909. It was only thwarted by the farmers' representatives in the Riksdag who were afraid to give legal support to the lock-out that the proposed legislation entailed for fear that the equivalent right of trade unions to take sympathetic action might encourage agricultural workers to seek the support of their better organized colleagues in manufacturing.

The third respect in which Britain and Sweden differ is in the role played by the employers' confederation. In Britain the National Confederation of Employers' Organizations (later the British Employers' Confederation) emerged only in 1919, largely on the initiative of the government, and never played a major role in collective bargaining. In Sweden the employers' confederation, the SAF, was formed in 1902 in the wake of the general strike in support of political suffrage and quickly assumed a major role; in 1906 it imposed a management-rights clause on trade unions in the form of the 'December Compromise' and in 1909 conducted an extremely effective lock-out; it subsequently became the employers' main bargaining agent. In Britain employers saw no need for an employers' confederation: industry or branch employers' organizations such as the Engineering Employers' Federation were well established, quite capable of looking after the interests of their own members and reluctant to see their power diminished. In Sweden the employers outside of the engineering industry were too weak to take on the trade unions by industry. Indeed, SAF was only one of several multi-industry employers' organizations in its early years and could claim to have truly national coverage only after the affiliation of the Halsingborg and Malmö organizations in 1906 and 1907 respectively.

With the virtue of hindsight, then, it is very easy to criticize Colonel Dyer and his fellow engineering employers for introducing the 'Provisions for Avoiding Disputes' that would become a 'shop stewards' charter' or their successors for failing to restructure industrial relations in the 1920s. The individuals concerned, like their Swedish counterparts, were not omniscient, however, and certainly did not possess the gift of hindsight. Moreover, they were not, as some commentators seem to imply, entirely free agents. They dealt with the problem as they saw it and within the constraints that they experienced; and, of these constraints, the history of employers' relationship with trade unions was as important as, if not more important, than their market situation which, in any event, allowed them a fair amount of discretion.

It is also interesting to reflect that it is not only Colonel Dyer and his colleagues who would have found some of the recent comments about the inability of British employers to take collective action rather odd, but also many of his contemporaries in other countries. The willingness of the engineering employers to mount a long-standing lock-out was held up in a number of countries as an example of what employers could do if only they were to stick together. Indeed, believe it or not, the engineering employers' organization provided the direct model for employers' organizations in a number of other countries; one example is the metalworking employers' organization in Milan.[21]

CONCLUDING REMARKS

To conclude with a statement of the obvious: although the structure of collective bargaining may be important, it is not the only institution that deserves close analysis. One institution or set of institutions that requires further analysis is the internal and external form of the labour market itself; there is a growing body of evidence for example, to suggest that the provisions for training are especially important in understanding personnel management practices.[22] Another area of importance is the functional composition of management which, notwithstanding the attention that the design of organisations has received following the pioneering work of Chandler,[23] has been virtually ignored: the balance between production or engineering and finance, for example, appears to be very significantly different from one country to another.[24] The full implications of the different institutional arrangements of share ownership also remain to be fully examined.

The emphasis on the need for an historical perspective is also something that has wider relevance. It is important not only to explain how institutions emerge and change, but also, difficult though it is, to capture something of the significance of the interaction between the main actors and of the critical incidents in their relationship. A prime candidate here for further attention would be government–industry relations. Indeed, it is unlikely that the employer-behaviour jigsaw will ever be complete without the essential pieces that such a study would provide.

It also seems that little real progress will be made in understanding employer behaviour unless and until internationally comparative research is taken more seriously. This is not to decry the extremely valuable one-country research, most of which is itself comparative, that has been going on. There are dangers, however, in seeing issues through the eyes of one's own country only – witness the fundamentally different theoretical conclusions which have been drawn about the logic of collective action on the part of employers by Olson,[25] on the one hand, and Offe and Wiesenthal,[26] on the other. Ideally, too, three or more countries should be included in the comparison: frustrating though it initially may be, the apparently 'black and white' situation in a two-country comparison can quickly turn into 'mid-grey' in a third country.

NOTES

1 K. Sisson, *The Management of Collective Bargaining: An International Comparison* (Oxford, 1987).
2 F. Sellier, *La Confrontation sociale en France, 1936–1981* (Paris, 1984), ch. 2.
3 B. Brizay, *Le Patronat* (Paris, 1975).
4 See, for example, G. P. Ammassari, *La politica della Confindustria* (Naples, 1976); A. Collidà, L. De Carlini, G. Mossetto and R. Stefanelli, *La politica del padronato italiano* (Bari, 1972); Intersind, *Dieci anni di attività contrattuale, 1958–1968* (Rome, 1968).
5 S. B. Levine, 'Employers' Associations in Japan', in J. P. Windmuller and A. Gladstone (eds), *Employers' Associations and Industrial Relations: A Comparative Study* (Oxford, 1984), pp. 318–56.
6 O. Kahn-Freund, 'The Legal Framework' in A. Flanders and H. A. Clegg (eds), *The System of Industrial Relations in Great Britain* (Oxford, 1954); Kahn-Freund, 'Labour Law' in M. Ginsberg (ed.) *Law and Opinion in England in the Twentieth Century* (London, 1959). A. D. Flanders, 'Industrial Relations: What Is Wrong with the System?', in *Management and Unions: The Theory and Reform of Industrial Relations* (London, 1970), pp. 83–128.
7 Kahn-Freund, 'Labour Law', pp. 262–3.
8 H. A. Clegg, *The Changing System of Industrial Relations in Great Britain* (Oxford, 1979), pp. 116–19.
9 ibid., p. 117.
10 H. A. Clegg, *Trade Unionism under Collective Bargaining: A Theory Based on Comparisons of Six Countries* (Oxford, 1976).
11 Kahn-Freund, *Labour and the Law*, 2nd edn (London, 1977), pp. 54–5.
12 ibid., p. 54.
13 ibid., p. 53.
14 A. Fox, 'Corporatism and Industrial Democracy: The Social Origins of Present Forms and Methods in Britain and Germany', in *Industrial Democracy: International Views* (Warwick, 1977); *History and Heritage: The Social Origins of the British Industrial Relations System* (London, 1985).
15 See for example, F. C. Pierson, 'Prospects for Industry-Wide Bargaining', *Industrial and Labor Relations Review* 3 (Apr. 1950), pp. 341–61; 'Recent Employer Alliances in Perspective', *Industrial Relations* 1 (Oct. 1961) pp. 39–57; L. Ulman, 'Competitive and Connective Bargaining', *Scottish Journal of Political Economy* 21 (1974); G. K. Ingham, *Strikes and Industrial Conflict* (London, 1974); P. Jackson and K. Sisson, 'Employers' Confederations in Sweden and the UK and the Significance of Industrial Infrastructure', *British Journal of Industrial Relations* 14 (1976), pp. 306–23.
16 C. Kerr, J. T. Dunlop, F. Harbison and C. Meyer, *Industrialism and Industrial Man* (2nd edn, Harmondsworth, 1973).
17 Flanders, 'Industrial Relations'.
18 A. M. Ross, 'Prosperity and Labor Relations in Europe: The Case of West Germany', *Quarterly Journal of Economics* 76 (Aug. 1962), pp. 331–59; E. M.

Kassalow, *Trade Unions and Industrial Relations: An International Comparison* (New York, 1969).

19 See, for example, C. E. Bonnett, *Employers' Associations in the United States: A Study of Typical Associations* (New York, 1922); J. R. Commons and associates, *History of Labour in the United States* (1966; original edn 1918 and 1935) and Chapter 4 by Harris in this volume.

20 E. Wigham, *The Power to Manage: A History of the Engineering Employers' Federation* (London, 1973), p. 63.

21 G. Baglioni, *L'ideologia della borghesia industriale nell'Italia industriale* (Turin, 1974).

22 NEDO/MSC, *Competence and Competition* (London, 1984).

23 A. D. Chandler, *The Visible Hand: The Managerial Revolution in American Business* (Cambridge, Mass., 1977); A. D. Chandler and H. Daems, *Managerial Hierarchies: Comparative Perspectives on the Rise of the Modern Industrial Enterprise* (Cambridge, Mass., 1980).

24 P. Armstrong, 'Competition between the Organisational Professions and the Evaluation of Management Control Strategies', in K. Thompson (ed.), *Work, Employment and Unemployment* (Oxford, 1974).

25 M. Olson, *The Logic of Collective Action* (New York, 1969).

26 C. Offe and H. Wiesenthal, 'Two Logics of Collective Action: Theoretical Notes on Social Class and Organisational Form', in M. Zeitlin (ed.), *Political Power and Social Theory* (New York, 1980), pp. 67–115; cf. P. C. Schmitter, and W. Streeck, 'The Organization of Business Interests: A Research Design to Study the Associative Action of Business in the Advanced Industrial Societies of Western Europe'.

Conclusion
National models and international variations in labour management and employer organization

Steven Tolliday and Jonathan Zeitlin

THE PROBLEM OF NATIONAL MODELS

This book has shown that employer labour policies, both individual and collective, display considerable variation across space and time. But how far do such variations polarize around distinctive national models? And if, as we argued in the Introduction, the objective constraints of markets and technology are insufficient to impose uniform labour strategies on employers, what of other forces operating 'behind the backs' of the actors themselves – notably national culture? Are the apparently subjective choices of employers – along with those of other social actors – in fact determined at a deeper level by the values, norms and practices of the culture into which they have been socialized?[1] This concluding chapter begins by considering the relationship between culture, institutions and strategies in defining national models, before building on the findings of the preceding chapters to construct a systematic comparative analysis of international variations in labour management within the enterprise, and in employer organization and collective action.

Culture looms large in popular interpretation of international variations in economic performance, notably in the abundant literature on 'the British disease' or 'the Japanese miracle'.[2] But it has a chequered career in academic and theoretical accounts. In the 1950s and 1960s the mainstream of organization theory, typified by the work of Clark Kerr and his associates in the United States, stressed the growing universality of the social order arising from progressive convergence in markets and technology.[3] Later theorists adapted this framework to give culture a more central role. Thus Child, for example, has argued that alternative solutions to organizational problems might be 'functionally equivalent' and that culture might determine the choice between them, thereby becoming an additional 'contingency' for organizational design.[4]

In these analyses 'culture' has generally been defined as sets of norms and values acquired through early socialization which condition actors to evaluate and respond to situations in a predetermined fashion. As many critics have observed, however, it is difficult to establish clear links between national culture in this sense and organizational behaviour, since norms and values may be ambiguous, contested and susceptible to change over time.[5] For this reason, other writers have insisted that culture is a dynamic historical phenomenon, which empowers as well as constrains actors in adapting to changing situations. Dore's comparative studies of Japanese and British industry, for example, treat culture simultaneously as a set of normative predispositions and as a set of social institutions which reward and reinforce varying value systems differently. Thus the Japanese employ-ment system, in his view, can be understood partly as an adaptation of pre-existing institutions, partly as a conscious attempt to create new arrange-ments consonant with dominant cultural values, and partly as the result of selective borrowing from other industrial nations. At the same time, however, Dore also emphasizes the role of objective differences in the timing of industrialization in explaining the contrasting evolution of employment systems in Britain and Japan, while arguing that the demands of interna-tional competition are pushing Britain towards a partial convergence with the Japanese model.[6]

Perhaps the most sustained attempt to overcome the limitations of the concept of 'national culture' in analysis of international differences in enterprise management and industrial relations is the work of the Labor-atoire d'Economie et Sociologie du Travail (LEST) at the University of Aix-en-Provence under Marc Maurice and his associates. The core of this work is a detailed comparison of 'twin factories' matched by economic and technological characteristics conducted in France and the Federal Republic of Germany during the 1970s, and supported by broader organizational and labour-market surveys at national level.[7] These studies uncovered systematic variations between the two countries across industrial sectors (metalworking, chemicals) and technologies (unit, batch/line, and conti-nuous-process production) in the composition of the work-force, the mechanisms of mobility and career development, the hierarchy of manage-ment and supervision, the pattern of wage differentials, the organization of work and the structure of industrial relations. They found that French factories had a substantially higher proportion of white-collar staff overall and of low-skilled workers within the manual labour force, much higher levels of indirect, supervisory and administrative personnel and much narrower spans of supervisory control. Wage differentials were larger at each level of the hierarchy in France – between blue- and white-collar employees, skilled and unskilled, senior and junior managers – and there was also a much greater dispersion of earnings between firms, industries and sectors within the national economy.

These differences are associated with a deeper contrast in the underlying principles of job design between the two countries. French firms use their own criteria to define jobs to which workers have to adapt, while German firms instead start by taking account of the workers' qualifications and then organize the jobs according to their capabilities. The result is that French work organization corresponds closely to a bureaucratic or Taylorist model, with a large authoritarian hierarchy supervising a mass of low-skilled workers predominantly engaged on fragmented, individualized tasks. German work organization, instead, more closely resembles the craft model, with a smaller and more technically orientated hierarchy collaborating with teams of highly skilled workers able to turn their hand to a variety of tasks with a minimum of direct supervision.

Franco-German variations in work organization, the LEST researchers argue, are linked in turn to national differences in systems of education, training and the production of skills. In France, job assignment and promotion depend primarily on a combination of general educational attainment and in-firm seniority. Hence the administrative decisions of firms are central to workers' careers and French firms have a powerful role in shaping occupational stratification. In Germany, on the other hand, job mobility depends on the acquisition of public vocational qualifications, notably craft apprenticeship, while general education is much less important. Hence workers can be moved easily between tasks without any necessary effect on their status or salary.

According to the LEST analysis, finally, these variations in work organization and training in French and German factories both give rise to and are shaped by fundamental differences between the two countries in the structure of industrial relations and collective action. The organizational logic of French firms homogenizes their work-force by subjecting it to a unified system of job classification, while at the same time isolating workers from one another both within and across companies by the fragmentation of individual tasks and pay rates. French unions therefore seek to mobilize all employees in a given firm in pursuit of their bargaining objectives, generalizing the best results across the economy through industry-wide contracts or government-set minimum wage rates. Management responds by discriminating between workers individually within the enterprise and seeking to shift labour conflicts into the national arena where a minimalist settlement can be reached based on the ability to pay of the weakest firms in each industry. The professional logic of German firms, conversely, links workers to one another across the labour market through a common system of vocational qualifications, while at the same time binding its employees to the company by productivity bonuses and the cooperative, polyvalent organization of work. German unions and employers alike therefore subordinate local conflicts to wider objectives in industry-wide bargaining, resolving disputes in particular firms through negotiations between company management and works councils under statutory co-determination procedures which prohibit recourse to strike action.

National differences in the pattern of professional identity and collective action, on this view, are at once a product of the legal and institutional rules of the industrial-relations system in each country and an independent factor reinforcing the underlying structure of each system. Thus the centralization and comprehensiveness of collective bargaining in the Federal Republic of Germany homogenizes wages and conditions within each industry, strengthening the authority of trade unions and employers' associations over their members, which is in turn a necessary condition for the successful operation of the bargaining system. In France, conversely, the limited scope and weak institutionalization of collective bargaining give rise to wide disparities in wages and conditions between firms, undermining the authority of trade unions and employers' associations, and encouraging in turn the settlement of industrial disputes by minimalist national agreements and statutory regulations.

The LEST studies convincingly identify deep-seated differences in employer labour policies between France and the Federal Republic of Germany, and their methodology has been extended effectively to a wider range of national cases and problems. A replication of the 'twin plants' study in Britain revealed a third set of national variations,[8] while the LEST approach has also been used to identify systematic differences between these three countries in the use of new microelectronic technologies.[9]

But how are such pervasive national differences to be explained? The LEST researchers emphatically reject 'culturalist' explanations of national differences in terms of a 'value system' that 'provides a normative orientation for action and for the system of roles and expectations that defines the position of the actors in each subsystem'. In such models,

> once the social system and its dominant system of values is known, the actors are in a sense given. The relation between the actors and the system is no longer problematic; it is completely determined. The actors are dependent on the social system, in which the real independent variable is the system of values.[10]

Instead of culture, therefore, the LEST researchers prefer to speak of a 'societal effect'. National differences arise from an interaction between processes of education/socialization, organization and industrial relations in which actors simultaneously construct the system and are constructed by it. Hence 'the actor as we conceive him', Maurice *et al.* write,

> fits into a set of rules, but at a deeper level identifies also with it, since he is at the same time a player, creator of the game and prisoner of its forms. The rules help to define the identity of [the] actor, and his professional and relational practices in turn help to establish the rules.[11]

Despite its theoretical sophistication and empirical fruitfulness, there are a number of substantive difficulties with the LEST approach.[12] First, its radical holism contains an inherent tendency towards that very structural determinism which its progenitors are at such pains to avoid. Little real independence remains to the actors when their actions are so tightly constrained by their socialization that they become 'prisoners' of a game, condemned to re-enact its rules in every situation whatever their conscious intentions. Despite their desire to develop an interactive model, the determining weight of society upon organization seems invariably to become the driving force.[13] Significantly, too, other attempts to apply the LEST approach often fall back in practice on the rejected category of national culture.[14]

Second, however great the pressures for uniformity within each national system, some internal heterogeneity inevitably persists. Even in France itself, the LEST's own subsequent research has thrown up evidence of significant variations in work organization between firms which cannot be fully accounted for in terms of structural differences in products or technology.[15] Moreover, the LEST research makes no attempt to take into account either the impact of foreign-owned multinational corporations (whose work organization may be more influenced by the parent than the host country), or the impact of large communities of migrant workers who have experienced a different national process of socialization (despite the fact that in some of their paired plants immigrants constituted between half and two-thirds of the work-force).[16]

A final and related problem is that of change over time. Despite its insistence on the need for a diachronic and dynamic approach, the LEST framework remains static and synchronic. Existing national systems are seen as embodiments of an underlying organizational logic. But how did these distinctive national models initially come into being as unified systems of action rather than mere 'crystallizations of accidental historical differences'?[17] In so far as they have addressed this issue, the LEST researchers seek to explain the origins of such national differences by historical variations in the pattern of industrialization, technical education and state intervention. But, as in Dore's parallel project, these explanations remain *ad hoc* and incomplete, while also entailing an objectivist determinism that violates their methodological insistence on the subjective autonomy of social actors.[18] Similar difficulties, finally, arise in considering the future of each national model. Like any system of action, national patterns of work organization, training and industrial relations always contain both stabilizing and destabilizing tendencies. Why, therefore, should the actors necessarily reinforce the coherence of the national model by their responses to novel situations, as the LEST researchers suggest, rather than upset or transform it through the intended or unintended consequences of their actions?[19]

It follows from these critical observations that national models of labour management should be understood not as homeostatic and self-reproducing systems of action but as complex and contingent historical constructions whose unity and coherence always remain open empirical questions. In each case, it is necessary to identify specific mechanisms – institutional, legal, political – which ensure the homogeneity of the national model across time and space.[20] And the unity and coherence of the national model will itself tend to vary depending on the extent to which the regulation of the labour market, training and industrial relations is permissive or prescriptive, centralized or decentralized – conditions which differ considerably across major developed countries such as France, the Federal Republic of Germany and Great Britain.

Peculiarities of the British?

With these theoretical considerations in mind, we can return to the problem of the 'peculiarities of the British' raised in previous chapters. British employers are often presented as internationally distinctive in terms of their limited exercise of direct control over production, their weak development of managerial and supervisory hierarchies, and the fragile solidarity of their collective associations. Recent research, including the chapters in this volume, largely confirms the validity of this characterization of British employers' labour policies for major sectors of the economy over long periods of time. There is no shortage of general explanations for these features of their behaviour, notably the influence of a national culture marked by the strength of 'individualism', '*laissez-faire*' or 'anti-industrial' values.[21] Yet there are serious theoretical problems in interpreting these characteristics as an expression of a broader set of national peculiarities.

British employers' labour policies may have differed sharply from those of some (though by no means all) of their foreign counterparts. But it would be wrong to interpret these differences as deviations from some 'normal' course of national development derived from a stylized account of the experience of another country such as the United States, Germany or Japan.[22] As we argued in the Introduction, there is no theoretical justification for treating any particular set of labour policies – such as direct control, bureaucratic management or associational solidarity – as a privileged or superior model imposed on successful employers by the objective logic of markets and technologies. In other industrial countries similar debates can be observed about the impact of a singular pattern of development on employer labour policies, often taking *Britain* as the bench-mark or norm against which their own national peculiarities are measured. Thus as the chapters by Harris, Homburg and Plumpe illustrate, historians speak of the 'exceptionalism' of American employers in resisting trade-union recognition and collective bargaining or the *Sonderweg* (special path) of German employers in combining these objectives with an equivocal attitude to parliamentary democracy.[23] As Keith Sisson points out in his chapter in this volume, not only is there 'no one dominant model' for employer labour strategies, but many international contrasts lose their starkness when a wider range of cases are considered: thus, 'the apparently "black and white" situation in a two-country comparison can quickly turn into "mid-grey" in a third country'. (see p. 270).

Each national experience may therefore be considered 'peculiar' or 'exceptional' in different respects. Hence each case must be analysed as the product of a distinctive national history, rather than as a deviation from some universal evolutionary model of 'normal' development. Accordingly the potential distinctiveness of every country's development path must be acknowledged, and it must be accepted that the unity and coherence of each national model will itself vary depending on the institutional mechanisms that generate uniformity across individual sectors, regions and firms. The sections which follow explore the implications of this approach for the characterization and explanation of international variations in labour management and employer organization respectively.

INTERNATIONAL VARIATIONS: LABOUR MANAGEMENT

Britain

Before the Second World War, labour management in much of British manufacturing industry was based on an indigenous variant of craft production which exhibited little tendency towards the assertion of direct control through deskilling technology or bureaucratic methods. Among the central features of this system of production was its heavy reliance on skilled, autonomous workers for the performance of a varied range of tasks that required considerable know-how and discretion. Even large-scale machinery in British workshops typically remained flexible, general-purpose equipment, and many tasks continued to be performed wholly by manual methods well into the twentieth century. Much managerial authority was devolved to craft-trained foremen or supervisors, and subcontracting was prevalent in a variety of forms both within and between enterprises. Although certain skills were 'picked up' on the job rather than through craft apprenticeship, workers changed firms frequently in many occupations and few enterprises developed much in the way of internal labour markets or company welfare programmes. At the same time, however, most British employers remained intensely cost-conscious, constantly seeking to cheapen and intensify skilled labour within the existing craft organization of production by a variety of methods from the extension of the working day and the manipulation of incentive payment systems to the multiplication of apprentices and the substitution of boys or 'handymen' for adult tradesmen on simpler and more repetitive tasks.[24]

The archetypal case of British craft production was the shipbuilding industry. Reid's chapter in this volume shows that until the 1950s most British ships were one-off products built to order by squads of skilled workers with little direct supervision. These workers used mainly hand-tools, often hired their own assistants and followed the work from yard to yard according to the cycle of construction. Less extreme forms of craft organization, as Zeitlin's chapter demonstrates, also characterized much of British engineering, particularly the heavier capital-goods sectors which dominated the industry's output before 1914. Similar combinations of manual methods, skill-intensive technologies and devolved management were common not only in classic craft sectors catering for local markets such as printing and construction, but also in the 'operative trades' such as cotton textiles, iron and steel and coalmining which comprised the core of Britain's staple export industries.[25] Even in newer sectors such as motor vehicles which expanded rapidly between the wars, British employers deliberately opted for more labour-intensive methods than their American counterparts, relying on incentive systems rather than tight supervision and machine-pacing to drive production.[26]

Many of these distinctive features can be explained by the pattern of demand for the products. Bureaucratic administration of production and large-scale investment in special-purpose equipment could only be justified by a large and stable demand for a standardized product. But most British manufacturers catered for highly differentiated markets at home and abroad that afforded little opportunity for mass production. Complex capital goods such as ships or heavy machinery were typically built to customer specifications, limiting the possibility of systematic production planning; while sharp fluctuations in demand discouraged investment in expensive machinery that might stand idle during the trough of the business cycle. Even in lighter consumer trades, such as motor vehicles, that made substantial use of interchangeable parts, competition revolved more around models and designs than price alone, and manufacturers emphasized productive flexibility and continuous productivity improvement rather than special-purpose machinery and economies of scale. These product-market influences were in turn reinforced by the relative cheapness and abundance of skilled labour in Britain, particularly compared to the United States.

The labour policies of British employers were shaped not only by narrowly economic forces but also by the broader institutional and political environment. Craft organization of production was buttressed in many sectors by strong occupational unions which sought to protect the market value of their members' skills by controlling access to the trade, establishing rights over a particular job territory, and standardizing wage rates and working conditions across as wide a territory as possible. At the same time, moreover, such unions also enhanced the attractiveness of craft methods to employers by organizing the supply of transferable skills, guaranteeing worker quality and accepting large wage differentials between apprentices and journeymen. In other sectors such as cotton textiles or iron and steel where few workers served a craft apprenticeship, the central constraint on employers' freedom of action came instead from union-backed collective-bargaining procedures that linked wages to work effort and regulated internal promotion to the more skilled jobs. Each of these tendencies in workplace industrial relations was reinforced from the 1870s onwards by state policies that promoted collective bargaining and trade-union recognition but did not impose in return a restrictive legal framework guaranteeing managerial prerogative, as occurred in the United States or Germany.[27]

In addition, however, British employers' labour policies reflected the internal organization of their firms and their own strategic choices as well as the constraints of the external environment. Most sectors of British industry were dominated by fragmented, family-owned firms, often specialized in a single phase of the production process. There was a limited amount of cartelization and monopoly, but even where some concentration of capital occurred, few centralized management-control structures emerged until the merger wave of the 1960s and 1970s. Firms of this type had much less capacity than their American or German counterparts to develop extensive in-house schemes for training, promotion or welfare; and their managerial and supervisory hierarchies likewise remained less elaborated.[28] But this persistence of family control and decentralized management, like the continued reliance on skilled labour in the production process, was as much a product of conscious preference as of structural constraints. Thus as Reid documents in the case of shipbuilding, British employers were actively sceptical of the economic and technological benefits of product standardization, scientific management and large-scale mechanization, and rejected proposals to assume direct responsibility for the payment and supervision of important sections of the work-force.[29] To some extent, as Reid suggests, these entrepreneurial choices may in turn have been influenced by deeper cultural and political values predisposing employers towards respect for workers' autonomy and self-reliance. But as he also observes, such values could give rise to sharply contrasting styles of labour management and attitudes towards trade unions between employers from different regions even within a single industry.

While a modified version of craft production remained the dominant model of labour management in Britain before the Second World War, a second pattern which placed significantly greater emphasis on paternalism, bureaucracy and company welfare, flourished alongside it in other sectors such as railways, gas works, chemicals, food processing, drink and tobacco. The major firms in these sectors were typically larger, more bureaucratic and more oligopolistic, and made more extensive use of large-scale, capital-intensive and continuous process technologies employing considerable numbers of semi-skilled, often female, workers. Stability of employment in these firms was greater, at least for the core work-force, and internal systems of training, grading and promotion were also more common. Firms such as the London and North Western Railway, South Metropolitan Gas, Cadbury, Rowntree, Imperial Tobacco, Unilever and Imperial Chemical Industries (ICI) pioneered the development of systematic personnel management in Britain, and invested most heavily in company welfare programmes, particularly occupational pensions, first on an *ex gratia* and then on a contributory basis. In some cases, such as railways and gasworks, these firms remained highly resistant to dealings with outside trade unions. But even where unions were recognized, as in chemicals and confectionery, such companies typically preferred in-house systems of consultation and representation confined to their own employees.[30]

As in the case of craft production, many features of this second model of labour management can be explained by the economic and technological characteristics of the industries concerned. Britain's rapid urbanization during the nineteenth century created a mass market for cheap, standardized consumer perishables such as chocolate, margarine, beer, cigarettes and soap, as well as services such as rail transport and gas lighting, a sharp contrast to the demand pattern of other sectors of the economy. Oligopolistic concentration in these industries was accompanied by investments in large-scale process technologies and distribution networks that required greater continuity of operations, leading to more stable employment of workers whose skills became more firm-specific and costly to replace.[31] Yet such arguments cannot be pushed too far, since other sectors like iron and steel shared certain key characteristics – notably continuous-process technology – without embracing bureaucratic methods of labour management.

The personnel policies of such 'progressive' companies in Britain were linked to the development of managerial hierarchies for the coordination and control of their increasingly complex and diverse businesses. But the adoption of such organizational forms was not simply a response to environmental pressures. It also depended on the contingent outcome of firms' internal decision-making processes, notably conflicts between family owners and professional managers, or external relations with other firms.[32] ICI's precocious diversification between the wars, for example, was strongly influenced by its close association with the American DuPont company through patent-sharing arrangements and other ties.[33] Entrepreneurial choices therefore loomed large in the adoption of paternalistic or bureaucratic labour policies. Many of the leading figures concerned were Quakers, Unitarians or Congregationalists whose religious values led them to regard their firms as trusts which imposed moral responsibilities for the well-being of their work-force. Not all non-conformist enterprises adopted similar policies, however, and other pioneers of systematic personnel administration and company welfare were not motivated by religious concerns.[34] Even within a single sector, finally, similar firms might adopt sharply different attitudes towards trade unionism, as in the case of the north and south London gas companies or the North Eastern and North Western railway companies.[35]

While British firms were internationally distinctive in their approach to labour management before 1945, the postwar years have seen a far-reaching transformation of both their structures and their strategies. The first and most striking development has been the rapid rise of industrial concentration. The merger waves of the 1900s and the 1920s began to alter the fragmented structure of British industry, but for the bulk of the economy, the decisive changes occurred during the great merger boom of the 1950s and 1960s. Between 1953 and 1970, the share of the 100 largest firms in net manufacturing output rose from 26 to 40 per cent, mainly as a result of mergers rather than internal growth, and the output share of manufacturing firms with under 200 employees fell substantially and only recovered slightly in the 1980s.[36] Merger activity and conglomeration have reached new heights during the past decade, in contrast to the trend towards deconcentration and corporate break-ups observable elsewhere.[37] As a result of these developments, the British economy is now one of the most concentrated in the world: the share of manufacturing output produced by the top 100 firms is considerably larger than in the United States, the Federal Republic of Germany or Japan, while its small-firm sector has declined much further in size and importance.[38]

These changes in ownership patterns were matched by wholesale shifts in the internal structure of company management. Before the Second World War, large British firms were typically organized either on functional lines or as loose holding companies in which the merged units retained a large measure of autonomy, often managed by their previous owners. During the 1950s and 1960s, however, these forms of organization were rapidly displaced by multi-divisional structures. Of the 100 large British companies studied by Channon, for example, the proportion organized on multi-divisional lines increased from 13 per cent in 1950 to 30 per cent in 1960 and 72 per cent in 1970, while diversification similarly rose from 25 per cent in 1950 to 45 per cent in 1960 and 60 per cent in 1970.[39]

Concentration and divisionalization also had important implications for labour policies. Personnel and industrial-relations functions have become increasingly specialized and professionalized within large multi-plant companies, while key issues are frequently decided by corporate planners above the level of the individual establishments.[40] On the shop floor, as Tolliday shows in the case of the motor industry, these changes were often accompanied by sweeping attempts to move away from indirect forms of labour control through the adoption of work-study methods, tighter supervision and the substitution of measured day-work for payment by results.[41] In many industries, too, large companies have run down their commitment to the production of transferable skills through apprenticeship programmes in favour of narrower forms of on-the-job training for their own work-force.[42] Some larger British firms, finally, have introduced internal labour-market policies and company welfare programmes, notably occupational pensions, though their scope and coverage typically remains more limited than in other advanced economies.[43]

The transformation of labour management in postwar Britain was clearly influenced by changes in the economic environment. From the mid-1950s onwards, competitive pressures intensified as a result of the dismantling of internal controls and restrictive trade agreements together with the reduction of external tariff barriers. But institutional factors also played a crucial role in shaping the pace and direction of changes in British business organization. Among the most important of these was government policy. From the First World War onwards, civil servants and politicians, convinced of the benefits of industrial concentration and mass production, had sought with limited success to promote rationalization and restructuring, particularly in older, depressed sectors such as steel, coal, cotton textiles and shipbuilding.[44] As in private industry, however, the real turning-point came during the 1960s. While Conservative governments had begun to encourage concentration in the late 1950s and early 1960s, the 1964–70 Labour Government pursued their commitment to the technological modernization of British industry by sponsoring a series of far-reaching mergers aimed at creating 'national champions' in sectors such as motor vehicles, aerospace, electrical manufacturing, computers and mechanical engineering.[45] During the 1970s governments of various political stripes extended nationalization from industries like coal, railways and steel to failing firms in aerospace, shipbuilding, motor cars and machine tools; and it was public-sector companies such as British Steel, British Leyland and the National Coal Board which undertook the most ambitious (and financially disastrous) investments in new mass-production facilities.[46]

Concentration policies, however, were only part of the story. For the vast majority of mergers the institutional organization and regulation of the British stock market were more crucial. The dispersion of share ownership among financial institutions pursuing short-term strategies of portfolio investment, the weakness of legal constraints on hostile take-overs and the possibility of purchasing assets with unsecured company paper all combined to make acquisitions an attractive alternative to internal growth for many British firms, particularly during stock-market booms when share prices soared. During the 1980s these conditions fuelled a merger wave of unprecedented proportions, despite an ostensible shift in government policy away from concentration towards the promotion of greater competition.[47]

Some commentators, finally, have suggested that British firms' adoption of multi-divisional structures was influenced by their desire to regain managerial control over the labour process from strong shop-steward organizations based on the individual factory.[48] Although this claim is clearly over-drawn, Tolliday's chapter on the motor industry shows that such motives did play a significant role in the introduction of new systems of payment and supervision, and as Jones's chapter demonstrates, British management more generally has become obsessed with the chimera of direct control over labour on the shop floor since the 1960s. In contrast to their Japanese counterparts, British managers focus on the reduction of direct labour costs with little reference to their place in the overall cost structure or the wider financial and commercial objectives of the enterprise. Similarly, when introducing new, automated technologies such as Flexible Manufacturing Systems or Computer-Aided Design, British managers often pursue the control or elimination of manual labour at the expense of productive flexibility and product diversification. The irony here, as Tolliday points out, is that British manufacturers embraced direct control at precisely the moment when US multinationals like Ford were recognizing its limitations in the light of both local institutional conditions and changing patterns of international competition.[49]

As these examples suggest, the transformation of British enterprise management cannot be explained without reference to firms' own strategic choices. Before 1914, as we have seen, American strategies of mass production and scientific management were received with considerable scepticism by large sections of British industry. From the First World War onwards, however, and even more after the Second, a growing body of business opinion came to regard the American model as technologically superior to indigenous practice, even though managers often continued to insist on its limited applicability to British conditions. When deteriorating performance made change appear imperative during the 1950s and 1960s, British firms accordingly turned to the American model as the most plausible remedy for their malaise despite the radical shifts in management structure and practice that it required. The resulting reorganizations were often overseen directly by American management consultancies such as McKinsey and Co., which was used by nearly one-quarter of the top 100 British companies between 1950 and 1970, while US-trained engineers also played an important part in the implementation of new payment systems and production methods.[50]

In many cases, however, these new management structures and methods were simply grafted onto older forms of organization. Great difficulties were often experienced in integrating the constituent units of merged companies, and overlaps between strategic and operational management remain common within multi-divisional firms.[51] Concentration of ownership did not necessarily result in concentration of production or economies of scale, and the share of output manufactured in the largest plants did not rise proportionately with the output share of the largest firms. The performance of merged companies accordingly proved disappointing both in terms of profitability and efficiency gains.[52]

Top management in these large, multi-industrial groups is generally dominated by financial considerations, with little commitment to product innovation or productive organization in any specific sector.[53] Production managers often have little formal training and are confined to narrow spheres of responsibility and specialized roles, without the autonomy or experience to innovate in their own right.[54] White-collar staffs contain large numbers of subaltern employees cut off from the line of authority, while the proportion of technically trained personnel remains low by international standards.[55] Such companies have experienced major problems in coordinating design, manufacturing and marketing functions, and production itself is internationally distinctive in its poor organization. British manufacturing in the 1980s continued to be characterized by missed delivery dates, poor quality control, under-utilization of new technology, pervasive skill shortages and a weak capacity for product innovation. Domestic manufacturers have largely failed to participate in the broader international shift towards product diversification and productive flexibility, locking themselves into declining markets for low-value goods. The result was a rapidly deteriorating balance of trade in manufactures during the 1980s, despite increased exports and a sharp upturn in productivity growth, itself largely a product of extensive de-manning and fuller utilization of existing capacity during a period of buoyant domestic demand.[56] Under these conditions, Britain has become one of the most internationalized economies in the western world, as US, European and most recently Japanese multinationals have stepped in to take charge of the physical and human resources which British manufacturers seem incapable of utilizing effectively.[57]

The United States

The case most often contrasted to the dominant craft model of British enterprise management is that of the United States. Between the mid-nineteenth century and the First World War, US industrialists elaborated the principles of the 'American system of manufactures', originally developed for the fabrication of firearms with interchangeable parts, into a full-fledged system of mass production using special-purpose machinery and unskilled, often immigrant, labour to turn out large volumes of standardized goods. With appropriate modifications, the mass-production model came to characterize the core sectors of the American economy not only in assembly industries such as sewing machines, farm equipment, bicycles, automobiles, rubber tyres and electrical products, but also in process industries such as oil, steel, food processing, glass and chemicals. These product and production strategies went hand-in-hand with a growing movement towards the systematic management of labour, including but by no means confined to Taylorism. On the shop floor, this movement often involved the analysis and sub-division of tasks, the introduction of new systems of supervision and incentive payment, and the concentration of production planning in a separate department. Within the wider enterprise, systematic management developed in parallel with movements towards professional, bureaucratic personnel policies, from centralized hiring and firing through internal systems of training and promotion to company welfare programmes, employee-representation plans and company unions.[58]

As in the case of Britain, this American model of enterprise management was the outcome in no small measure of a distinctive set of environmental conditions. The extraordinary development of mass production in the United States would hardly have been possible without its vast national market, its relatively egalitarian income distribution, and the unparalleled willingness of its immigrant consumers to accept standardized substitutes for traditional products. The production methods of American manufacturers were also influenced by the peculiarities of the US labour market. The scarcity of workers initially encouraged firms to invest in labour-saving technologies, and the extension of these methods was subsequently facilitated by the abundant flow of unskilled immigrants willing to accept the arduous discipline of the new mass-production jobs.[59]

In the United States, too, however, labour management was shaped not only by narrowly economic factors, but also by the wider institutional and political environment. The radical scope of managerial work reorganization and corporate personnel policies, for example, was facilitated by the relative weakness of craft unionism in the expanding sectors of the American economy before the New Deal.[60] Subsequently, as Jones's chapter shows, the triumph of industrial unionism in the 1930s and 1940s played an important part in the consolidation of the narrow job classifications, rigid seniority rules and bureaucratic grievance procedures that became characteristic of American mass-production companies in the postwar period.[61] In each of these phases, moreover, the labour policies of US companies were decisively influenced by legal and political intervention at the local and national levels. Many of the difficulties of American unions before the 1930s arose directly from judicial hostility to any form of worker collective action, and from the willingness of elected officials and government officers to use the police and the military for strike-breaking purposes. Government policies and judicial decisions during and after the New Deal were likewise crucial for the development of the legalistic, contractual system of industrial relations that came to regulate labour management in unionized companies.[62]

The dependence of this American model of labour management on specific environmental conditions is underlined by the experience of US multinationals such as Ford in Britain. As Tolliday shows, the smaller size and greater diversity of the British market defeated Henry Ford's attempt to transplant his American product, production and labour strategies during the 1920s, necessitating important modifications to stave off commercial annihilation. Government policies and the institutional structure of British industrial relations (multi-unionism, decentralization of authority and the legal unenforceability of collective agreements) similarly obliged Ford's successors to retreat from their American strategy of direct control over labour first by negotiating with full-time trade-union officials, then by recognizing shop stewards, and finally by accepting – if only tacitly – a measure of local bargaining over work-loads, manning and grading.[63]

Internal organization and strategic choices as well as external constraints shaped the labour policies of American enterprises. The late nineteenth and early twentieth centuries saw a remarkable process of horizontal concentration and vertical integration in American industry, partly as a consequence of judicial decisions prohibiting looser combinations among firms and partly of growing investment in large-scale technologies. Concentration and integration in turn gave rise to the development of powerful managerial hierarchies initially to coordinate the increasingly interdependent phases of production and distribution and later to monitor performance and allocate capital across firms' diversified business activities. The managerial systems pioneered on the railroads, as Chandler suggests, served as the template for this process of corporate reorganization, in sharp contrast to Britain where the techniques of railway administration had relatively little influence on the management of manufacturing firms.[64]

Nor was American employers' commitment to mass-production methods a simple response to their economic circumstances. Many of the innovations associated with the 'American system of manufacturers' were inspired by design conceptions elaborated outside the market. Thus military goals and finance provided the crucial impetus for the development of firearms with interchangeable parts, and it was at the federal armouries that the new technology emerged and many of the mechanics were trained who would later apply it in private industry. The technological choices of American manufacturers were similarly shaped by a utopian vision of automatic machine production which, though never fully realized, nevertheless helped to transform the factory along the prophesied lines.[65] Undoubtedly, too, American employers' approach to labour management was influenced by their deep attachment to individualist values and unilateral control associated with a liberal conception of property rights, although their interpretation of these values differed sharply from that of their British counterparts.[66]

As in Britain, however, a significant measure of internal diversity in employer labour strategies remained visible within the United States itself. The persistence of craft production in the United States has usually been seen as confined to sectors such as printing, construction and women's garments in which a host of small and medium-sized firms manufactured a wide range of specialized products for competitive, unstable markets.[67] But similar conditions, as Howell Harris's chapter shows, also prevailed across large sections of the American metalworking industry well into the 1930s. Hence when metalworking employers in cities such as Philadelphia drove out unions during the 'open shop' campaign of the early 1900s, rather than introducing deskilling machinery or systematic management they instead reorganized the local labour market to ensure an abundant supply of 'independent' skilled workers for firms predominantly engaged in craft production for fluctuating niche markets. Even in the United States, therefore, such sectors provided a significant basis for the survival of an alternative pattern of labour management.[68]

Within the mass-production sector itself, moreover, the uniformity of American labour management can easily be overstated. Detailed studies of the scientific-management movement have shown that the reform of work practices was often less systematic and far-reaching than its proponents recommended, while Taylor's own schemes for redeploying labour were never fully implemented even in companies whose reorganization he personally supervised.[69] In personnel management, too, large firms' continued to rely on the crude 'drive' system of supervision before 1914, while more ambitious corporate employment reforms often lapsed during the

1920s.[70] Even on the railroads, the supposed pioneers of bureaucratic management, the arbitrary action of local foremen and supervisors continued to determine recruitment, discipline, job assignments, pay, promotions and welfare benefits for more than a generation until the reforms that followed the great strike wave of 1877.[71] In mass-production enterprises, similarly, it was only the coming of industrial unionism during the 1930s and 1940s that consolidated pre-existing employment practices such as seniority and job classifications into a comprehensive bureaucratic system.[72] Within the increasingly important non-union sector, finally, more flexible patterns of work organization, labour deployment and skill development have persisted, along with internal systems of employee consultation and representation.[73]

Germany

German labour management is often assimilated to the American mass-production model in contrast to British craft production. But recent research suggests that the German model has been distinctive, combining elements found in both Britain and the United States. As in the United States, German firms in core sectors of the economy like coal, iron and steel, mechanical engineering, electrical products and chemicals were often large, vertically integrated concerns enjoying a significant degree of market power. Such firms, like their American counterparts, constructed complex managerial hierarchies for the planning and supervision of production, as well as for marketing, research and product development.[74] These large German manufacturers, as Homburg's chapter shows in the case of Siemens, also developed substantial internal labour markets, using in-firm systems of training, promotion and welfare provision to bind workers to the enterprise. As in the United States, finally, many German employers bitterly resisted trade-union recognition before the First World War, promoting 'yellow' company-based alternatives. And as Plumpe's chapter points out, heavy industry's continuing hostility to collective bargaining helped to wreck the Weimar system of compulsory arbitration during the late 1920s and early 1930s.[75]

But as Homburg and others have shown, unlike their American counterparts, giant firms like Siemens, AEG, Krupp, Borsig, Mannesmann and the Guttehoffnungshütte (GHH) continued to make extensive use of skilled workers and universal machines throughout the inter-war period, and to devolve authority over the direction of production to craft-trained *meister* or foremen. Despite their enthusiasm for rationalization and standardization, moreover, German manufacturers largely rejected the adoption of American techniques of scientific management as incompatible with their flexible work organization and diversified range of products. In some sectors, like electrical manufacturing or to a lesser extent iron and steel, German employers during the 1920s also began to accommodate collaboration with union-influenced factory councils within their vision of *werksgemeinschaft* or plant community. Thus before the Second World War large sections of German industry had already come to display the distinctive form of craft organization observed by the LEST researchers during the 1970s.[76]

As in Britain and the United States, these labour policies can be explained in part by structural features of their economic and institutional environment. As a late developer with a limited domestic market, German industry turned to flexibility and specialization in order to break into international markets already occupied by British and American manufacturers. German exporters accordingly concentrated on technologically advanced capital goods manufactured in small batches to customer specifications such as electrical generators, precision machinery, optical equipment or fine chemicals rather than on mass-produced consumer goods as in the United States, and they also relied more heavily than their British counterparts on customization and product innovation in older sectors such as textile machinery.[77] This pattern of specialization was likewise encouraged by the widespread availability of apprenticed skilled workers first from the state-protected artisan or *handwerk* sector and later from the public system of vocational training, as well as by the flow of scientifically trained manpower from the state-sponsored technical universities.[78]

As in the United States, moreover, trade-union weakness reinforced by government hostility gave large German firms a relatively free hand in labour management before 1914.[79] By the time such employers were forced to negotiate with trade unions, the latter were already organized on industrial rather than craft lines, while their predominantly skilled workforce largely shared management's commitment to 'German quality work', flexible job assignments and *werksgemeinschaft*.[80] The subsequent penetration of outside unions into the 'plant community' has been limited, as Plumpe emphasizes, by the restrictive works-council legislation that emerged from the political upheavals of the two world wars. But there is also considerable evidence that the legal framework of co-determination and works councils' statutory rights to consultation over layoffs, promotions and transfers have pushed postwar German employers towards manpower policies based on long-term planning, internal flexibility and broad training, particularly since the legislative reforms of the 1970s.[81]

As in Britain and the United States, German employers' distinctive style of labour management was also shaped by the internal organization of their firms and their own strategic choices. Thus the rapid progress of concentration and integration across as well as between sectors was stimulated by the spread of cartelization – tolerated and at times encouraged by the state – as well as by the close ties between the major firms and universal banks anxious to safeguard their large industrial investments.[82] Public bureaucracy, in contrast to the United States and Britain, provided the template for professional management in many large-scale German enterprises, and also served as a model for the status and career structure of the new white-collar employees, initially known as *privatbeamte* or private civil servants.[83]

The labour policies of German employers have also reflected a conscious rejection of American management methods, and large German enterprises have generally eschewed multi-divisional structures in favour of functional organization in which centralized design, research and marketing departments ensure cross-fertilization between separate craft workshops and facilitate customization and the development of new products.[84] In many cases, too, the German model of enterprise management was doubtless influenced by pre-capitalist traditions of authoritarian paternalism taken over from the aristocratic *Junkers* who dominated Prussian agriculture and public administration. Much more than their British or American counterparts, however, the cultural values of German employers have undergone significant transformations during the course of this century.[85]

As in other countries considerable variations in labour policies can also be observed within Germany itself. Unlike Britain or the United States, however, the major cleavage within German industry is not between craft and mass-production sectors, but rather between regions dominated by large, autarkic concerns and those characterized by more decentralized complexes of small and medium-sized firms. The autarkic, vertically integrated model of enterprise management discussed above emerged in poor, agricultural regions such as the Ruhr, Westphalia and parts of northern Germany and Bavaria which had little tradition of proto-industrial manufacturing. Firms in these regions grew large quickly because the absence of a pre-existing infrastructure forced them to internalize a wide range of processes and functions. The high capital requirements of this strategy in turn drew them into close relationships with investment banks, and the need to recruit and retain a vast labour force in isolated areas further encouraged them to develop welfare policies such as company housing.[86]

The decentralized form of industrial organization, by contrast, grew up in the older manufacturing regions of southern and western Germany such as Baden-Württemberg, Saxony and the *Bergisches Land* (Solingen, Remscheid, Wupperthal). There an abundance of handicraft skills and the survival of corporate institutions allowed firms in industries such as textiles, machinery, furniture, edge tools, cutlery and automobile components to remain small family enterprises specializing on particular products or phases of production. Other functions such as finance, marketing, training and research and development were externalized to an extensive local infrastructure of cooperative banks, trade associations, public research institutes and municipal government. Subcontracting has remained widespread in these regions, and even larger firms such as Robert Bosch are more closely integrated into the surrounding economy than their counterparts elsewhere in Germany. Before the 1920s local craft societies were often more important in these areas than industrial unions, and labour relations there remain less centralized today than in other German regions. Both models of German industrial organization are equally committed to the manufacture of customized goods for specialized export markets using flexible, skill-intensive methods. But the decentralized form – which is linked directly to the 'industrial districts' of the nineteenth century – has been gaining ground in recent years as a result of the increased volatility of international markets and rising costs of product development, while there are growing signs of decentralization within historically autarkic firms themselves.[87]

Japan

Since the mid-1970s the focus of international contrasts in labour management has shifted increasingly to Japan. Japanese manufacturers' extraordinary success in world markets across a wide range of sectors from automobiles and machine tools to computers and consumer electronics has led many western observers to regard their management practices as a new model of productive efficiency that foreign competitors will fail to emulate at their peril. There is little agreement about the precise nature of Japanese management or the sources of its competitive advantage, but recent research presents a reasonably clear picture of work organization and employment policies in large Japanese companies.

The central feature of work organization in Japan highlighted by these accounts is the systematic pursuit of productive flexibility even by mass manufacturers turning out high volumes of standardized goods. Like the West Germans, but unlike the Americans, Japanese manufacturers typically eschew narrow work assignments and job classifications, relying instead on teams of broadly skilled, polyvalent workers able to cope with a variety of tasks. As in Germany, there is little bureaucratization of production management, and supervisors are integrated into work-teams rather than hierarchically separated from them. In Japan, however, this broad skill base is produced by rotating workers across jobs within each enterprise rather than through a national system of occupational training or craft apprenticeship as in Germany. As Jones shows in his study of Flexible Manufacturing Systems, moreover, new microelectronic technologies in Japanese companies are assimilated into pre-existing flexible work practices rather than used to substitute for human skills and knowledge.[88]

This flexible model of work organization both permits and reflects a series of celebrated innovations in large-scale manufacturing which have played an important part in Japanese companies' international competitive success, from 'just-in-time' systems of inventory control, quick die-changes, short machine set-ups and small batch production of components to 'mixed-model' assembly lines and 'total quality control' through the integration of production and inspection.[89] Over time, these piecemeal innovations have allowed the Japanese to capitalize on their productive flexibility by speeding up the introduction of new models and widening their product ranges, fragmenting the market into a series of specialized niches.[90] Thus the Japanese system has gradually moved from an unprecedentedly flexible type of mass production towards flexible specialization, understood as a modern, innovative form of craft organization that combines great product variety with rapid throughput and high total volume.[91]

The most distinctive feature of employment policies in large Japanese firms has been their extensive development of internal labour markets. 'Permanent employment', seniority wages and promotions, company welfare benefits and enterprise unionism form the central pillars of what has come to be known as the 'Japanese employment system'. While a significant amount of job-changing continues to occur, particularly during periods of labour-market tightness, large Japanese companies prefer to recruit core workers at the beginning of their careers and train them internally. These largely male workers are then offered a high degree of job security with the company – maintained if necessary through transfers between plants or even affilitated firms – until the age of compulsory retirement in their mid- to late fifties. A major component of the monthly wage is related to length of service and other company-specific factors, and seniority plays a crucial part in promotions and career progression, as in much of American mass-production industry. In Japan, as in France, however, management has retained much greater discretion in promotions and job assignments, and 'merit' payments based on supervisors' assessments play a significant part in the determination of individual workers' wages. Company welfare is particularly important in Japan because of the absence of a developed system of state provision, and non-wage benefits cover a wide sphere from health insurance and subsidized housing or housing loans to cheap goods at company stores and company-sponsored leisure activities. Taken together, these employment policies have produced what Koike terms the 'white-collarization' of manual workers in large Japanese companies, fostering a broadly shared sense of 'enterprise community' among their members, reminiscent of but more intense than the German concept of *werksgemein-schaft*.[92] The Japanese employment system, finally, is capped off by the prevalence of trade unions organized around the individual enterprise rather than the craft or industry. These unions have generally adopted a cooperative outlook towards company policies, and often include past or future managers and supervisors among their officers, though their active representation of workers' interests through collective bargaining and joint consultation makes them much more than simple management tools.[93]

As in other countries, the distinctiveness of Japanese labour policies can be explained in part by structural features of markets and technology. Thus Dore, for example, attributes the internalization of labour management within large, bureaucratic enterprises primarily to Japan's position as a 'late developer'. In this view, the higher capital requirements and more sophisticated technology of heavy industries such as steel, shipbuilding or electrical machinery, coupled with a shortage of indigenous skills, pushed Japanese companies to internalize a wider range of functions and to adopt more bureaucratic employment policies to train and retain their workers than comparable firms in early industrializing countries such as Great Britain.[94] Similarly, the flexibility of Japanese work organization can be linked to the small initial size and diversity of the domestic market for industrial goods, together with postwar manufacturers' desperate drive to catch up with western standards of productivity and quality as quickly as possible. These characteristics in turn led Japanese entrepreneurs in sectors such as textiles and automobiles both to modify imported western technology for smaller batch sizes and to increase the flexibility of mass production methods through policies of continuous rationalization and product upgrading.[95]

As in the other countries we have discussed, institutional factors also played an important part in shaping the evolution of the Japanese employment system. The spread of flexible work practices and enterprise unionism were facilitated by the relative weakness of craft organization in Tokugawa Japan, where unlike Europe there were few links between guilds or journeymen's associations in different towns. In Japan as in the United States, conversely, the development of job security and seniority-based systems of promotion and wage determination owed much to workers' struggles between the 1920s and the 1940s to force management to live up to the half-hearted promises of their own personnel policies. It was only with the defeat of industrial unionism in the late 1940s, moreover, that the enterprise-based model of labour organization was reaffirmed and firms regained a wider margin of discretion in internal manpower management.[96]

State policies likewise exerted a formative influence on the evolution of Japanese employment practices. From the early 1900s onwards and especially between the wars, Japanese bureaucrats and politicians debated a variety of competing proposals for labour reform ranging from the regulation of working conditions through the creation of works councils to legal support for trade-union organization and collective bargaining. Although comprehensive legislative guarantees of labour standards, minimum wages and trade-union rights were only enacted during the postwar American occupation, the reform proposals of these 'social bureaucrats' during the preceding period arguably stimulated large Japanese enterprises to develop their own programmes of job security, company welfare and employee representation. The postwar defeat of industrial unionism, finally, owed much to the abrupt reversal of pro-labour policies by the American occupation authorities and Japanese government after the onset of the Cold War in 1948.[97]

As in other countries, however, the labour policies of Japanese employers were a result not only of the pressures of the external environment but also of the internal organization of firms and their own strategic choices. As in the United States and Germany, the creation of internal labour markets in Japan was associated with the development of large, horizontally concentrated, vertically integrated and sectorally diversified enterprises run by complex hierarchies of professional managers. As in Germany, too, industrial concentration and market control were underpinned by a far-reaching system of trade associations and cartels, often operating under government sponsorship. But unlike the United States, where multi-divisional corporations exercised tight control over their subsidiaries, the flexibility of Japanese manufacturers was enhanced by the greater autonomy allowed to their operating units by the prewar *zaibatsu* and the postwar industrial groups, which often remain loose federations of complementary firms with reciprocal shareholdings under the aegis of a trading company and an in-house bank.[98]

Although Japanese employers were keenly interested in mass production and scientific management, like their German counterparts they were rarely prepared to impose a rigid system of task fragmentation, narrow job assignments and bureaucratic production planning on their factories. Before the Second World War, Japanese attempts to introduce scientific management were concentrated in government enterprises such as naval dockyards and the national railways, together with certain large private textile and electrical manufacturers. Even in these cases, moreover, Taylorist methods were often introduced in a selective and piecemeal way, without necessarily resulting in the development of narrow work-roles.[99] In employment policies, similarly, Japanese managers borrowed selectively from a variety of foreign models, drawing for example on the company unionism of American firms such as US Steel during the 1920s or the unitary corporatism of Nazi Germany during the Second World War.[100] No doubt the labour policies of Japanese employers are also consonant with certain values of traditional Japanese culture, notably the 'beautiful customs' of familism and paternalism often invoked by opponents of independent trade unionism before the Second World War. But as we have seen, the Japanese employment system was not a residue of pre-industrial practices but rather a twentieth-century creation whose characteristics were the outcome of bitter internal struggles and debates as well as of external influences.[101]

Within Japan itself, as in western countries, a large measure of diversity in employment practices has also persisted. As many commentators have pointed out, the 'Japanese employment system' applies fully only to core workers within large private enterprises – roughly 25 per cent of the total work-force. The predominant view of employment conditions for Japan's 'peripheral work-force' is that they are simply the obverse of those prevailing in the core: low wages, insecurity and limited career progression. The small and medium-sized firms which employ the bulk of the work-force, on this view, are largely composed of dependent subcontractors whose exploitation forms a vital buffer underpinning the security and prosperity of workers in large companies.[102]

But recent research on the small-firm sector in Japan presents a different picture. This work has drawn attention to the technological dynamism and economic autonomy of many, though by no means all, small and medium-sized Japanese enterprises. A significant proportion of these firms manufacture specialized products with advanced equipment for international markets, and most subcontractors work for a plurality of customers while often in turn subcontracting to other firms. As in south-west Germany and other parts of western Europe, Japanese small firms frequently cluster in geographically compact industrial districts where trade associations, credit unions and local government combine to provide a wide range of infrastructural services needed to offset the disadvantages of a fragmented industrial structure.[103] One important but little-noted consequence is that the overall wage gap between workers in large and small firms is no greater than in other western economies, and has narrowed sharply since the loose labour markets of the 1950s.[104] The remaining wage gap between employees of similar ages in firms of different sizes narrows still further when account is taken of the high prospects that skilled workers in small firms have of moving either into self-employment or into supervisory and white-collar positions.[105] Employment conditions in this sector are thus distinguished by higher levels of job-changing, vertical mobility and new firm formation than in the core. But Koike has demonstrated that high levels of work-force seniority and internal skills formation can also be observed within the majority of small Japanese firms themselves.[106] Labour management in the small-firm sector can thus be understood as a hybrid form combining elements of the decentralized craft model characteristic of western industrial districts and the bureaucratic, internalizing model dominant in large Japanese companies.

INTERNATIONAL VARIATIONS: EMPLOYER ORGANIZATION AND COLLECTIVE ACTION

Britain

Like British labour management, the British model of employer organization has long been regarded as internationally distinctive; and it too has undergone a fundamental transformation during the postwar period. From the 1890s through the 1960s core sectors of the British economy such as engineering, shipbuilding, coalmining, textiles and iron and steel were characterized by widespread but restricted forms of employer solidarity. Employers in these sectors were organized into broadly representative associations which bargained collectively with trade unions over wages, hours and working conditions, first at a regional and then (with the partial exception of coal) at a national level.[107] British employers were among the first in the world to form continuous associations of this type, and as Sisson's chapter observes, their example often served as an inspiration for the creation of similar organizations abroad. Through much of this period, the British system of industry-wide bargaining was widely admired by foreign observers, and domestic employers' associations could be favourably compared in strength and cohesion with those of other European countries such as France or Italy.

Compared with their Scandinavian or German counterparts, however, it is the limited internal coherence and capacity for sustained offensive action of British employers' organizations that stand out. Employer organization in Britain has been notably weak at the inter-industrial level, and peak associations such as the National Confederation of Employers' Organizations (NCEO), the Federation of British Industries (FBI) or the Confederation of British Industry (CBI) have never played much role in coordinating the labour policies of their affiliates.[108] Even at a sectoral or regional level, as the chapters by Reid and Zeitlin show, although British employers' associations in industries such as shipbuilding and engineering succeeded in forging common fronts against the unions in periods of crisis, they were rarely able to acquire sustained influence over the strategies of individual firms. Few associations thus possessed much disciplinary power over their members; the centralization of resources and decision-making often remained limited; and financial guarantees of future solidarity were largely absent.[109] Attempts to prevent competitive bidding for labour through the use of enquiry or discharge notes usually broke down in practice, and systems of strike insurance and organized provision of blacklegs were in decline by the early 1920s.[110] In shipbuilding, as in other industries such as cotton spinning or iron and steel, the proposals of aggressive employers to attack job controls and restructure payment systems were repeatedly blocked by other firms' reluctance to bear the costs of a protracted stoppage.[111] Even in engineering, where the Engineering Employers' Federation (EEF) was more seriously committed to the collective defence of managerial prerogatives, the conflicting interests of its members in different districts and subsectors made it difficult to obtain support for a national lock-out to contain resurgent craft militancy between 1898 and 1922 or again in the late 1930s. Despite considerable variations from sector to sector, finally, collective agreements typically remained loose procedural or framework arrangements which left considerable discretion on many issues in the hands of individual firms.[112]

This model of industry-wide bargaining by national employers' organizations reached its apogee in the interwar years of high unemployment, weakened trade unions and increasingly regulated markets. During these years employers' organizations dominated collective bargaining and were often able to use their national strength to extract concessions from the unions during trade downturns or choke off local demand for improved wages and conditions in areas of relative prosperity. Under the changed circumstances of the postwar period, however, British employers' organizations came under increasing strain as a widening gap opened up in many industries between nationally agreed wages and conditions on the one hand and those conceded by individual firms on the other. By the mid-1960s, the Donovan Commission could identify a conflict between two systems of industrial relations in Britain: a formal system of national bargaining between employers' associations and trade unions, and an informal system of workplace bargaining between managers and shop stewards.[113] From that point onwards, the national bargaining system began to disintegrate rapidly in many industries. By the late 1970s workplace or company bargaining rather than national wage agreements had become the primary determinant of manual workers' earnings in key sectors of private manufacturing such as engineering and chemicals, while national disputes procedures were increasingly marginalized or ignored. Employers' organizations in these industries accordingly began to transform themselves from bargaining agents to providers of advice and services, as large firms seeking to develop company-based labour policies outside the framework of national agreements either resigned altogether or withdrew to new categories of associate membership.[114] The most dramatic such development came in engineering, where in 1989 the EEF decided to discontinue national negotiations over substantive issues during a protracted dispute over reductions in working hours, thereby bringing to an end nearly a century of involvement in multi-employer bargaining.[115]

How can we account for the emergence and subsequent transformation of this distinctive model of employer organization in Britain? One explanation widely canvassed during the 1970s and 1980s concerns the role of national culture and individualistic attitudes in inhibiting the development of employer solidarity. British employers, on this view, have differed from their counterparts elsewhere primarily in a lesser willingness to subordinate their individual autonomy to the demands of collective action on a long-term basis.[116] Whatever the merits of this view as an account of British employers' social attitudes, however, the postulation of deep-rooted cultural continuities can hardly provide much guide to explaining the profound changes in organizational behaviour which have taken place over the past century. Equally importantly, there is considerable evidence that British employers seriously attempted at key moments to strengthen the authority of their organizations and enhance the influence of collective agreements over the labour policies of individual firms. After the First World War, as Zeitlin's chapter argues, the EEF sought to reach a comprehensive national agreement with the engineering unions which would have established a standard code of working practice across the industry as a whole, bringing under joint regulation such key areas of managerial prerogative as payment systems, grading and training. After the Second World War, too, British engineering employers made determined efforts to rebuild their collective solidarity and stem the tide of workplace bargaining. During the late 1940s and 1950s, for example, the EEF tried to unify its members by coordinating resistance to union claims for general wage advances, culminating in a major national lock-out in 1957. And again in the 1960s the Federation sought to revive the effectiveness of the industry's disputes procedure by lobbying for legal enforceability of collective agreements and statutory penalties for unofficial strikers.[117] In each of these cases, the strength of support for such proposals among employers is as striking as their ultimate failure; nor does internal dissension, however significant, appear to have played the decisive part in determining any of these outcomes.

A more promising line of explanation focuses on the role of industrial structure and company organization. Well into the twentieth century, as we saw above, many sectors of British industry continued to be marked by a fragmented, competitive structure, while few companies had created effective organizational capabilities for labour management within the enterprise. These characteristics exerted a double influence on the development of employer organization and collective bargaining. On the one hand, British employers in industries such as iron and steel or engineering lacked both the incentives and the power that led their American and German counterparts to sweep away trade unionism and impose the open shop, so that some form of collective bargaining accordingly became unavoidable.[118] On the other hand, multi-employer bargaining offered positive benefits to individual firms in such industries by helping them to regulate competition in product and/or labour markets, and by allowing them to devolve responsibility for labour management to external organizations. As we also saw, however, the structure of British industry was transformed during the postwar period by the growing concentration of ownership, the spread of the multi-divisional company and the professionalization of all areas of management. Large diversified firms in oligopolistic industries gradually became less willing to accept the constraints of national agreements on their freedom of action, and they saw little need for assistance from outside bodies in framing their internal labour strategies. The resulting growth of managerial hierarchies and corporate personnel polices in turn helped to precipitate the decline of multi-employer bargaining and collective organization in many sectors of British industry from the mid-1960s onwards.[119]

This type of explanation clearly has considerable force. Not only are changes in industrial structure and company organization closely associated with chronological shifts in the pattern of collective action among British employers, but similar factors also appear important in accounting for sectoral variations within each period. Thus during the heyday of multi-employer bargaining before the Second World War, collective organization was generally weakest in sectors such as chemicals and confectionery where large, hierarchical companies had already developed their own personnel policies and welfare programmes.[120] More recently, on the other hand, employers' organizations and national bargaining have survived best in those industries such as footwear, textiles, printing, construction and clothing whose fragmented, competitive structure most closely resembles the earlier dominant model.[121] But such arguments break down, as Sisson's chapter points out, when the comparison is extended to the international level. For in other European countries such as the Federal Republic of Germany, Sweden, France or Italy, large firms have continued to play an active part in multi-employer bargaining – including foreign multinationals, such as Ford, which have always refused to join employers' associations in Britain. Even at a sectoral level, moreover, the correlation between industrial structure and employer organizations is far from perfect. Thus as Gospel himself has shown, one of the tightest national agreements in interwar Britain was negotiated by the Flour Milling Employers' Federation which was dominated by a handful of large, paternalistic companies.[122] Over the past two decades, conversely, the scope and effectiveness of multi-employer organization and bargaining has also declined significantly in highly competitive small-firm industries such as construction.[123]

Within any given industrial structure, therefore, a spectrum of bargaining arrangements are possible, and changing patterns of collective organization cannot be explained without reference to the strategic choices of employers themselves. As the chapters in this volume demonstrate, British employers' own decisions, individual and collective, clearly played a crucial role in both the rise and the subsequent decline of national bargaining. But as the chapters also show, these choices depended at each point not only on employers' internal deliberations, but also on a process of strategic interaction with the state and trade unions.

Thus the organizational practices and bargaining strategies of British employers were shaped not only by the changing structure of their industries but also by the trajectory of public policy. From the 1890s onwards civil servants and politicians alike became committed to the extension of collective bargaining as a distinctly British method for reconciling economic efficiency and social peace. Liberal ministers such as Gladstone, Mundella and Lloyd George pressurized recalcitrant employers to recognize trade unions and accept compromise settlements on the railways, in the mines and on the docks. The officials of the Board of Trade Labour Department, many of them ex-trade unionists, constituted a similar force for conciliation and arbitration in industrial disputes; and this tradition was continued in a lower key by the Ministry of Labour after its formation in 1916.[124] In engineering, as Zeitlin shows, the EEF's fear of government intervention in case of a renewed lock-out was a key factor behind its pursuit of a negotiated accommodation with the unions between 1908 and 1922. The emergence of national wage bargaining in many industries was closely associated with the compulsory arbitration system introduced by the state during the First World War; and government policies also sought to diffuse collective bargaining into sectors where economic forces did not encourage its spontaneous emergence through measures such as fair-wage resolutions, trade boards and Whitley Councils.[125]

But if public policy stimulated collective organization among British employers and circumscribed their opportunities for collective action, it also inhibited the development of employers' associations into more author-itative bodies. Thus the abstentionist regime of labour law confirmed by the Trade Disputes Act of 1906 discouraged the effective centralization of collective bargaining by granting far-reaching immunities from civil pro-secution to unofficial as well as official strikers; while unlike in countries such as Sweden, Germany or the United States, collective agreements were allowed to remain voluntary arrangements without binding force on either party.[126] At the peak level, similarly, the relative weakness of organizations such as the NCEO, the FBI and the CBI owed much to the enduring hold of parliamentary sovereignty on the British state and its consequent ambivalence towards such experiments in corporatist concertation as the National Industrial Conference of 1919–21, the Mond–Turner talks of 1927–33 or the National Economic Development Council of the 1960s.[127]

During the postwar period, similarly, the state has played a crucial role in the decline of multi-employer bargaining and collective organization in Britain. Thus in the 1957 engineering lock-out, for example, the Conserva-tive government's concern for the impact of a prolonged dispute on the balance of payments led them to pull the rug out from under the EEF whose resistance to trade-union wage demands it had hitherto encouraged.[128] During the 1950s and 1960s, as Tolliday's chapter illustrates in the case of Ford, continuing pressure from both Conservative and Labour govern-ments to avoid serious outbreaks of industrial conflict pushed the motor employers to abandon their long-standing opposition to shop-steward organization and paved the way for the extension of workplace bargaining. The Donovan Commission gave official sanction to the spread of factory and company agreements, while productivity bargaining offered firms an increasingly attractive means of escaping from the constraints of incomes policies.[129] Since 1979, finally, government policy and labour-law reform have consciously promoted the growth of employer individualism by a variety of means such as removing legal immunities for sympathetic strikes, abolishing fair-wages resolutions and wages councils, privatizing nation-alized companies and dismantling national bargaining arrangements in public services.[130]

Trade unions as well as the state have exercized a formative influence on the shifting pattern of employer organization and collective bargaining in Britain. Thus during the second half of the nineteenth century, it was the ability of short-lived unions of operatives to disrupt production during upturns of trade that led employers in cyclical export industries like coal, textiles and iron and steel to pioneer early forms of collective wage determinations such as sliding scales, joint boards and third-party arbi-tration. It was also the ability of craft unions to impose unilateral regulation on individual firms that led employers in sectors like engineering, ship-building, construction and printing to create industry-wide federations and disputes procedures during the 1890s and 1900s.[131] In engineering, as Zeitlin argues, the federal structure of the Amalgamated Engineering Union (AEU) and the weakness of its executive played a decisive role in undermining negotiations with the EEF to create a more centralized and comprehensive bargaining system after the First World War. The limited authority of trade unions over their members, like that of employers' associations, owed much to the negative immunities conferred by British labour law; but whenever reform proposals were debated between the Taff Vale decision of 1901 and the Employment Act of 1980, it was the unions that emerged as the staunchest defenders of the voluntarist system.[132] During the 1950s and 1960s, moreover, unions such as the AEU and the Transport and General Workers Union contributed significantly to the growth of workplace bargaining by throwing their support behind shop-steward organization and giving retrospective sanction to unofficial strikes, as in the case of the 1969 dispute at Ford described by Tolliday. During the 1980s, too, the EEF's decision to withdraw from national bargaining had its roots in the inability of the AEU executive to deliver its members' support for a proposed agreement exchanging workplace flexibility for shorter hours.[133]

Sweden and Germany

Sweden and Germany are the cases most often contrasted to the British model of employer organization and collective bargaining. Through most of this century employers' organizations in these countries have been characterized by their remarkable cohesion and capacity for strategic action. Perhaps the most striking example is that of *Svenska Arbetgivareföreningen* (SAF), the Swedish Employers' Confederation, which established the national framework of industrial relations through its historic agreements of 1906 and 1938 with the *Landsorganisationen i Sverige* (LO), the Swedish Confederation of Labour. From the early 1950s through the mid-1980s, SAF bargained over wages on behalf of its affiliates at a multi-industrial level, and the Confederation still plays a key role in the coordination of sectoral negotiations. Decision-making within SAF is extremely centralized, and until 1982 no affiliated association could enter into a collective agreement without its formal approval. Member firms that fail to uphold their obligations to SAF or its affiliates are subject to substantial fines, and the organization seeks to control wage drift through financial penalties for violation of collective agreements. Crucial to the centralization of authority within SAF is the highly developed system of mutual strike insurance, which has underpinned its strategic use of sympathetic lock-outs to meet trade-union challenges by widening the scope of conflict, from the formative confrontations of the 1900s to the most recent national dispute of 1980.[134] As key affiliates such as *Verkstadsförening* (VF), the Engineering Employers' Federation, have become more independent of SAF during the 1980s, they too have begun to build up their own strike-insurance funds to finance sectoral lock-outs.[135] Within this institutional framework, it is hardly surprising that Swedish collective agreements typically cover a wider range of issues in greater detail than their British counterparts, from bonus systems, payment by results and wage-drift compensation to training, health and safety, technological change, job security, pensions and investment.[136]

In Germany, on the other hand, the focus of collective bargaining is sectoral and regional rather than national and inter-industrial, but employers have been strongly organized at each of these levels. Under the Wilhelmine Reich and the Weimar Republic, peak associations of business were directed more at relations with the state than with labour, despite a short-lived experiment at bipartite cooperation with trade-union leaders in the *Zentralarbeitsgemeinschaft* (ZAG), or Central Working Community of Employers and Employees, between 1918 and 1924.[137] Under the Federal Republic, however, the *Bundesvereinigung der Deutschen Arbeitgeberverbände* (BDA), the Confederation of German Employers' Organizations, maintains a mutual strike-insurance fund for its sectoral affiliates and helps to coordinate their bargaining strategies on non-wage questions such as working hours and paid holidays through its secret '*Tabu-Katalog*' of prohibited concessions.[138] Before 1914 and again from the mid-1920s, as the chapters by Homburg and Plumpe show, sectoral employers' associations in large-scale industries such as coal, iron and steel and to a lesser extent electrical manufacturing deployed their collective strength to resist rather than negotiate with trade unions. Strike-insurance funds, sympathetic lockouts, leaving certificates, blacklists, employer-controlled employment exchanges and standardization of payment systems were among the methods used with varying degrees of success to harmonize the labour strategies of individual firms and reinforce collective solidarity during this period.[139]

After 1945, as Plumpe documents, West German employers were forced to come to terms with trade unionism, collective bargaining and co-determination even in the heavy industries of the Ruhr. But national employers' organizations in sectors such as iron and steel and engineering have maintained a strong role in coordinating regional bargaining through sympathetic lock-outs, mutual assistance to struck firms in meeting urgent contracts, and fines for non-compliance with association rules. As in Sweden, German collective agreements on subjects such as the operation of payment systems are considerably more comprehensive, detailed and binding on individual firms than would normally be the case in Britain.[140] In recent years, however, some tendencies towards decreasing uniformity have been observable, with growing regional differentiation and collective agreements setting the framework for more customized arrangements negotiated by works councils.[141]

As in Britain, national culture has often been adduced to account for the associative behaviour of Swedish and German employers. Thus Swedish 'communitarianism' and cultural and religious homogeneity are sometimes held to underlie the high levels of collective solidarity displayed by employers and workers alike. In Germany the weakness of liberal values and the strength of pre-capitalist corporate traditions have figured even more prominently in historical explanations of employer strategy and organizations. Despite evident cultural similarities between the two countries, however, Swedish and German employers' attitudes to liberalism have been quite different, and as we observed in the previous section, those of the latter have shifted considerably over time.[142] At a micro level, moreover, Homburg shows that the cultural norms of metalworking employers did not in themselves prevent periodic breaches of collective solidarity such as poaching of skilled workers in Berlin's tight labour market during the 1920s.

As in Britain, too, industrial structure has played a key role in explanations of the effectiveness of employer organization in Sweden and Germany. High early levels of concentration and cartelization, it is often argued, underpinned the success of sectoral employers' associations in both countries, while the domination of the Swedish economy by a small number of oligopolistic export sectors is also held to account for its long history of centralized multi-industrial bargaining.[143] Concentration and cartelization undoubtedly do facilitate collective organization and strategy formation among employers by relaxing competitive pressures, reducing the number of actors involved in key decisions and increasing the resources available for their implementation. The German iron and steel cartels, for example, regularly deployed their economic leverage to promote association and influence the policies of their customers in the machine-building and finishing sectors during both the Wilhelmine and the Weimar periods.[144]

But the historical relationship between concentration and collective organization in these countries is far from straightforward. Thus the centralization of organization among Swedish employers largely preceded the development of industrial concentration, while German employers were able to rebuild cohesive associations after the Second World War despite the dismantlement of their cartels. Substantial domestic competition has always existed in key sectors of the Swedish economy such as engineering, while in Germany, too, it was in competitive sectors such as book printing that employers first began to perfect the techniques of sympathetic lock-outs and national collective bargaining during the late nineteenth century.[145] Even within concentrated sectors such as Ruhr iron and steel, Plumpe demonstrates that there were bitter disagreements among employers over co-determination and the Schuman Plan during the late 1940s and early 1950s, and important divisions over labour strategy could likewise be observed within the SAF at key turning-points between the 1900s and the 1980s.[146] Nor does this line of argument stand up better to international comparisons: in Britain, as we have seen, the growth of industrial concentration accompanied the decline rather than reinforcement of collective action among employers; while the centralization of employer organization in Denmark approaches that of Sweden on the basis of a much more fragmented industrial structure.[147]

Strategic choice is thus just as important in explaining the relative strength of collective solidarity among employers in Sweden and Germany as in accounting for its relative weakness in Britain. There is widespread agreement, for example, that SAF's policies played a decisive role in the successive phases of centralization in Swedish industrial relations during the 1900s, the 1930s and the 1950s, even at the cost of squeezing out marginal firms unable to meet the burden imposed by national wage settlements. During the 1980s VF, the Engineering Employers' Federation, has been the driving force behind the demand for decentralized bargaining; but many Swedish employers still see real benefits in centralization as a private-sector substitute for incomes policy, and fears of an impending wage explosion prompted all sectors other than engineering to return to central negotiations under SAF auspices in 1989.[148] In Germany, too, employers were arguably the dominant actors in shaping the pattern of industrial relations before 1933, stimulating the formation of industrial unions in the 1890s by their ability to defeat localized craft societies through sympathetic lock-outs, allying with national union leaders to contain radical factory councils during the revolution of 1918–19, and undermining first peak-level concertation and then sectoral collective bargaining during the 1920s. After the Second World War, of course, German employers' scope for manoeuvre was substantially curtailed, but even then, as Plumpe points out, they were still able to block the extension of parity co-determination to sectors other than coal and steel, obtain a restrictive legal framework for works councils and contain union militancy within industry-wide bargaining arrangements.

As in Britain, however, the strategic calculations of Swedish and German employers were also shaped at key moments by the behaviour of the state and the unions. During the 1890s and 1900s the Swedish state, like its British counterpart, promoted employer recognition of trade unions by its unwillingness to deploy repressive force in industrial disputes.[149] Once both sides of industry had become organized, a series of unstable coalition governments reinforced the 'December Compromise' of 1906 (in which SAF committed itself to collective bargaining in exchange for LO's recognition of managerial prerogatives) by intervening against hardline employers in the lock-out of 1908 while refusing to protect militant workers in the general strike of 1909.[150] In contrast to Britain, a Conservative-dominated government then made collective agreements legally binding in 1928, imposing a peace obligation on both parties during the life of the contract, with disputes over its interpretation to be settled by a special Labour Court. Fear of further state intervention also proved an important stimulus to subsequent voluntary compromises between SAF and LO. Thus the Saltsjöbaden 'Basic Agreement' of 1938 which committed the two peak associations to national negotiations before strikes or lock-outs could occur was framed against the threat of legislation to introduce compulsory arbitration by the Social Democratic government whose recovery programme was being disrupted by a rash of industrial disputes. And the centralization of wage bargaining during the 1950s likewise owed much to the desires of both SAF and LO to avoid the imposition of official incomes policies.[151] Since 1982, finally, the macro-economic preoccupations of Social Democratic administrations have made them the staunchest defenders of centralized collective bargaining, using tax concessions and political pressure to broker renewed national wage agreements in 1985–6 and abortively proposing a statutory incomes policy in February 1990.[152]

In Germany unlike Sweden, the Wilhelmine state underwrote employer resistance to trade unions by legal support for organized strike-breaking and statutory restrictions on strike activity.[153] The state and the courts also promoted the cartelization process which reinforced employer organization in the labour market by granting tariff protection, making cartel agreements legally enforceable, pushing raw-materials suppliers to accommodate the needs of export customers, and even in extreme cases imposing compulsory syndicalization of marketing.[154] During the First World War, however, government policy and the exigencies of the war economy encouraged collaboration between employers and trade-union leaders, setting the stage for the Stinnes–Legien Agreement of 1918 whereby the former accepted collective bargaining while the latter accepted the continued existence of private property.[155] Weimar labour law placed the state's authority behind this compromise by creating statutory works councils, giving binding force to collective agreements and providing for compulsory arbitration where no agreement could be reached; and it was heavy-industrial employers' growing resentment of these policies which helped to turn them against the Republic itself during the late 1920s and early 1930s.[156]

After 1945, as Plumpe shows, the Allied occupation authorities and the Adenauer Government brokered the crucial compromises over deconcentration and parity co-determination which enabled Ruhr employers to restore their organizational unity. The postwar regime of labour law in turn has strongly fostered sectoral bargaining between employers' associations and industrial unions through a combination of positive and negative sanctions. Thus the legal right to strike is confined to national trade unions, and works councils are subject to a *friedenpflicht* or peace obligation; strikes and lock-outs are prohibited during the life of an agreement with heavy fines for violations, and disputes over contract interpretation are subject to the binding decision of the Labour Court; and collective agreements may be extended by public officials to cover all workers and employers in any particular industry.[157] In contrast to Britain, too, German law provides statutory support for employer organization throughout the economy by a compulsory system of Chambers of Industry, Commerce and *Handwerk* (artisanry) which exercise a variety of public functions, most notably in the area of vocational training.[158] Since 1982, however, the Kohl government has sought with limited success to weaken the public framework of German industrial relations – in some cases against the opposition of the BDA itself – by measures such as refusing to extend industry-wide agreements to civil servants, making public assistance to troubled firms conditional on wage cuts, and denying social-security payments to workers laid off by strikes and lock-outs.[159]

In both countries, finally, the emergent patterns of employer organization and collective action also owed much to the strategies of trade unions themselves. Thus the formation of SAF in 1902 was a direct response to that of LO in 1898, and the former's policies of centralized strike insurance and sympathetic lock-outs were stimulated by the latter's use of mutual-assistance funds to finance general strikes over political as well as industrial issues.[160] The centralized negotiating procedures created by the Saltsjöbaden Agreement could not have worked had the LO not revised its rules to acquire control over strike decisions and the right to participate in the contract negotiations of member unions, nor could centralized bargaining have been sustained during the postwar period had Swedish unions not come to see it as an effective instrument for the implementation of a solidaristic wages policy.[161] During the 1980s, too, LO's macroeconomic distributional objectives have made the Confederation a formidable opponent of decentralized bargaining, and its refusal to accept industry-level settlements was a major factor behind the national wage agreement of 1986. At the same time, however, some unions within LO such as the Metal Workers, whose members' earnings have been compressed by the solidaristic wage policy, see definite advantages in sectoral bargaining, while bitter inter-union rivalries between representatives of blue- and white-collar workers, as well as between those of the public and private sectors, has been a crucial factor in destabilizing peak-level wage negotiations.[162] A final and unexpected impetus to more decentralized bargaining has emerged from the 'Development Agreements' which gave workers rights to participate in company decisions over capital investments, rationalization and work organization under the union-sponsored Co-determination Act of 1976.[163]

In Germany as in Britain, the leap-frogging tactics of craft societies provided the stimulus for the formation of defensive employers' associations in fragmented industries during the late nineteenth century. Unlike in Britain, however, the transformation of the craft societies into industrial unions closely linked to the Social Democratic Party spurred Wilhelmine employers to block worker organization in large-scale industry by building strong offensive associations.[164] The organizational structure of German trade unions ensured that collective bargaining once established under the Weimar Republic would assume an industry-wide form, while the centralization of industrial relations was decisively reinforced after 1945 by structural reforms that rationalized the prewar unions into twelve industrial organizations and created a unified peak-level confederation. The centralization of employers' organizations during the 1950s and 1960s was largely a response to the coordinated bargaining strategies adopted by unions like IG Metall which sought to win major contract breakthroughs by concentrating its resources in industrial disputes on particularly prosperous firms and regions.[165] Since the 1970s German unions have continued to pursue industry-wide objectives such as the 35-hour week through centralized negotiations with employers' organizations, most notably in the national metalworkers' strike of 1984. As in Sweden, however, advocates of greater decentralization have gained increasing ground within the unions' own ranks during the 1980s, in part as an unintended consequence of the enhanced co-determination powers over the manpower policies of individual firms conferred on works councils by the union-sponsored legislation of the early 1970s, though no similar divisions have opened up between workers in the public and private sectors.[166]

France and Italy

If the solidarity of Swedish and German employers contrasts sharply with that of their British counterparts, other international comparisons are less invidious. In France and Italy, as we have already noted, employer organization and collective action have been generally weaker and less cohesive than in Britain for most of this century. In France, for example, peak associations of employers have been orientated more towards the state and the political system than to relations with organized labour, with little bargaining autonomy or authority over their constituents outside periods of crisis. Thus the *Confédération Générale de la Production Française* (General Confederation of French Production, CGPF) was founded in 1919 in response to government initiatives and languished in relative inactivity until its reorganization in response to the strikes of the Popular Front era.[167] Its successor, the *Confédération National du Patronat Français* (National Confederation of French Employers, CNPF), was not permitted to sign binding agreements on behalf of its affiliates with the trade unions until the strike explosion of 1968; and after a series of inter-industrial agreements during the late 1960s and early 1970s over non-wage issues such as job security, unemployment insurance and monthly pay for blue-collar workers, the bargaining activity of the Confederation has once again subsided. Although CNPF officials have periodically sought to exercise a leadership role in industrial relations and social policy, their initiatives have generally been circumscribed by internal political constraints as well as by external competition from other business organizations.[168]

As in Britain and Germany, employer organization in France has historically been more developed at the sectoral and regional levels than at that of the peak confederation. Perhaps the best-known example is that of the *Union des Industries Métallurgiques et Minières* (Union of Metallurgical and Mining Industries, UIMM). From its formation at the turn of the century, the UIMM has run a relatively effective strike-insurance scheme, and the association has played an important if fluctuating role in coordinating the labour strategies of its members both through unilateral arrangements and agreements with trade unions. Like most French employers' associations, the UIMM has long preferred to bargain over wages at a regional rather than a national or sub-sectoral level, though during the past two decades it has been prepared to sign national agreements on some non-wage issues such as job classifications (1975) or work-time restructuring (1986). Like other sectoral associations, too, the UIMM strongly opposed any form of company bargaining until the 1980s, and most national agreements have been consciously designed as 'closed accords' (*accords parfaits*) which could not be renegotiated at lower levels.[169]

As at the confederal level, however, sectoral employers associations in France are also marked by a lack of cohesion and limited authority over their members. The UIMM, for example, is a loose federation of some 100 regional chambers, and its bargaining strategies are effectively constrained by the position of the weakest firms in each area. The minimum wages set by collective agreements are typically below those fixed by law, leaving a wide discretionary margin to each enterprise, and the UIMM's heterogeneous membership has strongly resisted proposals to bargain over actual earnings rather than nominal rates. Often, too, no agreement at all can be reached at the local level, and employers' associations are reduced to issuing non-binding guidelines for wage increases to their members, while derogations from associational policy on other issues such as working hours have become increasingly common during the 1980s.[170] Despite industrial and regional variations, therefore, French employers' organizations at whatever level have rarely been able to go beyond limited defensive strategies aimed at maximizing the freedom of individual firms, and their internal coherence seems if anything to have diminished further over the past decade.

Employer organization in Italy historically resembles the French model, although the two countries have evolved in significantly different directions over the past two decades. As Contini's chapter shows, *Confindustria*, the peak association of Italian employers, has concentrated its energies even more than the CNPF on relations with the political system, while also lacking much in the way of authority or sanctions over its constituent associations and firms. Like the CNPF, too, *Confindustria* has suffered from severe problems of internal cohesion and factionalism – exemplified by the independent policies pursued by large firms such as Fiat – as well as from external rivalries with separate organizations representing public enterprises, small business and the artisanal sector. Unlike the CNPF, however, *Confindustria* served as the main employers' representative in collective negotiations over wage as well as non-wage issues during the 1940s and 1950s, and it has continued to exercise an important bargaining role despite the widespread development of sectoral and plant-level agreements since the late 1960s. Thus *Confindustria* successfully sought to reinvigorate peak-level bargaining by signing the landmark agreement of 1975 which created a new wage-indexation system, the *scala mobile*; and throughout the 1980s it has remained a key player in centralized negotiations with the unions, and at times the government, over cost-of-living increases as well as non-wage issues such as youth-training contracts.[171]

As in the French model, too, Italian employer organization at the sub-confederal level combines elements of both territorial and sectoral representation. Until the 1970s, there were no sectoral organizations in major industries such as metalworking, and heterogeneous regional associations such as *Assolombarda* (the Association of Lombard Industrialists) looked to *Confindustria* to prevent potentially dangerous concessions by better-off sectors or firms. But with the rise of plant bargaining after the 'hot autumn' of 1969, large metalworking firms found it necessary to create a separate organization, *Federmeccanica*, to control leap-frogging wage advances, and triennial contract negotiations between sectoral unions and employers' associations covering a wide range of wage and non-wage issues have become the cornerstone of Italian industrial relations. At the same time, however, sectoral and territorial organization are closely intertwined, and the regional associations remain important in the coordination of plant bargaining, the provision of information to firms and the administration of local disputes resolution procedures. The cumulative result of these developments, in sharp contrast to the French model, has been the emergence of a flexible but robust system of 'articulated bargaining' in which Italian employers' organizations, while lacking the power and resources of their Swedish or German counterparts, nevertheless play a major part in substantive negotiations at each level from the confederal through the sectoral and regional to that of the individual plant.[172]

As in the case of Britain, national culture has figured prominently in explanations of the relative weakness of employer organization in France and Italy. In France, in particular, employers' reluctance to be drawn into binding organizational commitments and their defensive use of association as a shield against plant bargaining have often been attributed to cultural attitudes such as a conception of the firm as an 'extended family circle' and a deep-seated aversion to face-to-face conflict.[173] While such attitudes are undoubtedly widespread in French industry, however, they cannot account for observed variations in employer behaviour. Thus more solidaristic forms of employer organization and collective bargaining had become established in a number of industries before 1914, and 'local industrial systems' with similar characteristics survived in certain regions until external interventions by state and trade-union officials brought them closer to the national model during the 1950s.[174] At the confederal level, too, the CNPF enjoyed considerable success in negotiating authoritative inter-professional agreements for a number of years after 1968, and the gradual disintegration of its centralized-bargaining strategy during the mid-1970s was due less to resistance from its own affiliates than to the decreasing willingness of left-wing trade unions to sign such agreements and of governments to finance their consequences through expansionary macroeconomic policies.[175]

The cultural attitudes of Italian employers present many similarities to those of their French counterparts, but their associational behaviour has developed in different directions. Thus before 1914, Italian employers in cities like Turin had formed relatively cohesive associations inspired by the German model which sought to establish stable bargaining relationships with trade unions, and despite significant internal divisions these organizations proved moderately effective in coordinating resistance to the massive strikes and factory occupations that convulsed the country between 1919 and the fascist seizure of power in 1922.[176] Since 1969, similarly, the culture of Italian employers, however construed, has not prevented them from participating in a system of articulated bargaining that has at the same time expanded the scope of collective agreements and enhanced the importance of wider organization for the individual enterprise.

As in Britain, Sweden and Germany, industrial structure has also occupied a central place in explanations of the associative behaviour of French and Italian employers. France and Italy are among the most dualistic of the advanced economies, and the resulting split between large corporations and small family firms has often been held responsible for undermining the cohesion of employers' associations and pushing them towards minimalist bargaining strategies.[177] Separate organizations of small business are more developed in these countries than elsewhere, and tensions between firms of different sizes have figured prominently in the internal politics of employers' associations in both cases. In France, for example, the reorganization of the CGPF was triggered off by a revolt of small and medium employers against the Matignon agreement of 1936; the CNPF from its formation was obliged to concede an independent role to the *Confédération Générale des Petites et Moyennes Entreprises* (General Confederation of Small and Medium Enterprises, CGPME); and both organizations have faced recurrent challenges from more radical movements of small business throughout the postwar period.[178] In Italy, too, as Contini points out, small firms acted as a brake within *Confindustria* on the more positive bargaining strategies promoted by Fiat and other large enterprises at a number of points betwen the 1930s and the 1970s, while also spearheading the drive for reform of the *scala mobile* during the 1980s. In both countries, however, employers' organizations have generally found political mechanisms for reconciling the interests of large and small enterprises, and the divisions between the two groups have rarely proved decisive in shaping their policies. Thus after 1968–9 both the CNPF and *Confindustria* were able to reform their organization and bargaining strategies despite opposition from small business, while large firms in each country have been at least as active as small ones in seeking to push employers' associations in neo-liberal and anti-union directions during the 1980s. In Italy, in fact, trade-union density is highest in industrially decentralized regions such as Emilia-Romagna, where even the smallest firms are organized into artisan associations and largely respect the terms of collective agreements.[179]

As in other countries, therefore, structural factors have left a significant margin for strategic choice in the development of collective organization and action among French and Italian employers. In France, for example, the relative atrophy of employers' organizations between the wars was largely a product of their rejection of union overtures for collective bargaining after the defeat of the 1920 general strike; and the CNPF likewise passed over opportunities to establish a more cooperative bargaining relationship with the ex-Catholic *Confédération Français Democratique du Travail* (French Democratic Confederation of Labour, CFDT), first in the early 1960s and then in the late 1970s.[180] At the same time, however, French employers were largely successful in defeating proposals to extend collective bargaining beyond the sectoral level from the 1950s through the 1970s, while their adoption of new strategies of employee involvement and human-resource management has paved the way for the diffusion of company agreements during the 1980s.[181] In Italy, too, as Contini demonstrates, many of *Confindustria*'s difficulties during the 1960s stemmed from the organization's misguided forays into electoral politics, as well as from its earlier rejection of overtures for more decentralized bargaining from the non-Communist trade unions. The revival of the confederation's influence over the past two decades, conversely, owes much to its strategic reorientation towards collaboration with the union confederations and government during the 1970s, and to the ascendancy within its ranks of forces favouring negotiated rather than unilateral approaches to employment flexibility during the 1980s.

But as in other countries, too, the strategic choices of French and Italian employers were formulated in close relationship with those of their inter-locutors in the state and the unions. In contrast to Sweden or Germany, as Sisson observes, public policy in postwar France and Italy has inhibited the development of employer solidarity by vesting workers with an unrestricted right to strike while ruling lock-outs illegal. In France, more broadly, the state has played a decisive role in shaping the trajectory of industrial relations and employer organization from the turn of the century to the present. Widespread government intervention in settling industrial disputes before 1914 – often on the side of the strikers – discouraged the formation of more cohesive organizations among workers and employers alike, and government repression was also crucial in the defeat of the labour move-ment after the First World War.[182] Both the Matignon Agreement of 1936 and the Grenelle Accords of 1968, the two formative settlements between French employers and unions, were likewise a direct result of government mediation. Where no bilateral agreement can be reached between the parties, the state has regularly stepped in to impose a legislative solution, and statutory regulation covers a wide range of issues in France that are largely governed by collective bargaining elsewhere, from minimum wages and maximum hours through working conditions and employment security to forms of worker representation. Legislation has likewise exercised a strong influence over bargaining structure, from the acts of 1936 and 1950 that institutionalized collective agreements at the sectoral level to the

Auroux Laws of 1982 which gave workers rights of direct expression within the enterprise and obliged employers to bargain with the unions each year at company level.[183] From Millerand in the 1900s, Thomas during the First World War and Blum in the 1930s to Delors in the 1960s and Mitterand in the 1980s, politicians and government officials have periodically sought to encourage collective bargaining by organized workers and employers as a means of overcoming the polarization and conflictuality of French industrial relations. But unlike in other countries such as Sweden, on each occasion the French state's pervasive interventionism and reluctance to share its sovereignty with corporate groups ultimately led employers and unions alike to look towards political rather than negotiated solutions to industrial conflicts.[184]

In Italy, too, the state has played a less visible but no less important role than that of its French counterpart in the evolution of employer organization and collective bargaining. A major stimulus to employer organization after the turn of the century came from Giolitti's encouragement of trade-union activity as part of a broader political opening to the left, while his repeated interventions in industrial disputes both before and after the First World War undercut employer unilateralism and pushed many industrialists to abandon their support for the liberal state.[185] The postwar system of centralized collective bargaining, as Contini observes, was a direct inheritance from the fascist regime; while the predominant position of employers during the 1950s owed much to the close relationship between *Confindustria* and the Christian Democratic Party. From the late 1950s onwards, however, the left-wing Christian Democrats began to distance themselves from *Confindustria*, while the public enterprises they controlled withdrew from the organization and broke the employers' front by pursuing an independent strategy of sectoral and plant negotiations with the unions. Unlike in France, where the resolute response of the stable Gaullist regime soon absorbed the impact of May 1968, in Italy the incoherent policies of a succession of weak centre-left governments both prolonged the industrial conflicts of the 'hot autumn' and gave legal ratification to the strikers' conquests through the *Statuto dei diritti dei lavoratori* (Charter of Workers' Rights) of 1970.[186]

While the Italian state proved an unreliable partner for corporatist projects of 'political exchange' with unions and employers during the late 1970s and early 80s, its mediation has nevertheless played a crucial part in the successful resolution of disputed issues through bilateral collective bargaining since the mid-1980s. Thus the government facilitated the 1986 accord between *Confindustria* and the unions on reform of the *scala mobile* through a combination of tax concessions and public-employment initiatives, while also pressing the employers back to the bargaining table during the contract-renewal disputes of 1990. As in the 1960s, moreover, public enterprises have also helped to push private employers away from unilateral strategies by signing separate protocols of collaboration with the

314   *Steven Tolliday and Jonathan Zeitlin*

unions.[187] At the local level, too, public authorities have played a vital part in brokering consensual solutions to the employment problems created by industrial restructuring, while also helping to reinforce the associational solidarity of small firms through the provision of collective services, particularly in 'red' regions such as Emilia-Romagna.[188] In contrast to its French counterpart, therefore, the Italian state appears to have compensated for its lesser autonomy from civil society by using public resources to facilitate the resolution of politically unmanageable conflicts through bilateral agreements between private interest groups.[189]

In neither country, finally, can the organizational choices of employers be fully understood without reference to those of trade unions. In France particularly, the predominant characteristics of national unions – their politicization, ideological divisions and weak representativeness – have repeatedly discouraged employers from regarding them as potentially reliable bargaining partners. Even before the Communist split of 1921, the *Confédération Générale du Travail* (General Confederation of Labour, CGT) was divided into competing 'reformist' and 'revolutionary' wings, and conflicts between the two groups were instrumental in undermining emergent collective bargaining arrangements in the Parisian metalworking industry after the First World War.[190] The reunification of the CGT during the run-up to the Popular Front was crucial for the breakthrough of collective bargaining in June 1936, but the Confederation's inability to control subsequent strikes and its insistence on the rigid application of the 40-hour week to continuous-process industries such as metallurgy soon proved instrumental in undermining employers' initial willingness to negotiate.[191]

After the Liberation, political disputes over wage restraint and the advent of the Cold War soon fractured the reconstruction coalition, and Communist, Catholic and Socialist trade unionists divided once again into hostile and competing camps. Through most of the postwar period, Communist-controlled CGT pursued an avowedly 'maximalist' strategy, subordinating industrial grievances to political objectives and refusing to sign collective agreements or treating them as trampolines for subsequent demands rather than as binding agreements, while its ideological rejection of plant-level bargaining as a form of enterprise corporatism reinforced employer preference for sectoral negotiations. Fear of being outflanked by the CGT in turn acted as a powerful constraint on the adoption of more contractual bargaining strategies by other unions, notably the CFDT, even at moments when employers themselves were more favourably disposed to collaboration.[192] After May 1968, for example, both the major confederations rejected proposals from government and employers for *contrats de progrès* which would have exchanged wage increases tied to productivity for plant-level guarantees of industrial peace; and union reservations likewise proved crucial to the collapse of centralized negotiations with the CNPF over working conditions in 1975 and over employment flexibility in 1984.[193]

While the developments of the 1980s mark a partial break with the historic traditions of French trade unions, the outcome has only served to exacerbate their underlying organizational weakness. Despite the CFDT's ardent support for the Auroux Laws, for example, none of the unions has succeeded in establishing an effective presence at the level of the enterprise, and the ensuing wave of worker discussion groups and company agreements has largely been shaped by employer initiatives. While both the CGT and the CFDT have de-emphasized political action as a result of their disappointing experiences with the left in power under Mitterand, they have been slow to find alternative strategies, and the resulting disorientation has favoured the smaller 'reformist' confederations which had maintained their distance from the government. French trade unions are now more fragmented and less representative than at any time in the recent past, further diminishing the incentives for employers to subordinate their individual strategies to the demands of collective organization.[194]

Much of the contrast between the recent evolution of employer organization in France and Italy has its roots in the divergence of union strategies in the two countries. From the 1900s through the 1950s the structural and ideological characteristics of Italian trade unions closely resembled those of their French counterparts, with similar consequences for the development of collective bargaining with employers' organizations. Thus between 1906 and 1922, the inability of reformist trade unions such as the *Federazione Italiana degli Operai Metallurgici* (Federation of Italian Metalworkers, FIOM) to control strikes and recurrent challenges to their authority from anarcho-syndicalist and Communist groups led employers to lose faith in the possibility of a negotiated settlement with organized labour.[195] After the fall of fascism, similarly, the predominantly political orientation of the *Confederazione Generale Italiana del Lavoro* (General Confederation of Italian Labour, CGIL) and the resulting split between Communist, Catholic and Social-Democratic trade unionists spurred employers to adopt unilateral strategies. The CGIL's firm commitment to centralized bargaining also reinforced that of *Confindustria*, undercutting the position of its representatives on the *commissioni interne* (internal commissions) which had sprung up in the plants at the end of the war.[196]

From the 1960s onwards, however, the strategic orientation of Italian unions began to change significantly. Like the CFDT, the ex-Catholic *Confederazione Italiana dei Sindacati Lavoratori* (Italian Confederation of Workers' Unions, CISL) had become convinced of the desirability of plant bargaining by its contacts with American trade unionists during the 1950s; but unlike the CGT, which was more tightly controlled by its Communist Party, the CGIL had also slowly begun to move in the same direction as a result of its reverses in elections for the *commissioni interne*. Trade-union support paved the way for the breakthrough of workplace organization during the 'hot autumn' of 1969, while the growing unity of three main confederations ensured a continuing link between the emergent forms of plant bargaining and wider negotiations with employers' organizations and government at other levels.[197] During the late 1970s, as Contini notes, the unrelenting conflictuality of factory councils in large companies such as Fiat provoked a unilateralist reaction from employers, while the limited authority of union confederations over their affiliates and the resurgence of political divisions between them also helped to scupper tripartite negotiations with *Confindustria* and the government over incomes policies during the mid-1980s.[198] Unlike their French or British counterparts, on the other hand, Italian unions during the 1980s proved willing to negotiate flexibility agreements with employers on issues such as work organization, wage structure, working hours and employment conditions in return for a significant voice in their implementation. This strategy of 'bargained flexibility' in turn has played an important part in reducing the influence of anti-union employers within *Confindustria* and maintaining the articulation between different levels of negotiation in Italian industrial relations.[199]

The United States and Japan

Employers' associations vary widely in strength and cohesion across countries such as Britain, Sweden, Germany, France and Italy, and no single dominant pattern can be identified. But as Sisson's chapter points out, there are also major industrial economies – most notably the United States and Japan – in which such organizations appear to play little formal role in labour management or collective bargaining. In the United States in particular, there is no comprehensive peak organization of business, while the coverage of sectoral and territorial associations is also fragmentary and incomplete. Even more importantly, since the breakthrough of mass-production unionism during the 1930s and 40s, single-employer bargaining, often centralized at the company level, has become the dominant form of labour negotiations in large-scale industries such as automobiles, rubber, agricultural equipment, electrical manufacturing, telecommunications and to a lesser extent steel. Some large corporations like IBM, Polaroid, Grumman Aircraft or Burlington Mills were never unionized at all, while many others such as DuPont, Proctor & Gamble, Goodyear, Mobil Oil and General Electric (GE) have won increased freedom to pursue firm-specific labour policies through the opening of new non-union plants since the 1960s.[200]

At the same time, however, it would be wrong to suppose that American industrial relations were completely atomized. In 1975, for example, multi-employer arrangements accounted for 45.8 per cent of all workers covered by collective agreements, and regional or industry-wide bargaining between unions and employers' associations predominated in sectors such as garments, construction, printing, coalmining, trucking, longshoring, entertainment, hotels, restaurants and other services.[201] Even in large-scale manufacturing, moreover, there is extensive coordination of contract negotiations both within and across industries through mechanisms such as pattern and coalition bargaining. From the 1940s onwards, industrial unions such as the United Auto Workers, the United Steel Workers and the United Rubber Workers have sought with considerable success to standardize wages, working conditions and fringe benefits for their members by targeting a particular company in each bargaining round and imposing the resulting settlement pattern on other firms in the same and related industries. Until the late 1970s large companies in these industries generally acquiesced in pattern bargaining as a means of taking labour costs out of competition, while also in some cases developing more formal coalitions to influence the emergent settlement. In steel, for example, the major companies formed a Coordinating Committee under the leadership of US Steel and Bethlehem which bargained collectively on their behalf with the Steel Workers between 1956 and 1985; after less successful experiments with joint negotiating committees, the airlines similarly provided themselves with collective strike insurance under a Mutual Aid Plan from 1958 to its statutory dissolution in 1978.[202] During the 1980s, however, there has been a significant erosion of pattern bargaining in economically troubled industries like automobiles, steel, meatpacking and airlines, while the spread of non-unionism has likewise diminished the coverage of multi-employer agreements in sectors like construction, coal and trucking. But despite the evident diversification of settlement patterns, both formal and informal structures of coordination still remain important points of reference for employers across much of American industry, including the non-union sector.[203]

Although employer association membership is much more widespread in Japan than the United States, the predominance of company-level bargaining is also greater. Outside the public sector, as we saw above, the overwhelming majority of collective agreements are negotiated between company management and enterprise unions rather than industrial, craft or professional organizations. Only shipping and textiles are currently covered by formal multi-employer agreements, though industry-wide bargaining arrangements have previously existed in other sectors such as coalmining, private railways, brewing, glass, docks and phosphates. Even more than in the United States, however, the apparent de-centralization of Japanese industrial relations conceals widespread coordination of bargaining by employers at the national, sectoral and regional levels. Thus *Nikkeiren*, the Japan Federation of Employers' Associations, which covers 90 per cent of all unionized workers, does not engage directly in collective bargaining nor is it authorized to sign collective agreements on behalf of its affiliates. But the organization nevertheless has played a central role in shaping employers' collective response to the unions' spring bargaining offensive (or '*shuntō*'), particularly since the wage explosion of 1974, seeking to establish a uniform national norm through a combination of information gathering, participation in joint consultation forums, publication of guidelines, government lobbying and informal pressure on key groups of firms. At the sectoral and regional levels, too, there are a variety of arrangements such as 'diagonal', 'group' and 'associational' bargaining which fall little short of industry-wide agreements, while large companies in industries such as steel and metal-working have long issued simultaneous 'one-shot' wage offers which are normally accepted by the unions and go on to set the pattern for other major sectors. Through such forms of synchronized and coordinated bargaining, national wage settlements in Japan have become increasingly standardized and responsive to economic fluctuations since the mid-1970s without recourse to formal incomes policies.[204]

Even more than in other countries, perhaps, explanations of employer collective action in the United States and Japan have frequently revolved around national culture. American employers' fierce proprietorial independence, it is widely believed, made them unwilling to share control over their affairs with external business organizations as with unions or the state. Collective action in this view could never become more than a means of advancing firms' short-term interests, and when associations did form they were more likely to pursue belligerent than bargaining objectives.[205] Japanese employers' paternalistic outlook, it is often claimed, made them no less reluctant to recognize outside trade unions than their American counterparts, while deep-seated cultural preferences for cooperation over competition are likewise held to account for firms' adherence to collective wage norms despite the absence of formal multi-employer agreements.[206] But whatever the broader validity of these characterizations of American or Japanese business values, such explanations are difficult to square with finer-grained evidence about employer behaviour in the two countries at specific points in time. Thus as Harris's chapter documents, from the 1900s through the 1930s open-shop metal employers in cities such as Philadelphia maintained mutual strike-insurance schemes, non-union labour bureaux and collective training programmes whose effectiveness far surpassed those of their British contemporaries as described by Zeitlin. In Japan, conversely, the failure of *Nikkeiren* to enforce its wage guide-lines between 1969 and 1974 offers clear testimony to the insufficiency of cultural cohesion alone to guarantee employer solidarity.[207]

As in other countries, a second type of explanation for the distinctiveness of employer collective action in the US and Japan focuses on industrial structure. In both countries, the argument runs, the predominance of company bargaining reflects the rapid development of large, professionally managed, multi-plant firms in core sectors of the economy. In contrast to Britain, for example, the financial and managerial resources of large American and Japanese enterprises enabled them to sweep away craft unionism and break free of multi-employer agreements, while also ensuring that collective bargaining (once established) would be based on the plant or company rather than the occupation or industry. In these concentrated sectors, oligopolistic price-leadership structures have underpinned the emergence of industry wage patterns, while the broader standardization of wage settlements in Japan has also been facilitated by the prevalence of multi-industry groups, cartels and extensive subcontracting relationships between large and small firms. On the other hand, as in Britain, multi-employer bargaining has persisted in fragmented, competitive sectors where small and medium-sized firms have an incentive to standardize labour costs and join forces against more powerful unions. Just as pattern and multi-employer bargaining had their roots in a pre-existing industrial structure, so too have these practices been undercut by the growing volatility of markets in the United States during the 1980s.[208]

As in previous cases, there is evident force to these arguments. Yet the examples of Sweden and Germany demonstrate that industrial concentration may reinforce rather than subvert centralized multi-employer bargaining, while similar patterns of dualism may be accommodated within looser industry-wide agreements as in France and Italy. Even within the United States and Japan, moreover, the correspondence between industrial organization and bargaining structure is far from perfect. Thus in the US, as Harris's chapter shows, industry-wide bargaining and employer organization have largely disappeared even from fragmented, competitive sectors such as small-scale metalworking, while in Japan there are fewer formal multi-employer agreements than the country's decentralized industrial structure might lead one to expect. And if the turbulent competitive conditions of the 1970s and 1980s have weakened the coordination of bargaining in the United States, the reverse appears true in Japan where employers have stepped up their efforts to standardize wage settlements both within and across industries.

In these countries too, therefore, bargaining structure and collective action have been shaped not only by industrial organization, but also by the strategic choices of employers themselves. In the United States, as Harris's chapter illustrates, the open-shop drive of the 1900s was not confined to giant mass-production corporations like US Steel, Ford or International Harvester, but also encompassed the host of small and medium-sized machine shops and foundries that formed the mainstay of multi-employer bargaining in countries like Britain. Within the largest firms, as we saw above, corporate personnel policies consciously promoted worker identification with the enterprise during the non-union era: yet the centralization of labour management at the company level also created strong incentives for a parallel centralization of bargaining once unionization had been achieved. In some cases, notably General Motors, top management saw company-level bargaining as a vital means of containing workplace militancy during the postwar period, though other firms such as GE or American Telegraph & Telephone (AT&T) preferred instead to play local unions off against one another in plant-by-plant negotiations.[209] During the 1980s, managerial strategies of concession bargaining, work-rule reform and union avoidance have been the driving forces behind the erosion of industry patterns and multi-employer agreements.[210]

In Japan, too, managerial opposition was the decisive factor behind the curtailment of industry-wide bargaining before the Second World War. In 1919 and again in 1929, for example, associations of small and medium employers from Osaka and Tokyo publicly endorsed legislation which would have legalized craft and industrial unions, only to withdraw their support under pressure from the large industrialists of the Japan Industrial Club who had been more successful in maintaining a union-free environment.[211] Resistance to progressive labour legislation was also the trigger for the formation in 1931 of *Zensanren* (National Federation of Industrial Organizations), the first peak organization of Japanese business; while the development of local and regional associations was a product of industrialists' struggle to refashion Tokugawa institutions of corporate self-regulation and collective services after the western-inspired liberalization of the Meiji restoration.[212] From the 1920s onwards, as we noted above, large Japanese firms like their American counterparts consciously set out to bind workers to the enterprise through seniority-based wage systems, welfare benefits and company unions; and management also played a crucial role in the consolidation of enterprise bargaining during the late 1940s and early 1950s by sponsoring splits within radical unions and refusing to deal with 'outside' organizations.[213] Since the late 1950s, finally, large firms in industries such as steel and automobiles have consciously sought to take labour costs out of competition, and the resulting trend towards wage standardization has been crucial to *Nikkeiren*'s more recent success in coordinating *shuntō* settlements on an economy-wide basis.[214]

In few countries has business enjoyed a freer hand in labour management than in the United States and Japan. Yet as in other cases, the organization and strategies of American and Japanese employers have nevertheless been shaped by those of the state and the unions. In the United States, as we observed above, the success of the open-shop drive before 1914 depended heavily on the favourable attitude of the judiciary, while pressure from the federal government played a key part in the acceptance of collective bargaining by the mass-production corporations during the 1930s and 40s. From the 1900s through the 1960s industry-wide bargaining arrangements have often fallen foul of the anti-trust acts, as the courts have repeatedly prohibited attempts to control product-market competition through the enforcement of collective agreements, whether by trade unions or employers' associations.[215] New Deal labour policies reinforced this trend by favouring plant or company rather than craft or industrial bargaining units and prohibiting unions from pushing demands for multi-employer negotiations to the point of a strike; the Taft–Hartley Act of 1947 further undermined the effectiveness of industry-wide agreements by banning practices such as the secondary boycott and the pre-entry closed shop. During the 1940s, the National War Labor Board consciously promoted pattern bargaining in industries like steel and meatpacking as part of its wage-restraint policies, while the regulatory regimes introduced between the wars exerted a similar influence on the transportation and communications sectors. During the 1980s, conversely, the major impetus towards decentralization of bargaining in industries such as airlines, trucking and telecommunications has come from public deregulation policies.[216]

The Japanese state also supported employer resistance to union organization before the mid-1920s, but during the late 1920s and early 1930s, in contrast to the United States, factional divisions between ministries and political parties also blocked the passage of progressive labour laws. Following the strike wave of 1919, the Home Ministry pressed industrialists to alleviate worker discontent by creating their own works councils and company unions; while the military regime which came to power in 1936 abolished independent unions and employers' associations, enrolling workers alongside management in compulsory corporate organizations within each enterprise known as *sanpō*.[217] After the Second World War, the Supreme Commander for the Allied Powers (SCAP) and Japanese social bureaucrats pushed through far-reaching legislation guaranteeing workers' freedom to organize, strike and bargain collectively as part of a broader programme of democratization. But the new unions proved unexpectedly radical, and with the onset of the Cold War, SCAP reversed course in 1947, abandoning its previous opposition to the formation of *Nikkeiren*, amending labour law to give government greater powers to intervene in industrial relations, and throwing its weight behind the large firms' campaign to replace industry-wide with enterprise bargaining.[218] During the postwar period, as in the 1930s, state agencies such as the Ministry of International Trade and Industry (MITI) have fostered the development of sectoral and regional business associations as privileged interlocutors for their industrial policies, endowing them with public responsibilities and powers, though the results have not always turned out as the bureaucracy intended.[219] Since the mid-1970s, finally, the Japanese government has played a leading role in bolstering employers' response to *shuntō* by involving union leaders in tripartite concertation processes and persuading them to moderate wage demands in exchange for tax cuts, reductions in working hours and more active employment policies.[220]

Despite their comparative weakness, trade unions in both countries have nevertheless exerted a formative influence on the evolution of bargaining structure and employer organization. In the United States, as in Britain, local autonomy and craft rivalries inhibited the development of centralized bargaining between unions and employers' associations in industries such as metalworking: as Harris observes, for example, unions' inability to prevent local strikes was a central motive for the repudiation of trade agreements by organizations such as the National Metal Trades' Association and the National Founders' Association during the early 1900s. In other sectors such as coalmining, garments and trucking, by contrast, centralized bargaining arrangements were imposed on fragmented employers by strong, authoritative union leaders like John L. Lewis, Sidney Hillman and Jimmy Hoffa as a means of stabilizing their industries.[221] Plant-specific demands such as seniority rules loomed large in the organization of mass-production firms during the 1930s; while union objectives such as wage equalization and fringe benefits were likewise crucial to the centralization of bargaining in companies such as Ford, International Harvester and AT&T.[222] As we have seen, too, pattern bargaining was first and foremost a union strategy, and despite its decline during the 1980s, union efforts to maintain a 'level playing-field' for wage costs between companies have proved an important force for competitive stability in troubled industries such as steel, airlines and telecommunications.[223]

In Japan, as in France and to a lesser extent Italy, ideological divisions between rival union confederations have reduced the political clout of organized labour and discouraged management from regarding them as potential bargaining partners. During the inter-war period, for example, the Communist *Hyōgikai* (Japan Council of Labour Unions) split off from the moderate *Sōdōmei* (Japan General Federation of Labour) to pursue a militant class-struggle line which soon attracted government repression; the radical *Sambetsu* (Japanese Congress of Industrial Organizations) was forcibly dissolved during the government's 'Red Purge' of 1950; and the right-wing *Dōmei* (Japan Confederation of Labour) broke away from the left-wing *Sōhyō* (General Council of Japanese Trade Unions) in 1964.[224] Even during the heady postwar period, however, Socialist and Communist unions remained strongly committed to organizing workers on an enterprise basis; and Japanese unionists of all stripes focused their demands on company-specific goals such as job security, seniority wages and the elimination of status distinctions between blue- and white-collar employees.[225] As in the United States, moreover, it was the union confederations that initiated the *shuntō* system of national pattern bargaining, while coalitions such as *Tekkōrōren* (the Japanese Federation of Iron and Steel Workers' Unions) and the International Metalworkers' Federation–Japan Council (IMF–JC) played a growing role in the sectoral coordination of enterprise negotiations. Nor would *shuntō* have proved an effective means of containing inflation during the 1970s and 1980s without the willingness of 'realistic' unions such as *Dōmei* and the IMF–JC to moderate their wage demands in return for a measure of influence on government economic policies.[226]

CONCLUSIONS

The chapters in this volume offer powerful testimony to the historical variation of employer labour policies, both individual and collective, across such major industrial economies as Britain, France, Italy, Germany, Sweden, the United States and Japan. But are such national differences a thing of the past to be swept away by the growing integration of the world economy and the current wave of innovation in technology and manufacturing organization? Here, too, this volume documents the persistent diversity of employers' responses to the challenges posed by their changing environment.

Since the mid-1970s, as we observed in the Introduction, the changing conditions of international competition – epitomized by the dramatic ascendency of Japan – have pushed manufacturing firms in the advanced economies to shift their strategies away from mass production towards greater flexibility. But as the British case demonstrates, there is little reason to expect different national economies to converge around a single model of productive organization. Even where a significant proportion of domestic firms persistently fail to meet competitive pressures, the result may simply be a slow and uneven process of decline coupled with a growing presence of foreign direct investment. Similarly, as Jones shows in the case of Flexible Manufacturing Systems, the same equipment may be used in very different ways in countries such as Britain, the United States and Japan depending on institutional factors such as government policy, labour law and trade-union structure, as well as on firms' own organization and strategies. As in the case of mass production, finally, there may be a variety of routes to flexibility, and a multiplicity of hybrid forms intermediate between the two pure models of mass production and flexible specialization. Thus internal labour markets, for example, may play a more important part in achieving product diversity and productive flexibility within large, diversified companies than within the small-firm industrial districts of Germany, Italy or Japan. And firms of either size may strike different balances between flexibility and rigidity in different spheres of operations, from product design and production technology to work organization and relations with suppliers. Today as in the past, therefore, neither markets nor technology dictate a uniquely efficient form of labour management, and historical differences in national institutions continue to exercise a powerful influence over firms' strategic choices.

Turning from the individual to the collective sphere, a similar picture can be traced. Pervasive volatility in the international economy and company-level experiments in work reorganization have everywhere strained established patterns of collective action and employer organization. Yet these pressures have not resulted in a universal trend towards the atomization of industrial relations or the disintegration of employers' associations. While centralized bargaining structures have declined significantly in countries such as Sweden, France, Britain and the United States, employers' organizations have maintained or even enhanced their importance in other cases such as Germany, Italy and Japan. Present conditions clearly favour looser forms of articulation between different levels of bargaining, but even where decentralization has proceeded furthest many employers continue to feel the need for greater coordination of their individual labour strategies.

Today as in the past, employer organization and collective action may assume a variety of forms, and as this book has shown, the outcome will depend not simply on markets and technology but also on the interaction between the strategic choices of employers, trade unions and the state.

NOTES

1 For a critical discussion of culture as a force determining actor's choices 'behind their backs', see D. Gambetta, *Were They Pushed or Did They Jump? Educational Choices in Italy* (Cambridge, 1987), ch. 1; and J. Elster, *Ulysses and the Sirens* (2nd edn, Cambridge, 1984), pp. 137–9.

2 M. J. Wiener, *English Culture and the Decline of the Industrial Spirit, 1850–1980* (Cambridge, 1980); J. C. Abegglen, *The Japanese Factory* (Glencoe, Ill., 1958); *idem, Management and the Worker: The Japanese Solution* (Tokyo, 1973); M. Morishima, *Why has Japan 'Succeeded'? Western Technology and the Japanese Ethos* (Cambridge, 1982).

3 C. Kerr, J. T. Dunlop, F. H. Harbison and C. Meyer, *Industrialism and Industrial Man* (2nd edn, Cambridge, Mass., 1973; 1st edn, 1960); cf. also C. Kerr, *The Future of Industrial Societies* (Cambridge, Mass., 1983).

4 J. Child, 'Culture, Contingency and Capitalism in the Cross-National Study of Organizations', *Research in Organizational Behaviour* 3 (1981).

5 See, for example, the discussions of the literature in A. Sorge and M. Warner, *Comparative Factory Organisation: An Anglo-German Comparison of Management and Manpower in Manufacturing* (Aldershot, 1986); and C. Lane, *Management and Labour in Europe: The Industrial Enterprise in Germany, Britain and France* (Aldershot, 1989).

6 R. Dore, *British Factory–Japanese Factory: The Origins of National Diversity in Industrial Relations* (London, 1973); *Flexible Rigidities: Industrial Policy and Structural Adjustment in the Japanese Economy, 1970–80* (London, 1986); *Taking Japan Seriously: A Confucian Perspective on Leading Economic Issues* (London, 1987). A related exploration of the connections between variations in national culture, industrial institutions and historical change can be found in the work of Duncan Gallie: see his *In Search of the New Working Class: Automation and Social Integration within the Capitalist Enterprise* (Cambridge, 1978); and *Social Inequality and Worker Radicalism in France and Britain* (Cambridge, 1983). For a useful discussion of these writers, see Lane, *Management and Labour*, pp. 31–3.

7 M. Maurice, F. Sellier and J.-J. Silvestre, *The Social Foundations of Industrial Power: A Comparison of France and Germany* (trans. A. Goldhammer, Cambridge, Mass., 1986).

8 M. Maurice, A. Sorge and M. Warner, 'Societal Differences in Organizing Manufacturing Units: A Comparison of France, West Germany, and Great Britain', *Organization Studies* 1 (1980); Sorge and Warner, *Comparative Factory Organisation*, pt II.

9 F. Eyraud, M. Maurice and F. Rychener, 'Variabilité des formes de la division du travail et technologies nouvelles: le cas de l'utilisation des machines outils à commande numérique en France, en Grande Bretagne et en RFA', in J. H. Jacot (ed.), *Travailleur collectif et relations Science-Technologie-Production* (Paris, 1984); M. Maurice, F. Eyraud, A. d'Iribarne and F. Rychener, 'Des entreprises face aux technologies flexibles: une analyse de la dynamique du changement', *Sociologie du travail* (1988); *idem, Des entreprises en mutation dans la crise: apprentissages des technologies flexibles et emergence de*

nouveaux acteurs (research report, LEST, Aix-en-Provence, 1988); A. Sorge, G. Hartmann, M. Warner and I. Nicholas, *Microelectronics and Manpower in Manufacturing: Applications of Computer Numerical Control in Great Britain and West Germany* (Aldershot, 1983); and Sorge and Warner, *Comparative Factory Organisation*, pt III.

10 The reference is to the theories of Talcott Parsons: see Maurice *et al., Social Foundations*, p. 221, and cf. their discussion of the concept of culture in the work of Crozier, pp. 226–7.

11 M. Maurice, F. Sellier and J.-J. Silvestre, 'Rules, Contexts and Actors: Observations Based on a Comparison between France and West Germany', *British Journal of Industrial Relations* 32 (1984), pp. 361–2.

12 For a sympathetic but critical overview, see M. Rose, 'Universalism, Culturalism and the Aix Group: Promise and Problems of a Societal Approach to Economic Institutions', *European Sociological Review* 1 (1985).

13 Cf. Maurice *et al., Social Foundations*, pp. 247–8.

14 See, for example, Maurice *et al.,* 'Societal Differences', p. 60; and cf. Sorge and Warner, *Comparative Factory Organization*, ch. 2, esp. p. 33.

15 Maurice *et al., Des entreprises en mutation*, esp. pt II; and F. Eyraud, M. Maurice, A. d'Iribarne and F. Rychener, 'Developpements des qualifications et apprentissage par l'entreprise des nouvelles technologies: le cas des machines-outils à commande numérique dans l'industrie mécanique', *Sociologie du travail* (1984).

16 Maurice *et al., Social Foundations*, p. 77.

17 ibid., p. 195.

18 See M. Maurice and F. Sellier, 'Societal Analysis of Industrial Relations: A Comparison between France and West Germany', *British Journal of Industrial Relations* 30 (1982); F. Sellier, *La Confrontation sociale en France, 1936–1981* (Paris, 1984); and Sorge and Warner, *Comparative Factory Organisation*, ch. 13. Cf. also Maurice *et al., Social Foundations*, pp. 183–4, on the limited relevance of historical explanations.

19 In their most recent work, Maurice *et al.* distinguish between 'innovatory' and 'reproductive' changes, but their main examples of the former involve individual firms breaking with their own past history in response to the broader attractions of the national model: see *Des entreprises en mutation*, esp. pts II and IV.

20 For a stimulating discussion of the institutional mechanisms of coherence in the French system of industrial relations, see J. Saglio, 'Les négociations de branche et l'unité du systeme français de relations professionelles: le cas des négociations de classification', *Droit social* (1987).

21 See, for example, O. Kahn-Freund, *Labour Relations; Heritage and Adjustment* (Oxford, 1979); H. Phelps Brown,, *The Origins of Trade Union Power* (Oxford, 1984); and A. Fox, *History and Heritage: The Social Origins of the British Industrial Relations System* (London, 1985).

22 Most discussions of the 'peculiarities of the British' take their point of departure from the Anderson–Nairn–Thompson debate of the 1960s, in which British social and political development was discussed as 'peculiar' in relation to a normative model derived from a selective reading of French and German history. See P. Anderson, 'Origins of the Present Crisis', and T. Nairn, 'The English Working Class', *New Left Review* 23 (1964); E. P. Thompson, 'The Peculiarities of the English', *Socialist Register* (1965); and P. Anderson, *Arguments within English Marxism* (London, 1980), esp. ch. 2.

23 On 'American exceptionalism', see also S. Jacoby, 'American Exceptionalism Revisited: The Importance of Management', in *idem* (ed.), *From Masters to Managers: Historical and Comparative Perspectives on Employers* (New York, 1991); and on the German *Sonderweg*, see D. Blackbourn and G. Eley, *The*

Peculiarities of German History (Oxford, 1984). For a good discussion of the problems of this style of argument, see A. R. Zolberg, 'How Many Exceptionalisms?', in I. Katznelson and A. R. Zolberg (eds), *Working-Class Formation: Nineteenth-Century Patterns in Western Europe and the United States* (Princeton, 1986).

24 For general overviews, see C. More, *Skill and the English Working Class, 1870–1914* (London, 1980); A. Reid, 'The Division of Labour and Politics in Britain, 1880–1920', in W. J. Mommsen and H. G. Husung (eds), *The Development of Trade Unionism in Great Britain and Germany, 1880–1914* (London, 1985): R. Harrison and J. Zeitlin (eds), *Divisions of Labour: Skilled Workers and Technological Change in Nineteenth-Century Britain* (Brighton, 1985); and J. Zeitlin, 'From Labour History to the History of Industrial Relations', *Economic History Review*, 2nd ser., 51 (1987).

25 On cotton textiles, see W. Lazonick, 'Industrial Relations and Technological Change: The Case of the Self-Acting Mule', *Cambridge Journal of Economics* 3 (1979); *idem*, 'Production Relations, Labour Productivity and Choice of Technique: British and US Cotton Spinning', *Journal of Economic History* 51 (1981); M. Freifeld, 'Technical Change and the Self-Acting Mule: A Case Study of Skill and the Sexual Division of Labour', *Social History* 11 (1986); and M. Savage, 'Women and Work in the Lancashire Cotton Industry', in J. A. Jowitt and A. J. McIvor (eds), *Employers and Labour in the English Textile Industries* (London, 1988). On iron and steel, see B. Elbaum and F. Wilkinson, 'Industrial Relations and Uneven Development: A Comparative Study of the American and British Steel Industries', *Cambridge Journal of Economics* 3 (1979); F. Wilkinson, 'Collective Bargaining in the Steel Industry during the 1920s', in A. Briggs and J. Saville (eds), *Essays in Labour History, 1918–39* (London, 1977); and G. Tweedale, *Sheffield Steel and America: A Century of Commercial and Technological Interdependence* (Cambridge, 1987). On coalmining, see R. Harrison (ed.), *The Independent Collier: The Coal Miner as Archetypal Proletarian Reconsidered* (Brighton, 1980); and M. Daunton, 'Down the Pit: Work in the Great Northern and South Wales Coal Fields, 1870–1914', *Economic History Review*, 2nd ser., 34 (1981).

26 In addition to Tolliday's chapter in this volume, see his 'Management and Labour in Britain, 1896–1939', in S. Tolliday and J. Zeitlin (eds), *The Automobile Industry and Its Workers: Between Fordism and Flexibility* (Cambridge, 1986); 'High Tide and After: Coventry's Engineering Workers and Shopfloor Bargaining, 1945–80', in B. Lancaster and T. Mason (eds), *Life and Labour in a Twentieth-Century City: The Case of Coventry* (Coventry, 1986); and W. Lewchuk, *American Technology and the British Vehicle Industry* (Cambridge, 1987).

27 For overviews, see Zeitlin, 'Labour History'; Reid, 'Division of Labour'; and R. Tarling and F. Wilkinson, 'The Movement of Real Wages and the Development of Collective Bargaining in the UK, 1855–1920', *Contributions to Political Economy* 1 (1982).

28 L. Hannah, *The Rise of the Corporate Economy* (2nd edn, London, 1983); P. L. Payne, 'The Emergence of the Large-Scale Company in Great Britain, 1870–1914', *Economic History Review*, 2nd ser., 20 (1967); D. F. Channon, *The Strategy and Structure of British Enterprise* (Cambridge, Mass., 1973); S. Tolliday, *Business, Banking and Politics: The Case of British Steel, 1918–1939* (Cambridge, Mass., 1987); R. Fitzgerald, *British Labour Management and Industrial Welfare, 1846–1939* (London, 1988), esp. chs 4 and 7; J. Melling, ' "Non-Commissioned Officers": British Employers and their Supervisory Workers, 1880–1920', *Social History* 5 (1980); and *idem*, 'Employers, Industrial Housing, and the Evolution of Company Welfare Policies in Britain's Heavy

Industries', *International Review of Social History* 26 (1981).

29 For similar choices in engineering and cotton spinning, see J. Zeitlin, 'Between Flexibility and Mass Production: Product, Production and Labour Strategies in British Engineering, 1840–1955', in C. Sabel and J. Zeitlin (eds), *Worlds of Possibility: Flexibility and Mass Production in Western Industrialization* (forthcoming); G. Saxonhouse and G. Wright, 'New Evidence on the Stubborn English Mule and the Cotton Industry, 1878–1920', *Economic History Review*, 2nd ser., 37 (1984), and exchange with W. Lazonick, *Economic History Review*, 2nd ser., 40 (1987).

30 For a valuable survey, see Fitzgerald, *British Labour Management*.

31 ibid.; Hannah, *Rise of the Corporate Economy; idem*, 'Visible and Invisible Hands in Great Britain', in A. D. Chandler, Jr, and H. Daems (eds), *Managerial Hierarchies: Comparative Perspectives on the Rise of the Modern Industrial Enterprise* (Cambridge, Mass., 1980); W. H. Fraser, *The Coming of the Mass Market, 1850–1914* (London, 1980); and J. B. Jefferys, *Retail Trading in Britain, 1850–1950* (Cambridge, 1954).

32 For an extensive discussion of these issues in the case of steel companies, see Tolliday, *Business, Banking and Politics*.

33 For the influence of DuPont on ICI, see W. J. Reader, *Imperial Chemical Industries*, vol. II (Oxford, 1975), and Hannah, *Corporate Economy*, p. 117; and for similar influence of Sears, Roebuck & Co. on the organization of retail merchandising in Marks and Spencer, see G. Rees, *St. Michael: A History of Marks and Spencer* (London, 1969), pp. 113ff.

34 For contrasting views on the role of religion in company welfare policies, see Fitzgerald, *British Labour Management*, pp. 179–84; J. Child, 'Quaker Employers and Industrial Relations', *Sociological Review*, new ser., 12 (1964); C. Dellheim, 'The Creation of a Company Culture: Cadbury's, 1861–1931', *American Historical Review* 92 (1987); M. Rowlinson, 'The Early Application of Scientific Management at Cadbury', *Business History* 30 (1988); and D. J. Jeremy (ed.), *Business and Religion in Britain* (Aldershot, 1988).

35 Fitzgerald, *British Labour Management*, chs 2–3. For the pro-union policies of the North Eastern Railway Company, see R. J. Irving, *The North Eastern Railway Co., 1870–1914* (Leicester, 1976).

36 Hannah, *Corporate Economy*, pp. 144–5.

37 A. D. Cosh, A. Hughes, K. Lee and A. Singh, 'Institutional Investment, Mergers and the Market for Corporate Control', *International Journal of Industrial Organization* 7 (1989).

38 S. J. Prais, *The Evolution of Giant Firms in Britain* (Cambridge, 1976).

39 D. F. Channon, *The Strategy and Structure of British Enterprise* (Cambridge, Mass., 1973), esp. p. 239. Cf. also P. Steer and J. Cable, 'Internal Organization and Profit: An Empirical Analysis of Large UK Companies', *Journal of Industrial Economics* 27 (1978); and R. S. Thompson, 'Diffusion of the M-Form Structure in the UK: Rate of Imitation, Inter-Firm and Inter-Industry Differences', *International Journal of Industrial Organization* 1 (1983).

40 W. Brown (ed.), *The Changing Contours of British Industrial Relations* (Oxford, 1981), pp. 26–40; E. Batstone, *The Reform of Workplace Industrial Relations* (Oxford, 1988), ch. 2; N. Kinnie, 'Bargaining within the Enterprise: Centralized or Decentralized', *Journal of Management Studies* 24 (1987); and P. Marginson, 'Centralized Control or Establishment Autonomy', in P. Marginson, P. K. Edwards, R. Martin, J. Purcell and K. Sisson, *Beyond the Workplace: Managing Industrial Relations in Multi-Establishment Enterprises* (Oxford, 1988).

41 For a survey of these developments, see Batstone, *Workplace Industrial Relations*, ch. 4. For historical case studies, in addition to Tolliday's chapter in

this volume, see his 'High Tide and After'; and M. Terry and P. K. Edwards (eds), *Shopfloor Politics and Job Controls: The Post-War Engineering Industry* (Oxford, 1988).

42 D. Finegold and D. Soskice, 'The Failure of Training in Britain: Analysis and Prescription', *Oxford Review of Economic Policy* 4 (1988); and S. J. Prais (ed.), *Productivity, Education and Training* (London, 1989).

43 L. Hannah, *Inventing Retirement: The Development of Occupational Pensions in Britain* (Cambridge, 1985), esp. pp. 65–72. On the limited development of internal labour markets in postwar Britain more generally, see H. Gospel, *Markets, Firms and the Management of Labour: The British Experience in Historical Perspective* (forthcoming); and D. Marsden, *The End of Economic Man? Custom and Competition in Labour Markets* (Brighton, 1986), esp. ch. 7.

44 For reviews of inter-war experience, see M. W. Kirby, 'Industrial Policy', in S. Glynn and A. Booth (eds), *The Road to Full Employment* (London, 1986); Hannah, *Corporate Economy*, ch. 3; and Tolliday, *Business, Banking and Politics*, esp. pt III.

45 On postwar industrial policies, see A. Graham, 'Industrial Policy', in W. Beckerman (ed.), *The Labour Government's Economic Record, 1964–70* (London, 1972); and S. Young with A. V. Lowe, *Intervention in the Mixed Economy* (London, 1974).

46 K. Williams, C. Haslam, A. Wardlow and J. Williams, 'Accounting for Failure in the Nationalized Enterprises – Coal, Steel and Cars since 1970', *Economy and Society* 15 (1986); K. Williams, C. Haslam and J. Williams, *The Breakdown of Austin-Rover* (Leamington Spa, 1987).

47 K. Williams, J. Williams and D. Thomas, *Why Are the British Bad at Manufacturing?* (London, 1983), pp. 76–91; J. Fairburn and J. Kay (eds), *Mergers and Merger Policy* (Oxford, 1989); and Cosh *et al.,* 'Institutional Investment'.

48 P. Marginson, 'The Multidivisional Firm and Control over the Work Process', *International Journal of Industrial Organization* III (1985).

49 For a fuller development of these arguments, see P. Hirst and J. Zeitlin, *Reversing Industrial Decline? Industrial Structure and Policy in Britain and her Competitors* (Oxford, 1989); and 'Flexible Specialization and the Competitive Failure of UK Manufacturing', *Political Quarterly* 60 (1989).

50 Channon, *Strategy and Structure*, esp. p. 239; A. Carew, *Labour under the Marshall Plan: The Politics of Productivity and the Marketing of Management Science* (Manchester, 1988), esp. ch. 9.

51 Even after the initial period of transition to the M-Form structure, many British companies continue to blur the line between strategic and operational decision-making within large, heterogeneous divisions: see C. W. L. Hill and J. F. Pickering, 'Divisionalization, Decentralization and Performance of Large United Kingdom Companies', *Journal of Management Studies* 23 (1986).

52 Prais, *Giant Firms*; A. Hughes, 'The Impact of Merger: A Survey of Empirical Evidence for the UK', in Fairburn and Kay, *Mergers and Merger Policy.*

53 The classic case is that of GEC: see the detailed examination of its internal organization and performance in Williams *et al., Why Are the British. . .?* ch. 3.

54 In addition to Jones's chapter in this volume, see A. Campbell, W. Currie and M. Warner, 'Innovation, Skills and Training: Micro-Electronics and Manpower in the United Kingdom and West Germany', in Hirst and Zeitlin, *Reversing Industrial Decline?*; Sorge *et al., Microelectronics and Manpower;* and Prais, *Productivity, Education and Training.*

55 Maurice *et al.,* 'Societal Differences'; and Sorge and Warner, *Comparative Factory Organisation* pt II.

56 For general reviews of British manufacturing performance during the 1980s, see Hirst and Zeitlin, *Reversing Industrial Decline?; idem,* 'Flexible Specialisation'; and K. Coutts and W. Godley, 'The British Economy under Mrs. Thatcher', in *Political Quarterly* 60 (1989).

57 For the role of foreign multinationals in the British economy, see J. Dunning, *US Industry in Britain* (London, 1973); J. M. Stoppard and L. Turner, *Britain and the Multinationals* (London, 1986); S. Young, N. Hood and J. Hamill, *Foreign Multinationals and the UK Economy* (London, 1988). For the recent growth of Japanese direct investment, see M. Trevor, *Under Japanese Management* (London, 1983); J. Dunning, *Japanese Participation in British Industry* (London, 1986); and N. Oliver and B. Wilkinson, *The Japanization of British Management* (Oxford, 1988).

58 For overviews of these developments, see D. A. Hounshell, *From the American System to Mass Production, 1800–1932* (Baltimore, 1984); O. Mayr and R. C. Post (eds), *Yankee Enterprise: The Rise of the American System of Manufactures* (Washington, DC, 1981); D. Nelson, *Managers and Workers: Origins of the New Factory System in the United States, 1880–1920* (Madison, 1975); *idem, Frederick W. Taylor and the Rise of Scientific Management* (Madison, 1980); and S. Jacoby, *Employing Bureaucracy: Managers, Unions and the Transformation of Work in American Industry, 1900–1945* (New York, 1985).

59 N. Rosenberg, *Perspectives on Technology* (Cambridge, 1976); S. B. Saul (ed.), *Technological Change: The United States and Britain in the Nineteenth Century* (London, 1970); H. J. Habakkuk, *American and British Technology in the Nineteenth Century* (Cambridge, 1962); and C. Sabel and J. Zeitlin, 'Historical Alternatives to Mass Production: Politics, Markets and Technology in Nineteenth-Century Industrialization', *Past and Present* 108 (1985).

60 In addition to the chapter by Harris in this volume, see D. Montgomery, *Workers' Control in America* (Cambridge, 1979); *idem, The Fall of the House of Labour: The Workplace, The State and American Labor Activism, 1865–1925* (Cambridge, 1987); and D. Brody, *Workers in Industrial America,* (New York, 1980), chs 1–3.

61 For an historical elaboration of this argument, see S. Tolliday and J. Zeitlin, 'Shop-Floor Bargaining, Contract Unionism and Job Control: An Anglo-American Comparison', in *idem, Automobile Industry.*

62 On the role of the law and the state in the development of American industrial relations, see H. Harris, 'The Snares of Liberalism? Politicians, Bureaucrats and the Shaping of Federal Labour Relations Policy in the United States, ca. 1915–47', in S. Tolliday and J. Zeitlin (eds), *Shop Floor Bargaining and the State* (Cambridge, 1985); C. Tomlins, *The State and the Unions: Labour Relations, Law and the Organized Labour Movement in America, 1880–1960* (Cambridge, 1985); W. E. Forbath, 'The Shaping of the American Labor Movement', *Harvard Law Review* 102 (1989); Brody, *Workers in Industrial America,* chs 3 and 5; and K. Stone, 'The Postwar Paradigm in American Labor Law', *Yale Law Review* 90 (1981).

63 See Tolliday, 'Management and Labour', and his chapter in this volume. For the difficulties experienced by French and Italian automobile manufacturers in emulating the 'Fordist' model, see Tolliday and Zeitlin, *Automobile Industry,* esp. chs 2, 3 and 6; as well as Contini's chapter in this volume.

64 See A. D. Chandler, Jr, *The Visible Hand: The Managerial Revolution in American Business* (Cambridge, Mass., 1977); and N. Lamoreaux, *The Great Merger Movement in American Business, 1895–1904* (Cambridge, 1985). For the impact of legal regulation on American corporate organization, see M. Keller, 'Regulation of Large Enterprise: The United States in Comparative

Perspective', in Chandler and Daems, *Managerial Hierarchies*. For the limited influence of the railways on the development of management structures elsewhere in British industry, see T. R. Gourvish, 'The Railways and the Development of Managerial Enterprise in Britain, 1850–1939', in K. Koybayashi and H. Morikawa (eds), *Development of Managerial Enterprise* (Tokyo, 1986).

65　On the military origins of the American system of manufactures, see M. Roe Smith, *Harpers' Ferry Armory and the New Technology* (Ithaca, NY, 1977); *idem*, 'Military Entrepreneurship', in Mayr and Post, *Yankee Enterprise*; Hounshell, *American System*, ch. 1; and for a contrasting view, D. Hoke, *Ingenious Mechanics: The Rise of the American System of Manufactures in the Private Sector* (New York, 1989). For automatic machine production as a utopian vision or 'technological paradigm', see Sabel and Zeitlin, 'Historical Alternatives', esp. pp. 171–4.

66　See, for example, Jacoby, 'American Exceptionalism'.

67　See, for example, R. M. Jackson, *The Formation of Craft Labor Markets* (New York, 1984); and, more generally, S. Berger and M. J. Piore, *Dualism and Discontinuity in Industrial Societies* (Cambridge, 1980).

68　In the 1970s, for example, roughly 70 per cent of all metalworking production in the United States consisted of small batches: see 'Machine-Tool Technology', *American Machinist* (Oct. 1980), fig. 2, p. 106. Additional evidence of the importance of craft production in American industrial development can be found in the work of Philip Scranton: see his *Proprietary Capitalism: The Textile Manufacture at Philadelphia, 1800–1885* (Cambridge, 1983); *Figured Tapestry: Production, Markets and Power in Philadelphia Textiles, 1885–1941* (Cambridge, 1989); and *Endless Novelty: The Other Side of American Industrialization* (New York, forthcoming).

69　See especially D. Nelson, *Frederick W. Taylor; Managers and Workers;* and *American Rubber Workers and Organized Labor, 1900–1941* (Princeton, 1988).

70　Jacoby, *Employing Bureaucracy*; and D. M. Gordon, R. Edwards and M. Reich, *Segmented Work, Divided Workers: The Historical Transformation of Labor in the United States* Cambridge, 1982), pp. 128–35.

71　W. Licht, *Working for the Railroad: The Organization of Work in the Nineteenth Century* (Princeton, NJ, 1983).

72　Jacoby, *Employing Bureaucracy*, chs 7–8; R. Schatz, *The Electrical Workers: A History of Labour at General Electric and Westinghouse, 1923–60* (Urbana, IL, 1983), chs 3 and 5; and Tolliday and Zeitlin, 'Shop-Floor Bargaining'.

73　T. Kochan, H. Katz and R. McKersie, *The Transformation of American Industrial Relations* (New York, 1986), esp. ch. 3; and F. K. Foulkes, *Personnel Policies in Large Non-Union Companies* (Englewood Cliffs, NJ, 1980).

74　For synthetic overviews, see J. Kocka, 'Entrepreneurs and Managers in German Industrialization', in P. Mathias and M. Postan (eds), *The Cambridge Economic History of Europe*, vol. VII (1978); *idem*, 'The Rise of the Modern Industrial Enterprise in Germany', in Chandler and Daems, *Managerial Hierarchies*; and A. D. Chandler, Jr, *Scale and Scope*, (Cambridge, Mass., 1990), pt IV. For a Chandlerian study of three major companies, see W. Feldenkirchen, 'Big Business in Interwar Germany: Organizational Innovation at Vereinigte Stahlwerke, IG Farben, and Siemens', *Business History Review* 61 (1987).

75　For these policies, see, in addition to the chapters in this volume, D. Geary, 'The Industrial Bourgeoisie and Labour Relations in Germany, 1871–1933', in D. Blackbourn and R. Evans (eds), *The German Bourgeoisie* (London, 1991); E. G. Spencer, *Management and Labor in Imperial Germany: Ruhr Industrialists as Employers, 1896–1914* (New Brunswick, NJ, 1984); D. F. Crew, *Town in the*

Ruhr: A Social History of Bochum, 1860–1914 (New York, 1979), chs 4–6; B. Weisbrod, 'Economic Power and Political Stability Reconsidered: Heavy Industry in Weimar Germany', *Social History* 4 (1979); and H. James, *The German Slump: Politics and Economics, 1924–1936* (Oxford, 1986), esp. ch. 6.

76 See also A. Lüdtke, 'Workplace Revisited: Rationalisation, Necessity-Cooperation and *"Eigensinn"* Amongst Factory Workers in Germany, 1920–40' (unpublished paper, Max-Planck-Institut für Geschichte, Göttingen, 1988); G. Herrigel, 'Industrial Order and the Politics of Industrial Change: Mechanical Engineering', in P. Katzenstein (ed.), *Industry and Political Change in West Germany: Towards the Third Republic* (Ithaca, NY, 1989); Herrigel , 'Industrial Organization and the Politics of Industry: Centralized and Decentralized Production in Germany' (Ph.D. thesis, Massachusetts Institute of Technology, 1990); and M. J. Piore and C. Sabel, *The Second Industrial Divide* (New York, 1984), pp. 142–8. On the limitations of rationalization between the wars, see also R. Brady, *The Rationalization Movement in German Industry* (Berkeley, 1933), esp. ch. 7 on machine tools; and James, *German Slump*, ch. 4. For a contrasting view which emphasizes the success of rationalization in sectors such as refrigerators, prime movers and steel, see Chandler, *Scale and Scope*, ch. 14.

77 Herrigel, 'Industrial Order'; *idem*, 'Industrial Organization'; and C. Sabel, G. Herrigel, R. Deeg and R. Kazis, 'Regional Prosperities Compared: Massachusetts and Baden-Württemberg in the 1980s', *Economy and Society* 18 (1989). Chandler argues that economies of scope were more important than those of scale in explaining the growth of large, diversified German companies in sectors like heavy machinery and chemicals, while German manufacturers of light machinery were also forced to develop more specialized products by the strength of American competition in the domestic market: see *Scale and Scope*, chs 11–12.

78 J. J. Lee, 'Labour in German Industrialization', in Mathias and Postan, *Cambridge Economic History of Europe*; and R. R. Locke, *The End of the Practical Man: Entrepreneurship and Higher Education in Germany, France and Great Britain, 1880–1940* (Greenwich, Conn., 1984).

79 K. Saul, 'Repression or Integration? The State, Trade Unions and Industrial Disputes in Imperial Germany', in Mommsen and Husung, *Trade Unionism*; J. A. Moses, *Trade Unionism in Germany from Bismarck to Hitler* (London, 1982), vol. 1, ch. 5; and Spencer, *Management and Labor in Imperial Germany*.

80 On the structure and policies of German unions, see Mommsen and Husung, *Trade Unionism*, esp. chs 11–13; Moses, *Trade Unionism in Germany*; and Piore and Sabel, *Second Industrial Divide*, pp. 144–5. For the unions' commitment to 'German quality work', see Lüdtke, 'Workplace Revisited', p. 14.

81 For a forceful statement of this view, see W. Streeck, 'Codetermination: the Fourth Decade', in B. Wilpert and A. Sorge (eds), *International Perspectives on Organizational Democracy* (New York, 1984).

82 For a valuable survey, see W. Feldenkirchen, 'Concentration in German Industry', in H. Pöhl (ed.), *The Concentration Process in the Entrepreneurial Economy* (Stuttgart, 1988).

83 For an overview, see J. Kocka, 'Capitalism and Industrialization in German Industrialization before 1914', *Economic History Review*, 2nd ser., 34 (1981).

84 Herrigel, 'Industrial Order'; *idem*, 'Industrial Organization'; and J. Cable and M. J. Dirrheimer, 'Hierarchies and Markets: An Empirical Test of the Multidivisional Hypothesis in West Germany', *International Journal of Industrial Organization* 1 (1983).

85 For the influence of pre-capitalist values on German employers, see H. U.

Wehler, *The German Empire, 1871-1918* (Leamington Spa, 1985); and the critical discussion in G. Eley, 'Capitalism and the Wilhelmine State', *Historical Journal* 21 (1978); and Geary, 'Industrial Bourgeoisie'. For contrasting views on the extent of postwar transformations, cf. V. Berghahn, *The Americanization of West German Industry, 1945-73* (Leamington Spa, 1986); and Plumpe's chapter in this volume.

86   This contrast is based on Herrigel, 'Industrial Order' and 'Industrial Organization'. A partial exception to this pattern was the Berlin electrical manufacturing industry: large firms there, as Homburg's chapter shows, drew their workers from a volatile metropolitan labour market and were necessarily less autarkic than their counterparts in regions like the Ruhr.

87   Herrigel, 'Industrial Order' and 'Industrial Organization'; Sabel *et al.,* 'Regional Prosperities Compared'; and R. Boch, 'The Rise and Decline of "Flexible Production": The Cutlery Industry of Solingen since the Eighteenth Century', in Sabel and Zeitlin, *Worlds of Possibility.*

88   The best English-language survey of work organization in Japan is K. Koike, *Understanding Industrial Relations in Modern Japan* (London, 1988).

89   M. Cusumano, *The Japanese Automobile Industry* (Cambridge, Mass., 1985); R. Schonberger, *Japanese Manufacturing Techniques* (New York, 1982); and A. Sayer, 'New Developments in Manufacturing: The Just-in-Time System', *Capital and Class* 30 (1986).

90   For the case of automobiles, see Cusumano, *Japanese Automobile Industry*; D. Friedman, 'Beyond the Age of Ford: The Strategic Basis of Japanese Success in Automobiles', in J. Zysman and L. Tyson (eds), *American Industry in International Competition* (Ithaca, NY, 1983); and Tolliday and Zeitlin, *Automobile Industry,* esp. the Introduction and chs 8-9.

91   The extent to which Japanese manufacturers have moved away from, rather than refined and perfected, mass-production methods remains highly controversial. For a representative spectrum of views, cf. Tolliday and Zeitlin, *Automobile Industry*; C. F. Sabel, 'Flexible Specialization and the Re-emergence of Regional Economies', in Hirst and Zeitlin, *Reversing Industrial Decline?,* esp. pp. 38-40; Friedman, 'Beyond the Age of Ford'; *idem, The Misunderstood Miracle: Industrial Development and Political Change in Japan* (Ithaca, NY, 1988); K. Dohse, U. Jurgens and T. Malsch, 'From "Fordism" to "Toyotism"? The Social Organization of the Labour Process in the Japanese Automobile Industry', *Politics and Society* 15 (1985); M. Kenney and R. L. Florida, 'Beyond Mass Production: Production and the Labor Process in Japan', *Politics and Society* 17 (1988); Sayer, 'New Developments in Manufacturing'; and *idem,* 'Post-Fordism in Question', *International Journal of Urban and Regional Research* 13 (1989).

92   Koike, *Industrial Relations*; R. Clark, *The Japanese Company* (New Haven, 1979); R. Cole, *Work, Mobility and Participation: A Comparative Study of American and Japanese Industry* (Berkeley, 1979); Dore, *British Factory-Japanese Factory*; and A. Gordon, *The Evolution of Labor Relations in Japan: Heavy Industry, 1853-1955* (Cambridge, Mass., 1985).

93   T. Shirai, 'A Theory of Enterprise Unionism', in T. Shirai (ed.), *Industrial Relations in Contemporary Japan* (Madison, 1983); K. Kozo, 'The Japanese Enterprise Union and its Functions', in T. Shigeyoshi and J. Bergmann (eds), *Industrial Relations in Transition: The Cases of Japan and the Federal Republic of Germany* (Tokyo, 1984); C. Deutschmann, 'Economic Restructuring and Company Unionism - The Japanese Model', *Economic and Industrial Democracy* 8 (1987); and Koike, *Industrial Relations,* ch. 7. For case studies of Nissan and Toyota, see Cusumano, *Japanese Automobile Industry,* ch. 3; and R. Okayama, 'Industrial Relations in the Japanese Automobile Industry, 1945-70:

The Case of Toyota', in Tolliday and Zeitlin, *Automobile Industry*.

94 Dore, *British Factory–Japanese Factory*, esp. chs 14–15. See also R. Cole, 'The Late Developer Hypothesis: An Evaluation of its Relevance for Japanese Employment Practices', *Journal of Japanese Studies* 4 (1978); Dore, 'More on Late Development', *Journal of Japanese Studies* 5 (1979); and *idem*, 'Industrial Relations in Japan and Elsewhere', in A. M. Craig (ed.), *Japan: A Comparative View* (Princeton, 1979).

95 On textiles, see the special Anglo-Japanese conference issue of *Textile History*, 19/2 (1988); and T. Nakaoka, 'The Role of Domestic Technical Innovation in Foreign Technology Transfer: The Case of the Japanese Cotton Textile Industry', *Osaka City University Economic Review* 18 (1982). On automobiles, see Cusumano, *Japanese Automobile Industry*; and Piore and Sabel, *Second Industrial Divide*, pp. 223–6.

96 For a masterful synthesis, see Gordon, *Labor Relations in Japan*.

97 S. Garon, *The State and Labor in Modern Japan* (Berkeley, 1988); and Gordon, *Labor Relations in Japan*, chs 6–10. On the occupation authorities and the postwar defeat of industrial unionism, see also J. Moore, *Japanese Workers and the Struggle for Power, 1945–47* (Madison, 1983); Cusumano, *Japanese Automobile Industry*, ch. 3; and Okayama, 'Japanese Automobile Industry'.

98 M. Aoki, 'The Japanese Firm in Transition', in K. Yamamura and Y. Yasuba (eds), *The Political Economy of Japan, vol. I: The Domestic Transformation* (Palo Alto, Calif, 1987); J. C. Abegglen and G. Stalk, Jr, *Kaisha: The Japanese Corporation* (New York, 1985); Clark, *Japanese Company*; Dore, *Flexible Rigidities*, ch. 3; and J. Cable and H. Yasuki, 'Internal Organisation, Business Groups and Corporate Performance: An Empirical Test of the Multidivisional Hypothesis in Japan', *International Journal of Industrial Organization* 3 (1985). For historical discussions, see H. Morikawa, 'The Development of Multi-Industrial Concentration in Modern Japan', in Pöhl, *Concentration Process*; and J. Hirschmeier and T. Yui, *The Development of Japanese Business, 1600–1973* (London, 1975).

99 Cole, *Work, Mobility and Participation*, pp. 108–11, 121–223; C. Littler, *The Development of the Labour Process in Capitalist Societies* (London, 1982), pp. 156–8; T. Nakase, 'The Introduction of Scientific Management in Japan and Its Characteristics – Case Studies of Companies in the Sumitomo Zaibatsu', in K. Nakagawa (ed.), *Labor and Management* (Tokyo, 1979); S. Sasaki, 'Scientific Management Movements in Pre-War Japan', *Japanese Yearbook on Business History* 4 (1987); and E. Daito, 'Railways and Scientific Management in Japan, 1907–30', *Business History* 31 (1989).

100 For an attentive treatment of this theme, see Garon, *State and Labor in Modern Japan*.

101 Gordon, *Labour Relations in Japan*; Garon, *State and Labor in Modern Japan*; and Dore, *British Factory–Japanese Factory*.

102 For recent restatements of the conventional view, see Norma J. Chalmers, *Industrial Relations in Japan: The Peripheral Workforce* (London, 1989); and R. Steven, *Classes in Contemporary Japan* (Cambridge, 1983).

103 Friedman, *Misunderstood Miracle*, chs 4–5; Dore, *Flexible Rigidities*, chs 7–9; and H. T. Patrick and T. P. Rohlen, 'Small-Scale Family Enterprises', in Yamamura and Yasuba, *Political Economy of Japan*.

104 Koike, *Industrial Relations*, pp. 42–4; Friedman, *Misunderstood Miracle*, pp. 141–3. Wage differentials by sex, however, are unusually high in Japan for workers over 30 years old, demonstrating the continuing exclusion of women from internal career ladders in both large and small firms.

105 Friedman, *The Misunderstood Miracle*, pp. 143–6.

106 Koike, *Industrial Relations*, pp. 180–205, esp. p. 191.

107 For general surveys, see W. R. Garside and H. Gospel, 'Employers and Managers: Their Organization Structure and Changing Industrial Strategies', in C. J. Wrigley (ed.), *A History of British Industrial Relations, 1875–1914* (Brighton, 1982); H. Gospel, 'Employers and Managers: Organization and Strategy, 1914–39', in C. J. Wrigley (ed.), *A History of British Industrial Relations, vol. 2: 1914–39* (Brighton, 1986); Commission on Industrial Relations, *Employers' Organisations and Industrial Relations* (London, 1972); H. A. Clegg, *The Changing System of Industrial Relations in Britain* (Oxford, 1979), pp. 62–100; and E. Armstrong, 'Employers' Associations in Great Britain', in J. Windmuller and A. Gladstone (eds), *Employers' Associations and Industrial Relations* (Oxford, 1984).

108 Gospel, 'Employers and Managers'; T. Rodgers, 'Work and Welfare: The NCEO and the Unemployment Problem, 1919–36' (Ph.D. thesis, University of Edinburgh, 1981); J. Turner (ed.), *Businessmen and Politics: Studies of Business Activity in British Politics, 1900–45* (London, 1985); S. Blank, *Government and Industry in Britain: The Federation of British Industries in Politics, 1945–65* (Farnborough, 1973); and W. Grant and D. Marsh, *The Confederation of British Industry* (London, 1977).

109 For other sectoral case studies which illustrate the fragility of employer solidarity in Britain, see R. Bean, 'Employers' Associations in the Port of Liverpool, 1890–1914', *International Review of Social History* 21 (1976); R. Church, *The History of the British Coal Industry, vol. III: 1830–1913, Victorian Pre-eminence* (Oxford, 1986), pp. 651–74; Jowitt and McIvor, *Employers and Labour in the English Textile Industries*, chs 1–3; and J. McKenna and R. Rodger, 'Control by Coercion: Employers' Associations and the Establishment of Industrial Order in the Building Industry of England and Wales, 1860–1914', *Business History Review* 59 (1985).

110 For the decline of organized strikebreaking, see A. McIvor, 'Employers' Organization and Strikebreaking in Britain, 1880–1914', *International Review of Social History* 29 (1984).

111 For the cases of cotton spinning and iron and steel, see Lazonick, 'Industrial Relations and Technical Change', and Elbaum and Wilkinson, 'Industrial Relations and Uneven Development'.

112 For a useful overview of sectoral variations in the scope and form of multi-employer bargaining, see Commission on Industrial Relations, *Employers' Organizations*, pp. 18–27; and for case studies of industries characterized by more cohesive bargaining arrangements, see H. Gospel, 'The Development of Bargaining Structure: The Case of Electrical Contracting, 1914–39', in Wrigley, *Industrial Relations. vol. 2*, and 'Product Markets, Labour Markets, and Industrial Relations: The Case of Flour Milling', in *Business History* 31 (1989).

113 Royal Commission on Trade Unions and Employers' Associations, *Report (Donovan Commission)* (Cmnd. 3623, London, 1968); A. Flanders, *Management and Unions* (London 1970).

114 W. Brown (ed.), *The Changing Contours of British Industrial Relations* (Oxford, 1978); Commission on Industrial Relations, *Employers' Organisations*; and K. Sisson, *The Management of Collective Bargaining* (Oxford, 1987). In industries such as coal, rail, iron and steel and shipbuilding, however, the postwar shift to single-employer bargaining was the result of nationalization rather than of any change in company strategies.

115 A. McKinlay and D. McNulty, 'Open Secrets and Hidden Agendas: Working Time, Flexibility and Industrial Relations in British Engineering', in P. Blyton and J. Morris (eds) *Towards a Flexible Future?* (London, 1990); and W. Grant, 'The Organization of Business Interests in the UK Machine Tool Industry', *IIM/LMP Discussion Paper* 83–21 (Wissenschaftszentrum Berlin, 1983).

116 See, for example, Phelps Brown, *Trade Union Power*, pp. 98–130.
117 E. Wigham, *The Power to Manage: A History of the Engineering Employers' Federation* (London, 1973), chs 8–10; H. Clegg and R. Adams, *The Employers' Challenge: A Study of the National Engineering and Shipbuilding Disputes of 1957* (Oxford, 1957); S. Tolliday, 'Government, Employers and Shop Floor Organization in the British Motor Industry, 1939-69', in Tolliday and Zeitlin, *Shop Floor Bargaining*; and J. Salmon, 'Wage Strategy, Redundancy and Shop Stewards in the Coventry Motor Industry', in Terry and Edwards, *Shopfloor Politics*.
118 For a comparative study of iron and steel, see Elbaum and Wilkinson, 'Industrial Relations and Uneven Development'.
119 For this general argument, see Gospel, *Management of Labour*; 'The Management of Labour: Great Britain, the US, and Japan', *Business History* 30 (1988); and 'The Development of Management Organization: A Historical Perspective', in K. Thurley and S. Wood (eds), *Industrial Relations and Management Strategy* (Cambridge, 1983).
120 Gospel, *Management of Labour*.
121 In addition to the chapter by Sisson in this volume, see his *Management of Collective Bargaining*; and Commission on Industrial Relations, 'Employers' Organisations'.
122 Gospel, 'Product Markets'.
123 On the declining effectiveness of disputes procedures and collective agreements in construction, see Donovan Commission, *Report*, pp. 17–18; and T. Austrin, 'The "Lump" in the UK Construction Industry', in T. Nichols (ed.), *Capital and Labour* (London, 1980).
124 For overviews see C. J. Wrigley, 'The Government and Industrial Relations' and R. Davidson, 'Government Administration', in Wrigley, *Industrial Relations, vol. 1*; and R. Lowe, *Adjusting to Democracy: The Ministry of Labour In British Politics, 1916-39* (Oxford, 1986).
125 For examples of statutory support for the extension of collective bargaining, see O. Kahn-Freund, *Labour and the Law* (London, 1972), pp. 76–90; B. Bercusson, *Fair Wages Resolutions* (London, 1978); D. Sells, *British Trade Boards: A Study in Industrial Democracy* (Washington, DC, 1939); F. J. Bayliss, *British Wages Councils* (Oxford, 1962); and R. Charles, *The Development of Industrial Relations in Britain, 1911-39* (London, 1973).
126 Kahn-Freund, *Labour and the Law*; R. Lewis, 'The Historical Development of British Labour Law', *British Journal of Industrial Relations* 14 (1976); Phelps Brown, *Trade Union Power*, pp. 28–55; and K. D. Brown, 'Trade Unions and the Law', in Wrigley, *Industrial Relations, vol. 1*.
127 R. Lowe, 'The Failure of Consensus in Britain: The National Industrial Conference, 1919-21', *Historical Journal* 21 (1978); *idem, Adjusting to Democracy*; and S. Blank, 'Britain: The Politics of Foreign Economic Policy, the Domestic Economy and the Problem of Pluralist Stagnation', in P. Katzenstein (ed.), *Between Power and Plenty* (Madison, 1978).
128 Clegg and Adams, *Employers' Challenge*; Wigham, *Power to Manage*, ch. 8.
129 Brown, *Changing Contours*; and M. Nightingale, 'UK Productivity Dealing in the 1960s', in Nichols, *Capital and Labour*.
130 J. MacInnes, *Thatcherism at Work* (Milton Keynes, 1987); P. Fosh and C. Littler (eds), *Industrial Relations and the Law in the 1980s* (Aldershot, 1985); and R. Mailly, S. J. Dimmock and A. S. Sethi, *Industrial Relations in the Public Services* (London, 1989).
131 For a general overview, see Tarling and Wilkinson, 'Movement of Real Wages'.
132 Brown, 'Trade Unions and the Law'; R. Currie, *Industrial Politics* (Oxford,

1979); Lowe, *Adjusting to Democracy*, ch. 4; M. Moran, *The Politics of Industrial Relations* (London, 1977); and A. Flanders, 'The Tradition of Voluntarism', *British Journal of Industrial Relations* 12 (1974).

133 McKinlay, 'Open Secrets'.

134 See in addition to Sisson's chapter in this volume, his *Management of Collective Bargaining*, pp. 74–5, 92–6; G. Skogh, 'Employers' Associations in Sweden', in Windmuller and Gladstone, *Employers' Associations*; L. Bengtsson, A. C. Eriksson and P. Sederblad, 'The Associative Action of Swedish Business Interests: The Swedish Employers' Confederation and Centralized Collective Bargaining in 1980, 1981 and 1983', *IIM/LMP Discussion Paper* 84–24 (Wissenschaftszentrum Berlin, 1984); and T. L. Johnston, *Collective Bargaining in Sweden* (London, 1962), ch. 2.

135 Bengtsson *et al.*, 'Swedish Business Interests', pp. 59–67, 72.

136 See, for example, Sisson, *Management of Collective Bargaining*, p. 116; P. Swenson, *Fair Shares: Unions, Pay, and Politics in Sweden and West Germany* (Ithaca, NY, 1989), p. 103.

137 T. Pierenkemper, 'Trade Associations in Germany in the Late Nineteenth and Early Twentieth Centuries', in H. Yamazaki and M. Miyamoto (eds), *Trade Associations in Business History* (Tokyo, 1988); V. R. Berghahn and D. Karsten, *Industrial Relations in West Germany* (Oxford, 1987), pp. 146–8, 154–60; and G. Feldman, 'German Interest Group Alliances in War and Inflation', in S. Berger (ed.), *Organizing Interests in Western Europe* (Cambridge, 1981).

138 R. F. Bunn, 'Employers' Associations in the Federal Republic of Germany', in Windmuller and Gladstone, *Employers' Associations*; Berghahn and Karsten, *Industrial Relations in West Germany*, pp. 18–23; and Sisson, *Management of Collective Bargaining*, pp. 74–5, 104–6.

139 In addition to the chapters in this volume, see Spencer, *Management and Labor in Imperial Germany*, pp. 102–110; and Swenson, *Fair Shares*, pp. 34–41.

140 See also Bunn, 'Employers' Associations in Germany', pp. 184–5; Berghahn and Karsten, *Industrial Relations in West Germany*, pp. 21, 25–6; and Sisson, *Management of Collective Bargaining*, pp. 75, 117–18.

141 W. Streeck, 'Industrial Relations in West Germany: Agenda for Change', *IIM/LMP Discussion Paper* 87–5 (Wissenschaftszentrum, Berlin, 1987), esp. pp. 25–6; and H. Kern and C. F. Sabel, 'Trade Unions and Decentralized Production: A Sketch of Strategic Problems in the West German Labor Movement' (unpublished paper, MIT, January 1990).

142 On Swedish communitarianism and cultural homogeneity as influences on interest group behaviour, see H. Heclo and H. Madsen, *Policy and Politics in Sweden* (Philadelphia, 1987), p. 22; and the critical comments in J. Fulcher, 'On the Explanation of Industrial Relations Diversity: Labour Movements, Employers and the State in Britain and Sweden', *British Journal of Industrial Relations* 26 (1988). On the culture of German employers, see the sources cited in note 85 above.

143 For a classic statement of this argument, see G. Ingham, *Strikes and Industrial Conflict: Britain and Scandinavia* (London, 1974); and cf. also S. Lash and J. Urry, *The End of Organized Capitalism*, (Cambridge, 1987), ch. 2.

144 G. Feldman and U. Nocken, 'Trade Associations and Economic Power: Interest Group Development in the German Iron and Steel and Machine Building Industries, 1900–1933', *Business History Review* 49 (1975), p. 421; and U. Nocken, 'Inter-Industrial Conflicts and Alliances as Exemplified by the AVI-Agreement', in H. Mommsen, D. Petzina and B. Weisbrod (eds), *Industrielles System und politiche Entwicklung in der Weimarer Republik* (Düsseldorf, 1974), pp. 698–9.

145 For these arguments, see P. Jackson and K. Sisson, 'Employers' Confederations

in Sweden and the UK: The Significance of Industrial Infrastructure', *British Journal of Industrial Relations* 14 (1976); Fulcher, 'Industrial Relations Diversity', p. 252; and Swenson, *Fair Shares*, pp. 34–42.

146 For strategic divisions within SAF, see B. Schiller, 'Years of Crisis, 1906–14', in S. Koblik (ed.), *Sweden's Development from Poverty to Affluence, 1750–1970* (Minneapolis, 1975); J. Elster, *The Cement of Society* (Cambridge, 1989), pp. 177–8; and Bengtsson *et al., 'Swedish Business Interests'.

147 For the combination of fragmented industry with centralized bargaining in Denmark, see W. Galenson, *The Danish System of Labor Relations* (Cambridge, Mass., 1952); and B. Amoroso, 'Development and Crisis of the Scandinavian Model of Labour Relations in Denmark', in G. Baglioni and C. Crouch (eds) *European Industrial Relations: The Challenge of Flexibility* (London, 1990).

148 K. Ahlén, 'Swedish Collective Bargaining Under Pressure: Inter-union Rivalry and Incomes Policies', *British Journal of Industrial Relations* 27 (1989), pp. 334–5, 345–6.

149 Jackson and Sisson, 'Employers' Confederations', p. 311; but cf. the discussion of the 1899 Åkarp Law which made coercion of non-strikers punishable by imprisonment in Fulcher, 'Industrial Relations Diversity', p. 254.

150 Schiller, 'Years of Crisis'.

151 Jackson and Sisson, 'Employers' Confederations', pp. 311–12; Swenson, *Fair Shares*, pp. 42–60; and Johnston, *Collective Bargaining in Sweden*, pp. 34–6, 115–16, 144–54.

152 Ahlén, 'Swedish Collective Bargaining'; A. Martin, 'The End of the "Swedish Model?" Recent Developments in Swedish Industrial Relations', *Bulletin of Comparative Labour Relations* 16 (1987); and R. Taylor, 'Shards of a Broken Model', *Financial Times*, 21 Feb. 1990.

153 See the sources cited in note 79 above.

154 E. Maschke, 'Outline of the History of German Cartels from 1873 to 1914', in F. Crouzet, W. H. Chaloner and W. M. Stern (eds), *Essays in European Economic History, 1789–1914* (London, 1969); G. Feldman, 'The Collapse of the Steel Works Association, 1912–1919', in H. U. Wehler (ed.), *Sozialgeschichte Heute. Festschrift für Hans Rosenberg zum 70. Geburstag* (Göttingen, 1974); and Feldman, *Iron and Steel in the German Inflation, 1916–1923* (Princeton, 1977), pp. 27–159.

155 G. Feldman, *Army, Industry and Labor in Germany, 1914–18* (Princeton, 1966); and 'German Business Between War and Revolution: The Origins of the Stinnes-Legien Agreement', in G. A. Ritter (ed.), *Enstehung und Wandel der modernen Gesellschaft. Festschrift für Hans Rosenberg zum 65. Geburstag* (Berlin, 1970).

156 For the impact of labour law and compulsory arbitration on Weimar industrial relations, see O. Kahn-Freund, *Labour Law and Politics in the Weimar Republic* (ed. and introduced by R. Lewis and J. Clark, Oxford, 1981); and Weisbrod, 'Economic Power and Political Stability'. For a thoughtful if inevitably partisan survey of the acrimonious debate over German industrialists' role in the rise of Hitler, see D. Geary, 'Employers, Workers and the Collapse of the Weimar Republic', in I. Kershaw (ed.), *Weimar: Why Did German Democracy Fail?* (London, 1990).

157 Berghahn and Karsten, *Industrial Relations in West Germany*, chs 3–4; and W. Streeck, *Industrial Relations in West Germany: A Case Study of the Car Industry* (London, 1984), ch. 3.

158 W. Grant and W. Streeck, 'Large Firms and the Representation of Business Interests in the UK and West German Construction Industry', in A. Cawson (ed.), *Organized Interests and the State* (London, 1985); W. Streeck, K. Hilbert,

K. H. van Kevelaer, F. Maier and H. Weber, 'The Role of the Social Partners in Vocational Training and Further Training in the Federal Republic of Germany', *IIM/LMP Discussion Paper* 87–12 (Wissenschaftszentrum, Berlin, 1987); and Streeck, 'The Territorial Organization of Interests and the Logics of Associative Action: The Case of Artisanal Interest Organizations in West Germany', in W. D. Coleman and H. J. Jacek (eds) *Regionalism, Business Interests and Public Policy* (London, 1989).

159 W. Streeck, 'Neo-Corporatist Industrial Relations and the Economic Crisis in West Germany', in J. Goldthorpe (ed.), *Order and Conflict in Contemporary Capitalism* (Oxford, 1984); Streeck, 'Industrial Relations in West Germany'; and S. J. Silvia, 'The West German Labor Law Controversy: A Struggle for the Factory of the Future', *Comparative Politics* 20 (1988).

160 Schiller, 'Years of Crisis'; Fulcher, 'Industrial Relations Diversity'; Jackson and Sisson, 'Employers' Confederations'; and Johnston, *Collective Bargaining in Sweden*, pp. 68–78.

161 Swenson, *Fair Shares*, pp. 51–60, 84–95, 102–7; Martin, 'Trade Unions in Sweden'; and Johnston, *Collective Bargaining in Sweden*, pp. 39–47.

162 Ahlén, 'Swedish Collective Bargaining'; Martin, 'End of the "Swedish Model?" '; and S. Lash, 'The End of Neo-Corporatism?: The Breakdown of Centralized Bargaining in Sweden', *British Journal of Industrial Relations* 23 (1985).

163 Ahlén, 'Swedish Collective Bargaining', pp. 332–3, 336–7.

164 Swenson, *Fair Shares*, pp. 34–42; Moses, *Trade Unionism in Germany,* chs 4, 6–7; and Mommsen and Husung, *Trade Unionism*, chs 11–13.

165 Berghahn and Karsten, *Industrial Relations in West Germany*, chs 2 and 6; Streeck, *Industrial Relations in West Germany*, ch. 2; and A. S. Markovits and C. S. Allen, 'Trade Unions and Economic Crisis: The West German Case', in P. Gourevitch, A. Martin, G. Ross, S. Bornstein, A. Markovits and C. Allen, *Unions and Economic Crisis: Britain, West Germany, and Sweden* (London, 1984).

166 Swenson, *Fair Shares*, pp. 72–84, 95–102, 216–22; Streeck, 'Industrial Relations in West Germany'; and Kern and Sabel, 'Trade Unions and Decentralized Production'.

167 I. Kolboom, *La Revanche des patrons: le patronat français face au front populaire* (Paris, 1986); and H. W. Ehrmann, *Organized Business in France* (Princeton, 1957), ch. 1.

168 J. Bunel and J. Saglio, 'Employers' Associations in France', in Windmuller and Gladstone, *Employers' Associations*; Bunel and Saglio, *L'Action patronale, du CNPF au petit patron* (Paris, 1979); Ehrmann, *Organized Business in France*; and H. Weber, *Le Parti des patrons: Le CNPF (1946–1986)* (Paris, 1986).

169 Bunel and Saglio, 'Employers' Associations in France' and *L'Action patronale*; Sellier, *La Confrontation sociale*, esp. chs 2 and 6; and Sisson, *Management of Collective Bargaining*, pp. 35–40.

170 Sellier, *La Confrontation sociale*, pp. 56–62, 66–70, 202–13, 220–4; D. Segrestin, 'Recent Changes in France', in Baglioni and Crouch, *European Industrial Relations*, esp. pp. 104–6.

171 See, in addition to the chapter by Contini in this volume, A. Martinelli and T. Treu, 'Employers' Associations in Italy', in Windmuller and Gladstone, *Employers' Organizations*; R. J. Flanagan, D. W. Soskice and L. Ulman, *Unionism, Economic Stabilization, and Incomes Policy* (Washington, DC, 1983), ch. 9; M. Regini, 'Social Pacts in Italy', in I. Scholten (ed.), *Political Stability and Neo-corporatism* (London, 1987); Ministero del Lavoro e della Previdenza Sociale, *Report '88: Labour and Employment Policies in Italy*

(Rome, 1988), ch. 4; and S. Negrelli and E. Santi, 'Industrial Relations in Italy', in Baglioni and Crouch, *European Industrial Relations*.

172 Martinelli and Treu, 'Employers' Associations in Italy', esp. pp. 276–9, 282–3; Sisson, *Management of Collective Bargaining*, pp. 22–7; Ministero del Lavoro, *Report '88*, ch. 4; and Negrelli and Santi, 'Industrial Relations in Italy', esp. pp. 181–3, 186–8.

173 On the cultural attitudes of French employers, see Bunel and Saglio, 'Employers' Associations in France' and *L'Action patronale*, esp. ch. 1; and for similar explanations of disunity among Italian employers, see J. La Palombara, *Interest Groups in Italian Politics* (Princeton, 1964), p. 416.

174 For the development of collective bargaining in France before 1914, see P. Stearns, 'Against the Strike Threat: Employer Policies Towards Labor Agitation in France, 1900–14', *Journal of Modern History* 40 (1968); and Sisson, *Management of Collective Bargaining*, p. 143. On the role of employer organization and collective agreements in 'local industrial systems' such as Oyonnax (plastics), Lyon (silk), and St Etienne (ribbons), see M. F. Raveyre and J. Saglio, 'Les systèmes industriels localisés: elements pour une analyse sociologique de PME industriels', *Sociologie du travail* (1984); and Sabel and Zeitlin, 'Historical Alternatives', esp. pp. 149–50, 156–60.

175 Weber, *Le Parti des patrons*, pp. 171–231; but cf. also the greater emphasis given to employer resistance in Bunel and Saglio, 'Employers' Associations in France', pp. 256–60, and *L'Action patronale*, chs 4–7.

176 M. Abrate, *La lotta sindacale nell'industrializzazione in Italia* (Turin, 1967); but cf. S. Ortaggi, 'Padronato e classe operaia a Torino negli anni 1906–1911', *Rivista di storia contemporanea* 8 (1979).

177 On the dualistic structure of the French and Italian economies, see S. Berger, 'The Traditional Sector in France and Italy', in Berger and Piore, *Dualism and Discontinuity*. For its impact on employer organization in the two countries, see, in addition to the chapter by Contini in this volume, Bunel and Saglio, 'Employers' Associations in France', pp. 251–2; and Sellier, *La Confrontation sociale*, pp. 42–52.

178 See Kolboom, *La Revanche des patrons*; Weber, *Le Parti des patrons*, pp. 107–23; and S. Berger, 'Regime and Interest Representation: The French Traditional Middle Classes', in *idem, Organizing Interests*.

179 For English-language surveys, see C. Trigilia, 'Small-firm Development and Political Subcultures in Italy', in E. Goodman and J. Bamford, with P. Saynor (eds), *Small Firms and Industrial Districts in Italy* (London 1989); and S. Brusco, 'The Emilian Model: Productive Decentralisation and Social Integration', *Cambridge Journal of Economics* 6 (1982).

180 On employers' response to the 1920 General Strike, see Sisson, *Management of Collective Bargaining*, p. 145; and on the 'missed appointments' between the CNPF and the CGT, see Weber, *Le Parti des patrons*, pp. 151–5, 239–42.

181 Segrestin, 'Recent Changes in France', esp. pp. 105, 110–12, 119; and F. Eyraud and R. Tchobanian, 'The Auroux Reforms and Company-Level Industrial Relations in France', *British Journal of Industrial Relations* 23 (1985).

182 On state intervention in strikes before 1914, see G. Friedman, 'Strike Success and Union Ideology: The United States and France, 1880–1914', *Journal of Economic History* 48 (1988); and on the role of the government in the 1920 General Strike, see C. Maier, *Recasting Bourgeois Europe: Stabilization in France, Germany and Italy in the Decade after World War I* (Princeton, 1975), pp. 154–58.

183 For a forceful statement of this view, see Sellier, *La Confrontation sociale*, esp. ch. 3.

184 J. F. Stone, *The Search for Social Peace: Reform Legislation in France, 1890–*

1914 (Albany, NY, 1985), pp. 139–57; M. Reberioux and P. Fridenson, 'Albert Thomas, pivot du reformisme francais', *Le Mouvement sociale* 87 (1974); A. Hennebicque, 'Albert Thomas et le regime des usines de guerre, 1915–17', in P. Fridenson (ed.), *1914–18: l'autre front* (Paris, 1975); A. Rossiter, 'Popular Front Economic Policy and the Matignon Negotiations', *Historical Journal* 30 (1987); *idem*, 'The Blum Government, the Conseil National Economique and Economic Policy', in M. S. Alexander and H. Graham (eds), *The French and Spanish Popular Fronts* (Cambridge, 1989); A. Prost, 'Le climat social', and J. P. Rioux, 'La conciliation et l'arbitrage obligatoire des conflits du travail', in R. Remond and J. Bourdin (eds), *Edouard Daladier, chef de gouvernement* (Paris, 1977); see B. Moss, 'La réforme de la legislation du travail sous la Ve Republique: un triomphe du modernisme', *Le Mouvement social* 148 (1989); Segrestin, 'Recent Changes in France', esp. pp. 108–11; and J. Goetschy, 'The Neo-corporatist issue in France', in Scholten, *Political Stability and Neo-corporatism*.

185 Abrate, *La lotta sindacale*.

186 For this contrast, see M. Salvati, 'May 1968 and the Hot Autumn of 1969: The Responses of Two Ruling Classes', in Berger, *Organizing Interests*.

187 In addition to Contini's chapter in this volume, see Regini, 'Social Pacts in Italy'; Ministero del Lavoro, *Report '88*, ch. 4; and Negrelli and Santi, 'Industrial Relations in Italy', esp. pp. 164–71, 182, 184–6.

188 I. Regalia, 'Non più apprendisti stregoni? sindicati e istituzioni in periferia', *Stato e mercato* 19 (1987); and Trigilia, 'Small-firm Development'.

189 For a broader development of this view, see P. Lange and M. Regini (eds), *State, Market and Social Regulation: New Perspectives on Italy* (Cambridge, 1989).

190 Sisson, *Management of Collective Bargaining*, pp. 144–6; N. Papayannis, 'Masses revolutionnaires et directions reformistes: les tensions au cours des grèves des metallurgistes français en 1919' and B. Abhervé, 'Les origines de la grève des métallurgistes parisiens, juin 1919', both in *Le Mouvement social* 93 (1975).

191 J. Jackson, *The Popular Front in France: Defending Democracy 1934–38* (Cambridge, 1988), pp. 73–112, 264–8; Rossiter, 'Popular Front Economic Policy' and 'Blum Government'; and Kolboom, *La Revanche des patrons*.

192 G. Ross, *Workers and Communists in France: From Popular Front to Eurocommunism* (Berkeley, 1982); and P. Lange, G. Ross and M. Vannicelli, *Unions, Change and Crisis: French and Italian Union Strategy and the Political Economy, 1945–80* (London, 1982), pt I.

193 Moss, 'La réforme de la legislation du travail', p. 76–7; Weber, *Le Parti des patrons*, pp. 222–7, 237–42, 344–57; and Segrestin, 'Recent Changes in France', pp. 107–10.

194 Segrestin, 'Recent Changes in France'; Moss, 'La réforme de la legislation du travail', pp. 85–91; and Eyraud and Tchobanian, 'Auroux Reforms'.

195 Abrate, *La lotta sindacale*; and M. Clark, *Antonio Gramsci and the Revolution that Failed* (New Haven, 1977).

196 Lange *et al.*, *Unions, Change and Crisis*, pp. 100–17; and B. Salvati, 'The Rebirth of Italian Trade Unionism', in S. J. Woolf (ed.), *The Rebirth of Italy, 1943–50* (London, 1972).

197 See, in addition to the chapter by Contini in this volume, Lange *et al.*, *Unions, Change and Crisis*, pp. 117–41; and I. Regalia, M. Regini and E. Reyneri, 'Labour Conflicts and Industrial Relations in Italy', in C. Crouch and A. Pizzorno (eds), *The Resurgence of Class Conflict in Western Europe since 1968*, vol. I (London, 1978).

198 Regini, 'Social Pacts in Italy'; M. Golden, *Labor Divided: Austerity and*

Working-Class Politics in Contemporary Italy (Ithaca, NY, 1988); and Negrelli and Santi, 'Industrial Relations in Italy', pp. 164–71.

199 Negrelli and Santi, 'Industrial Relations in Italy', esp. pp. 175–179; and M. Regini and C. F. Sabel (eds), *Strategie di riaggustimento industriale* (Bologna, 1989).

200 For an overview of American employers' associations, see M. Derber, 'Employers' Associations in the United States', in Windmuller and Gladstone, *Employers' Associations*; for a survey of bargaining structure in American industry, see T. A. Kochan and H. C. Katz, *Collective Bargaining and Industrial Relations* (2nd edn, Homewood, Ill. 1988), ch. 5; and on the non-union sector, see Kochan *et al.*, *Transformation of American Industrial Relations*, ch. 3.

201 Kochan and Katz, *Collective Bargaining*, esp. p. 122; Derber, 'Employers' Associations in the United States', esp. p. 83; and G. G. Somers (ed.), *Collective Bargaining: Contemporary American Experience* (Madison, 1980), chs 1–3.

202 Kochan and Katz, *Collective Bargaining*, pp. 136–40; C. Bourdon, 'Pattern Bargaining, Wage Determination, and Inflation: Some Preliminary Observations on the 1976–78 Wage Round', in M. J. Piore (ed.), *Unemployment and Inflation* (White Plains, NY, 1979); Somers, *Collective Bargaining*, chs 4–5, 7; D. B. Lipsky and C. B. Donn, *Collective Bargaining in American Industry* (Lexington, Mass., 1987), chs 2–6. For the Steel Companies Coordinating Committee, see J. Stieber, 'Steel', in Somers, *Collective Bargaining*, pp. 164–75; and J. P. Hoerr, *And the Wolf Finally Came: The Decline of the American Steel Industry* (Pittsburgh, 1988), esp. pp. 229–35, 474–6; for the airlines' Mutual Aid Plan, see P. Capelli, 'Airlines', in Lipsky and Donn, *Collective Bargaining*, pp. 140, 152–3.

203 On the decline of pattern and multi-employer bargaining during the 1980s, see Kochan *et al.*, *Transformation of American Industrial Relations*, ch. 5. But for evidence of the continuing resilience of industry patterns, see the case studies of automobiles, agricultural machinery, tyres, telecommunications and airlines in Lipsky and Donn, *Collective Bargaining*; and for the emergence of new employers' associations in non-union construction, see D. Q. Mills, 'Construction', in Somers, *Collective Bargaining*, pp. 49–50, 89–91.

204 For general surveys, see S. B. Levine, 'Employers' Associations in Japan', in Windmuller and Gladstone, *Employers' Associations*; and K. Kōshiro, 'Development of Collective Bargaining in Postwar Japan', in Shirai, *Industrial Relations in Contemporary Japan*. For more detailed discussions of *shuntō*, see H. Shimada, 'Wage Determination and Information Sharing: An Alternative Approach to Incomes Policy?', *Journal of Industrial Relations* 25 (1983); I. Kume, 'Changing Relations among the Government, Labor, and Business in Japan after the Oil Crisis', *International Organization* 42 (1988); Dore, *Flexible Rigidities*, pp. 101–7; and *idem, Taking Japan Seriously*, ch. 4.

205 Jacoby, 'American Exceptionalism'; and cf. the discussion in H. Harris, 'Getting it Together: The Metal Manufacturers' Association of Philadelphia, c. 1900–1930', in Jacoby, *Masters to Managers*.

206 For these views, see Dore, *British Factory–Japanese Factory*, ch. 14; *Flexible Rigidities*, pp. 101–7, 129–31; and *Taking Japan Seriously*, ch. 4.

207 Kume, 'Changing Relations', pp. 666–7. For similar breaches of solidarity in the steel industry during the 1950s and 60s, see S. Yonekura, 'The Long and Winding Road of the Postwar Japanese Iron and Steel Industry', in E. Abe and Y. Suzuki (eds), *Changing Patterns of International Rivalry: Some Lessons from the Steel Industry* (Tokyo, 1991).

208 For these arguments, see Sisson, *Management of Collective Bargaining*, ch. 7; L. Ulman, 'Competitive and Connective Bargaining', *Scottish Journal of*

Political Economy 21 (1974); J. Haydu, 'Employers, Unions, and American Exceptionalism: Pre-World War I Open Shops in the Machine Trades in Comparative Perspective', *International Review of Social History* 33 (1988); Levine, 'Employers' Associations in Japan'; Kōshiro, 'Collective Bargaining in Japan'; Kochan and Katz, *Collective Bargaining*, ch. 4; and Kochan *et al.*, *Transformation of American Industrial Relations*, ch. 5.

209 H. J. Harris, *The Right to Manage: Industrial Relations Policies of American Business in the 1940s* (Madison, 1982), esp. ch. 5; Tolliday and Zeitlin, 'Shop-Floor Bargaining', and N. Lichtenstein, 'Reutherism on the Shop Floor: Union Strategy and Shop-Floor Conflict in the USA, 1946–70', in Tolliday and Zeitlin, *Automobile Industry*; Schatz, *Electrical Workers*, ch. 9; J. Kuhn, 'Electrical Products', in Somers, *Collective Bargaining*; W. E. Hendricks, 'Telecommunications', in Lipsky and Donn, *Collective Bargaining*; and M. Koch, D. Lewin and D. Sockell, 'The Determinants of Bargaining Structure: A Case Study of AT&T', in *Advances in Industrial and Labor Relations*, vol. 4 (Greenwich, Conn., 1987).

210 For an overview, see Kochan *et al.*, *Transformation of American Industrial Relations*.

211 Garon, *State and Labor in Modern Japan*, pp. 45–7, 165–72.

212 On employer resistance to labour legislation and the formation of *Zensanren*, see ibid., pp. 182, 191–2, 198, 203–4; and A. Gordon, 'Business and the Corporate State: The Business Lobby and Bureaucrats on Labor, 1911–41', in W. D. Wray (ed.), *Managing Industrial Enterprise: Case Studies from Japan's Pre-war Experience* (Cambridge, Mass., 1989). On employers' associations and the struggle for collective self-regulation after the Meiji liberalization, see M. Miyamoto, 'The Development of Business Associations in Prewar Japan', and T. Fujita, 'Local Trade Associations in Prewar Japan', in Yamazaki and Miyamoto, *Trade Associations*.

213 Gordon, *Labor Relations in Japan*, ch. 10; Cusumano, *Japanese Automobile Industry*, ch. 3; and Okayama, 'Japanese Automobile Industry'.

214 Kōshiro, 'Collective Bargaining in Postwar Japan', pp. 222–6.

215 Derber, 'Employers' Association in the United States', pp. 101–2; D. Ernst, 'The Labor Exemption, 1908–14', *Iowa Law Review* 74 (1989); and *idem*, 'The Danbury Hatters Case, 1903–1917' (unpublished paper presented to the conference 'Perspectives on American Labor History: The Wisconsin School and Beyond', Madison, 9–10 Mar. 1990).

216 For the influence of public policy on the development of bargaining structures since the 1930s, see Kochan and Katz, *Collective Bargaining*, pp. 125–7; Harris, 'Snares of Liberalism?'; Tomlins, *The State and the Unions*, pts II–III; and Piore and Sabel, *Second Industrial Divide*, pp. 120–4. On the role of regulation and deregulation, see Capelli, 'Airlines'; H. M. Levinson, 'Trucking'; Hendricks, 'Telecommunications'; and Koch *et al.* 'Determinants of Bargaining Structure'.

217 Garon, *State and Labor in Modern Japan*; and Gordon, *Labor Relations in Japan*, chs 6–8; *idem*, 'Business and the Corporate State'; W. M. Fletcher III, *The Japanese Business Community and National Trade Policy, 1920–42* (Chapel Hill, NC, 1989), ch. 5.

218 On SCAP and the 'reverse course', see Garon, *State and Labor in Modern Japan*, pp. 235–42; Gordon, *Labor Relations in Japan*, chs 9–10; and Moore, *Japanese Workers and the Struggle for Power*. On the longer-term influence of the postwar legislation on Japanese industrial relations, see T. A. Hanami, 'The Function of the Law in Japanese Industrial Relations', in Shirai, *Industrial Relations in Contemporary Japan*; and W. B. Gould IV, *Japan's Reshaping of American Labour Law* (Cambridge, Mass., 1988).

219 For contrasting views of the relationship between the Japanese state and

business associations, see C. Johnson, *MITI and the Japanese Miracle* (Palo Alto, Calif., 1982); R. J. Samuels, *The Business of the Japanese State* (Ithaca, NY, 1987); Friedman, *Misunderstood Miracle*; and Dore, *Flexible Rigidities*, chs 6–9.

220 Kume, 'Changing Relations'; Shimada, 'Wage Determination'; and Dore, *Flexible Rigidities*, pp. 101–7, and *Taking Japan Seriously*, ch. 4.

221 For these cases, see the articles on Lewis, Hillman and Hoffa in M. Dubofsky and W. Van Tine (eds), *Labor Leaders in America* (Urbana, Ill., 1987); W. H. Miernyk, 'Coal', in Somers, *Collective Bargaining*; J. T. Carpenter, *Competition and Collective Bargaining in the Needle Trades, 1911–1967* (Ithaca, NY, 1972); and Levinson, 'Trucking'.

222 Tolliday and Zeitlin, 'Shop-Floor Bargaining'; Schatz, *Electrical Workers*, chs 5–6; Lichtenstein, 'Reutherism on the Shop Floor'; R. L. Seeber, 'Agricultural Machinery', in Lipsky and Donn, *Collective Bargaining*; Hendricks, 'Telecommunications'; and Koch *et al.,* 'Determinants of Bargaining Structure'.

223 Hoerr, *And the Wolf Finally Came*, esp. ch. 18; Capelli, 'Airlines'; Hendricks, 'Telecommunications'; and Koch *et al.,* 'Determinants of Bargaining Structure'.

224 Garon, *State and Labor in Modern Japan*; T. Shirai, 'Japanese Labor Unions and Politics', in *idem, Industrial Relations in Contemporary Japan*; and T. J. Pempel and K. Tsunekawa, 'Corporatism without Labor? The Japanese Anomaly', in P. C. Schmitter and G. Lehmbruch (eds), *Trends Toward Corporatist Intermediation* (London, 1979).

225 Gordon, *Labor Relations in Japan*, esp. ch. 9; Kōchiro, 'Collective Bargaining in Postwar Japan', pp. 210–11, 217–18; and E. Daito, 'Seniority Wages and Labour-Management: Japanese Employers' Wage Policy', in Shigeyoshi and Bergmann, *Industrial Relations in Transition*.

226 Kōshiro, 'Collective Bargaining in Postwar Japan', pp. 215, 219–22; Shimada, 'Wage Determination'; Kume, 'Changing Relations'; and Gordon, *State and Labor in Modern Japan*, pp. 242–8.

Index

Abraham, David 18
Abrate, M. 208
Adenauer, Konrad 193–4, 196, 197, 306
'After Japan' programme 101, 102
Aglietta, M. 235
Agnelli, Gianni 214, 216, 217, 218, 219, 220, 221, 224
Agnelli, Giovanni 204, 206
Agnelli, Umberto 217
Ahlener Programm 189
Alfa Romeo 208, 217, 219
Allgemeine Elektricitäts Gesellschaft (AEG) 150, 151, 152, 157, 166, 289
Amalgamated Engineering Federation (AEF) 97, 98
Amalgamated Engineering Union (AEU) 67, 68, 69, 70, 71, 72, 73, 76, 84, 85, 90, 301, 302
Amalgamated Society of Engineers (ASE) 54, 55, 56, 57, 58, 59, 60, 61, 62, 64, 65, 66, 68, 76, 267
Amalgamated Union of Engineering Workers (AUEW) 98, 99
American Federation of Labor (AFL) 83, 118, 133, 142
American Foundrymen's Association 118
American Telegraph & Telephone (AT&T) 319, 322
'Americanization' 91, 176, 177
apprenticeship, *see* trade unions
Arbeitgeberverband für rheinisch-westfalische Eisen- und Metallindustrie (Employers' Association for the Iron and Metal Industry of North Rhine-Westphalia) 188, 190
Arbeitgemeinschaft Eisen und Metal (Working Group of the Iron and Metal Industry) 190

Arbeitnordwest 185
arbitration and conciliation 66, 75, 120, 186, 305, 306
Armstrong, William 54, 55
Armstrong-Whitworth 63
Arthur, Brian 17
Assolombarda (Association of the Industrialists of Lombardy) 210, 310
Auroux Laws 313, 315
Austin 82
Austin Rover 106, 107, 108
Autobianchi 219
automation, *see* technology

Baden-Württemberg 291
Baldwin Locomotive 125, 126
Barnes, George 59, 60
Beckett, Terence 98
Berg, Fritz 193, 194, 197
Bergmann 150, 152, 157
Berlin 148, 150, 151, 152, 153, 154, 155, 157, 158, 159, 160, 161, 162, 163, 164, 165, 166, 167, 168, 169, 178, 182
Bessant, J. 238, 250
Bethlehem Steel 317
Betriebsfrieden 191
Betriebsgemeinschaft 170, 192
Beutler, Wilhelm 190, 191, 198, 199
Bevin, Ernest 179
Beynon, Hugh 91, 92, 98
Birmingham 63, 72
blacklists 45, 55, 63, 66, 71, 128, 130, 131, 155, 157, 297, 303, 307
Blakeman, Leslie 89, 97
Blum, Leon 313
Board of Trade 56, 60, 61, 300
Boddy, D. 234
Boilermaker's Society 36, 37, 39, 46
Bonnett, C. 141
Borsig 150, 152, 157, 159, 289

Bosch, Robert 291
Braverman, H. 7, 8
Briggs Bodies 88, 89, 93
British Aerospace 246
British Employers' Confederation
  (BEC) 261
British Leyland (BL) 13, 95, 105, 106,
  107, 108, 284
British Leyland Motor Corporation
  (BLMC) 87, 95
British Motor Corporation (BMC) 86,
  87, 95, 108
British Steel 13, 284
Brizay, B. 257
Browne, Benjamin 56
Brownlie, J. T. 68
Buchanan, D. 234, 236, 248, 251
*Bundesverband der Deutschen
  Industrie* (BDI) Federation of
  German Industries 190, 192, 193, 194,
  195, 196, 197
*Bundesvereinigung der Deutschen
  Arbeitgeberverbände* (BDA)
  Confederation of German Employers'
  Organizations 192, 193, 197, 303, 306
Burawoy, Michael 9
Burlington Mills 316

Cadburys 138, 281
Caldwell, Philip 104
Cameron, Lord 88
Cammell-Laird 67
Carron, William 89
Catholics 207, 209, 210, 213, 215, 216,
  218, 219, 312, 314, 315
Cefis, Eugenio 211, 216, 218
Chandler, Alfred 4, 5, 6, 13, 156, 269,
  288
Channon, D. 283
Child, J. 273
Christlich-Demokratische Union
  (CDU) 189, 192, 193, 194, 197
Citrine, Walter 84, 85
Clegg, H. 259, 260, 261
closed shop 66, 99, 320
Clydeside 37, 38, 39, 40, 43, 55, 59, 61,
  63, 64, 65, 68, 72
Co-Determination Act (1976) (Sweden)
  307
co-determination, *see* trade unions
Cold War 182, 294, 314, 321
Collective Agreements Act (1928) 266,
  268
Communist Party 84, 85, 89, 107, 155,

178, 180, 181, 182, 183, 189, 193, 207,
  208, 212, 219, 221, 224, 312, 314, 315,
  322
Computer-Aided Design (CAD)/
  Computer-Aided Manufacturing
  (CAM) 237, 244, 246, 247, 248, 249,
  284
Computer-Integrated Manufacturing
  (CIM) 237, 238, 243, 246
Computer Numerical Control (CNC)
  237, 247, 250
Conagricoltura 211
Confapi 207
Confcommercio 211
Confederation of British Industry (CBI)
  261, 297, 301
*Confédération Français Democratique
  du Travail* (CFDT) French
  Democratic Confederation of Labour
  312, 314, 315
*Confédération Générale de la
  Production Français* (CGPF)
  General Confederation of French
  Production 308, 311
*Confédération Générale des Petites et
  Moyennes Entreprises* (CGPME)
  General Confederation of Small and
  Medium Enterprises 311
Confédération Générale du Travail
  (CGT) General Confederation of
  Labour 314, 315
*Confédération National du Patronat
  Français* (CNPF) National
  Confederation of French Employers
  308, 309, 310, 311, 314
*Confederazione Generale dell'Industria
  Italiana* (*Confindustria*) General
  Confederation of Italian Industry
  204–25, 309, 311, 312, 313, 315, 316
*Confederazione Generale Italiana del
  Lavoro* (CGIL) General
  Confederation of Italian Labour 221,
  315
*Confederazione Italiana dei Sindacati
  Lavoratori* (CISL) Italian
  Confederation of Workers' Unions
  315
*Confederazione Italiana dei Sindacati
  Lavoratori* (CISL) 209, 213, 214, 221
Congress of Industrial Organizations
  (CIO) 83
Conservative government 246, 284, 301
contingency theory, *see* theories of the
  firm

Contini, G. 309, 311, 312, 313, 316
Control Commission for Germany/
  British Element (CCG/BE) 177, 178,
  179, 180, 183, 188, 195, 196
Costa, Angelo 207, 208, 209, 210, 221
Coventry 71, 72, 73
Coventry Association 63, 71, 73
craft production, *see* technology
Craxi, Benito 220, 221
Cyert, R. 12

Dagenham (works) 82, 83, 84, 87, 88,
  90, 91, 93, 96, 100
Delors, J. 313
demarcation, *see* trade unions
Democrazia Cristiana (DC) Christian
  Democratic Party 207, 208, 209, 210,
  211, 212, 213, 214, 215, 216, 218, 219,
  222, 223, 224, 313
Democrazia Proletaria 221
Denmark 304
Denny, William 40
Department of Employment and
  Productivity 97
Department of Industry 247
Department of Labor and Industry 133,
  142
Department of Labor Conciliation
  Service 134
Department of Trade and Industry 251
Detroit 82, 83, 91
Deutsch Gewerkschaftsbund (DGB)
  German Trade Union Federation
  178, 193, 197
Deutsche Arbeitsfront (DAF) 178, 186,
  187
Deutsche Kohlenbergbauleitung
  (DKBL) 194, 195, 196
Deutscher Metallarbeiter-Verband
  (German Union of Metalworkers)
  155
Dinkelbach, C. 187
direct control, *see* theories of the firm
Dōmei (Japan Confederation of Labor)
  322
Donovan Commission 97, 298, 301
Dore, R. 274, 277, 293
DuPont 282, 316
Durcan, J. 94
Dyer, Colonel 55, 268, 269

Edison 210, 211
Edwardes, Michael 105, 106, 107
Edwards, Paul 8, 9, 10

Eight-hour day 55, 56, 135
Einaudi, Luigi 207, 208
Emilia-Romagna 311, 314
Employee Involvement (EI) 102, 104
Employers Associations: *see also* under
  individual associations; cohesion of
  2, 19–22, 36–40, 46–7, 52–3, 54–7,
  58–9, 60, 61, 62, 63–8, 70–6, 117–18,
  122–5, 132–4, 157, 158, 159, 162, 163,
  165, 169, 186, 187, 189–90, 193, 194–
  9, 208, 211–12, 214–22, 257, 261–3,
  265–7, 269, 276, 297–302, 302–8, 308–
  23; future of 323–4; lock-outs 38, 52,
  53, 54, 55, 56, 57, 58, 59, 60, 61, 62,
  64, 67, 69, 70, 72, 73, 120, 126, 155,
  174, 213, 268, 269, 285, 299, 301, 302,
  303, 305, 306, 307, 312; political
  activities 20, 22, 38, 40, 47–8, 53, 61,
  63–6, 67, 75, 76, 125, 134, 170, 171,
  177, 189, 192, 193, 194–9, 204, 205,
  206, 207, 266–7, 300–1, 302, 305, 306,
  307, 312–15, 320–1, 322; regional 36–
  7, 38, 53, 54, 55, 56, 59, 60, 62, 63,
  64, 65, 66, 67–8, 71, 72, 73, 74, 75,
  117–43, 155, 157, 158, 176–99, 206–7,
  222, 261, 264, 296, 297, 303, 308–10,
  315–16; sectoral 36–7, 52, 53, 54, 55,
  56, 59, 60, 62, 64, 65, 66, 70, 71, 72,
  73, 74, 117–18, 155, 185, 206–7, 222,
  257, 261, 262, 264, 297, 299, 300, 301,
  303, 308–10, 315–16, 371, 321–2;
  theories of 19–22, 117, 140–3, 259–61,
  269–70, 274–8, 323–4
Employment Act of 1980 302
engineering industry 22, 52–76, 84, 268,
  297, 298, 299, 300, 301, 302, 305
Engineering Employers' Federation
  (EEF) 39, 52, 53, 55, 56, 57, 58, 59,
  60, 61, 62, 63, 64, 65, 66, 67, 68, 69,
  70, 71, 72, 73, 74, 75, 76, 84, 268,
  297, 298, 299, 300, 301, 302, 305
Ente Nazionale Idrocarburi (ENI) 210,
  211, 212, 216, 218
Erdmann, Gerhard 192, 193
European Coal and Steel Community
  198, 208
European Monetary System 220

*Facharbeiter mit höchstwertiger
  Leistung* 153
Fanfani, Amintore 210, 216
fascism 178, 188, 204, 205, 206, 207,
  209, 315
Feather, Vic 84, 85

Federal Republic of Germany (FRG),
  see Germany
Federation of British Industry (FBI)
  297, 301
*Federazione Italiana degli Operai
  Metallurgici* (FIOM) Federation of
  Italian Metalworkers 315
Federmeccanica 222, 310
Ferruzzi 218
Fiat (*Fabbrica Italiana Automobili
  Torino* – Italian Automobile Works
  of Turin) 204, 205, 206, 208, 210,
  212, 213, 214, 216, 217, 218, 219, 220,
  221, 223, 224, 309, 316
First World War 36, 37, 41, 43, 44, 45,
  53, 57, 58, 62–7, 75, 76, 133, 134, 148,
  149, 152, 155, 156, 185, 186, 264, 265,
  283, 285, 286, 289, 298, 300, 302, 306,
  312, 313, 314
Flanders, Allan 97, 259
flexibility and flexible specialization,
  see technology
Flexible Manufacturing System (FMS)
  237, 238, 239, 240, 241, 242, 244, 245,
  246, 247, 248, 249, 250, 251, 284, 292,
  323
Flour Milling Employers' Federation 300
Ford, Henry 287
Ford Motor Company 11, 81–114, 149,
  169, 191, 205, 219, 262, 284, 300, 301,
  302, 319, 322
Fordism 81, 82, 101, 149, 150, 206, 235,
  236, 237, 238, 239, 241, 242, 246, 247,
  251, 252
Foreman's Mutual Benefit Society 44
Foundrymen's Club 118, 123
Fox, Alan 48, 263
France 256, 257, 258, 264, 265, 266,
  274, 275, 276, 277, 278, 293, 297, 300,
  308, 309, 310, 311, 312, 313, 314, 315,
  316, 319, 322, 323
Freeman, C. 245
Frei Demokratische Partei (FDP) 192
Friedman, Andrew 7, 8, 9, 233, 234
Friedman, Henry 99
Friedman, Milton 3, 4
Friedmann, Wolfgang 178, 179
Fujitsu Fanuc 243

Gantt, H. 169
General and Municipal Workers Union
  (GMWU) 90
General Electric Company (GE) 59,
  127, 136, 139, 316, 319

General Motors 319
George, Lloyd 60, 63, 67, 76, 300
German National Board for Efficiency
  Engineering 167, 168
Germany, 2, 13, 14, 105, 147, 148, 149,
  150, 156, 163, 170, 171 (147–171)
  (175–199), 256, 257, 258, 263, 264,
  265, 266, 274, 275, 276, 278, 280, 283,
  289, 291, 292, 295, 296, 300, 301, 302,
  303, 304, 305, 306, 307, 308, 311, 312,
  316, 319, 322
Geyer, Michael 147
Ghidella, Vittorio 220
Gilbreth, F. 160
Goodyear 316
Gordon, D. 8
Gospel, Howard 20
Gourevitch, P. 18
Great Britain 11, 13, 14, 36, 48, 52, 53,
  82, 98, 108, 180, 224, 231, 232, 234,
  237, 240, 245, 250, 251, 256, 257, 258,
  259, 261, 262, 263, 264, 265, 266, 267,
  268, 274, 276, 278, 279, 280, 281, 282,
  283, 286, 287, 288, 289, 290, 291, 294,
  296, 298, 300, 301, 303, 304, 305, 306,
  307, 308, 310, 311, 312, 316, 318, 319,
  321, 322, 323
Grenelle Accords 312
Grumman Aircraft 316
Guttehoffnungshütte (GHH) 190, 192,
  193, 196, 289

Halewood 87, 90, 91, 92, 93, 99, 100,
  103, 104
Harris, Howell 75, 278, 288, 318, 319,
  321
Harris-Burland 180, 184
Hayden, Bill 101, 102
Haydu, J. 142, 143
Hegner, Kurt 160, 161, 162, 164, 165
Henderson, A. P. 59
Henle, Gunter 194, 197
High Commission for Germany 194–5
Hill, John 42, 43
Hillman, Sidney 322
Hitler, A. 170
hochqualifizierte Facharbeiten 153
Hoesch 195
Hoffa, Jimmy 322
Homburg, H. 278, 289, 303, 304
Hunter, G. V. 38
Hyman, Richard 11
Hyogikai (Japan Council of Labour
  Unions) 322

IBM 316
IG Metall (Metalworkers' Union) 196, 262, 307
Imperial Chemical Industries (ICI) 281, 282
Imperial Tobacco 281
In Place of Strife 97
Industrial Relations Act (1971) 97, 109, 267
Industrial Revolution 147
Istituto per la Ricostruzione Industriale (IRI) 209, 214, 218, 219, 222
International Association of Machinists (IAM) 121, 122, 125, 126, 134
International Harvester 117, 319, 322
International Labour Office 206
International Metalworkers' Federation–Japan Council (IMF–JC) 322
Intersind 211, 213, 215
Iron Molders' Union (IMU) 118, 119, 120, 121, 122, 125, 126, 128, 132, 134
Iron Trade Employers' Association (ITEA) 54, 55, 56
Italy 2, 204–27, 256, 257, 258, 264, 265, 266, 297, 300, 308, 309, 310, 311, 312, 313, 315, 316, 319, 322, 323

Japan 2, 10, 13, 14, 22, 100, 101, 102, 232, 237, 240, 243, 245, 256, 257, 263, 264, 265, 266, 274, 278, 283, 292, 293, 294, 295, 316, 317, 318, 319, 320, 322, 323
Japan Industrial Club 320
Jarres, Karl 187
Joint Negotiating Committee (JNC) 84, 85
Joint Works Committee (JWC) 85, 87
Jones, Bryn 11, 97, 98, 242, 284, 287, 292, 323
Junkers 291

Kahn-Freund, O. 259, 262, 263
Kelly, John 10, 11
Kerr, Clark 273
Keynesian 207
Klöckner Trust 187, 194, 195
Knights of Labor 266
Kochan, T. 242
Koike, K. 293, 296
Kommunistische Partei Deutschlands (KPD) 182
Kost, Heinrich 194, 197

Labor Bureau (Philadelphia) 126, 127, 128, 129, 130, 131, 132, 134, 135, 138, 139
Laboratoire d'Economie et Sociologie du Travail (LEST) 274, 275, 276, 277, 290
Labour Government 93, 96, 97, 107, 181, 247, 284, 301
Lamoreaux, N. 13, 14
Lancashire 54, 60, 66, 73
Lancia 219
Landsorganisationen i Sverige (LO) Swedish Confederation of Labour 302, 305, 307
Landtag 189
Lazonick, William 5
legal regulation 64, 74, 75, 88, 93, 94, 97, 109, 133, 137, 142, 180, 181, 185–6, 187, 188, 190, 191, 192, 193, 194–8, 258, 259–61, 262–3, 266, 267, 268, 280, 287, 290, 294, 301, 302, 305, 306, 312, 313, 315, 320, 321
Lehr, Robert 187, 194
Lewchuk, Wayne 81, 108
Lewis, John L. 322
Liberal Party 61, 210
Lithgow, James 40
lock-outs, *see* Employers' Associations
London 54, 56, 84, 178, 181, 183, 282
London and North Western railway 281
London Business School 13
Lorenz, Edward 41
Lovell, John 36
Lucchini, Luigi 221
Luce, W. R. 181
Ludwig Loewe & Co. 150, 152, 157, 160, 166

M-Form corporation 4, 13
machine manning, *see* trade unions
Management Information Systems 232, 239
managerial prerogatives 38, 46, 52, 53, 55, 56–7, 58–9, 61, 62, 64, 66, 68, 69, 73, 74, 75, 76, 82, 86, 89, 90, 91, 94, 97, 100, 103, 106, 107, 121, 149, 155, 159, 162, 165, 169, 170, 213, 243, 256, 260, 267, 284, 297, 298
Manchester 56, 73, 82
Mannesman 195, 289
March, J. 12
Marglin, S. 8
Marsden, D. 94
Marshall Plan 182

Marxism 3, 6, 7, 8, 9, 10, 11, 14, 18, 19, 20, 48, 147, 235, 236
Mason, Tim 147
mass production, *see* technology
Matignon Agreement 312
Mattei, Enrico 210, 211, 212
Maurice, Marc 274, 276
Mazda 102
McKinlay, Alan 39
McKinsey and Co. 285
Measured Day Work (MDW) 95, 96, 105
Mediobanca 218, 219
Meiji 320
Melling, Joseph 43
Meredeen, S. 96
Merloni, Vittorio 221
Metal Manufacturers' Association of Philadelphia (MMA) 117–43
Millerand, J. 313
Ministro per la Costituente (Economic Commission of the Ministry for the Promulgation of the Constitution) 208
Ministry of Aircraft Production (MAP) 83
Ministry of International Trade and Industry (MITI) 321
Ministry of Labour 85, 88, 89, 93, 94, 96, 109, 300
Ministry of Munitions 63, 64, 65
Mitterand, F. 313, 315
Mobil Oil 316
Moede, Walter 166, 167
Mond–Turner talks 301
Montanmitbestimmung (Parity Co-determination Law) 179, 180, 181, 183, 184, 189, 190, 192–89, 208
Montecatini 211
Montedison 211, 215, 216, 218, 219, 224
Moore, Les 99
Mosse, George L. 147
Motor Industry Joint Council 93
Mundella 300
Mussolini 204, 205

National Association of Manufacturers (NAM) 121
National Board of Industrial Standards 158
National Cash Register 117
National Civic Federation 142
National Coal Board 13, 284
National Committee for Time Studies

and Time Rate Setting 158, 163, 164
National Confederation of Employers' Organizations (NCEO) 67, 75, 268, 297, 301
National Economic Development Council 301
National Economic Development Office 247
National Federation of Engineering and Shipbuilding Employers 55
National Founders Association (NFA) 118, 119, 120, 121, 122, 126, 132, 134, 321
National Industrial Conference 301
National Joint Negotiating Committee (NJNC) 84, 85, 87, 88, 89, 90, 93, 96, 97, 98, 99, 105
National Labor Relations Board (NLRB) 83
National Metal Trades Association (NMTA) 121, 122, 127, 134, 140, 321
National Socialist 147, 170, 171, 178, 186, 189, 192, 198, 295
National War Labor Board (NWLB) 134, 136, 320
Nazi, *see* National Socialist
neo-classical economics 3, 13, *see also*, theories of the firm
New Deal 140, 287, 320
New York Agreement 120, 121
Nikkeiren (Japan Federation of Employers' Associations) 257, 317, 318, 320, 321
Noble, D. 233
Nord-westliche Gruppe des Vereins Deutscher Eisen- und Stahlindustrieller (Northwestern Group of the Association of the Iron and Steel Industrialists – VdESI) 184–5
North Rhine-Westphalia 193, 194, 197, 262
numerical control (NC) 232, 234, 237

Offe, C. 19, 20, 22, 270
Olivetti 213, 214
Olson, Mancur 18, 19, 270
open shop 54, 57, 82, 117–43, 266, 288, 318, 319
Osram 166, 167
Overtime and Night Shift Agreement (Sept. 1920) 68, 71, 72

Palloix, C. 235

Partito Communista Italiana (PCI) 212, 219
peace obligation 258, 262, 268
Pennsylvania (Commonwealth of) 122, 127, 133
Pennsylvania Manufacturers' Association (PMA) 133
Perry, Percival 83
personnel management 91, 92, 108, 136, 137, 139, 156, 157, 159, 167, 169, 195, 196, 198, 199, 238, 239, 286, 287, 299
Pfahler, William 119
Philadelphia 75, 117, 118, 119, 120, 121, 122, 123, 125, 126, 127, 128, 129, 130, 131, 132, 133, 134, 135, 136, 137, 139, 140, 141, 142, 288, 318
Pininfarina, Sergio 221
Pirelli 212, 216, 217, 218, 219, 224
Plumpe, W. 278, 289, 290, 303, 304, 306
Polaroid 316
Pollock, David 41, 42
Popular Front 308, 314
Premium Bonus System 44
procedural agreements, *see* trade unions
Proctor & Gamble 316
Provisions for Avoiding Disputes 268
Prussia 291

Quaker 137, 138, 139, 282
Quality Circles 104
Quality of Work Life 142

Ramsey, Bob 98
rationalization 93, 101, 158, 159, 168, 169, 289
Raymond, Walter 192, 193
Reichswirtschaftsrat (Reich Economic Council) 189, 191
Reid, A. 279, 281, 297
Reusch, Hermann 192, 194, 196, 197
Rheinisch-Westfälisches Kohlensyndikat (RWKS) Rhenish-Westphalian Coal Syndicate 185
Rolls Royce 246
Roots, Paul 98
Rossoni, Edmondo 204
Rowntrees 138, 281
Ruhr 176, 180, 188, 189, 190, 194, 195, 198, 291, 303, 304, 306

Sabel, C. 239, 244
Salewski, Wilhelm 190, 191, 198, 199
Saltsjöbaden 'Basic Agreement' 305, 307

Salvemini, Gaetano 204, 205
Sambetsu (Japanese Congress of Industrial Organizations) 322
Sapelli, G. 205
Scanlon, H. 97, 98
Schmitter, P. 20, 21
Schlesinger, Georg 166
Schmoller, Gustav 148, 149, 150, 169
Schuckert and Co. 152
Schumacher, Kurt 182
Schuman Plan 194, 195, 196, 197, 208, 304
scientific management 58, 72, 95, 96, 130, 149, 157, 160–5, 165–9, 288, 295
Scott, Joe 87
Scott, P. J. 236, 237, 238, 239, 250
Second World War 41, 52, 73, 83, 176, 177, 198, 235, 261, 264, 279, 281, 283, 285, 290, 295, 298, 299, 304, 305, 320, 321
SED (*Socialistiche Einheitspartei Deutschlands*) 182
Sellier, M. 257
Senker, P. 248
shipbuilding 35–49
Shipbuilding Employer's Federation (SEF) 36, 37, 61, 62, 66, 67
shop stewards 66, 67, 72, 73, 83, 84, 85, 88, 89, 90–109, 239, 268, 284, 287, 301, 302
Shop Representatives 85, 88
shuntō 257, 317, 320, 321, 322
Siemens 150, 151, 152, 153, 155, 156, 157, 158, 159, 166, 167, 169, 170, 289
Sisson, Keith 231, 278, 316
skill and skilled workers, *see* technology
Smith, Adam 140
Smith, Allan 60, 62, 64, 65, 66, 67, 68, 69, 71, 73, 76
Smith, Rowland 84
Socialist Party (Italy) 214, 219, 223, 224
Socialists 207, 208, 212, 213, 219, 220, 221, 222, 314, 322
Società Italiana dell'Automobile (SIDA) 213
Sōdōmei (Japan General Federation of Labor) 322
Sōhyō (General Council of Japanese Trade Unions) 322
Soviet Union 177, 180, 182
Sozialdemokratische Partei Deutschlands (SPD) 180, 181, 182, 183, 192, 193, 307
Stahltreuhändervereinigung (Union of

Steel Trustees) 195, 196
standardization, *see* technology
Statuto dei diritti dei lavoratori
  (Charter of Workers' Rights) 313
Stinnes–Legien Agreement (1918) 185,
  192, 306
Storey, John 10
Stove Founders' National Defense
  Association 119
Streeck, W. 20, 21, 95
strikes, *see* trade unions
Supreme Commander for the Allied
  Powers (SCAP) 266, 321
Svenska Arbetsgivareföreningen (SAF)
  Swedish Employers' Confederation
  268, 302, 304, 305, 307
Sweden 22, 256, 257, 258, 263, 264, 266,
  267, 268, 300, 301, 302, 303, 304, 305,
  306, 308, 311, 312, 313, 316, 319, 322,
  323

Tabu-Katalog 303
Taft–Hartley Act 320
Taylor, Frederick W. 7, 130, 149, 160,
  169, 288
Taylorism 58, 149, 150, 235, 240, 241,
  244, 252, 275, 286, 295
technology 6, 16–17; automation 7, 55,
  56, 102–3, 104, 106, 107, 231–52, 284;
  craft production 3, 5, 7, 8, 16, 17, 35,
  40–8, 55, 105, 118–21, 123, 126, 129,
  141, 152, 238, 250, 275, 279, 280, 281,
  282, 288, 289, 290, 291, 292, 296, 323;
  flexibility and flexible specialization
  16, 17, 151–2, 232, 237, 239, 242, 244,
  251, 279, 280, 286, 289, 290, 291,
  292–4, 323; mass production 3, 4, 5,
  7, 8, 9, 11, 16, 17, 81, 82, 83, 137,
  206, 212–13, 242, 244, 247, 281, 285,
  286, 287, 288, 289, 290, 294, 323; skill
  and skilled workers 3, 5, 7, 10, 11, 17,
  35, 41, 42, 43, 45, 46, 47, 53, 54, 55,
  56, 60, 61, 72, 118, 121, 123, 127, 128,
  129, 130, 131, 132, 136, 138, 141, 150,
  151, 152, 153, 155, 157, 233, 238, 239,
  241, 244, 250, 274, 275, 279, 280, 281,
  282, 283, 285, 288, 289, 290, 291, 292,
  294, 296, 323; standardization 7, 8,
  16, 17, 37, 41, 42, 43, 46, 47, 53, 82,
  83, 137, 151–2, 235, 236, 280, 281,
  282, 285, 286, 287, 288, 323
Tekkororen (Japanese Federation of
  Iron and Steel Workers' Unions) 322
Terms of Settlement (ASE, 1898) 57,

58, 59, 62, 260
Terry, M. 107
Thatcher, M. 104, 106, 107
Theories of the firm 2–17; contingency
  theory 12, 273, 274; cultural 142–3,
  273–7, 291, 298, 303–4, 310, 318;
  direct control 3, 7, 8, 9, 10, 11, 35,
  44, 48, 74, 75, 82, 103, 104, 105, 106,
  107–8, 231, 232–6, 250–2, 284, 285;
  managerial 3, 4, 5, 12, 13, 234–5;
  Marxist 3, 6–11, 13, 233–6; neo-
  classical 3, 4, 5, 6, 13, 14, 15, 17;
  transaction costs 4, 5, 6, 10
Thomas, A. 313
Tokugawa Japan 294, 320
Tolliday, Steven 11, 283, 284, 287, 301,
  302
Total Quality campaign 220
Toyota 102
Trade Associations 54, 55, 56, 184, 185,
  187, 188, 190, 192, 206, 207, 265, 304
Trade Disputes Act 301
Trade Union Act (1871) 263
Trade Unions: *see also* under individual
  unions 19, 22; co-determination 179,
  180, 181, 182, 183, 184, 187, 188, 189,
  190, 192–9, 290, 307; Company
  Unions 156, 157, 266, 289, 293, 322;
  demarcation and machine manning,
  job controls 38, 55, 56, 57, 61, 64, 66,
  67, 68, 74, 89, 91, 95, 104, 118, 121,
  126, 238, 241, 244, 245, 267, 280, 297;
  procedural agreements 36, 54, 55, 56,
  57, 58, 59, 60, 61, 62, 64, 67, 69, 70,
  71, 72, 73, 76, 83, 84, 85, 93, 97–8,
  99, 100, 106, 109, 120, 142, 259, 260,
  287, 297, 299, 301, 303; strikes 36, 38,
  54, 55, 56, 57, 58, 59, 60, 61, 62, 64,
  65, 67, 69, 72, 73, 83, 84, 85, 89, 90,
  94, 95, 96, 97, 98, 99, 100, 103, 104,
  119, 120, 122, 125–6, 131, 132, 133,
  135, 136, 138, 155, 179, 189, 196, 197,
  213, 217, 222, 261, 287, 299, 301, 302,
  305, 306, 307, 308, 312, 313, 314, 318,
  320, 321; training (apprenticeship) 41,
  46, 58, 66, 67, 68, 70, 72, 73, 75, 118,
  127, 128, 130, 138, 153, 157, 166–7,
  238, 244, 279, 280, 285, 286, 290, 292,
  298, 309; wage bargaining and wage
  systems 36, 37, 44, 45, 52, 54, 57, 59,
  60, 61, 62, 63, 65, 66, 67, 68, 69, 70,
  71, 72, 73, 132, 153, 157, 160, 161,
  163, 164, 165, 206, 209, 213, 220, 221,
  222, 238, 257, 258, 264, 265, 267, 275,

276, 280, 283, 294, 296, 297, 298, 301,
302, 303, 305, 306, 307, 308, 309, 310,
312, 314, 316, 317, 318, 320, 322;
works councils 179, 180, 181, 182,
186, 187, 188, 189, 191, 192–9, 290,
303, 305
Trades Union Congress (TUC) 83, 84,
85, 178
training, *see* trade unions
transaction costs, *see* theories of the
firm
Transport and General Workers' Union
(TGWU) 90, 93, 97, 98, 99, 302
Treasury Agreement (March 1915) 63
Turner, H. 85, 89, 94

*Union des Industries Métallurgiques et
Minières* (UIMM) Union of
Metallurgical and Mining Industries
308, 309
Unione Italiana dei Lavoratori (UIL)
209, 213, 221
United Automobile Workers (UAW)
83, 97, 317
United Rubber Workers 317
United Society of Boilermakers and
Iron and Steel Shipbuilders
(USBISS) 37
United States (US) 2, 4, 10, 13, 14, 22,
37, 47, 75, 83, 84, 109, 142, 179, 180,
204, 224, 232, 235, 237, 240, 241, 242,
244, 245, 247, 256, 257, 258, 260, 263,
264, 265, 266, 273, 278, 280, 283, 284,
285, 286, 287, 288, 289, 290, 291, 294,
295, 301, 316, 317, 318, 319, 320, 321,
322, 323
United Steel Workers 317
University of Pennsylvania 122, 139, 140
Upper Clyde Shipbuilders 46
US Steel 14, 117, 317, 319

Valetta, Vittorio 206, 208, 212, 213, 214
Vauclain, Samuel 126
Verband Berliner Metallindustrieller
(Berlin Metalworking Employers'
Association) 155, 157, 158
Verein für Socialpolitik 148
Verein für die bergbaulichen Interessen
(Association of the Coal Mining
Industry) 184
*Verein zur Wahrung der gemeinsamen
wirtschaftlichen Interessen in*

*Rheinland und Westfalen
Langnamverein* (Association to
Protect the Common Economic
Interests in Rhineland and
Westphalia) 185
Vereinigte Stahlwerke 187, 195
Verkstadsförening (VF) Swedish
Engineering Employers' Federation
302, 305
Volksgemeinschaft 170
von Siemens, Carl Friedrich 158, 167

Waeland, Derek 103
wage bargaining and wage systems, *see*
trade unions
Wagner Act 266
Weimar Republic 158, 170, 177, 181,
185, 186, 187, 189, 191, 192, 289, 303,
304, 306, 307
Weir, William 64
Weisbrod, B. 186
Weisenthal, H. 19, 20, 22, 270
Werksgemeinschaft 186, 187, 290, 293
West Germany, *see* Germany
Westinghouse 127, 136, 139
Westphalia 291
Whitley Councils 300
Wigham, E. 267
Wilhelmine Reich 303, 304, 306, 307
Wilkinson, B. 233
Williams, K. *et al* 13, 94, 106
Williamson, Oliver 4, 5, 6, 10
Willman, Paul 81, 95, 106
Winch, G. 106
Windolf, Paul 20
Winter, Sidney 14
*Wirtschaftsvereinigung Eisen- und
Stahlindustrie* (Iron and Steel
Industry Trade Association) 187, 188,
190
works councils, *see* trade unions
Works Constitution Law 193, 197, 199
Works Council Law 179, 188, 191, 192

Zechenverband 185
Zeitlin, J. 142, 279, 297, 298, 300, 301,
318
Zensanren (National Federation of
Industrial Organizations) 320
Zentralarbeitsgemeinschaft (ZAG)
Central Working Committee of
Employers and Employees 192, 303